DOCUMENTS OF CATHERINE THE GREAT

DOCUMENTS OF CATHERINE THE GREAT

The Correspondence with
Voltaire and the *Instruction* of 1767
in the English text of 1768

EDITED BY
W. F. REDDAWAY, M.A.
Fellow of King's College
Cambridge

CAMBRIDGE
AT THE UNIVERSITY PRESS
1931

CAMBRIDGE UNIVERSITY PRESS
Cambridge, New York, Melbourne, Madrid, Cape Town,
Singapore, São Paulo, Delhi, Tokyo, Mexico City

Cambridge University Press
The Edinburgh Building, Cambridge CB2 8RU, UK

Published in the United States of America by Cambridge University Press, New York

www.cambridge.org
Information on this title: www.cambridge.org/9781107694859

First published 1931
First paperback edition 2011

A catalogue record for this publication is available from the British Library

ISBN 978-1-107-69485-9 Paperback

To

A. P. GOUDY

CONTENTS

Introduction . . . . *page* ix

The Correspondence with Voltaire, Letters I to CLIX *pages* 1–213

THE GRAND INSTRUCTIONS

Chap. I. That Russia is an European State . . . *page* 216
II. Of the Extent of the Russian Empire . . . 216
III. Of the Safety of the Institutions of Monarchy . 217
IV. That there must be a political Body, to whom the Care and strict Execution of these Laws ought to be confided 217
V. Of the Situation of the People in general . . 219
VI. Of the Laws in general 220
VII. Of the Laws in particular 222
VIII. Of Punishments 225
IX. Of the Administration of Justice in general . . 228
X. Of the Forms of criminal Courts 235
XI. That a Society of Citizens requires a certain fixed Order 256
XII. Of the Propagation of the human Species in a State 257
XIII. Of handicraft Trades and Commerce . . . 262
XIV. Of Education 271
XV. Of the Nobility 273
XVI. Of the middling Sort of People 275
XVII. Of the Cities 276
XVIII. Of Inheritances 278
XIX. Of the Composition of Laws 282
XX. Of the different Statutes which require Explanation 285

Chap. XXI. Of good Order, otherwise termed Police . . . 295

XXII. Of the Expences, Revenues, and publick Management of the Finances; that is, of the Oeconomy of the State, otherwise termed the Direction of the Exchequer . . . 300

Notes 311

Table of Events, 1762–77 330

Index 339

INTRODUCTION

(i)

"Vive l'adorable Catherine!" cried Voltaire.

"Vous êtes devenue ma passion dominante.... Je me mets à vos pieds, je les baise beaucoup plus respectueusement que ceux du pape.... Je me mets à vos pieds avec adoration de latrie."

"Je prends hardiment ce titre de votre favorite", replied the Empress, "Je baiserai de bon cœur cette main qui a écrit tant de belles choses.... Je ne cesserai de vous souhaiter l'âge de Mathusalem."

Thus wrote two creators of the eighteenth century in the years in which that century reached and passed its height. Both were adventurers with those cosmopolitan careers in which the age abounded. The dictator of French learning had been safer in Berlin than in Paris, and now posed as a Swiss. The German princess, ever studiously Russian, had long dreaded the Petersburg Bastille, and now lay in peril of deposition. In externals, indeed, no two correspondents could be more unlike. Voltaire, when the interchange began, verged on seventy, while Catherine had not half his years. Like Thiers, he was "all brain", while in face and frame he formed the prototype of the frail Leo XIII, ablest and most gentle of modern popes. Catherine, but a few years earlier, had charmed young Poniatowski into forgetting that Siberia existed. With her black hair and long eyelashes, her skin of dazzling whiteness, her lips made for kisses, her perfect hands and arms, her pleasant voice and active bearing, he adored a mistress at once captivating and noble, who turned with perfect ease from the gayest trifling to the most serious calculations. In gaiety indeed she resembled Voltaire, and like him she remained gay long after youth had flown. Her immense vitality produced what he owed to his more subtle insight and long-practised pose.

Their gaiety informs a correspondence which illuminates the

years 1763–77, years which form the very pith and marrow of the century. For Europe, freed from the internecine strife which began in 1740, had now turned hopefully to the advancement of civilisation, and, ere Voltaire died, achieved astonishing success. Cook and others only less eminent explored the earth, while the scientists computed its density and explained its structure. Within a decade, hydrogen, nitrogen and oxygen were discovered. Coke, Watt, Arkwright, Hargreaves, Wedgwood—such names were pledges that what the scientist might discover would be applied to the benefit of man. Inoculation and steam power were introduced. Meanwhile the science of government shared in the advance. A young Italian expounded the relations between crime and punishment: a Portuguese statesman condemned slavery. Autocrats in other lands showed themselves eager for new light, but while they turned towards Montesquieu, Rousseau produced a mirage or a new illumination. Religious intolerance at least was condemned by all progressive men. While Wesley was becoming a national institution, the Jesuit hold was broken, and the French philosophers gained the ear of educated Europe. "Si l'opinion est la reine du monde", wrote Voltaire to D'Alembert, "les philosophes gouvernent cette reine."

The movement of the human mind in these years shook economic theory no less than physical, political and religious. While Adam Smith was working out his system, Necker and Turgot stood opposed. In this electric atmosphere, moreover, art flourished. For the age, with its classical dignity, proportion and restraint, it could be claimed that in it every article that the French peasant saw around him was a thing of beauty. While Johnson talked with Boswell, and Goldsmith, Sterne, Sheridan and Smollett charmed mankind, Lessing and Goethe were discovering new avenues to the emotions. Conscious of its progressive civilisation, Europe was at this time justly proud.

(ii)

In 1762 Voltaire had been for a generation the unquestioned patriarch of literary Europe. "For a poet", said Rameau's nephew, "there is Voltaire." "And who else?" "Voltaire."

"And for a third?" "Voltaire." "And a fourth?" "Voltaire." A century after his death, John Morley could still describe him as the very eye of modern illumination, the most trenchant writer in the world. This rank was the reward of his prose, and not least of his 14,000 letters.

Frederick the Great, the foremost contemporary monarch, and the most vindictive, forgave him everything rather than be shut out from his correspondence. This, which no mortal has surpassed and of which Frederick saw but a tiny fraction, made Voltaire "the newsvendor of Europe" and a really considerable power. In Russia, where the educated and fashionable aped the French, his name had become generic for a man of letters. Russians placed their sons *dans les Voltaire*, as Swiss families, brought up on Crusoe, became Robinson on desert islands. Until 1762, however, when "almost with a saucer of cherry brandy at her lips" the daughter of the great Peter died, Voltaire could claim no pupil on the Russian throne. Through five campaigns, indeed, Elizabeth's troops on the east of Prussia, like those of Louis XV on the west, had been striving to crush that champion of Philosophy, the "wicked man, who turned holy things into ridicule and never went to church".

The summer of 1762, however, witnessed the sudden rise of a new planet as radiant as Voltaire himself. Startled in the spring by the news that Peter III, Elizabeth's successor, had changed sides, thus saving Prussia, Europe learned in the summer that he had been assassinated and that his widow had seized the crown. Voltaire, trembling for "philosophy"[1] in its struggle with priest-ridden monarchy, saw Frederick restored to power and a philosopher-empress installed in Russia. For Catherine, although perhaps "the most political woman in history", was also his devoted pupil. Their mutual magnetism triumphed over distance. Next year a contact was established which only death could break.

The actual intermediary seems to have been Pictet, Catherine's

[1] The inverted commas, or a precautionary P, warn the reader that there is no question of metaphysics (which D'Alembert indeed associated with medicine and theology as the greatest absurdities produced by man) but rather of an enthusiasm for a "fertilising medley of new notions" poured out by literary men interested in natural science.

gigantic secretary from Geneva. Voltaire, dreading some government onslaught which would renew his acquaintance with the Bastille, had bought four estates near the Swiss frontier, thus becoming a citizen of Berne and of Geneva as well as of France. Secure at Ferney within this "sort of quadrilateral", he could write of himself as an old Swiss loving freedom, while orthodox French became "les Welches", the un-French W hall-marking them as barbarians. Both to him and to his correspondents the curiosity of the French post office was well known, and his letters were not seldom phrased to instruct or defy or hoodwink the ministers of Louis XV.

Voltaire was already deeply interested in Russia. Ivan Shuvalov, a Russian Maecenas, had commissioned him to write a history of Peter the Great, and the consummate courtier sent one graceful compliment after another from Geneva to Petersburg. Now it was congratulation on taking Colberg from the Prussians, now condolence on the death of Elizabeth, now defence of her father's reforms against the doctrinaire strictures of Rousseau. His admiration for Russia was no less sincere than the investigation which evoked it. The laws of history, he declared, allowed no palliative or disguise of Peter's condemnation of his son to death. But the five great non-Greek churches of Petersburg, monuments of the spirit of toleration, formed an example to other nations. Poltava, where the Swedish king was overthrown and Peter's new creation made secure, gave the opportunity for a great spread of civilisation and was therefore to Voltaire the only battle which has promoted the happiness of the human race. To him Elizabeth was not the crapulous illiterate but the clement empress who sentenced no man to death. The rumour ran that her successor had been poisoned or strangled by his wife, and Voltaire believed that she herself would soon be overthrown. But he was prepared to welcome her as the fourth woman to defend the great Peter's work and above all as the upholder of toleration.

Within a month of Peter's murder, indeed, Pictet was vindicating his mistress and the Russian nation in a letter to Voltaire. The Tsar, wrote Catherine's secretary, had sunk into open and incessant debauchery, and his people had naturally replaced him by "the worthiest and greatest empress whom the world had ever known". His letter crossed one to Shuvalov, in which Voltaire made light of the assassination. Like the Jesuits of old, he declared, Providence makes use of every means, and a drunkard's death from colic at least teaches us to be sober. Another, dated Ferney, 25 September 1762, extols Catherine for her offer to print the menaced *Encyclopaedia* in Russia. Before the year ended, Pictet reported his mistress, "qui les sait presque toutes par cœur", as clamouring for Voltaire's works, and the Russian court for permission to act his latest plays. Thus was the way prepared for empress and patriarch to correspond direct.

(iii)

It is much to be deplored that during its first three years the correspondence between Catherine and Voltaire survives only in fragments. With the aid of drafts which may never have been copied and sent, or, if sent, may have failed to arrive, it is possible, however, to outline their relations. The foundation of their intercourse was their need of one another for the achievement of their purposes in life. Catherine, it is true, was sincerely grateful to the "philosopher" whose works had formed her mind and style, and, when she was on the verge of suicide, had relieved the spiritual starvation and social torment of her existence. As an amateur of intellectual exchanges, she relished in Voltaire's letters that which she derived also from other "philosophers", notably from Diderot and Grimm, by word of mouth. But with their common master, her senior by five and thirty years, she could never chatter as artlessly as sometimes with the disciples. To her Voltaire must be the arbiter of her credit and of Russia's in the eyes of the enlightened world. Whether or no the topic was political, her letters to Voltaire were always in some degree documents of state.

Voltaire, on the other hand, found in Catherine an ally of rising value as her hold on the Russian sceptre grew more firm. All his most cherished projects she might attain or at least advance. While Jesuit influence appeared to be supreme in

France, Voltaireans ruled or seemed likely to rule in Prussia, Russia, Denmark, Sweden, the Empire, and perhaps elsewhere. This handful of enlightened despots might defy the priests and spread over non-Latin Europe the liberty which won Voltaire's enthusiastic admiration among the English, Dutch and Swiss. Compared with this great hope, Catherine's power to subsidise the "philosophers" and their protégés was in Voltaire's eyes a small though real merit. While some English statesmen looked vaguely to the new northern star to preserve Europe from Bourbon domination, Voltaire formed the precise and not unfounded belief that the empress was ready to free her own oppressed subjects and those of the Turks and Poles. The historian of the great Peter was eager for fresh Poltavas.

Such were the realities which underlay the embroidered surface of their correspondence. Waliszewski, the Polish *advocatus diaboli*, sneeringly reminds us that in Voltaire's letters to D'Alembert Catherine becomes simply *la belle Cateau*, or *Cateau* without the *belle*, and that the two philosophers agree that such converts give "philosophy" but little cause to boast. Catherine, moreover, for all her incense, kept her nephews away from the patriarch and himself from Petersburg. "For God's sake", she implored Grimm in March 1778, "advise the octogenarian to remain in Paris. What should he do here? He would die, here or by the wayside, of cold, weariness and bad roads....Tell him that *Cateau* is only good to see from a distance. That *Cateau* tickled me not a little." An unprejudiced reader may think that neither of these letters convicts the writers of hypocrisy in their mutual compliments. In their age, indeed, epistolary courtesy had become somewhat mechanical, as when, for example, a young noble ascribed the success of his courtship to the renown of his parents' virtues. Nothing in the Catherine-Voltaire letters was more dangerous to truth than Frederick's excuse for not inviting "the divine Emily" with Voltaire lest her radiance, added to Voltaire's, should be too blinding for his merely mortal vision. A compliment in a letter meant neither more nor less than a bow on meeting in the street.

(iv)

Whether sincere or not, the letters of Voltaire to Catherine were unquestionably written by Voltaire. Is the converse true? According to the article on Catherine in the eleventh edition of the *Encyclopaedia Britannica*, "the letters to Voltaire attributed to her are not hers, and were probably composed for her by Andrei Shuvalov". The writer gives neither his name, nor his authority, nor his reasons, but he declares that all other accounts of Catherine have been superseded by Waliszewski's. He appears, that is to say, to rely upon a Polish scholar not only to treat dispassionately the career of the partitioner of Poland but also to pronounce upon the genuineness of correspondence in a foreign language. Waliszewski's translator, it is interesting to note, remarks that his *Roman d'une impératrice* (22e édition, ouvrage couronné par l'académie française, prix Thérouanne) "is not written in Parisian French: it has the colloquialisms of a foreigner, wishing to be more native than the natives". On a question of French style, Waliszewski's verdict could not compare in weight with that of M. Rambaud, who pronounces Catherine's memoirs (those intimate confessions which were unquestionably her own) to be written "en très bon français".

But has Waliszewski proved that Catherine's letters to Voltaire were written for her? The passage upon which the encyclopaedist may rely occurs in book III, chapter ii of the *Roman*. It is conspicuously unconvincing. The author first quotes the verdict of M. Quérard, who is certain that not one of the letters to Voltaire was written by an empress to whom "la langue française était peu familière". M. Quérard places them among his *Supercheries littéraires dévoilées*, because he finds them, as compared with Catherine's instructions to the brother of Louis XVI, so far superior in style and sense as to establish a difference of authorship. He makes no account of two vital considerations—that the letters were written in Catherine's prime, the instructions, in her old age; and that in 1763 her usual vehicle was French, for which she gradually substituted Russian as she grew older. Blind to the weakness of M. Quérard's reasoning, Waliszewski half adopts his conclusion, which he then proceeds to demolish without realising that he is doing so. Catherine, he declares, certainly wrote her own letters to Grimm. These letters contain a passage from which he quotes at length. It was written near Moscow on 10 May 1775. Catherine loved dogs, and it was her order to have "Sutherland" stuffed that, according to Ségur, the weeping Chief of Police attempted to carry out on a naturalised court banker of that name. At this time "Anderson" was with his mistress, who thus depicts the scene and much of her own character as well.

"Mais le moyen d'écrire? ne voilà-t-il pas Tom Anderson qui demande à être couvert; il s'est placé vis-à-vis de moi sur un fauteuil; j'ai le bras gauche et lui la patte droite appuyés sur une croisée ouverte, qu'on pourrait prendre pour une porte d'église, si elle n'était au troisième étage. De cette croisée sir Anderson considère, primo, la rivière de Moscou, qui serpente et fait à la portée de la vue une vingtaine de coudes; il est inquiet, il aboie. C'est un vaisseau qui remonte la rivière; non, non, c'est outre le vaisseau une vingtaine de chevaux, qui passent la rivière à la nage pour aller paître sur les prés verts et couverts de fleurs qui forment l'autre côté du rivage et qui s'étendent jusqu'à une hauteur couverte de terres fraîchement labourées et qui appartiennent aux trois villages qui sont là devant mes yeux. A gauche est un petit couvent bâti en briques, entouré d'un petit bois, et puis des coudes de la rivière et des maisons de campagne, qui s'étendent jusqu'à la capitale, qu'on voit dans le lointain; la droite offre à la contemplation de M. Tom des hauteurs couvertes de bois épais, entre lequel on voit des clochers, des églises de pierre et de la neige aussi dans les creux des hauteurs. M. Anderson est fatigué de considérer une aussi belle vue apparemment, car le voilà qui s'emmaillotte dans sa couverture et qui va dormir. Si ma description appesantit vos paupières, vous pourrez, monsieur, en faire autant. Si vous êtes curieux, pour vous désennuyer, de connaître la race des Anderson dans son état présent, la voici. A la tête se trouve le chef de la race sir Tom Anderson, son épouse duchesse Anderson, leurs enfants, la jeune duchesse Anderson, monsieur Anderson. Tom Thomson, celui-ci s'est établi à Moscou sous la tutelle du prince Volkonski, gouverneur-général de la ville; il y a encore, outre ceux-ci, dont la réputation est faite, quatre ou cinq jeunes gens, qui promettent infiniment et qu'on élève dans les meilleures maisons des villes de Moscou et de Pétersbourg, comme par exemple dans celle du prince Orlof, de messieurs Narychkine, chez le prince Tufiakine. Sir Tom Anderson a épousé en secondes noces mademoiselle Mimi, qui depuis ce temps-là a pris le nom de Mimi Anderson, mais jusqu'ici il n'y a pas de lignée. Outre ces légitimes mariages,—puisqu'il faut dire les défauts comme les vertus des gens dans leur histoire,—M. Tom a eu plusieurs attachements illégitimes: la grande duchesse a plusieurs jolies chiennes, qui lui on mis martel en tête, mais jusqu'ici aucun de ses bâtards n'a paru, et il y a apparence qu'il n'y en a pas; quoi qu'on en dise, ce sont des calomnies."

The writer who could scribble thus in her unstudied written chat could assuredly produce anything which appears in the letters to Voltaire. Some two years later, in August 1777, her spirit and her French were equal to mocking Grimm and her son's German consort.

"Savez-vous la nouvelle du jour? Tandis que vous vous amusez à critiquer mes adresses de lettres, qui finissent par *Dieu sait où*, Euler nous prédit la fin du monde pour le mois de juillet de l'année qui vient; il fait venir tout exprès pour cela deux comètes, qui feront je ne sais quoi à Saturne, qui à son tour viendra nous détruire; or, la grande-duchesse m'a dit de n'en rien croire, parce que les prophéties de l'Evangile et de l'Apocalypse ne sont point encore remplies, et nommément l'Antechrist n'est point venu, ni toutes les croyances réunies. Moi, à tout cela je réponds comme le barbier de Séville: je dis à l'un: Dieu vous bénisse, et à l'autre: va te coucher, et je vais mon train, qu'en pensez-vous?"

Next year Voltaire died, and Catherine bewailed the fatal May which had robbed her also of Chatham. In letter after letter to Grimm she gave imperial commands for all to be done that could pay homage to the memory of her master *la divinité de la gaîté* and much more. Now it was a hundred complete editions of his works to form citizens, *des génies*, heroes and authors. Now, on December 11, *fête de St André*, *avec une gelée de* 16 *à* 17 *degrés*, again with a dog playing round her, she instructs Grimm to pay for Voltaire's library. Her own letters she gives to Grimm, but they are not to be copied or in any way made public. She continues in a passage of supreme interest to readers of this book:

"Je crains l'impression comme le feu; je n'écris pas assez bien pour cela, quoi qu'en disent Mad. Denis et ses amis. Faites cela, commentez mes lettres si vous croyez qu'il en vaille la peine, cela peut faire l'ouvrage le plus bouffon qu'il y eût jamais. Or, écoutez donc, s'il y a de la force, de la profondeur, de la grâce dans mes lettres ou expressions, sachez que je dois tout cela à Voltaire, car pendant fort longtemps nous lisions, relisions et étudiions tout ce qui sortait de sa plume, et j'ose dire que par là j'ai acquis un tact si fin que je ne me suis jamais trompée sur ce qui était de lui ou n'en était pas: la griffe du lion a une empoignure à elle que nul humain n'imita jusqu'ici, mais dont l'épître à Ninon du comte Schuvalov [sic] approche."

This is the Andrei Shuvalov who, in the judgment of the British encyclopaedist, probably wrote Catherine's letters for her. Nephew of Voltaire's Maecenas, he was one of Catherine's titular chamberlains and her "little one". When the correspondence began he was a lad of nineteen. Voltaire, who knew him well, ranked his French verse with the French prose of his own constant correspondents, Frederick the Great and Catherine herself. If he were a supreme artist he might perhaps have made the letters of his mistress to Voltaire what they plainly are—playful, witty, caressing, irreverent, politic, the natural expression of Catherine's personality. But to say that he may have had the ability and the opportunity to do so is very far from proving or even suggesting that he did. The most accommodating chamberlain could hardly be a pocket dictionary available at Petersburg, Tsarskoeselo, Moscow, Casan—wherever and whensoever Catherine desired to write to Voltaire or to add to a letter already written. When the correspondence was at its brightest, Andrei and his bride were actually guests of Voltaire. The copious letters in French written by Catherine to Grimm and others, moreover, appear no less conspicuous for grace and charm. Even M. Quérard would hardly suggest that Andrei Shuvalov made a third in company when she wrote to Grimm or that he drafted the dog-scene for her to copy. Did he compose her tribute to his own literary powers? And was Voltaire's keen palate deceived when he spoke of Frederick, Catherine and Shuvalov as three separate writers?

The question is one of far more than merely literary importance. Regarding Catherine's whole career the truth lies in extremes. Either she was a consummate hypocrite, as many have declared, or, as she claims, and as some concede, above all else sincere. The paragraph to Grimm last quoted, if fraudulent, would lower her place in history.

We may pertinently ask whether any ambitious female Philosopher would have risked so humbling an exposure? Hardly Catherine, who wrote many drafts to Voltaire which exist in the Russian archives before transcribing the letters themselves. If Shuvalov or another had made the draft it could easily have been preserved as a copy. But, apart from the labour, it would have been a refinement of hypocrisy for the empress to write out the document that was to be kept as well as that which was to be sent. In many cases, too, the document that Catherine sent, differs from that which Catherine wrote and kept.

Such a fraud, moreover, would have robbed the empress of one of her dearest pleasures—composition. As she confessed to Grimm, the sight of a new pen made her fingers itch to write. Tales, plays, journalism, as well as letters and memoirs, flowed from an author who could only think with a pen in her hand and who could not dictate. In spite of some natural tremors, for a professional scribe to forego the tremulous delight of an interchange with the patriarch of letters was a sacrifice that only some weighty personal or political necessity could impose, and what such necessity could there be? Only, it would seem, that her command of French was inadequate to such a correspondence.

That Catherine never mastered French, that through a half-century for public utterances or for the composition of her private memoirs she could and did always find and conceal a Shuvalov, this may be left for a Frenchman to assert and for a credulous encyclopaedist to repeat. But it is not difficult to prove that she was a first-rate linguist, that she had studied French abundantly, and that she spoke it with perfect ease. French was the customary language of the court circle in which she was brought up and the indispensable stock-in-trade of all ambitious North German princesses. Her mother left a noteworthy correspondence in that language. Among Catherine's French instructors were Mlle Cardel and others among the many Huguenots who had fled to Prussia. An ardent reader, she turned naturally to that literature which was as yet hardly challenged by German or by Russian.

"She had begun", wrote John Morley, "with the books in which most of the salt of old France was to be found, with Rabelais, Scarron, Montaigne; she cherished Molière and Corneille; and of the writers of the eighteenth century, apart from Voltaire, the author of Gil Blas was her favourite."

If it was her Russian that critics in the 'sixties praised, it was because they took her French for granted. In 1765, when a new British minister made his inaugural speech at Court, Catherine replied extempore in French, the language of her private intercourse, 1755–7, with Hanbury Williams, with his secretary Poniatowski and with Lord Buckingham, ambassador from 1762 to 1765. Just twenty years later, when a new French minister, dazzled by what he saw, forgot his inaugural address, Catherine adjusted hers to meet his improvisation.

Her letters in French, says Grot, who edited those addressed to Grimm between 1774 and 1796, "reveal in the author an uncommon practical knowledge of a foreign tongue, its spirit and idioms".

"Contemporaries", writes the learned German Dr Brückner, "with one accord praised the refinement of social intercourse at the Russian court. This proved the significance of going to school to the Philosophers of France....Of these scholars Catherine equalled the best in mind and wit."

Grimm, thoroughly Parisianised, found that no one surpassed her in readiness and preciseness of expression. Her swift sallies, the verve and grace of her conversation with foreign men of letters left an ineffaceable impression on his mind, and all was done in French. Thus, on the vital question, did Catherine write these letters or merely pretend to have written them? both the nature of the case and the weight of evidence enforce the verdict of M. Masson, who knew her well and wrote impartially after she was dead:

"If the Code of Laws drawn up by Catherine bespeak a mind capable of enlarged views and a sound policy, her letters announce the wit, graces and talents of a woman of still greater merit....She never had a man about her capable of writing her letters to Voltaire in French. Odart and Aubri, her secretaries at the time, did not write so well as herself. She was unquestionably the author."

(v)

The first of the long series which has been preserved appears to date from mid-October 1763. It was written at a time when Catherine's throne, though never solid, was becoming less insecure, when she was resolving to disappoint the British, whom she admired, and connect herself with the Prussians, whom she distrusted, when the question of the Polish succession threatened to become acute, and when she was opening wide the gates of Russia to colonists from other lands. Her letter answered that of September 1763 to Pictet, in which Voltaire plays over almost every Leitmotiv of his share of the coming correspondence.

"Mon cher géant, vraiment votre lettre est d'un vrai philosophe: vous êtes un Anacharsis, et d'Alembert n'a pas voulu l'être. Je ne sais pourquoi le philosophe de Paris n'a pas osé aller chez la Minerve de Russie: il a craint peut-être le sort d'Ixion.

"Pour votre Jean-Jacques, ci-devant citoyen de Genève, je crois que la tête lui a tourné quand il a prophétisé contre les établissements de Pierre le Grand. J'ai peut-être mieux rencontré quand j'ai dit que si jamais l'empire des Turcs était détruit, ce serait par la Russie; et sans l'aventure du Pruth, je tiendrais ma prophétie plus sûre que toutes celles d'Isaïe.

"Votre auguste Catherine seconde est assurément Catherine unique; la première ne fut qu'heureuse. J'ai pris la liberté de lui envoyer quelques exemplaires du second tome de *Pierre le Grand*, par M. de Balk. Je me flatte qu'elle y trouvera des vérités. J'ai eu de très-bons mémoires; je n'ai songé qu'au vrai: je sais heureusement combien elle l'aime.

"Ce qu'elle a daigné dicter à son géant me paraît d'un esprit bien supérieur. O qu'elle a raison, quand elle fait sentir cette fastidieuse prolixité d'écrits pour et contre les jésuites, et quand elle parle de ces quatre-vingts pages d'extraits sur des choses qu'on doit dire en dix lignes! que j'ai de vanité de penser comme elle! Mais on ne doit jamais rendre public ce qu'on admire, à moins d'une permission expresse; sans quoi il faudrait, je pense, imprimer toutes ses lettres.

"Savez-vous bien que madame la princesse sa mère m'honorait de beaucoup de bonté, et que je pleure sa perte? Si je n'avais que soixante ans, je viendrais me consoler en contemplant sa divine fille.

"Mon cher géant, mettez à ses pieds, je vous prie, ce petit papier pomponné. Si vous êtes bigle, vous verrez que je deviens aveugle et sourd. Elle daigne donc protéger la petite-fille de Corneille? Eh bien! n'est-il pas vrai que toutes les grandes choses nous viennent du Nord? Ai-je tort?

"Madame votre mère vous mandera les nouvelles de Genève. Pour moi, je suis si pénétré du billet que j'ai lu de votre auguste impératrice, que j'en oublie jusqu'à votre grande république. J'ai baisé ce billet: n'allez pas le lui dire au moins; cela n'est pas respectueux."

(vi)

Between the brilliant initial exchange of the autumn of 1763 and Letter II from the early summer of 1765, the relative positions of Catherine and Voltaire had greatly changed. Voltaire, now over seventy, lived on at Ferney, playing at squiredom, but working as hard in his way as Catherine in hers. The frequent bouts of illness, the honourable preoccupation with the victims of injustice, the thousand demands upon the time of the best-known figure of the day—none of these could sterilise the tireless author. Her letter is an acknowledgment of the first edition of his *Philosophie de l'histoire*. Almost one letter for every day that passed has been enshrined in his published correspondence.

But while in these twenty months Voltaire had steadily enlarged his fame, Catherine had vaulted to the head of Europe.

Despite rumours and some hushed-up tumults, despite, too, the fundamental illegality of her title, Russia now seemed more firmly hers. In Panin she possessed an honest and able statesman. Her great Prussian neighbour had pledged himself to her alliance, and that pledge at least, for his own safety's sake, he meant to keep. In 1764 he had helped her to force on Poland a king "who had but one title to reign—that he had been her lover". Already statesmen saw that the twenty million Poles must either become her vassals or cede provinces to her empire. In Denmark, and even in Sweden, she had supplanted Louis XV. Britain was hotly courting her alliance. What power, save the Turk, would venture to attack her? proudly asked Panin, and Turkish attack must open the fairest prospect for Russian conquests. At the same time Catherine was showing an untiring zeal to improve the lot of her subjects. One provincial governor received from her in a single month nearly twenty lessons in the duties of his office, each of several hours' duration. "Mettez le Russe dans le bon chemin, il est capable de tout", wrote the outgoing British ambassador in 1765, while the incoming Frenchman noted that she had already raised the revenue by fifteen million livres.

(vii)

The correspondence had been carried on no further than to July 1765 before it touched on what had then become Catherine's chief ambition. This was no less than to remodel the laws of Russia in accordance with the new principles proclaimed in France. To this great design she devoted a fifth part of the fifteen hours which made up her working day. The results appeared in 1767 when her so-called *Instruction* saw the light.

This *Instruction* or *Nakaz* has become inseparably linked with Catherine's name. It embodies that liberal policy which in 1767 won her the title of "the Great" in Russia, and for a time made her the cynosure of Europe. Voltaire pronounced it the finest monument of the century. In Kluchevsky's phrase, it was her "political confession", comprising, as she herself declared, all that she had to say. First promulgated in Russian, within four years it appeared in twenty-three versions, including one or more in almost every European language. In 1771 two thousand copies were prevented by a timid government from entering France. Catherine's son forbade it to be read in Russia. Its influence is by no means to be measured by the facts that it did not create a lasting Russian parliament nor achieve a Russian code. But a parliament and a code were what the contemporary world expected, and without them interest in the *Instruction* fell away. The very text became rare. The version here reprinted, bearing, in an age of literary pseudonyms, an untraced Russian name, remains until to-day the only one in English. Ten years ago, a French writer declared that since 1769 the *Instruction* had not been reproduced. Its rarity, however, has not prevented a host of historians from criticising it in general terms. Catherine, according to many of them, was a plagiarist and a hypocrite. With the sole design of self-advertisement she passed off the work of others as her own.

Those who indict Catherine for plagiarism see in the *Instruction* an ill-compounded hash of Montesquieu with a spice of Beccaria. "Every sentence", says the writer in the *Cambridge Historical Series*, "is directly inspired by Beccaria's *Dei delitti e delle pene*, or by Montesquieu's *L'Esprit des Lois*." According to Chechulin's analysis, not less than four-fifths of the whole was derived from the works of others. Fifteen of the first twenty chapters are based on Montesquieu, and in these only 62 sections out of 340 come from another source.

Catherine herself made not the smallest attempt to minimise her indebtedness to her teachers. Beccaria received a cordial invitation to make his home in Russia. She termed Montesquieu's book her breviary, and uttered the hope that if the author observed her work from the next world he would forgive the pillage for the sake of the twenty million Russians whose condition it would improve. To Frederick the Great she mocked at herself as a crow in peacock's feathers, claiming as her own no more than the arrangement and here and there a word or line. Pokrovsky, however, finds her not only a plagiarist but a stupid plagiarist, who summarised Montesquieu without the wit to understand him. To hoodwink the French censors,

Montesquieu had created an imaginary France which was really England, translating English liberties into terms of antiquated French institutions which he could safely praise. His sophisticated countrymen perfectly comprehended the device, and gleefully read between the lines. Catherine, on the other hand, copied maxims which in Panin's phrase would "renverser les murailles", such maxims as those which made the Senate the custodian of the laws and thus the guardian of the people against the sovereign's caprice and greed. Her ineptitude was most clearly displayed on the question of capital punishment. First, following Montesquieu, she holds in § 79 that a citizen merits death when he has taken life or offered so to do. But when in §§ 209–212 she quotes Beccaria it is to declare that in normal times to deprive a citizen of life must be unnecessary.

To much of this indictment the reply seems obvious. No sovereign is called upon to be an original jurist. To combine in one person a disposition to invent laws with autocratic power would be most dangerous to a state. What Russia required from Catherine was the ability to perceive that the existing laws were bad and the goodwill and energy to seek out better. Someone, by her command, must determine the principles of a better code, and someone, again by her command, must invent machinery for carrying those principles into effect. That Catherine saw the evil and that she showed apparent goodwill and energy, not even Pokrovsky can deny. By herself drafting the principles and decreeing the form of the legislative assembly she shortened the inevitable delay before achievement. Instead of wasting half her reign on attempting to think out the basis of a code, she turned to what has been acclaimed by enlightened men as the greatest book of the century in which she lived. *L'Esprit des Lois* had cost Montesquieu twenty if not forty years of toil. For two decades past all educated Europe had rejoiced in his wit and wisdom. To sneer at Catherine for passing off his maxims as her own is as senseless as to denounce George V for the composition of the king's speech. Such a plagiarist would be capable of publishing the Ten Commandments as his own hints on how to behave. As Diderot wrote, "Les 19 vingtièmes d'une nation sont condamnés à l'ignorance par leur état et leur imbécillité.

L'autre vingtième est à présent même très éclairé, et l'est sans effet". Catherine purposed to benefit both sections; the larger, which in Russia comprised far more than nineteen-twentieths, by the substance of her decrees; the smaller, which knew its Montesquieu, also by the programme which so open a homage to his principles implied. She brought Russia nearer to freedom in 1767 than did Alexander I after overthrowing Napoleon, or Alexander II after the defeat of Russian absolutism by the West, or Nicholas II after the unprecedented humiliations of 1905. This she did by proclaiming as her own so many of the principles of Montesquieu as she judged advantageous to Russia. Some of his maxims and illustrations she adapted, and once at least she proclaimed the direct opposite of what he wrote. Where she found the young Italian Beccaria more convincing she turned by preference to him. Bielefeld and Justi were also drawn upon, and the supplements contain undisguised sections from the *Encyclopaedia*. In all her compilation Catherine was nothing that is ordinarily meant by plagiarist, nor a hypocrite in any sense at all.

The obvious path towards a true appreciation of the *Instruction* is indicated by its author in words which she chose long afterwards for her tombstone. "In the year 1744 she went to Russia to marry Peter III.... Eighteen years of tediousness and solitude caused her to read many books. When she had ascended the throne of Russia, she wished to do good, and tried to bring happiness, freedom and prosperity to her subjects." As she herself declared, her mind was not creative. But she claimed to have found work easy and took credit for her power of distinguishing the salutary from the pernicious, a ruler's most priceless gift. In drawing up projects based on first principles she faithfully represented her age, and she surpassed most "projectors" in her power to begin to put these in execution. "I am a great beginner", she confessed, and the confession at least proves her sincerity. If we add that, as her whole life shows, she had unlimited ambition, unfailing courage, together with both the will and the power to conciliate, the *Instruction* appears as the natural product of the first years in which she sat firmly upon the throne.

Of this epoch (1765–6) she wrote shortly before her death an account which is indispensable to a just judgment of the *Instruction* and of herself. "For two years I read and wrote, and for eighteen months consulted no one, but was guided solely by my own heart and reason....When I thought that I had reached my goal, I began to show parts of my results to divers persons... including Prince Orlov and Count Nikita Panin. The latter said, 'These are principles to throw down walls'.[1] Prince Orlov rated my work very high and often wished to show it to others, but I never showed more than a sheet or two at once. Finally I composed the manifesto summoning delegates from the whole empire, the better to learn the conditions of every section. These assembled in Moscow in 1767. I summoned several persons of different ways of thinking...to hear the *Instruction*. Every part of it evoked division. I let them erase what they pleased, and they struck out more than half of what I had written...I bade them take [the remainder] as rules upon which an opinion can be based, not as a law."

These rules, described by our ambassador as not much bigger than the Standing Orders of the House of Lords, were to be read monthly as a guide to the deputies in their law-making. They were neither a code nor a decree establishing a parliament. Foreigners, however, persisted in believing them to be both, and the reputation both of Catherine and of the *Instruction* suffered.

To French diplomatists and statesmen, Catherine was the enemy who made Russia the tool of Britain. For more than ten months they had been discussing the report that she was working at a code of laws which, with the aid of an assembly, was designed to emancipate the slaves. Then, in October 1767, their consul at Moscow decried the whole proceeding. The meetings, he wrote, were reputed to be a comedy staged by despotism masquerading as humanity, and the *Instruction*, for all its casket of gold, "a compilation of the works of Montesquieu and of a book entitled *Du délit et des peines*".

England at the same time was suffering from a lack of intelligent representation in Russia. Macartney, an able commoner interpolated between two duller peers, had at last been

1 À renverser des murailles—quoted in French by the empress, who on this occasion wrote in Russian.

suffered to return home, and his successor had not yet arrived. He had praised Catherine's design, but the task of reporting on the *Instruction* itself devolved on the acid and uninitiated secretary of legation, Shirley. "It is scarce possible", he wrote, "to be more active than she is, better acquainted with the genius of her subjects, or more attentive to improve this great advantage", but as, in his judgment, these intentions did not proceed from principles of the purest nature, her actions, like false pearls, had more *éclat* but less value than the genuine ones.

Thinking thus, he penned the famous lines which have been taken for the verdict of his country. "Knowing the restless dispositions of her subjects, the great object of her policy is to occupy them at home and abroad as much as possible. This motive...sharpened by her vanity, has made her undertake to be the legislator of this empire; but in order to do it with safety she has taken care to have in the commission such people only who will follow her dictates and who will form pompous representation of her generosity, justice and moderation."

Shirley knew the Russians better than he knew the empress. The fulfilment of his prophecy of the fate of her project has given a false lustre to his estimate of herself. "Were even these laws to be brought to a certain degree of perfection", he argued, "the extreme want of respected and disinterested magistrates would still prevent her feeling the good effects." The dilemma which Peter the Great had striven to will away by harsh decrees kept fast hold on Russia. Good laws postulate good officials, but without good laws officials cannot be made good. Catherine avoided Peter's absurdities. She issued no such decree as "Let it be done everywhere as at Riga and Reval", nor did she import foreign laws with foreign prisoners to work them. But she was an optimist in an optimistic age, an age prone to believe all men endowed with like capacity, and at least capable of being transfigured by precepts based on reason. Catherine had sacrificed much of the wisdom of the Philosophers to the prejudices of her Russian critics. Though she stood firm in condemning torture, she had consented to strike out many of her aphorisms in favour of peasant freedom. The deputies were not to be told, as she had wished, that food and clothing must be made the legal right of everyone. But such slanders as that the whole proceeding was a comedy staged by despotism were refuted by all her conduct. How could her prestige be advanced by the calculated failure of an enterprise which was conspicuously her own?

That enterprise—the composition, discussion and promulgation of the *Instruction*, the election of the 564 deputies and their provision with *cahiers* designed to formulate the grievances of Russia, the solemn assembling at Moscow (11 August 1767), the seventy-seven plenary sessions and the nineteen special committees, the transplantation to Petersburg (February 1768); the struggle, seventy sessions long, with Law; in mid-December, the call to the colours against the Turks; the evaporation of the project in a war of five campaigns and a terrible rebellion—that enterprise, which for four years absorbed Catherine's attention was neither a calculated nor an unqualified failure. A few months before the tragic interruption, the British ambassador visited the assembly. He beheld with surprise "not a black gown or anything that looked like a lawyer in the House", and was astonished that a motion to declare all field officers noble was carried only by 242 votes to 213. He regarded the institution as a scaffolding, to be removed when Catherine's "noble edifice", the novel code, should be complete. Although committees functioned for six years more, posterity can point only to a collection of isolated points in which the *Instruction* and the debates influenced specific statutes. Half a century later, according to Speranski, there were more than 30,000 decrees since the code of Alexis and no fresh code. But the *Instruction* and the assembly did not therefore fail wholly to benefit Russia. A national parliament which had been active for seventeen months could not vanish without a trace. It had taught the empress what her people desired, and in some degree what they were. The deputies, like the later Duma, something of "an anthropological museum", had individually received an intensive training in public life. Above all, the crown had committed itself to ideas and principles which must stir up the stagnant Russia of tradition. Maxims which, to the rulers of a nation claiming to march at the head of civilisation, appeared subversive of authority and order had been proclaimed from the

Russian throne. "The government", declared Catherine, "which shackles natural freedom the least...best accords with the design of men in forming civil societies", and her subjects enshrined her aphorisms in a golden casket. Once saluted by their empress as fellow-beings born to the benefits of natural law, they might indeed be re-enslaved but hardly without hope. Voltaire might justly utter the *Nunc dimittis* of Simeon.

(viii)

With the outbreak of the Turkish war, foreign policy once again became Catherine's foremost care. Voltaire, more than any other man, could influence a section of European opinion and thereby promote the success of Russia. This success he ardently desired, as a victory of the freest thought in Europe over the most barbarous repression. The Poles, in his eyes, were the accomplices of the Turks and their rivals in persecution. The Catherine-Voltaire correspondence therefore blossomed with new life. From the first year of the war more letters survive than from the five preceding, and until 1774 a brisker *tempo* is maintained. Then, when the Turks lie prostrate, when Poland has undergone partition, when Pugachev's rebellion has been crushed, and when Voltaire has passed his eightieth birthday, the exchanges become less frequent. They cease only with Voltaire's death on the morrow of his apotheosis in Paris. His wit, his grace and his zeal for justice survived his powers of body. The last of the twelve thousand letters which remain were a card to his doctor: "Non in solo pane vivit homo sed in omni verbo quod oritur ex ore Tronchin", and three lines of congratulation to Lally on his father's vindication. "Le mourant ressuscite en apprenant cette grande nouvelle...il mourra content."

(ix)

This book has been compiled to meet an emergency, with little beyond local resources. It has not been possible to venture far into "the vast labyrinth of Voltaire" or to complete some fascinating but secondary tasks. The chief of these concerns the authorship of the English translation of the *Instruction*. This the title-page ascribes to Michael Tatischeff, a Russian gentleman, and the preface claims that a Russian work translated into English by a native of Russia must attract by its novelty.

In the age of Ossian and a thousand lesser impostures, a Russian gentleman translating from the Russian might well turn out to be an English or Irish gentleman translating from the French, especially when the same press, that of the Senate at Petersburg, which issued the Russian version issued a French version simultaneously. Many of the sections, moreover, existed verbatim in easily accessible French books such as Montesquieu, the *Encyclopaedia* and the translation of Beccaria. Yet the translator, who often rises to a high and sustained level of nervous eighteenth-century prose, is occasionally unintelligible. He is sometimes better than the French, sometimes immeasurably worse, and sometimes ignorant of what a contemporary Russian would most probably have known. I regard it as certain that the Russian version was used and the French frequently ignored, and I can hardly believe that any foreigner could have produced so idiomatic a translation by himself. But whether this is indeed a pure product of "the land of infinite possibilities", or whether a Russian gentleman drew unacknowledged help from Grub Street, or whether "Michael Tatischeff" conceals a literary hack or an agent of Russian propaganda, this is a problem towards the solution of which I can only hope that the Notes may contribute something.

For technical reasons which those who have printed in haste will divine, much that might normally have been expected in the Notes appears in the Index. From this Voltaire's innumerable allusions to the Classics "of which he talked so much and knew so little" have been excluded, together with such variations in proper names as anyone who is likely to use this book will readily penetrate. Giurgi on the Danube, for instance, appears also as Gorgora in Catherine's LXVII, Giurgevo in her CXVI and Giorgiova in Voltaire's C. The *Annual Register* for 1770–2 gives Giurgewo, and Georgova is also found. But when she first mentioned its capture (XXXVIII) Catherine was supposed to have written Giorgione. This traditional spelling remained in the French edition of 1882, although it professed to reproduce *Sbornik*, which has Giorgoue in the French text and in the Russian translation Giurgi or something like it. To index all these variants would be to lessen the usefulness of the book and to disguise the indifference of the eighteenth century to niceties of orthography and grammar.

My version of the *Correspondance* is based on the editions of 1822, 1877, and 1881–2, supplemented from the collection of MM. de Cayrol et François, and from the publications of the Russian Historical Society (*Sbornik*). I have seldom ventured on emendation, but where an obvious slip of the pen has produced nonsense, I have felt that the unscholarly character of my work might excuse me for substituting sense. No previous editor has resisted the temptation to help Catherine to spell: the responsibility for not standardising their efforts or modernising the text is mine. Comments on the *Instruction* are derived mainly from *Sbornik*, from the sumptuous Russian edition of Chechulin, from Ledieu's *Diderot; Observations*, and from the works of Brückner, Andreae (Berlin, 1912), Waliszewski, Kluchevsky (Petersburg, 1921) and Pokrovsky (Moscow, 1924).

W. F. REDDAWAY

CORRESPONDENCE
OF CATHERINE THE GREAT

I

DE L'IMPÉRATRICE

? *c.* 15 octobre 1763

J'ai mis sous les vers du portrait de Pierre-le-Grand, que M. de Voltaire m'a envoyés par M. de Balk, *Que Dieu le veuille!*

J'ai commis un péché mortel en recevant la lettre adressée au géant: j'ai quitté un tas de suppliques, j'ai retardé la fortune de plusieurs personnes, tant j'étais avide de la lire. Je n'en ai pas même eu de repentir. Il n'y a point de casuistes dans mon empire, et jusqu'ici je n'en étais pas bien fâchée. Mais voyant le besoin d'être ramenée à mon devoir, j'ai trouvé qu'il n'y avait point de meilleur moyen que de céder au tourbillon qui m'emporte, et de prendre la plume pour prier M. de Voltaire, très sérieusement, de ne me plus louer avant que je l'aie mérité. Sa réputation et la mienne y sont également intéressées. Il dira qu'il ne tient qu'à moi de m'en rendre digne; mais en vérité, dans l'immensité de la Russie, un an n'est qu'un jour, comme mille ans devant le Seigneur. Voilà mon excuse de n'avoir pas encore fait le bien que j'aurais dû faire.

Je répondrai à la prophétie de J.-J. Rousseau, en lui donnant, j'espère, aussi long-temps que je vivrai, un démenti fort impoli. Voilà mon intention; reste à voir les effets. Après cela, monsieur, j'ai envie de vous dire: *Priez Dieu pour moi.*

J'ai reçu aussi, avec beaucoup de reconnaissance, le second tome de *Pierre-le-Grand*. Si dans le temps que vous avez commencé cet ouvrage j'avais été ce que je suis aujourd'hui, j'aurais fourni bien d'autres mémoires. Il est vrai qu'on ne peut assez s'étonner du génie de ce grand homme. Je vais faire imprimer ses lettres originales, que j'ai ordonné de ramasser de toutes parts. Il s'y peint lui-même. Ce qu'il y avait de plus beau dans son caractère, c'est que, quelque colérique qu'il fût, la vérité avait toujours sur lui un ascendant infaillible: et pour cela seul il mériterait, je pense, une statue.

Je regrette aujourd'hui, pour la première fois de ma vie, de ne point faire de vers; je ne peux répondre aux vôtres qu'en prose, mais je peux vous assurer que depuis 1746, que je dispose de mon temps, je vous ai les plus grandes obligations. Avant cette époque je ne lisais que des romans, mais par hasard vos ouvrages me tombèrent dans les mains; depuis je n'ai cessé de les lire, et n'ai voulu d'aucuns livres qui ne fussent aussi bien écrits, et où il n'y eût autant à profiter. Mais où les trouver? Je retournai donc à ce premier moteur de mon goût et de mon plus cher amusement. Assurément, monsieur, si j'ai quelques connaissances, c'est à lui seul que je les dois. Mais puisqu'il se défend par respect de me dire qu'il baise mon billet, il faut, par bienséance, que je lui laisse ignorer que j'ai de l'enthousiasme pour ses ouvrages. Je lis à présent l'*Essai sur l'Histoire générale*: je voudrais savoir chaque page par cœur, en attendant les œuvres du grand Corneille, pour lesquelles j'espère que la lettre de change est expédiée.

CATERINE

II

DE L'IMPÉRATRICE

? *c.* juin 1765

L'impératrice de Russie est très obligée au neveu de l'abbé Bazin, de ce qu'il a bien voulu lui dédier l'ouvrage de son oncle, qui assurément n'a rien de commun avec Abraham Chaumeix, maître d'école à Moscou, où il enseigne l'*a b c* aux petits enfants. Elle a lu ce beau livre d'un bout à l'autre avec beaucoup de plaisir, et ne s'est point trouvée supérieure à ce qu'elle a lu, parce qu'elle fait partie de ce genre humain, si enclin à goûter les absurdités les plus étranges; elle est persuadée que ce livre ne manquera pas d'en éprouver sa part, et qu'à Paris il sera infailliblement livré au feu, au pied d'un grand escalier; ce qui lui donnera un lustre de plus.

Comme le neveu de l'abbé Bazin a gardé un profond silence sur le lieu de sa résidence, on a adressé cette réponse à M. de

Voltaire, si connu pour protéger et favoriser les jeunes gens dont les talents font espérer qu'ils seront un jour utiles au genre humain. Cet illustre auteur est prié de faire parvenir ce peu de lignes à sa destination; et si par hasard il ne connaissait point ce neveu de l'abbé Bazin, on est persuadé qu'il excusera cette démarche en faveur du mérite éclatant de ce jeune homme.

CATERINE

III

DE VOLTAIRE

24 juillet 1765, près de Genève

Madame, je n'ai pas manqué de chercher le neveu de l'abbé Bazin pour lui communiquer la lettre dont votre Majesté Impériale m'a honoré. C'est un homme retiré et obscur, mais votre gloire est venue jusqu'à lui; elle lui est chère, il connait l'étendue de votre génie, de votre esprit, de votre courage. Il vous admire d'avoir su reduire les prêtres à être utiles et dépendants. Si je n'étais pas si vieux que je le suis, je demanderais à votre Majesté, la permission d'assister avec lui au premier carouzel qu'on ait vu dans vos climats. Falestris ne donna jamais de carouzel, elle alla cajoler Aléxandre, mais Aléxandre serait venu vous faire sa cour.

On n'a point encore incendié le livre de l'abbé Bazin. On croit qu'il l'a composé dans vos états, car la vérité vient du nord, comme les colifichets viennent du midi.

Au reste, madame, le neveu Bazin m'a dit qu'il avait été très attaché à Madame la Princesse de Zerbst, mère de votre Majesté, il dit qu'elle était aussi fort belle et pleine d'esprit; et que si elle vivait, elle serait prête à mourir de joie en voyant les succès de sa fille.

Il y a un meilleur parti à prendre, c'est celui d'en être longtemps témoin. Que Votre Majesté Impériale me permette de me joindre au petit Bazin pour me mettre à vos pieds.

Je suis avec un profond respect, Madame, de Votre Majesté Impériale le très humble, et très obéissant serviteur.

VOLTAIRE

IV

DE L'IMPÉRATRICE

Le 11/22 auguste 1765

Monsieur, puisque, Dieu merci, le neveu de l'abbé Bazin est trouvé, vous voudrez bien qu'une seconde fois je m'adresse à vous pour lui faire parvenir dans sa retraite le petit paquet ci-joint, en témoignage de ma reconnaissance pour les douceurs qu'il me dit. Je serais très aise de vous voir assister tous les deux à mon carrousel, dussiez-vous vous déguiser en chevaliers inconnus. Vous en auriez tout le temps: la pluie continuelle qui tombe depuis plusieurs semaines m'a obligée de renvoyer cette fête au mois de juin de l'année prochaine.

Ma devise est une abeille qui, volant de plante en plante, amasse son miel pour le porter dans sa ruche, et l'inscription est l'*Utile*. Chez vous les inférieurs instruisent, et il serait facile aux supérieurs d'en faire leur profit: chez nous c'est tout le contraire; nous n'avons pas tant d'aisance.

L'attachement du neveu Bazin pour feu ma mère lui donne un nouveau degré de considération chez moi: je trouve ce jeune homme très aimable, et je le prie de me conserver les sentiments qu'il me témoigne. Il est très bon et très utile d'avoir de pareilles connaissances. Vous voudrez bien, monsieur, être assuré que vous partagez avec le neveu mon estime, et tout ce que je lui dis est également pour vous aussi.

CATERINE

P.S. Des capucins qu'on tolère à Moscou (car la tolérance est générale dans cet empire, il n y a que les jésuites qui ne sont pas soufferts), s'étant opiniâtrés cet hiver à ne vouloir pas enterrer un Français (qui était mort subitement), sous prétexte qu'il n'avait pas reçu les sacrements. Abraham Chaumeix fit un factum contre eux pour leur prouver qu'ils devaient enterrer un mort. Mais ce factum ni deux réquisitions du gouverneur ne purent porter ces pères à obéir. A la fin, on leur fit dire de choisir, ou de passer la frontière, ou d'enterrer ce Français. Ils partirent, et j'envoyai d'ici des augustins plus dociles, qui, voyant qu'il n'y avait pas à badiner, firent tout ce qu'on voulut.

Voilà donc Abraham Chaumeix devenu raisonnable en Russie; il s'oppose à la persécution. S'il prenait de l'esprit, il ferait croire les miracles aux incrédules. Mais tous les miracles du monde n'effaceront pas la tache d'avoir empêché l'impression de l'*Encyclopédie*.

Les sujets de l'Église souffrant des vexations souvent tyranniques, auxquelles les fréquents changements de maîtres contribuaient encore beaucoup, se révoltèrent vers la fin du règne de l'impératrice Élisabeth, et ils étaient à mon avénement plus de cent mille en armes. C'est ce qui fit qu'en 1762 j'exécutai le projet de changer entièrement l'administration des biens du clergé, et de fixer ses revenus. Arsène, évêque de Rostou, s'y opposa, poussé par quelques uns de ses confrères, qui ne trouvèrent pas à propos de se nommer. Il envoya deux mémoires où il voulait établir le principe absurde des deux puissances. Il avait déjà fait cette tentative du temps de l'impératrice Élisabeth; on s'était contenté de lui imposer silence; mais son insolence et sa folie redoublant, il fut jugé par le métropolitain de Novogorod et par le synode entier, condamné comme fanatique, coupable d'une entreprise contraire à la foi orthodoxe autant qu'au pouvoir souverain, déchu de sa dignité et de la prêtrise, et livré au bras séculier. Je lui fis grâce, et je me contentai de le réduire à la condition de moine.

V

DE VOLTAIRE

c. 30 septembre 1765

L'abeille est utile sans doute,
On la chérit, on la redoute,
Aux mortels elle fait du bien,
Son miel nourrit, sa cire éclaire:
Mais quand elle a le don de plaire,
Ce superflu ne gâte rien.

Minerve, propice à la terre,
Instruisit les grossiers humains,
Planta l'olivier de ses mains,
Et battit le dieu de la guerre.
Cependant elle disputa
La pomme due à la plus belle;
Quelque temps Pâris hésita,
Mais Achille eût été pour elle.

Madame, que votre majesté impériale pardonne à ces mauvais vers; la reconnaissance n'est pas toujours éloquente: si votre devise est une abeille, vous avez une terrible ruche; c'est la plus grande qui soit au monde; vous remplissez la terre de votre nom et de vos bienfaits. Les plus précieux pour moi sont les médailles qui vous représentent. Les traits de votre majesté me rappellent ceux de la princesse votre mère.

J'ai encore un autre bonheur, c'est que tous ceux qui ont été honorés des bontés de votre majesté sont mes amis; je me tiens redevable de ce qu'elle a fait si généreusement pour les Diderot, les d'Alembert, et les Calas. Tous les gens de lettres de l'Europe doivent être à vos pieds.

C'est vous, madame, qui faites les miracles; vous avez rendu Abraham Chaumeix tolérant; et, s'il approche de votre majesté, il aura de l'esprit; mais pour les capucins, votre majesté a bien senti qu'il n'était pas en son pouvoir de les changer en hommes, depuis que saint François les a changés en bêtes. Heureusement votre académie va former des hommes qui n'auront pas affaire à saint François.

Je suis plus vieux, madame, que la ville où vous régnez, et que vous embellissez. J'ose même ajouter que je suis plus vieux que votre empire, en datant sa nouvelle fondation du créateur Pierre-le-Grand, dont vous perfectionnez l'ouvrage. Cependant je sens que je prendrais la liberté d'aller faire ma cour à cette étonnante abeille qui gouverne cette vaste ruche, si les maladies qui m'accablent me permettaient, à moi pauvre bourdon, de sortir de ma cellule.

Je me ferais présenter par M. le comte de Schouvalof et par madame sa femme, que j'ai eu l'honneur de posséder quelques jours dans mon petit ermitage. Votre majesté impériale a été le sujet de nos entretiens, et jamais je n'ai tant éprouvé le chagrin de ne pouvoir voyager.

Oserai-je, madame, dire que je suis un peu fâché que vous vous appeliez Catherine? les héroïnes d'autrefois ne prenaient point de nom de saintes: Homère, Virgile, auraient été bien embarrassés avec ces noms-là; vous n'étiez pas faite pour le calendrier.

Mais, soit Junon, Minerve, ou Vénus, ou Céres, qui s'ajustent bien mieux à la poésie en tout pays, je me mets aux pieds de votre majesté impériale, avec reconnaissance et avec le plus profond respect.

VI

DE L'IMPÉRATRICE

A Pétersbourg, 17/28 novembre 1765

Monsieur, ma tête est aussi dure que mon nom est peu harmonieux; je répondrai par de la mauvaise prose à vos jolis vers. Je n'en ai jamais fait; mais je n'en admire pas moins pour cela les vôtres. Ils m'ont si bien gâtée, que je ne puis presque en souffrir d'autres. Je me renferme dans ma grande ruche; on ne saurait faire différents métiers à la fois.

Jamais je n'aurais cru que l'achat d'une bibliothèque m'attirerait tant de compliments: tout le monde m'en fait sur celle de M. Diderot. Mais avouez, vous à qui l'humanité en doit pour le soutien que vous avez donné à l'innocence et à la vertu dans la personne des Calas, qu'il aurait été cruel et injuste de séparer un savant d'avec ses livres.

Démétri, métropolite de Novogorod, n'est ni persécuteur, ni fanatique. Il n'y a pas un principe dans le mandement d'Alexis qu'il n'avouât, ne prêchât, ne publiât, si cela était utile ou nécessaire: il abhorre la proposition des *deux puissances*. Plus d'une fois il m'a donné des exemples que je pourrais vous citer. Si je ne craignais de vous ennuyer, je les mettrais sur une feuille séparée, afin de la brûler, si vous ne vouliez pas la lire.

La tolérance est établie chez nous: elle fait loi de l'état, et il est défendu de persécuter. Nous avons, il est vrai, des fanatiques qui, faute de persécution, se brûlent eux-mêmes; mais si ceux des autres pays en fesaient autant, il n'y aurait pas grand mal; le monde n'en serait que plus tranquille, et Calas n'aurait pas été roué. Voilà, monsieur, les sentiments que nous devons au fondateur de cette ville, que nous admirons tous deux.

Je suis bien fâchée que votre santé ne soit pas aussi brillante que votre esprit: celui-ci en donne aux autres. Ne vous plaignez point de votre âge, et vivez les années de Mathusalem, dussiez-vous tenir dans le calendrier la place que vous trouvez à propos de me refuser. Comme je ne me crois point en droit d'être chantée, je ne changerai point mon nom contre celui de l'envieuse et jalouse Junon: je n'ai pas assez de présomption pour prendre celui de Minerve; je ne veux point du nom de Vénus, il y en a trop sur le compte de cette belle dame. Je ne suis pas Cérès non plus; la récolte a été très mauvaise en Russie cette année: le mien au moins me fait espérer l'intercession de ma patronne là où elle est; et, à tout prendre, je le crois le meilleur pour moi. Mais, en vous assurant de la part que je prends à ce qui vous regarde, je vous en éviterai l'inutile répétition.

CATERINE

VII

DE VOLTAIRE

24 janvier 1766

Madame, la lettre dont votre majesté impériale m'honore m'a tourné la tête; elle m'a donné des patentes de prophète. Je ne me doutais pas que l'archevêque de Novogorod se fût en effet déclaré contre le système absurde des *deux puissances*. J'avais raison sans le savoir, ce qui est encore un caractère de prophétie. Les incrédules pourront m'objecter que cet archevêque ne s'appelle pas Alexis, mais Démétri. Je pourrai répondre avec tous les commentateurs qu'il faut de l'obscurité dans les prophéties, et que cette obscurité rend toujours la vérité plus claire. J'ajouterai qu'il n'y a qu'à changer *Alex* en *Démé*, et *is* en *tri*, pour avoir le véritable nom de l'archevêque. Il n'y aura certainement que des impies qui puissent ne se pas rendre à des preuves si évidentes.

Je suis si bien prophète, que je prédis hardiment à votre majesté la plus grande gloire et le plus grand bonheur. Ou les hommes deviendront entièrement fous, ou ils admireront tout ce que vous faites de grand et d'utile; cette prédiction même vient un peu, comme les autres, après l'événement.

Il me semble que si cet autre grand homme, Pierre Ier, s'était établi dans un climat plus doux que sur le lac Ladoga, s'il avait choisi Kiovie, ou quelque autre terrain plus méridional, je serais actuellement à vos pieds, en dépit de mon âge. Il est triste de mourir sans avoir admiré de près celle qui préfère le nom de Catherine aux noms des divinités de l'ancien temps, et qui le rendra préférable. Je n'ai jamais voulu aller à Rome; j'ai senti toujours de la répugnance à voir des moines dans le Capitole, et les tombeaux des Scipions foulés aux pieds des prêtres; mais je meurs de regret de ne point voir des déserts changés en villes superbes, et deux mille lieues de pays civilisés par des héroïnes. L'histoire du monde entier n'a rien de semblable; c'est la plus belle et la plus grande des révolutions: mon cœur est comme l'aimant, il se tourne vers le nord.

D'Alembert a bien tort de n'avoir pas fait le voyage, lui qui est encore jeune. Il a été piqué de la petite injustice qu'on lui fesait; mais l'objet qui est fort mince ne troublait point sa philosophie. Tout cela est réparé aujourd'hui. Je crois que l'*Encyclopédie* est en chemin pour aller demander une place dans la bibliothèque de votre palais.

Que votre majesté impériale daigne recevoir avec bonté ma reconnaissance, mon admiration, mon profond respect.

Feu l'abbé Bazin

VIII

A CATHERINE II

A Ferney par Genève, 21 juin 1766

Madame! C'est maintenant vers l'étoile du nord qu'il faut que tous les yeux se tournent. Votre Majesté Impériale a trouvé un chemin vers la gloire inconnue avant elle à tous les autres souverains. Aucun ne s'était avisé de répandre des bienfaits à sept ou huit cent lieues de ses états. Vous êtes devenue réellement la bienfaitrice de l'Europe; et vous avez acquis plus de sujets par la grandeur de votre âme, que d'autres n'en peuvent conquérir par les armes.

Il y a peut être de l'indiscrétion à oser implorer la protection de Votre Majesté pour les Sirven, après les bontés dont elle a comblé la famille Calas. Je sais ce que Votre Majesté fait de grand et d'utile pour ses peuples. Ce serait se rendre coupable envers eux que de vous supplier de détourner pour une malheureuse famille du Languedoc une partie de la source des biens que vous répandez en Russie. Je ne prends la liberté de vous écrire, Madame, que pour vous prier de modérer vos bontés. Le moindre secours nous suffira. Nous ne demandons que l'honneur de placer votre auguste nom à la tête de ceux qui nous aident à écraser le fanatisme et à rendre les hommes plus tolérants et plus humains.

J'ai une autre grâce à demander à Votre Majesté, c'est de daigner permettre que je communique le mémoire dont elle m'a honoré au sujet de cet évêque de Rostow puni pour avoir imaginé qu'il y avait deux puissances. Il n'y en a qu'une, Madame, et c'est celle qui est bienfaisante.

Je suis avec le plus profond respect et la plus vive reconnaissance, Madame, de Votre Majesté Impériale, le très humble très obéissant et très obligé serviteur.

VOLTAIRE

IX

DE L'IMPÉRATRICE

A Pétersbourg, 29 juin/10 juillet 1766

Monsieur, la lueur de l'étoile du nord n'est qu'une aurore boréale.

Les bienfaits répandus à quelques centaines de lieues, et dont il vous plaît de faire mention, ne m'appartiennent pas: les Calas doivent ce qu'ils ont reçu à leurs amis; M. Diderot, la vente de sa bibliothèque au sien; mais les Calas et les Sirven vous doivent tout. Ce n'est rien que de donner un peu à son prochain de ce dont on a un grand superflu; mais c'est s'immortaliser que d'être l'avocat du genre humain, le défenseur de l'innocence opprimée. Ces deux causes vous attirent la vénération due à de tels miracles. Vous avez combattu les ennemis réunis des hommes: la superstition, le fanatisme, l'ignorance, la chicane, les mauvais juges, et la partie du pouvoir qui repose entre les mains des uns et des autres. Il faut bien des vertus et des qualités pour surmonter ces obstacles. Vous avez montré que vous les possédez: vous avez vaincu.

Vous desirez, monsieur, un secours modique pour les Sirven: le puis-je refuser! me louerez-vous de cette action? y a-t-il de quoi? Je vous avoue que j'aimerais mieux qu'on ignorât ma lettre-de-change. Si cependant vous pensez que mon nom, tout peu harmonieux qu'il est, fasse quelque bien à ces victimes de l'esprit de persécution, je me remets à votre prévoyance, et vous me nommerez, pourvu seulement que cela même ne leur nuise pas. J'ai mes raisons pour le croire. Mes aventures avec l'évêque de Rostou ont été traitées publiquement, et vous en pouvez, monsieur, communiquer le mémoire à votre gré, comme une pièce authentique.

J'ai lu avec beaucoup d'attention l'imprimé qui accompagnait votre lettre. Il est bien difficile de réduire en pratique les principes qu'il contient. Malheureusement le grand nombre y sera longtemps opposé. Il est cependant possible d'émousser la pointe des opinions qui mènent à la destruction des humains.

Voici mot à mot ce que j'ai inséré, entre autres choses, à ce sujet, dans une instruction au comité qui refondra nos lois:

"Dans un grand empire, qui étend sa domination sur autant de peuples divers qu'il y a de différentes croyances parmi les hommes, la faute la plus nuisible au repos et à la tranquillité de ses citoyens serait l'intolérance de leurs différentes religions. Il n'y a même qu'une sage tolérance, également avouée de la religion orthodoxe et de la politique, qui puisse ramener toutes les brebis égarées à la vraie croyance. La persécution irrite les esprits; la tolérance les adoucit et les rend moins obstinés; elle étouffe ces disputes contraires au repos de l'état et à l'union des citoyens.".

Après cela suit un précis du Livre de l'*Esprit des Lois*, *Sur la magie*, etc., qu'il serait trop long de rapporter ici. Il y est dit tout ce qu'on peut dire pour préserver, d'un côté, les citoyens des maux que peuvent produire de pareilles accusations, sans cependant troubler, de l'autre, la tranquillité des croyances, ni scandaliser les consciences des croyants. J'ai cru que c'était l'unique voie praticable d'introduire le cri de la raison, que de l'appuyer sur le fondement de la tranquillité publique, dont chaque individu sent continuellement le besoin et l'utilité.

Le petit comte de Schouvalof, de retour dans sa patrie, m'a fait le récit de l'intérêt que vous avez bien voulu prendre à tout ce qui me regarde. Je finis par vous en marquer ma gratitude.

CATERINE

X

DE VOLTAIRE

22 décembre 1766

Madame, que votre majesté impériale me pardonne: non, vous n'êtes point l'*Aurore boréale*; vous êtes assurément l'astre le plus brillant du nord, et il n'y en a jamais eu d'aussi bienfesant que vous: Andromède, Persée, et Calisto, ne vous valent pas. Tous ces astres-là auraient laissé Diderot mourir de faim. Il a été persécuté dans sa patrie, et vos bienfaits viennent l'y chercher. Louis XIV avait moins de magnificence que votre majesté; il récompensa le mérite dans les pays étrangers, mais on lui indiquait ce mérite: vous le cherchez, madame, et vous le trouvez. Vos soins généreux pour établir la liberté de conscience en Pologne sont un bienfait que le genre humain doit célébrer, et j'ambitionne bien d'oser parler au nom du genre humain, si ma voix peut encore se faire entendre.

En attendant, madame, permettez-moi de publier ce que vous avez daigné m'écrire au sujet de l'archevêque de Novogorod, et sur la tolérance. Ce que vous écrivez est un monument de votre gloire; nous sommes trois, Diderot, d'Alembert, et moi, qui vous dressons des autels; vous me rendez païen: je suis avec idolâtrie, madame, aux pieds de votre majesté, mieux qu'avec un profond respect, *Le prêtre de votre temple*

XI

DE L'IMPÉRATRICE

A Pétersbourg, 29 décembre/9 janvier 1767

Monsieur, je viens de recevoir votre lettre du 22 décembre, dans laquelle vous me donnez une place décidée parmi les astres. Je ne sais si ces places-là valent la peine qu'on les brigue. Je ne voudrais point être mise au rang de ceux que le genre humain a adorés pendant si long-temps, par tout autre que vous et vos dignes amis dont vous me parlez. En effet, quelque peu d'amour-propre qu'on se sente, il est impossible de desirer de se voir l'égal des ognons, des chats, des veaux, des peaux d'ânes, de bœufs, de serpents, de crocodiles, des bêtes de toute espèce, etc., etc. Après cette énumération, quel est l'homme qui voulût des temples?

Laissez-moi donc, je vous prie, sur la terre; j'y serai plus à portée d'y recevoir vos lettres et celles de vos amis les d'Alembert et les Diderot: j'y serai témoin de la sensibilité avec laquelle vous vous intéressez à tout ce qui regarde les lumières de notre siècle, partageant si parfaitement ce titre avec eux.

Malheur aux persécuteurs! ils méritent d'être rangés parmi ces divinités. Voilà leur vraie place.

Au reste, monsieur, soyez persuadé que votre approbation m'encourage beaucoup.

L'article dont je vous ai fait part, et qui regarde la tolérance, ne paraîtra au grand jour qu'à la fin de l'été prochain.

Je me souviens de vous avoir écrit dans une lettre précédente ce que je pensais de la publication des pièces qui concernent l'archevêque de Novogorod: cet ecclésiastique a donné depuis peu encore une preuve des sentiments que vous lui connaissez. Un homme qui avait traduit un livre le lui porta: il lui dit qu'il lui conseillait de le supprimer, parce qu'il contenait les principes qui établissent les *deux puissances*.

Soyez assuré, monsieur, que tel titre que vous preniez, il ne nuira jamais chez moi à la considération qui est due à celui qui plaide avec toute l'étendue de son génie la cause de l'humanité.

CATERINE

L'imprimé ci-joint vous fera juger si la justice est de notre côté.

XII

DE VOLTAIRE

A Ferney, 27 février 1767

Madame, votre majesté impériale daigne donc me faire juge de la magnanimité avec laquelle elle prend le parti du genre humain. Ce juge est trop corrompu et trop persuadé qu'on ne peut répondre que des sottises tyranniques à votre excellent mémoire. Ne pouvoir jouir des droits de citoyen parce qu'on croit que le Saint-Esprit ne procède que du Père me paraît si fou et si sot, que je ne croirais pas cette bêtise, si celles de mon pays ne m'y avaient préparé. Je ne suis pas fait pour pénétrer dans vos secrets d'état; mais je serais bien attrapé si votre majesté n'était pas d'accord avec le roi de Pologne; il est philosophe, il est tolérant par principe; j'imagine que vous vous entendez tous deux, comme larrons en foire, pour le bien du genre humain, et pour vous moquer des prêtres intolérants.

Un temps viendra, madame, je le dis toujours, où toute la

lumière nous viendra du nord: votre majesté impériale a beau dire, je vous fais étoile, et vous demeurerez étoile. Les ténèbres cimmériennes resteront en Espagne; et à la fin même elles se dissiperont. Vous ne serez ni ognon, ni chatte, ni veau d'or, ni bœuf Apis; vous ne serez point de ces dieux qu'on mange, vous êtes de ceux qui donnent à manger. Vous faites tout le bien que vous pouvez au-dedans et au-dehors. Les sages feront votre apothéose de votre vivant; mais vivez long-temps, madame, cela vaut cent fois mieux que la divinité; si vous voulez faire des miracles, tâchez seulement de rendre votre climat un peu plus chaud. A voir tout ce que votre majesté fait, je croirai que c'est pure malice à elle, si elle n'entreprend pas ce changement: j'y suis un peu intéressé; car, dès que vous aurez mis la Russie au trentième degré, au lieu des environs du soixantième, je vous demanderai la permission d'y venir achever ma vie; mais, en quelque endroit que je végète, je vous admirerai malgré vous, et je serai avec le plus profond respect, madame, de votre majesté impériale, etc.

XIII

DE L'IMPÉRATRICE

A Moscou, le 15/26 mars 1767

Monsieur, j'ai reçu votre lettre du 27 février, où vous me conseillez de faire un miracle pour changer le climat de ce pays. Cette ville-ci était autrefois très accoutumée à voir des miracles, ou plutôt les bonnes gens prenaient souvent les choses les plus ordinaires pour des effets merveilleux. J'ai lu dans la préface du concile du tzar Ivan Basilewitz, que lorsque le tzar eut fait sa confession publique, il arriva un miracle: le soleil parut en plein midi, ses rayons donnèrent sur lui, et sur tous les pères rassemblés. Notez que ce prince, après avoir fait une confession générale à haute voix, finit par reprocher au clergé, dans des termes très vifs, tous ses désordres, et conjura le concile de le corriger lui et son clergé aussi.

A présent les choses sont changées. Pierre-le-Grand a mis tant de formalités pour constater un miracle, et le synode les remplit si strictement, que je crains d'exposer celui dont il vous plaît de me charger avant votre arrivée. Cependant, je ferai tout ce qui sera en mon pouvoir pour procurer à la ville de Pétersbourg un meilleur air. Il y a trois ans qu'on est après à saigner par des canaux les marais qui l'entourent, à abattre les forêts de sapins qui la couvrent au midi; et à présent il y a déjà trois grandes terres occupées par des colons, là où un homme à pied ne pouvait passer sans avoir de l'eau jusqu'à la ceinture: les habitants ont semé, l'automne dernière, leurs premiers grains.

Comme vous paraissez, monsieur, prendre intérêt à ce que je fais, je joins à cette lettre la moins mauvaise traduction française du *Manifeste* que j'ai signé le 14 décembre de l'année passée, et qui a été si fort estropié dans les gazettes de Hollande, qu'on ne savait pas trop ce qu'il pouvait signifier. En russe c'est une pièce estimée: la richesse et les expressions fortes de notre langue l'ont rendue telle. La traduction en a été d'autant plus pénible. Au mois de juin, cette grande assemblée commencera ses séances, et nous dira ce qui lui manque. Après quoi on travaillera à des lois que l'humanité, j'espère, ne désapprouvera pas. D'ici à ce temps-là, j'irai faire un tour dans différentes provinces, le long du Volga; et au moment peut-être que vous vous y attendrez le moins, vous recevrez une lettre datée de quelque bicoque de l'Asie.

Je serai là, comme partout ailleurs, remplie d'estime et de considération pour le seigneur du château de Ferney.

CATERINE

XIV

DE VOLTAIRE

26 mai 1767

Un voyage en Asie! allez-vous l'entreprendre,
Belle et sublime Thalestris?
Que ferez-vous dans ce pays?
Vous n'y verrez point d'Alexandre.

Hélas! votre majesté impériale ferait le tour du globe, qu'elle ne rencontrerait guère de rois dignes d'elle. Elle voyage comme

Cérès la législatrice, en fesant du bien au monde. Je ne sais point la langue russe; mais par la traduction que vous daignez m'envoyer, je vois qu'elle a des inversions et des tours qui manquent à la nôtre. Je ne suis pas comme une dame de la cour de Versailles, qui disait: C'est bien dommage que l'aventure de la tour de Babel ait produit la confusion des langues, sans cela tout le monde aurait toujours parlé français.

L'empereur de la Chine, Kang-hi, votre voisin, demandait à un missionnaire si on pouvait faire des vers dans les langues de l'Europe; il ne pouvait le croire.

Que votre majesté impériale daigne agréer mes sentiments et le très profond respect de ce vieux Suisse, etc.

XV

DE L'IMPÉRATRICE

A Casan, le 29 mai/9 juin 1767

Je vous avais menacé d'une lettre, de quelque bicoque de l'Asie; je vous tiens parole aujourd'hui.

Il me semble que les auteurs de l'*Anecdote sur Bélisaire*, et de la *Lettre sur les Panégyriques*, sont proches parents du neveu de l'abbé Bazin. Mais, monsieur, ne vaudrait-il pas mieux renvoyer tout panégyrique des gens après leur mort, crainte que tôt ou tard ils ne donnent un démenti, vu l'inconséquence et le peu de stabilité des choses humaines? Je ne sais si, après la révocation de l'édit de Nantes, on a fait beaucoup de cas des panégyriques de Louis XIV: les réfugiés, au moins, n'étaient pas disposés à leur donner du poids.

Je vous prie, monsieur, d'employer votre crédit auprès du savant du canton d'Uri, pour qu'il ne perde pas son temps à faire le mien avant mon décès.

Ces lois dont on parle tant, au bout du compte, ne sont point faites encore. Eh! qui peut répondre de leur bonté? C'est la postérité, et non pas nous, en vérité, qui sera à portée de décider cette question. Imaginez, je vous prie, qu'elles doivent servir pour l'Europe et pour l'Asie: et quelle différence de climat, de gens, d'habitudes, d'idées même!

Me voilà en Asie; j'ai voulu voir cela par mes yeux. Il y a dans cette ville vingt peuples divers, qui ne se ressemblent point du tout. Il faut pourtant leur faire un habit qui leur soit propre à tous. Ils peuvent se bien trouver des principes généraux; mais les détails? Et quels détails! J'allais dire: C'est presque un monde à créer, à unir, à conserver. Je ne finirais pas, et en voilà beaucoup trop de toutes façons.

Si tout cela ne réussit pas, les lambeaux de lettres que j'ai trouvés cités dans le dernier imprimé paraîtront ostentation (et que sais-je, moi?) aux impartiaux et à mes envieux. Et puis mes lettres n'ont été dictées que par l'estime, et ne sauraient être bonnes à l'impression. Il est vrai qu'il m'est bien flatteur et honorable de voir par quel sentiment tout cela a été cité chez l'auteur de la *Lettre sur les Panégyriques*; mais Bélisaire dit que c'est là justement le moment dangereux pour mon espèce. Bélisaire ayant raison partout, sans doute n'aura pas tort en ceci. La traduction de ce dernier livre est finie, et va être imprimée. Pour faire l'essai de cette traduction, on l'a lue à deux personnes qui ne connaissaient point l'original. L'un s'écria: Qu'on me crève les yeux, pourvu que je sois Bélisaire, j'en serai assez récompensé; l'autre dit: Si cela était, j'en serais envieux.

En finissant, monsieur, recevez les témoignages de ma reconnaissance pour toutes les marques d'amitié que vous me donnez; mais, s'il est possible, préservez mon griffonnage de l'impression.

CATERINE

XVI

DE VOLTAIRE

29 janvier 1768

Madame, on dit qu'un vieillard, nommé Siméon, en voyant un petit enfant, s'écria dans sa joi: Je n'ai plus qu'à mourir *puisque j'ai vu mon salutaire*. Ce Siméon était prophète, il voyait de loin tout ce que ce petit Juif devait faire.

Moi, qui ne suis ni Juif ni prophète, mais qui suis aussi vieux que Siméon, je n'aurais pas deviné en 1700 qu'un jour la Raison, aussi inconnue au patriarche Nicon qu'au sacré collége, et aussi mal voulue des papas et des archimandrites que des dominicains, viendrait à Moscou, à la voix d'une princesse née en Allemagne, et qu'elle assemblerait dans sa grand'salle des idolâtres, des musulmans, des grecs, des latins, des luthériens, qui tous deviendraient ses enfants.

C'est ce triomphe de la Raison qui est mon *salutaire*; et en qualité d'être raisonnable, je mourrai sujet, dans mon cœur, de votre majesté impériale, bienfaitrice du genre humain.

Je suis retiré auprès de la petite ville de Genève, où il n'y a pas vingt mille habitants, et la discorde règne depuis quatre ans dans ce trou, dans le temps que Catherine *seconde*, qui est bien la *première*, réunit tous les esprits dans un empire plus vaste que l'empire romain.

Je ne suis pas en tout de l'avis du respectable auteur de *l'Ordre essentiel des sociétés*: je vous avoue, madame, qu'en qualité de voisin de deux républiques, je ne crois point du tout que la puissance législatrice soit, de droit divin, copropriétaire de mes petites chaumières; mais je crois fermement que, de droit humain, on doit vous admirer et vous aimer.

Feu l'abbé Bazin disait souvent qu'il craignait horriblement le froid, mais que s'il n'était pas si vieux, il irait s'établir au midi d'Astracan, pour avoir le plaisir de vivre sous vos lois.

J'ai rencontré ces jours passés son neveu, qui pense de même. Le professeur en droit Bourdillon est dans les mêmes sentiments; ce pauvre Bourdillon s'est plaint à moi amèrement de ce qu'on l'avait trompé sur l'évêque de Cracovie. Je l'ai consolé en lui disant qu'il avait raison sur tout le reste, et que l'événement l'a bien justifié. Votre majesté impériale ne saurait croire à quel point ce pédant républicain vous est attaché, toute souveraine que vous êtes.

Je ramasse, madame, toutes les sottises sérieuses ou comiques de feu l'abbé Bazin et de son neveu, et même celles qu'on leur attribue; il y en a qu'on n'oserait envoyer au pape, mais qu'on peut mettre hardiment dans la bibliothèque d'une impératrice philosophe. Ce recueil assez gros partira dès qu'il sera relié.

L'empereur Justinien et le grand capitaine Bélisaire ont été impitoyablement déclarés damnés par la Sorbonne. J'en ai été très affligé, car je m'intéressais beaucoup à leur salut. Je ne sais pas encore bien positivement si votre église grecque est damnée aussi; je m'en informerai, madame, car je vous suis encore plus attaché qu'à l'empereur Justinien. Je souhaite que vous viviez encore plus long-temps que lui.

Que votre majesté impériale daigne agréer le profond respect, l'admiration, et l'attachement inviolable du vieux solitaire, moitié Français, moitié Suisse, cousin-germain du neveu de l'abbé Bazin.

XVII

DE VOLTAIRE

A Ferney, 15 novembre 1768

Madame, j'eus l'honneur de dépêcher à votre majesté impériale, le 15 mars dernier, à l'adresse du sieur B. Le Maistre, à Hambourg, un assez gros ballot, marqué I. D. R., N° 1.

Votre majesté a des affaires un peu plus importantes que celles de ce ballot. D'un côté elle force les Polonais à être tolérants et heureux, en dépit du nonce du pape; et de l'autre elle paraît avoir affaire aux musulmans, malgré Mahomet. S'ils vous font la guerre, madame, il pourra bien leur arriver ce que Pierre-le-Grand avait eu autrefois en vue, c'était de faire de Constantinople la capitale de l'empire russe. Ces barbares méritent d'être punis, par une héroïne, du peu d'attention qu'ils ont eue jusqu'ici pour les dames. Il est clair que des gens qui négligent tous les beaux-arts, et qui enferment les femmes, méritent d'être exterminés. J'espère tout de votre génie et de votre destinée. Moustapha ne doit pas tenir contre Catherine. On dit que Moustapha n'a point d'esprit, qu'il n'aime point les vers, qu'il n'a jamais été à la comédie, et qu'il n'entend point le français; il sera battu, sur ma parole. Je demande à votre majesté impériale la permission de venir me mettre à ses pieds, et de passer quelques jours à sa cour, dès qu'elle sera établie à Constantinople; car je pense très sérieusement que si jamais les Turcs doivent être chassés de l'Europe, ce sera par les Russes. L'envie de vous plaire les rendra invincibles.

Que votre majesté daigne agréer les souhaits et le profond

respect de votre admirateur, de votre très zélé, très ardent serviteur.

XVIII

DE L'IMPÉRATRICE

A Pétersbourg, 6/17 décembre 1768

Monsieur, je suppose que vous me croyez un peu d'inconséquence: je vous ai prié, il y a environ un an, de m'envoyer tout ce qui a jamais été écrit par l'auteur dont j'aime le mieux à lire les ouvrages; j'ai reçu au mois de mai passé le ballot que j'ai desiré, accompagné du buste de l'homme le plus illustre de notre siècle.

J'ai senti une égale satisfaction de l'un et de l'autre envoi: ils font depuis six mois le plus bel ornement de mon appartement, et mon étude journalière; mais jusqu'ici je ne vous en ai accusé ni la réception, ni fait mes remerciements. Voici comme je raisonnais: un morceau de papier mal griffonné, rempli de mauvais français, est un remerciement stérile pour un tel homme; il faut lui faire mon compliment par quelque action qui puisse lui plaire. Différents faits se sont présentés; mais le détail en serait trop long: enfin j'ai cru que le meilleur serait de donner par moi-même un exemple qui pût devenir utile aux hommes. Je me suis souvenue que par bonheur je n'avais pas eu la petite-vérole. J'ai fait écrire en Angleterre pour avoir un inoculateur: le fameux docteur Dimsdale s'est résolu de passer en Russie. Il m'a inoculée le 12 octobre. Je n'ai pas été au lit un seul instant, et j'ai reçu du monde tous les jours. Je vais tout de suite faire inoculer mon fils unique.

Le grand-maître de l'artillerie, le comte Orlof, ce héros qui ressemble aux anciens Romains du beau temps de la république, et qui en a le courage et la générosité, doutant s'il avait eu cette maladie, est à présent entre les mains de notre Anglais, et le lendemain de l'opération il s'en alla à la chasse dans une très grande neige. Nombre de courtisans ont suivi son exemple, et beaucoup d'autres s'y préparent. Outre cela, on inocule à présent à Pétersbourg dans trois maisons d'éducation, et dans un hôpital établi sous les yeux de M. Dimsdale.

Voilà, monsieur, les nouvelles du pôle. J'espère qu'elles ne vous seront point indifférentes.

Les écrits nouveaux sont plus rares. Cependant il vient de paraître une traduction française de l'instruction russe donnée aux députés qui doivent composer le projet de notre code. On n'a pas eu le temps de l'imprimer. Je me hâte de vous envoyer le manuscrit, afin que vous voyiez mieux de quel point nous partons. J'espère qu'il n'y a pas une ligne qu'un honnête homme ne puisse avouer.

J'aimerais bien de vous envoyer des vers en échange des vôtres; mais qui n'a pas assez de cervelle pour en faire de bons, fait mieux de travailler de ses mains. Voilà ce que j'ai mis en pratique: j'ai tourné une tabatière que je vous prie d'accepter. Elle porte l'empreinte de la personne qui a pour vous le plus de considération; je n'ai pas besoin de la nommer, vous la reconnaîtrez aisément.

J'oubliais, monsieur, de vous dire que j'ai augmenté le peu ou point de médecine qu'on donne pendant l'inoculation, de trois ou quatre excellents spécifiques que je recommande à tout homme de bon sens de ne point négliger en pareille occasion. C'est de se faire lire l'*Écossaise*, *Candide*, *l'Ingénu*, *l'Homme aux quarante écus*, et *la Princesse de Babylone*. Il n'y a pas moyen, après cela, de sentir le moindre mal.

P.S. La lettre ci-jointe était écrite il y a trois semaines. Elle attendait le manuscrit; on a été si long-temps à le transcrire et à le rectifier, que j'ai eu le temps, monsieur, de recevoir votre lettre du 15 novembre. Si je fais aussi aisément la guerre contre les Turcs que j'ai eu de facilité à introduire l'inoculation, vous courez risque d'être sommé à tenir bientôt la promesse que vous me faites de venir me trouver dans un gite où, dit-on, se sont perdus tous ceux qui en ont fait la conquête. Voilà de quoi faire passer cette tentation à qui la prendra.

Je ne sais si Moustapha a de l'esprit; mais j'ai lieu de croire qu'il dit: *Mahomet, ferme les yeux!* quand il veut faire des guerres injustes à ses voisins. Si le succès de cette guerre se déclare pour nous, j'aurai beaucoup d'obligation à mes envieux: ils m'auront procuré une gloire à laquelle je ne pensais pas.

Tant pis pour Moustapha s'il n'aime ni la comédie ni les vers. Il sera bien attrapé si je parviens à mener les Turcs au même spectacle auquel la troupe de Paoli joue si bien. Je ne sais si ce dernier parle français, mais il sait combattre pour ses foyers et son indépendance.

Pour nouvelle d'ici, je vous dirai, monsieur, que tout le monde généralement veut être inoculé, qu'il y a un évêque qui va subir cette opération, et qu'on a inoculé ici dans un mois plus de personnes qu'à Vienne dans huit.

Je ne saurais, monsieur, vous témoigner assez ma reconnaissance pour toutes les choses obligeantes que vous voulez bien me dire, mais surtout pour le vif intérêt que vous prenez à tout ce qui me regarde. Soyez persuadé que je sens tout le prix de votre estime, et qu'il n'y a personne qui ait pour vous plus de considération que

CATERINE

Je prends encore une fois la plume pour vous prier de vous servir de cette fourrure contre le vent de bise et la fraîcheur des Alpes, qu'on m'a dit vous incommoder quelquefois. Adieu, monsieur; lors de votre entrée dans Constantinople, j'aurai soin de faire porter à votre rencontre un bel habit à la grecque, doublé des plus riches dépouilles de la Sibérie. Cet habit est bien plus commode et plus beau que les habits étriqués dont toute l'Europe fait usage, et dont aucun sculpteur ne veut ni ne peut vêtir ses statues, crainte de les faire paraître ridicules et mesquines.

XIX

DE L'IMPÉRATRICE

8/19 décembre 1768

Monsieur, le porteur de celle-ci vous remettra de ma part trois paquets, numérotés 1, 2, et 3.

En ouvrant le premier, vous saurez ce que contiennent les deux autres. Je vous fais mille excuses d'avoir tardé si longtemps: cent choses ensemble m'ont empêchée de vous envoyer ces papiers. Le prince Kosloftsky, lieutenant de mes gardes, a regardé comme une faveur distinguée d'être envoyé à Ferney. Je lui en sais gré. Si j'étais à sa place, j'en ferais autant.

Adieu, monsieur; portez-vous bien, et soyez assuré que personne ne s'intéresse plus à tout ce qui vous regarde que

CATERINE

XX

DE VOLTAIRE

A Ferney, février 1769

Cette belle et noire pelisse
Est celle que perdit le pauvre Moustapha,
Quand notre brave impératrice
De ses musulmans triompha;
Et ce beau portrait que voilà,
C'est celui de la bienfaitrice
Du genre humain, qu'elle éclaira.

Voilà ce que j'ai dit, madame, en voyant le cafetan dont votre majesté impériale m'a honoré, par les mains de M. le prince Kosloftsky, capigibachi de vos janissaires, et surtout cette boîte tournée de vos belles et augustes mains, et ornée de votre portrait.

Qui le voit et qui le touche
Ne peut borner ses sens à le considérer;
Il ose y porter une bouche
Qu'il n'ouvre désormais que pour vous admirer.

Mais quand on a su que la boîte était l'ouvrage de vos propres mains, ceux qui étaient dans ma chambre ont dit avec moi:

Ces mains, que le ciel a formées
Pour lancer les traits des Amours,
Ont préparé déjà ces flèches enflammées,
Ces tonnerres d'airain dont vos fières armées
Au monarque sarmate assurent des secours;
Et la Gloire a crié, de la tour byzantine,
Aux peuples enchantés que votre nom soumet:
Victoire à Catherine!
Nazarde à Mahomet!

Qu'est devenu le temps où l'empereur d'Allemagne aurait, dans les mêmes circonstances, envoyé des armées à Belgrade, et où les Vénitiens auraient couvert de vaisseux les mers du Péloponèse? Eh bien! madame, vous triompherez seule. Montrez-vous seulement à votre armée vers Kiovie, ou plus loin, et je vous réponds qu'il n'y a pas un de vos soldats qui ne soit un héros invincible. Que Moustapha se montre aux siens, il n'en fera que de gros cochons comme lui.

Quelle fierté imbécile dans cette tête coiffée d'un turban à aigrette! Tous les rois de l'Europe ne devraient-ils pas venger le droit des gens, que la Porte ottomane viole tous les jours avec un orgueil si grossier?

Ce n'est pas assez de faire une guerre heureuse contre ces barbares, pour la terminer par une paix telle quelle; ce n'est pas assez de les humilier, il faudrait les reléguer pour jamais en Asie.

XXI

DE VOLTAIRE

A Ferney, 26 février 1769

Madame, quoi! pendant que votre majesté impériale se prépare à battre le grand-turc, elle forme un corps de lois chrétiennes. Je lis l'instruction préliminaire qu'elle a eu la bonté de m'envoyer. Lycurgue et Solon auraient signé votre ouvrage, et n'auraient pas été capables de le faire. Cela est net, précis, équitable, ferme, et humain. Les législateurs ont la première place dans le temple de la gloire, les conquérants ne viennent qu'après. Soyez sûre que personne n'aura dans la postérité un plus grand nom que vous; mais, au nom de Dieu, battez les Turcs, malgré le nonce du pape en Pologne, qui est si bien avec eux.

De tous les préjugés destructrice brillante,
Qui du vrai dans tout genre embrassez le parti,
Soyez à la fois triomphante
Et du saint-père et du mufti.

Eh! madame, quelle leçon votre majesté impériale donne à nos petits-maîtres français, à nos sages maîtres de Sorbonne, à nos Esculapes des écoles de médecine! Vous vous êtes fait inoculer, avec moins d'appareil qu'une religieuse ne prend un lavement. Le prince impérial a suivi votre exemple. M. le comte Orlof va à la chasse dans la neige, après s'être fait donner la petite-vérole: voilà comme Scipion en aurait usé, si cette maladie, venue d'Arabie, avait existé de son temps.

Pour nous autres, nous avons été sur le point de ne pouvoir être inoculés que par arrête du parlement. Je ne sais pas ce qui est arrivé à notre nation, qui donnait autrefois de grands exemples en tout; mais nous sommes bien barbares en certains cas, et bien pusillanimes dans d'autres.

Madame, je suis un vieux malade de soixante et quinze ans. Je radote peut-être, mais je vous dis au moins ce que je pense; et cela est assez rare quand on parle à des personnes de votre espèce. La majesté impériale disparaît sur mon papier devant la personne. Mon enthousiasme l'emporte sur mon profond respect.

XXII

DE VOLTAIRE

A Ferney...avril 1769

Madame, un jeune homme des premières familles de Genève, qui, à la vérité, a près de six pieds de haut, mais qui n'est âgé que de seize ans, assistant chez moi à la lecture de l'instruction que Votre Majesté Impériale a donnée pour la rédaction de ses lois, s'écria: "Mon Dieu, que je voudrais être Russe!" Je lui dis, en présence de sa mère: "Il ne tient qu'à vous de l'être; Pictet, qui est plus grand que vous, l'est bien; vous êtes plus sage et plus aimable que lui. Madame votre mère veut vous envoyer dans une université d'Allemagne apprendre l'allemand et le droit public; au lieu d'aller en Allemagne, allez à Riga; vous apprendrez à la fois l'allemand et le russe; et à l'égard du droit public, il n'y en a certainement point de plus beau que celui de l'impératrice".

Je proposai la chose à sa mère, et je n'eus pas de peine à l'y faire consentir. Ce jeune homme s'appelle *Galatin*; il est de la plus aimable et de la plus belle figure; sa mémoire est prodigieuse;

son esprit est digne de sa mémoire, et il a toute la modestie convenable à ses talents. Si Votre Majesté daigne le protéger, il partira incessamment pour Riga, après avoir commencé à suivre votre exemple en se faisant inoculer. Je suis fâché de n'offrir à Votre Majesté qu'un sujet; mais je réponds bien que celui-là en vaudra plusieurs autres.

Oserai-je prendre la liberté de demander à Votre Majesté à qui il faudra que je l'adresse à Riga? Sa mère ne peut payer pour lui qu'une pension modique. J'ose me flatter qu'il n'aura pas été un an à Riga, sans être en état de venir saluer Votre Majesté en russe et en allemand. Qu'est devenu le temps où je n'avais que soixante ans? Je l'aurais accompagné.

Si Votre Majesté va s'établir à Constantinople, comme je l'espère, il apprendra bien vite le grec; car il faut absolument chasser d'Europe la langue turque, ainsi que tous ceux qui la parlent. Enfin, madame, au nom de toutes vos bontés pour moi, j'ose vous implorer pour le jeune Galatin, et je puis répondre qu'il méritera toute votre protection.

J'attends les ordres de Votre Majesté Impériale.

XXIII

DE VOLTAIRE

A Ferney, 27 mai 1769

La lettre dont votre majesté impériale m'honore, en date du 15 avril, m'a fait plus de bien que le mois de mai. Le beau temps ranime un peu les vieillards, mais vos succès me donnent des forces. Vous daignez me dire que vous sentez que je vous suis attaché; oui, madame, je le suis et je dois l'être indépendamment de toutes vos bontés; il faudrait être bien insensible pour n'être pas touché de tout ce que vous faites de grand et d'utile. Je ne crois pas qu'il y ait dans vos états un seul homme qui s'intéresse plus que moi à l'accomplissement de tous vos desseins.

Permettez-moi de vous dire, sans trop d'audace, qu'ayant pensé comme vous sur toutes les choses qui ont signalé votre règne, je les ai regardées comme des événements qui me devenaient en quelque façon personnels. Les colonies, les arts de toute espèce, les bonnes lois, la tolérance, sont mes passions; et cela est si vrai, qu'ayant, dans mon obscurité et dans mon hameau, quadruplé le petit nombre des habitants, bâti leurs maisons, civilisé des sauvages, et prêché la tolérance, j'ai été sur le point d'être très violemment persécuté par des prêtres. Le supplice abominable du chevalier de La Barre, dont votre majesté impériale a sans doute entendu parler, et dont elle a frémi, me fit tant d'horreur, que je fus alors sur le point de quitter la France et de retourner auprès du roi de Prusse. Mais aujourd'hui, c'est dans un plus grand empire que je voudrais finir mes jours.

Que votre majesté juge donc combien je suis affligé quand je vois les Turcs vous forcer à suspendre vos grandes entreprises pacifiques pour une guerre qui, après tout, ne peut être que très dispendieuse, et qui prendra une partie de votre génie et de votre temps.

Quelques jours avant de recevoir la lettre dont je remercie bien sensiblement votre majesté, j'écrivis à M. le comte de Schouvalof, votre chambellan, pour lui demander s'il était vrai qu'Azof fût entre vos mains. Je me flatte qu'à présent vous êtes aussi maîtresse de Taganrock.

Plût à Dieu que votre majesté eût une flotte formidable sur la mer Noire! Vous ne vous bornerez pas sans doute à une guerre défensive; j'espère bien que Moustapha sera battu par terre et par mer. Je sais bien que les janissaires passent pour de bons soldats; mais je crois les vôtres supérieurs. Vous avez de bons généraux, de bons officiers, et les Turcs n'en ont point encore: il leur faut du temps pour en former. Ainsi toutes les apparences font croire que vous serez victorieuse. Vos premiers succès décident déjà de la réputation des armes, et cette réputation fait beaucoup. Votre présence ferait encore davantage. Je ne serais point surpris que votre majesté fît la revue de son armée sur le chemin d'Andrinople; cela est digne de vous. La législatrice du nord n'est pas faite pour les choses ordinaires. Vous avez dans l'esprit un courage qui me fait tout espérer.

J'ai revu l'ancien officier qui proposa des chariots de guerre dans la guerre de 1756. Le comte d'Argenson, ministre de la guerre, en fit faire un essai. Mais comme cette invention ne pouvait réussir que dans de vastes plaines, telles que celles de Lutzen, on ne s'en servit pas. Il prétend toujours qu'une demi-douzaine seulement de ces chars, précédant un corps de cavalerie ou d'infanterie, pourraient déconcerter les janissaires de Moustapha, à moins qu'ils n'eussent des chevaux de frise devant eux. C'est ce que j'ignore. Je ne suis point du métier des meurtriers; je ne suis point homme à projets; je prie seulement votre majesté de me pardonner mon zèle. D'ailleurs il est dit, dans un livre qui ne ment jamais, que Salomon avait douze mille chars de guerre dans un pays où il n'y eut avant lui que des ânes.

Et il est dit encore, dans le beau livre des Juges, qu'Adonaï était victorieux dans les montagnes, mais qu'il fut vaincu dans les vallées, parce que les habitants avaient des chars de guerre.

Je suis bien loin de desirer une ligue contre les Turcs; les croisades ont été si ridicules, qu'il n'y a pas moyen d'y revenir; mais j'avoue que si j'étais Vénitien, j'opinerais pour envoyer une armée en Candie, pendant que votre majesté battrait les Turcs vers Yassi ou ailleurs; si j'étais un jeune empereur des Romains, la Bosnie et la Servie me verraient bientôt, et je viendrais ensuite vous demander à souper à Sophie ou à Philippopolis de Romanie, après quoi nous partagerions à l'amiable.

Je vous supplierais de permettre que le nonce du pape en Pologne, qui a déchaîné si saintement les Turcs contre la tolérance, fût du souper; car je suppose qu'il serait votre prisonnier. Je crois, madame, que votre majesté lui en dirait tout doucement de bonnes sur l'horreur et l'infamie d'avoir excité une guerre civile, pour ravir aux dissidents les droits de la patrie, et pour les priver d'une liberté que la nature leur donnait, et que vos bienfaits leur avaient rendue; je ne sais rien de si honteux et de si lâche dans ce siècle. On dit que les jésuites polonais ont eu une grande part aux Saint-Barthélemi continuelles qui désolent ce malheureux pays. Ma seule consolation est d'espérer que ces turpitudes horribles tourneront à votre gloire: ou je me trompe fort, ou vos ennemis ne seront parvenus qu'à faire graver sur vos médailles: *Triomphatrice de l'empire ottoman, et pacificatrice de la Pologne.*

XXIV

DE L'IMPÉRATRICE

A Pétersbourg, le 3/14 juillet 1769

Monsieur, j'ai reçu, le 20 de juin, votre lettre du 27 mai. Je suis charmée d'apprendre que le printemps rétablit votre santé, quoique la politesse vous fasse dire que mes lettres y contribuent. Cependant je n'ose leur attribuer cette vertu. Soyez-en bien aise; car d'ailleurs vous pourriez en recevoir si souvent, qu'à la fin elles vous ennuieraient.

Tous vos compatriotes, monsieur, ne pensent pas comme vous sur mon compte; j'en connais qui aiment à se persuader qu'il est impossible que je puisse faire quelque chose de bien, qui donnent la torture à leur esprit pour en convaincre les autres; et malheur à leurs satellites, s'ils osaient penser autrement qu'ils ne sont inspirés! Je suis assez bonne pour croire que c'est un avantage qu'ils me donnent sur eux, parce que celui qui ne sait les choses que par la bouche de ses flatteurs les sait mal, voit dans un faux jour, et agit en conséquence. Comme, au reste, ma gloire ne dépend pas d'eux, mais bien de mes principes, de mes actions, je me console de n'avoir pas leur approbation. En bonne chrétienne, je leur pardonne, et j'ai pitié de ceux qui m'envient.

Vous dites, monsieur, que vous pensez comme moi sur différentes choses que j'ai faites, et que vous vous y intéressez. Eh bien! monsieur, sachez que ma belle colonie de Saratof monte à vingt sept mille âmes, et qu'en dépit du gazetier de Cologne, elle n'a rien à craindre des incursions des Turcs, des Tartares, etc.; que chaque canton a des églises de son rite, qu'on y cultive les champs en paix, et que de trente ans ils ne paieront aucune charge.

D'ailleurs nos charges sont si modiques, qu'il n'y a pas de paysan, en Russie, qui ne mange une poule quand il lui plaît, et que, depuis quelque temps, il y a des provinces où ils préfèrent les dindons aux poules; que la sortie du blé, permise avec certaines restrictions qui précautionnent contre les abus sans gêner le commerce, ayant fait hausser le prix de cette denrée, accommode si bien le cultivateur, que la culture augmente d'année en année, que la population est pareillement augmentée d'un dixième dans beaucoup de provinces depuis sept ans. Nous avons la guerre, il est vrai; mais il y a bien du temps que la Russie fait ce métier-là, et qu'elle sort de chaque guerre plus florissante qu'elle n'y était entrée.

Nos lois vont leur train: on y travaille tout doucement. Il est vrai qu'elles sont devenues causes secondes, mais elles n'y perdront rien. Ces lois seront tolérantes, elles ne persécuteront, ne tueront, ni ne brûleront personne. Dieu nous garde d'une histoire pareille à celle du chevalier de La Barre! On mettrait aux Petites-Maisons les juges qui oseraient faire de pareilles procédures.

Depuis la guerre, j'ai fait deux nouvelles entreprises: je bâtis Azof et Taganrock, où il y a un port commencé et ruiné par Pierre Ier. Voilà deux bijoux que je fais enchâsser, et qui pourraient bien n'être pas du goût de Moustapha. L'on dit que le pauvre homme ne fait que pleurer. Ses amis l'ont engagé dans cette guerre malgré lui et à son corps défendant. Ses troupes ont commencé par piller et brûler leur propre pays; à la sortie des janissaires de la capitale, il y a eu plus de mille personnes de tuées; l'envoyé de l'empereur, sa femme, ses filles, battues, volées, traînées par les cheveux, et sous les yeux du sultan et de son visir, sans que personne osât empêcher ce désordre: tant ce gouvernement est faible et mal arrangé!

Voilà donc ce fantôme si terrible, dont on prétend me faire peur!

L'on dirait que l'esprit humain est toujours le même. Le ridicule des croisades passés n'a pas empêché les ecclésiastiques de Podolie, soufflés par le nonce du pape, de prêcher une croisade contre moi, et les fous de soi-disants confédérés ont pris la croix d'une main, et se sont ligués de l'autre avec les Turcs, auxquels ils ont promis deux de leurs provinces. Pourquoi? afin d'empêcher un quart de leur nation de jouir des droits de citoyen. Et voilà pourquoi encore ils brûlent et saccagent leur propre pays. La bénédiction du pape leur promet le paradis: conséquemment les Vénitiens et l'empereur seraient excommuniés, je pense, s'ils prenaient les armes contre ces mêmes Turcs, défenseurs aujourd'hui des croisés, contre quelqu'un qui n'a touché ni en blanc ni en noir à la foi romaine.

Vous verrez encore, monsieur, que ce sera le pape qui mettra opposition au souper que vous me proposez à Sophie. Rayez, s'il vous plaît, Philippopolis du nombre des villes; elle a été réduite en cendres ce printemps par les troupes ottomanes qui y ont passé, parce qu'on voulait les empêcher de la piller.

Adieu, monsieur; soyez persuadé de la considération toute particulière que j'ai pour vous.

CATERINE

XXV

DE L'IMPÉRATRICE

A Pétersbourg, le 4/15 auguste 1769

J'ai reçu, monsieur, votre belle lettre du 26 février; je ferai mon possible pour suivre vos conseils. Si Moustapha n'est pas rossé, ce ne sera pas assurément votre faute, ni la mienne, ni celle de mon armée; mes soldats vont à la guerre contre les Turcs comme s'ils allaient à la noce.

Si vous pouviez voir tous les embarras dans lesquels ce pauvre Moustapha se trouve, à la suite du pas précipité qu'on lui a fait faire, contre l'avis de son divan et des gens les plus raisonnables, il y aurait des moments où vous ne pourriez vous empêcher de le plaindre comme homme, et comme homme très mal dans ses affaires.

Il n'y a rien qui me prouve plus la part sincère que vous prenez, monsieur, à ce qui me regarde, que ce que vous me dites sur ces chars de nouvelle invention; mais nos gens de guerre ressemblent à ceux de tous les autres pays: les nouveautés non éprouvées leur paraissent douteuses.

Vivez, monsieur, et réjouissez-vous, lorsque mes braves guerriers auront battu les Turcs. Vous savez, je pense, qu'Azof, à l'embouchure du Tanaïs, est déjà occupé par mes troupes. Le dernier traité de paix stipulait que cette place resterait abandonnée de part et d'autre: vous aurez vu par les gazettes que nous avons envoyé promener les Tartares dans trois différents endroits, lorsqu'ils ont voulu piller l'Ukraine: cette fois-ci ils s'en sont retournés aussi gueux qu'ils étaient sortis de la Crimée. Je dis gueux, car les prisonniers qu'on a faits sont couverts de lambeaux, et non d'habits. S'ils n'ont pas réussi selon leurs desirs chez nous, en revanche ils se sont dédommagés en Pologne. Il est vrai qu'ils y ont été invités par leurs alliés les protégés du nonce du pape.

Je suis bien fâchée que votre santé ne réponde pas à mes souhaits: si les succès de mes armées peuvent contribuer à la rétablir, je ne manquerai pas de vous faire part de tout ce qui nous arrivera d'heureux. Jusqu'ici je n'ai encore, Dieu merci, que de très bonnes nouvelles; de tous côtés on renvoie bien étrillé tout ce qui se montre de Turcs ou de Tartares, mais surtout les mutins de Pologne. J'espère avoir dans peu des nouvelles de quelque chose de plus décisif que des affaires de parti entre troupes légères.

Je suis avec une estime bien particulière, etc. CATERINE

XXVI

DE VOLTAIRE

A Ferney, 2 septembre 1769

Madame, la lettre dont votre majesté impériale m'honore, du 14 juillet, a transporté le vieux chevalier de la guerrière et de la législatrice Tomyris, devant qui l'ancienne Tomyris serait assurément peu de chose. Il est bien beau de faire fleurir une colonie aussi nombreuse que celle de Saratof, malgré les Turcs, les Tartares, la Gazette de Cologne, et le Courrier d'Avignon.

Vos deux bijoux d'Azof et de Taganrock, qui étaient tombés de la couronne de Pierre-le-Grand, seront un des plus beaux ornements de la vôtre, et j'imagine que Moustapha ne dérangera jamais votre coiffure.

Tout vieux que je suis, je m'intéresse à ces belles Circassiennes qui ont prêté à votre majesté serment de fidélité, et qui prêteront sans doute le même serment à leurs amants. Dieu merci, Moustapha ne tâtera pas de celles-là. Les deux parties qui composent le genre humain doivent être vos très obligées.

Il est vrai que votre majesté a deux grands ennemis, le pape et le padisha des Turcs. Constantin ne s'imaginait pas qu'un jour sa ville de Rome appartiendrait à un prêtre, et qu'il bâtissait sa ville de Constantinople pour des Tartares. Mais aussi il ne prévoyait pas qu'il se formerait un jour vers la Moskva et la Néva un empire aussi grand que le sien.

Votre vieux chevalier conçoit bien, madame, qu'il y a dans les confédérés de Pologne quelques fanatiques ensorcelés par des moines. Les croisades étaient bien ridicules; mais qu'un nonce du pape ait fait entrer le grand-turc dans sa croisade contre vous, cela est digne de la farce italienne. Il y a là un mélange d'horreur et d'extravagance dont rien n'approche: je n'entends rien à la politique, mais je soupçonne pourtant que parmi ces folies il y a des gens qui ont quelques grands desseins. Si votre majesté ne voulait que de la gloire, on vous en laisserait jouir; vous l'avez assez méritée; mais il paraît qu'on ne veut pas que votre puissance égale votre renommée: on dit que c'est trop à la fois. On ne peut guère forcer les hommes à l'admiration sans exciter l'envie.

Je vois, madame, que je ne pourrai faire ma cour à votre majesté, cette année, dans les états de Moustapha, le digne allié du pape. Il faut que je remette mon voyage à l'année prochaine. J'aurai, à la vérité, soixante et dix-sept ans, et je n'ai pas la vigueur d'un Turc; mais je ne vois pas ce qui pourrait m'empêcher de venir dans les beaux jours saluer l'étoile du nord et maudire le croissant. Notre madame Geoffrin a bien fait le voyage de Varsovie, pourquoi n'entreprendrais-je pas celui de Pétersbourg au mois d'avril? J'arriverais en juin, je m'en retournerais en septembre; et si je mourais en chemin, je ferais mettre sur mon petit tombeau: Ci gît l'admirateur de l'auguste Catherine, qui a eu l'honneur de mourir en allant lui présenter son profond respect.

Je me mets aux pieds de votre majesté impériale.

L'ermite de Ferney

XXVII

DE L'IMPÉRATRICE

A Pétersbourg, 15/26 septembre 1769

Monsieur, il n'y a rien de plus flatteur pour moi que le voyage que vous voulez entreprendre pour me venir trouver: je répondrais mal à l'amitié que vous me témoignez, si je n'oubliais en ce moment la satisfaction que j'aurais à vous voir, pour ne m'occuper que de l'inquiétude que je ressens en pensant à quoi vous exposerait un voyage aussi long et aussi pénible. La délicatesse de votre santé m'est connue; j'admire votre courage, mais je serais inconsolable si par malheur votre santé était affaiblie par ce voyage; ni moi, ni toute l'Europe, ne me le pardonnerions. Si jamais l'on fesait usage de l'épitaphe qu'il vous a plu de composer, et que vous m'adressez si gaiement, on me reprocherait de vous y avoir exposé. Outre cela, monsieur, il se pourrait, si les choses restent dans l'état où elles sont, que le bien de mes affaires demandât ma présence dans les provinces méridionales de mon empire, ce qui doublerait votre chemin et les incommodités inséparables d'une telle distance.

Au reste, monsieur, soyez assuré de la parfaite considération avec laquelle je suis, etc.

CATERINE

XXVIII

DE L'IMPÉRATRICE

A Pétersbourg, 22 septembre/3 octobre 1769

J'ai vu, monsieur, par votre lettre au comte de Schouvalof, que la prétendue dévastation de la nouvelle Servie, que les gazettes fanatiques ont tant prônée, vous avait donné quelque appréhension; cependant il est très vrai que les Tartares, quoiqu'ils aient attaqué nos frontières de trois côtés, ont trouvé partout une résistance convenable, et se sont retirés sans causer de dommages considérables. Toute cette expédition n'a duré que trois jours, durant un froid excessif, mêlé de vent et de neige; ce qui a causé beaucoup de perte aux Tartares, tant en hommes qu'en chevaux.

Mais que direz-vous, monsieur, lorsque vous saurez que les belles Circassiennes, indignées d'être renfermées dans le sérail de Constantinople, comme des animaux dans une écurie, ont persuadé à leurs pères et à leurs frères de se soumettre à la Russie? Le fait est que les Circassiens des montagnes m'ont prêté serment de fidélité. Ce sont ceux qui habitent le pays nommé Cabarda; et c'est une suite de la victoire qu'ont remportée nos Kalmoucs, soutenus de troupes régulières, sur les Tartares du Kouban, sujets de Moustapha, et qui habitent le pays que traverse la rivière de ce nom, au-delà du Tanaïs.

Adieu, monsieur, portez-vous bien, et moquons-nous de Moustapha le victorieux.

CATERINE

A propos, j'ai entendu dire qu'on avait défendu de vendre à Constantinople et à Paris mon *Instruction pour le Code*.

XXIX

DE VOLTAIRE

17 octobre 1769

Madame, le très vieux et très indigne chevalier de votre majesté impériale était accablé de mille faux bruits qui couraient et qui l'affligeaient. Voilà tout à coup la nouvelle consolante, qui se répand de tous côtés, que votre armée a battu complètement les esclaves de Moustapha vers le Niester. Je renais, je rajeunis, ma législatrice est victorieuse; celle qui établit la tolérance, et qui fait fleurir les arts, a puni les ennemis des arts: elle est victorieuse, elle jouit de toute sa gloire. Ah! madame, cette victoire était nécessaire; les hommes ne jugent que par le succès. L'envie est confondue. On n'a rien à répondre à une bataille gagnée: des lauriers sur une tête pleine d'esprit et d'une force de raison supérieure font le plus bel effet du monde.

On m'a dit qu'il y avait des Français dans l'armée turque; je ne veux pas le croire. Je ne veux pas avoir à me plaindre de mes compatriotes; cependant j'ai connu un colonel qui a servi en Corse, et qui avait la rage d'aller voir des queues de cheval; je lui en fis honte, je lui représentai combien sa rage était peu chrétienne; je lui mis devant les yeux la supériorité du nouveau Testament sur *l'Alcoran*; mais sur tout je lui dis que c'était un crime de lèse galanterie française de combattre pour de vilaines gens qui enferment les femmes, contre l'héroïne de nos jours. Je n'ai plus entendu parler de lui depuis ce temps-là. S'il est votre prisonnier, je supplie votre majesté impériale de lui ordonner de venir faire amende honorable dans mon petit château, d'assister à mon *Te Deum*, ou plutôt à mon *Te Deam*, et de déclarer à haute voix que les Moustapha ne sont pas dignes de vous déchausser.

Aurai-je encore assez de voix pour chanter vos victoires? J'ai l'honneur d'être de votre académie; je dois un tribut. M. le comte Orlof n'est-il pas notre président? Je lui enverrais quelque ennuyeuse ode pindarique, si je ne le soupçonnais de ne pas trop aimer les vers français.

Allons donc, héritier des Césars, chef du saint empire romain, avocat de l'église latine, allons donc. Voilà une belle occasion. Poussez en Bosnie, en Servie, en Bulgarie; allons, Vénitiens, équipez vos vaisseaux, secondez l'héroïne de l'Europe.

Et votre flotte, madame, votre flotte!...Que Borée la conduise, et qu'ensuite un vent d'occident la fasse entrer dans le canal de Constantinople!

Léandre et Héro, qui êtes toujours aux Dardanelles, bénissez la flotte de Pétersbourg. Envie, taisez-vous! peuples, admirez! C'est ainsi que parle le malade de Ferney; mais ce n'est pas un transport au cerveau, c'est le transport du cœur.

Que votre majesté impériale daigne agréer le profond respect et la joie de votre très humble et très dévot ermite.

XXX

DE L'IMPÉRATRICE

A Pétersbourg, 7/18 octobre 1769

Monsieur, vous direz que je suis une importune avec mes lettres, et vous aurez raison; mais prenez-vous-en à vous-même: vous m'avez dit plus d'une fois que vous souhaitiez d'apprendre la défaite de Moustapha: eh bien! ce victorieux empereur des Turcs a perdu la Moldavie entière. Yassi est pris; le visir s'est enfui en grande confusion au-delà du Danube. Voilà ce qu'un courrier m'annonce ce matin, et ce qui fera taire la Gazette de Paris, le Courrier d'Avignon, et le nonce, qui fait la Gazette de Pologne.

Adieu, monsieur; portez-vous bien, et soyez persuadé que je réponds bien à l'amitié que vous me témoignez.

CATERINE

XXXI

DE VOLTAIRE

A Ferney, 30 octobre 1769

Madame, votre majesté impériale me rend la vie, en tuant des Turcs. La lettre dont elle m'honore, du 22 septembre, me fait sauter de mon lit en criant: *Allah, Catharina!* J'avais donc raison, j'étais plus prophète que Mahomet: Dieu et vos troupes victorieuses m'avaient donc exaucé quand je chantais, *Te Catharinam laudamus, te dominam confitemur*. L'ange Gabriel m'avait donc instruit de la déroute entière de l'armée ottomane, de la prise de Choczin, et m'avait montré du doigt le chemin d'Yassi.

Je suis réellement, madame, au comble de la joie; je suis enchanté, je vous remercie, et, pour ajouter à mon bonheur, vous devez toute cette gloire à monsieur le nonce. S'il n'avait pas déchaîné le divan contre votre majesté, vous n'auriez pas vengé l'Europe.

Voilà donc ma législatrice entièrement victorieuse. Je ne sais pas si on a tâché de supprimer à Paris et à Constantinople votre *Instruction pour le code de la Russe*; mais je sais qu'on devrait la cacher aux Français; c'est un reproche trop honteux pour nous de notre ancienne jurisprudence ridicule et barbare, presque entièrement fondée sur les décrétales des papes, et sur la jurisprudence ecclésiastique.

Je ne suis pas dans votre secret; mais le départ de votre flotte me transporte d'admiration. Si l'ange Gabriel ne m'a pas trompé, c'est la plus belle entreprise qu'on ait faite depuis Annibal.

Permettez que j'envoie à votre majesté la copie de la lettre que j'écris au roi de Prusse: comme vous y êtes pour quelque chose, j'ai cru devoir la soumettre à votre jugement.

Que Dieu me donne de la santé, et certainement je viendrai me mettre à vos pieds l'été prochain pour quelques jours, ou même pour quelques heures, si je ne puis mieux faire.

Que votre majesté impériale pardonne au désordre de ma joie, et agrée le profond respect d'un cœur plein de vous.

L'ermite de Ferney

XXXII

DE L'IMPÉRATRICE

A Pétersbourg, 29 octobre/9 novembre 1769

Monsieur, je suis bien fâchée de voir, par votre obligeante lettre du 17 d'octobre, que mille fausses nouvelles sur notre compte vous aient affligé. Cependant il est très vrai que nous avons fait la plus heureuse campagne dont il y ait d'exemple. La levée du blocus de Choczin, par le manque de fourrages, était le seul désavantage qu'on pouvait nous donner. Mais quelle suite a-t-elle eue? La défaite entière de la multitude que Moustapha avait envoyée contre nous.

Ce n'est pas le grand-maître de l'artillerie, le comte Orlof, qui a la présidence de l'académie, c'est son frère cadet, qui fait son unique occupation de l'étude. Ils sont cinq frères; il serait difficile de nommer celui qui a le plus de mérite, et de trouver une famille plus unie par l'amitié. Le grand-maître est le second; deux de ses frères sont présentement en Italie. Lorsque j'ai montré au grand-maître l'endroit de votre lettre où vous me dites, monsieur, que vous le soupçonnez de ne pas trop aimer les vers français, il m'a répondu qu'il ne possédait pas assez la langue française pour les entendre. Et je crois que cela est vrai, car il aime beaucoup la poésie de sa langue maternelle.

J'espère, monsieur, que vous me donnerez bientôt des nouvelles de ma flotte. Je crois qu'elle a passé Gibraltar. Il faudra voir ce qu'elle fera: c'est un spectacle nouveau que cette flotte dans la Méditerranée. La sage Europe n'en jugera que par l'événement.

Je vous avoue, monsieur, que ce m'est toujours une satisfaction bien agréable, lorsque je vois la part que vous prenez à ce qui m'arrive.

Soyez persuadé que je sens tout le prix de votre amitié. Je vous prie de me la continuer et d'être assuré de la mienne.

CATERINE

XXXIII

DE VOLTAIRE

A Ferney, 28 novembre 1769

Madame, la lettre du 18 octobre, dont votre majesté impériale m'honore, me rajeunit tout d'un coup de seize ans, de sorte que me voilà un jeune homme de soixante ans, tout propre à faire une campagne dans vos troupes contre Moustapha. J'avais été assez faible pour être alarmé des fausses nouvelles de quelques gazettes qui prétendaient que les Turcs étaient revenus à Choczin, qu'ils s'en étaient rendus maîtres, et qu'ils rentraient en Pologne. Vous ne sauriez croire de quel poids énorme la lettre de votre majesté m'a soulagé.

Par les derniers vaisseaux arrivés de Turquie à Marseille, on apprend que le nombre des mécontents augmente à Constantinople, et que le sérail est obligé d'apaiser les murmures par des mensonges: triste ressource; la fraude est bientôt découverte, et alors l'indignation redouble. On a beau faire tirer le canon des Sept-Tours et de Topana pour de prétendues victoires, la vérité perce à travers la fumée du canon, et vient effrayer Moustapha sur ses tapis de zibeline.

Je ne serais point étonné que ce tyran imbécile (qu'il me pardonne cette expression) ne fût détrôné dans quatre mois, quand votre flotte sera près des Dardanelles, et que son successeur ne demandât humblement la paix à votre majesté. Il ne m'appartient pas de lire dans l'avenir, encore moins même dans le présent; mais je ne saurais m'imaginer que les Vénitiens ne profitent pas d'une si belle occasion. Il me semble que votre majesté prend Moustapha de tous les sens.

Quand une fois on a tiré l'épée, personne ne peut prévoir comment les choses finiront; je ne suis point prophète, Dieu m'en garde! mais il y a long-temps que j'ai dit que si l'empire turc est jamais détruit, ce ne sera que par le vôtre. Je me flatte que Moustapha paiera bien cher son amitié chrétienne pour le nonce du pape en Pologne. Tout ce que je sais bien certainement, c'est que, Dieu merci, votre majesté est couverte de gloire. Je ne suis plus indigné contre ceux qui l'ont contestée, car leur humiliation me fait trop de plaisir. Ce n'est pas sur les seuls Turcs que vous remportez la victoire, mais sur ceux qui osaient être jaloux de la fermeté et de la grandeur de votre âme, que j'ai toujours admirée.

Que votre majesté impériale daigne agréer mon remerciement, ma joie, mes vœux, mon enthousiasme pour votre personne, et mon profond respect.

XXXIV

DE L'IMPÉRATRICE

A Pétersbourg, 2/13 décembre 1769

Monsieur, nous sommes si loin d'être chassés de la Moldavie et de Choczin, comme la Gazette de France le publie, qu'il n'y a que quelques jours que j'ai reçu la nouvelle de la prise de Galatzo, place fortifiée sur le Danube, où un sérasquier et un bacha ont été tués, au dire des prisonniers. Mais, ce qu'il y a de bien vérifié, c'est qu'entre ces derniers se trouve le prince de Moldavie Maurocordato. Trois jours après, nos troupes légères amenèrent de Bucharest, capitale de la Valachie, le prince hospodar, son frère, et son fils, à Yassi, au lieutenant-général Stoffeln, qui y commande. Tous ces messieurs passeront leur carnaval, non pas à Venise, mais à Pétersbourg. Bucharest est occupé présentement par mes troupes. Il ne reste plus guère de postes aux Turcs dans la Moldavie, de ce côté-ci du Danube.

Je vous mande ces détails, monsieur, afin que vous puissiez juger de l'état des choses, qui assurément n'ont point un aspect affligeant pour tous ceux qui, comme vous, veulent bien s'intéresser à mes affaires.

Je crois ma flotte à Gibraltar, si elle n'a pas encore franchi ce détroit: vous saurez plus tôt de ses nouvelles que moi. Que Dieu conserve Moustapha! Il conduit si bien ses affaires, que je ne voudrais point que malheur lui arrivât. Ses amitiés, ses liaisons, tout y contribue: son gouvernement est si aimé de ses sujets, que les habitants de Galatzo se joignirent à nos troupes, au moment même de la prise, pour courir sur le misérable reste du corps turc qui venait de les quitter, et qui fuyait à toutes jambes.

Voilà, monsieur, ce que j'avais à vous dire en réponse à votre lettre, remplie d'amitiés, du 28 novembre. Je vous prie de me continuer ces sentiments, dont je fais un si grand cas, et d'être assuré des miens.

CATERINE

XXXV

DE VOLTAIRE

A Ferney, 2 janvier 1770

Madame, j'apprends que la flotte de votre majesté impériale est en très bon état à Port-Mahon; permettez que je vous en témoigne ma joie. On dit qu'on travaille, par les ordres de votre majesté, dans Azof, à préparer des galères et des brigantins. Moustapha sera bien surpris quand il se verra attaqué par le Pont-Euxin et par la mer Égée, lui qui ne sait ce que c'est que la mer Égée et l'Euxin, non plus que son grand-visir ni son mufti. J'ai connu un ambassadeur de la sublime Porte, qui avait été intendant de la Romélie; je lui demandai des nouvelles de la Grèce, il me répondit qu'il n'avait jamais entendu parler de ce pays-là. Je lui parlai d'Athènes, aujourd'hui Sétine; il ne la connaissait pas davantage.

Je ne puis me défendre de redire encore à votre majesté que son projet est le plus grand et le plus étonnant qu'on ait jamais formé; que celui d'Annibal n'en approchait pas. J'espère bien que le vôtre sera plus heureux que le sien: en effet, que pourront vous opposer les Turcs? Ils passent pour les plus mauvais marins de l'Europe, et ils ont actuellement très peu de vaisseaux. Léandre et Héro vous favoriseront du haut des Dardanelles.

L'homme qui avait la rage d'aller servir dans l'armée du grand-visir n'a point mis son projet en exécution. Je lui avais conseillé d'aller plutôt faire une campagne dans vos armées: il voulait voir, disait-il, comment les Turcs font la guerre; il l'aurait bien mieux vu sous vos drapeaux, il aurait été témoin de leur fuite.

Il paraît un manifeste des Géorgiens, qui déclare net qu'ils ne veulent plus fournir de filles à Moustapha. Je souhaite que cela soit vrai, et que toutes leurs filles soient pour vos braves officiers, qui le méritent bien; la beauté doit être la récompense de la valeur.

Suis-je assez heureux pour que les troupes de votre majesté aient pénétré d'un côté jusqu'au Danube; et de l'autre, jusqu'à Erzeroum? Je bénis Dieu, madame, quand je songe que vous devez tout cela à l'évêque de Rome et à son nonce apostolique; il ne s'attendait pas qu'il vous rendrait de si grands services.

Je remercie votre majesté de m'avoir fait connaître les cinq frères qui sont l'ornement de votre cour. Je commence à croire réellement qu'ils vous accompagneront à Constantinople.

J'ai écrit deux lettres à M. de Schouvalof depuis quatre mois; point de réponse. Il y a bien plus de plaisir à avoir affaire à votre majesté; elle daigne écrire; elle sait de quelle joie elle me comble en m'apprenant ses victoires: j'ai le plaisir de les apprendre tout doucement à ceux qu'on en croit fâchés. Le public fait des vœux pour votre prospérité, vous aime, et vous admire. Puisse l'année 1770 être encore plus glorieuse que 1769!

Je me mets aux pieds de votre majesté impériale.

Le vieillard des Alpes

XXXVI

DE L'IMPÉRATRICE

Le 8/19 janvier 1770

Monsieur, je suis très sensible de ce que vous partagez ma satisfaction sur l'arrivée de nos vaisseaux au Port-Mahon. Les voilà plus proche des ennemis que de leurs propres foyers; cependant il faut qu'ils aient fait gaiement ce trajet, malgré les tempêtes et la saison avancée, puisque les matelots ont composé des chansons.

Les Géorgiens en effet ont levé le bouclier contre les Turcs, et leur refusent le tribut annuel de recrues pour le sérail. Héraclius, le plus puissant de leurs princes, est un homme de tête et de courage. Il a ci-devant contribué à la conquête de l'Inde, sous le fameux Sha-Nadir. Je tiens cette anecdote de la propre bouche du père d'Héraclius, mort ici, à Pétersbourg, en 1762.

Mes troupes ont passé le Caucase cette automne, et se sont jointes aux Géorgiens. Il y a eu par-ci par-là de petits combats avec les Turcs; les relations en ont été imprimées dans les gazettes. Le printemps nous fera voir le reste.

D'un autre côté, nous continuons à nous fortifier dans la Moldavie et la Valachie, et nous travaillons à nettoyer cette rive-ci du Danube. Mais, ce qu'il y a de mieux, c'est qu'on sent si peu la guerre dans l'empire, qu'on ne se souvient pas d'avoir vu un carnaval où généralement tous les esprits fussent plus portés à inventer des amusements que pendant celui de cette année. Je ne sais si l'on en fait autant à Constantinople. Peut-être y invente-t-on des ressources pour continuer la guerre. Je ne leur envie point ce bonheur; mais je me félicite de n'en avoir pas besoin, et me moque de ceux qui ont prétendu qu'hommes et argent me manquaient. Tant pis pour ceux qui aiment à se tromper; ils trouvent aisément pour de l'argent des flatteurs qui leur en donneront à garder.

Puisque mon exactitude ne vous est point à charge, soyez assuré, monsieur, que je la continuerai pendant cette année

1770, que je vous souhaite heureuse. Que votre santé se fortifie comme Azof et Taganrock le sont déjà.

Je vous prie d'être persuadé de mon amitié et de ma sensibilité.

CATERINE

XXXVII

DE VOLTAIRE

A Ferney, 2 février 1770

Madame, votre majesté daigne m'apprendre que les hospodars de Valachie et de Moldavie ne feront pas leur carnaval à Venise; mais votre majesté ne pourrait-elle pas les faire souper avec quelque amiral de Tunis et d'Alger? On dit que ces animaux d'Afrique se sont approchés un peu trop près de quelques uns de vos vaisseaux, et que vos canons les ont mis fort en désordre: voilà un bon augure; voilà votre majesté victorieuse sur les mers comme sur la terre, et sur des mers que vos flottes n'avaient jamais vues.

Non, je ne veux plus douter d'une entière révolution. Les sultanes turques ne résisteront pas plus que les Algériens. Pour les sultanes du sérail de Moustapha, elles appartiennent de droit aux vainqueurs.

On m'assure que votre majesté très impériale est à présent maîtresse de la mer Noire, que M. de Tottleben fait des merveilles avec les Mingreliennes et les Circassiennes, que vous triomphez partout. Je suis plus heureux que vous ne pensez, madame; car, bien que je ne sois ni sorcier ni prophète, j'avais soutenu violemment qu'une partie de ces grands événements arriverait; non pas tout: je ne prévoyais pas qu'une flotte partirait de la Néva, pour aller vers la mer de Marmara.

Cette entreprise vaut mieux que les chars de Cyrus, et surtout que ceux de Salomon, qui ne lui servirent à rien; mes chars, madame, baissent pavillon devant vos vaisseaux.

Mais, en fesant la guerre d'un pôle à l'autre, votre majesté n'aurait-elle pas besoin de quelques officiers? Le roi de Sardaigne vient de réformer un régiment huguenot qui le sert lui et son père depuis 1689. La religion l'a emporté sur la reconnaissance; peut-être quelques officiers, quelques sergents de ce régiment ambitionneraient la gloire de servir sous vos drapeaux. Ils pourraient servir à discipliner des Monténégrins, si vos belliqueuses troupes ne voulaient pas d'étrangers. Je connais un de ces officiers, jeune, brave, et sage, qui aimerait mieux se battre pour vous que pour le grand-turc et ses amis, s'il en a. Mais, madame, je ne dois qu'admirer et me taire.

Daignez agréer la joie excessive, la reconnaissance sans bornes, le profond respect du vieil ermite des Alpes.

Votre majesté impériale a trop de justice pour ne pas gronder M. le chambellan, comte de Schouvalof, qui n'a point répondu à mes lettres d'enthousiaste.

XXXVIII

DE L'IMPÉRATRICE

18 février/1 mars 1770

Monsieur, en réponse à votre lettre du 2 février, je vous dirai que le hospodar de Moldavie est mort; que celui de Valachie, qui se trouve ici, a beaucoup d'esprit; que nous continuons à être les maîtres de ces deux provinces, malgré les gazettes qui nous en chassent souvent.

Le sultan avait fait un nouvel hospodar *in partibus infidelium*, auquel il avait ordonné d'aller avec une armée innombrable se mettre en possession de Bucharest: il ne trouva que six à sept mille hommes, avec lesquels il fut battu, comme il faut, au mois de janvier, et il pensa être fait prisonnier. La semaine passé, j'ai reçu la nouvelle de la prise de Giurgi sur le Danube, et de la défaite d'un corps turc de seize mille hommes sous cette place. Nous avons chanté le *Te Deum* pour cet avantage et pour tant d'autres remportés depuis le 4 de janvier.

On dit ma flotte partie de Mahon. Il faut espérer que nous en entendrons parler bientôt, et qu'elle prendra la liberté de donner un démenti à ceux qui soutiennent qu'elle est hors d'état d'agir. Je trouve très plaisant que l'envie ait recours au mensonge pour en imposer au monde. Un pareil associé est toujours prêt à faire banqueroute. Le peu de vaisseaux turcs qui existent manquent de matelots. Les musulmans ont perdu l'envie de se laisser tuer pour les caprices de sa hautesse.

M. Tottleben a passé le Caucase, et il est en quartier d'hiver en Géorgie. Mais, comme la mauvaise saison est courte dans ces pays, j'espère qu'il ouvrira bientôt la campagne.

Lorsque la première division de ma flotte relâcha en Angleterre, le comte Czernischef, alors ambassadeur à cette cour, était inquiet de ce que quelques vaisseaux avaient besoin de radoub, etc. L'amiral anglais leur dit de n'être point inquiets. Jamais expédition maritime de quelque importance, ajouta-t-il, ne s'est faite sans de pareils inconvénients: cela est neuf pour vous, chez nous c'est l'affaire de tous les jours.

Je souhaite, monsieur, que vous ayez le plaisir de voir vos prophéties s'accomplir: peu de prophètes peuvent se vanter d'un tel avantage.

Soyez assuré, monsieur, de mon amitié et de ma considération la plus distinguée.

CATERINE

XXXIX

DE VOLTAIRE

A Ferney, 10 mars 1770

Madame, j'aurais eu l'honneur de remercier plus tôt votre majesté impériale, si je n'avais pas été cruellement malade. Je n'ai pas la force de vos sujets; il s'en faut de beaucoup. Je me flatte surtout qu'ils auront celle de continuer à bien battre les Turcs.

Votre majesté m'a dit un grand mot, Je ne manque ni d'hommes ni d'argent: je m'en aperçois bien, puisqu'elle fait acheter des tableaux à Genève, et qu'elle les paie fort cher. La cour de France ne vous ressemble pas; elle n'a point d'argent, et elle nous prend le nôtre.

La lettre dont votre majesté a daigné m'honorer m'était bien nécessaire pour confondre tous les bruits qu'on affecte de répandre. Je me donne le plaisir de mortifier les conteurs de mauvaises nouvelles.

Le roi de Prusse vient de m'envoyer cinquante vers français fort jolis; mais j'aimerais mieux qu'il vous envoyât cinquante mille hommes pour faire diversion, et que vous tombassiez sur Moustapha avec toutes vos forces réunies. Toutes les gazettes disent que ce gros cochon va se mettre à la tête de trois cent mille hommes; mais je crois qu'il faut bien rabattre de ce calcul. Trois cent mille combattants, avec tout ce qui suit pour le service et la nourriture d'une telle armée, monteraient à près de cinq cent mille. Cela est bon du temps de Cyrus et de Tomyris, et lorsque Salomon avait quarante mille chars de guerre, avec deux ou trois milliards de roubles en argent comptant, sans parler de ses flottes d'Ophir.

Voici le temps où les flottes de votre majesté, qui sont un peu plus réelles que celles de Salomon, vont se signaler. La terre et les mers vont retentir, ce printemps, de nouvelles vraies et fausses. J'ose supplier votre majesté impériale de daigner ordonner qu'on m'envoie les véritables. Écrire un code de lois d'une main, et battre Moustapha de l'autre, est une chose si neuve et si belle, que vous excusez sans doute, madame, mon extrême curiosité.

J'ai encore une autre grâce à vous demander, c'est de vouloir bien vous dépêcher d'achever ces deux grands ouvrages, afin que j'aie le plaisir d'en parler à Pierre-le-Grand, à qui je ferai bientôt ma cour dans l'autre monde.

J'espère lui parler aussi d'un jeune prince Gallitzin, qui me fait l'honneur de coucher ce soir dans ma chaumière de Ferney. Je suis toujours enchanté de l'extrême politesse de vos sujets. Ils ont autant d'agrément dans l'esprit que de valeur dans le cœur. On n'était pas si poli du temps de Catherine Ire. Vous avez apporté dans votre empire toutes les grâces de madame la princesse votre mère, que vous avez embellies.

Vivez heureuse, madame; achevez tous vos ouvrages; soyez la gloire du siècle et de l'Europe. Je recommande Moustapha à vos braves troupes: ne pourrait-il pas aller passer le carnaval de 1771 à Venise avec Candide?

Je reçois une lettre de M. le comte de Schouvalof, votre chambellan, qui me fait voir qu'il a reçu les miennes, et que la pétaudière polonaise ne les a pas arrêtées.

Que votre majesté impériale daigne toujours agréer mon profond respect, mon admiration, et mon enthousiasme pour elle.

XL

DE L'IMPÉRATRICE

A Pétersbourg, le 20/31 mars 1770

Monsieur, j'ai reçu, il y a trois jours, votre lettre du 10 de mars. Je souhaite que celle-ci trouve votre santé tout à fait rétablie, et que vous parveniez à un âge plus avancé que celui de Mathusalem. Je ne sais pas au juste si les années de cet honnête homme avaient douze mois; mais je veux que les vôtres en aient treize, comme l'année de la liste civile en Angleterre.

Vous verrez, monsieur, par la feuille ci-jointe, ce que c'était que notre campagne d'été et celle d'hiver, sur le compte desquelles je ne doute point qu'on ne débite mille faussetés. C'est la ressource d'une cause faible et injuste que de faire flèche de tout bois. Les gazettes de Paris et de Pologne ayant mis sur notre compte tant de combats perdus, et l'événement leur ayant donné le démenti, elles se sont avisées de faire mourir mon armée par la peste. Ne trouvez-vous pas cela très plaisant? Au printemps apparemment les pestiférés ressusciteront pour combattre. Le vrai est qu'aucun des nôtres n'a eu la peste.

Je ne puis qu'être très sensible à votre amitié, monsieur; vous voudriez armer toute la chrétienté pour m'assister. Je fais grand cas de l'amitié du roi de Prusse; mais j'espère que je n'aurai pas besoin des cinquante mille hommes que vous voulez qu'il me donne contre Moustapha.

Puisque vous trouvez trop fort le compte de trois cent mille hommes, à la tête desquels on prétend que le sultan marchera en personne, il faut que je vous parle de l'armement turc de l'année passée; il vous fera juger de ce fantôme selon sa vraie valeur. Au mois d'octobre, Moustapha trouva à propos de déclarer la guerre à la Russie; il n'y était pas plus préparé que nous. Lorsqu'il apprit que nous nous défendions avec vigueur, cela l'étonna; car on lui avait fait espérer beaucoup de choses qui n'arrivèrent pas. Alors il ordonna que des différentes provinces de son empire, un million cent mille hommes se rendraient à Andrinople pour prendre Kiovie, passer l'hiver à Moscou, et écraser la Russie.

La Moldavie seule eut ordre de fournir un million de boisseaux de grains pour l'armée innombrable des musulmans. Le hospodar répondit que la Moldavie, dans l'année la plus fertile, n'en recueillait pas tant, et que cela lui était impossible. Mais il reçut un second commandement d'exécuter les ordres donnés; et on lui promit de l'argent.

Le train d'artillerie pour cette armée était à proportion de la multitude. Il devait consister en six cents pièces de canon, qu'on assigna des arsenaux; mais lorsqu'il s'agit de les mettre en mouvement, on laissa là le plus grand nombre, et il n'y eut qu'une soixantaine de pièces qui marchèrent.

Enfin, au mois de mars, plus de six cent mille hommes se trouvèrent à Andrinople; mais comme ils manquaient de tout, la désertion commença à s'y mettre. Cependant le visir passa le Danube avec quatre cent mille hommes. Il y en avait cent quatre-vingt mille sous Choczin, le 28 d'auguste. Vous savez le reste. Mais vous ignorez peut-être que le visir repassa, lui septième, le pont du Danube, et qu'il n'avait pas cinq mille hommes lorsqu'il se retira à Balada. C'était tout ce qui lui restait de cette prodigieuse armée. Ce qui n'avait pas péri, s'était enfui, dans la résolution de retourner chez soi.

Notez, s'il vous plaît, qu'en allant et en venant, ils pillaient leurs propres provinces, et qu'ils brûlèrent les endroits où ils trouvèrent de la résistance. Ce que je vous dis est vrai; et j'ai plutôt diminué qu'augmenté les choses, de peur qu'elles ne parussent fabuleuses.

Tout ce que je sais de ma flotte, c'est qu'une partie est sortie de Mahon, et qu'une autre va quitter l'Angleterre où elle a hiverné. Je crois que vous en aurez plus tôt des nouvelles que moi. Cependant je ne manquerai pas de vous faire part, en son temps, de celles que je recevrai, avec d'autant plus d'empressement que vous le souhaitez.

Vous me priez, monsieur, d'achever incessamment et la guerre et les lois, afin que vous en puissiez porter la nouvelle à Pierre-le-Grand dans l'autre monde: permettez que je vous dise que ce n'est pas le moyen de me faire finir de sitôt. A mon tour, je vous prie bien sérieusement de remettre cette partie le plus long-temps que faire se pourra. Ne chagrinez pas vos amis de ce monde, pour l'amour de ceux qui sont dans l'autre. Si là-bas, ou là-haut, chacun a le choix de passer son temps avec telle compagnie qu'il lui plaira, j'y arriverai avec un plan de vie tout prêt, et composé pour ma satisfaction. J'espère bien d'avance que vous voudrez m'accorder quelques quarts d'heure de conversation dans la journée: Henri IV sera de la partie, Sulli aussi, et point Moustapha.

Je vois toujours avec bien du plaisir le souvenir que vous avez de ma mère, qui est morte bien jeune, et à mon grand regret.

Soyez assuré, monsieur, de tous les sentiments que vous me connaissez, et de l'estime distinguée que je ne cesserai d'avoir pour vous.

CATERINE

XLI

DE VOLTAIRE

A Ferney, 10 avril 1770

Madame, mon enthousiasme a redoublé par la lettre du premier mars, dont votre majesté impériale a daigné m'honorer. Il n'y a point de prêtre grec qui soit plus enchanté de votre supériorité continuelle sur les circoncis, que moi misérable baptisé dans l'église romaine. Je me crois né dans les anciens temps héroïques, quand je vois une de vos armées au-delà du Caucase; les autres, sur les bords du Danube; et vos flottes, dans la mer Égée. Je plains fort le hospodar de la Moldavie. Ce pauvre Gète n'a pas joui long-temps de l'honneur de voir Tomyris. Pour le hospodar de la Valachie, puisqu'il a de l'esprit, il restera à votre cour.

Il ne reste plus d'autre ressource à vos ennemis que de mentir.

Les gazetiers ressemblent à M. de Pourceaugnac, qui disait, Il m'a donné un soufflet, mais je lui ai bien dit son fait.

Je m'imagine très sérieusement que la grande armée de votre majesté impériale sera dans les plaines d'Andrinople au mois de juin. Je vous supplie de me pardonner si j'ose insister encore sur les chars de Tomyris. Ceux qu'on met à vos pieds sont d'une fabrique toute différente de ceux de l'antiquité. Je ne suis point du métier des homicides. Mais hier, deux excellents meurtriers allemands m'assurèrent que l'effet de ces chars était immanquable dans une première bataille, et qu'il serait impossible à un bataillon ou à un escadron de résister à l'impétuosité et à la nouveauté d'une telle attaque. Les Romains se moquaient des chars de guerre, et ils avaient raison; ce n'est plus qu'une mauvaise plaisanterie quand on y est accoutumé; mais la première vue doit certainement effrayer, et mettre tout en désordre. Je ne sais d'ailleurs rien de moins dispendieux et de plus aisé à manier. Un essai de cette machine, avec trois ou quatre escadrons seulement, peut faire beaucoup de bien sans aucun inconvénient.

Il y a très grande apparence que je me trompe, puisqu'on n'est pas de mon avis à votre cour; mais je demande une seule raison contre cette invention. Pour moi, j'avoue que je n'en vois aucune.

Daignez encore faire examiner la chose; je ne parle qu'après les officiers les plus expérimentés. Ils disent qu'il n'y a que les chevaux de frise qui puissent rendre cette manœuvre inutile; car pour le canon, le risque est égal des deux côtés; et, après tout, on ne hasarde de perdre, par escadron, que deux charrettes, quatre chevaux, et quatre hommes.

Encore une fois, je ne suis point meurtrier; mais je crois que je le deviendrais pour vous servir.

Il y a quinze jours que les officiers du régiment de Montfort, que j'avais engagés à servir votre majesté impériale, ont pris parti: les uns sont rentrés au service savoyard, les autres sont allés en France; il y en a un qui a l'honneur d'être capitaine dans l'armée de Genève, consistant en six cents hommes. Genève est actuellement le théâtre de la plus cruelle guerre en-deçà du Rhin. Il y a eu même quatre personnes assassinées par-derrière, dans l'église militante de Calvin. Je m'imagine que dorénavant l'église grecque en usera ainsi, et qu'elle ne verra plus que le dos des musulmans; en ce cas, les chars ne seront bons qu'à courir après eux.

Je me mets aux pieds de votre majesté, comme le hospodar de Valachie, et j'envie sa destinée.

Que votre majesté impériale daigne toujours agréer le profond respect, la reconnaissance, et l'admiration du vieil ermite de Ferney.

J'ai reçu une belle lettre de M. le comte de Schouvalof, votre chambellan; mais il ne me dit point le jour où votre cour sera dans Stamboul.

XLII

DE VOLTAIRE

A Ferney, ce 18 mai 1770

Madame, les glaces de mon âge me laissent encore quelque feu; il s'allume pour votre cause. On est un peu Moustapha à Rome et en France; je suis Catherin, et je mourrai Catherin. La lettre dont votre majesté impériale daigne m'honorer, du 31 mars, me comblait de joie; les nouvelles qu'on répand aujourd'hui m'accablent d'affliction.

On parle de vicissitudes, et je n'en voulais pas; on dit que les Turcs ont repassé le Danube en force, et qu'ils ont repris la Valachie; il faudra donc les battre encore: mais c'était dans les plaines d'Andrinople que je voulais une victoire; ils envoient, dit-on, une flotte dans la Morée. On ajoute que les Lacédémoniens sont en petit nombre; enfin on me donne mille inquiétudes. Pour toute réponse, je maudis Moustapha, et je prie la sainte Vierge de secourir les fidèles. Je suis sûr que vos mesures sont bien prises en Grèce, que l'on a donné des armes aux Spartiates, que les Monténégrins se joignent à eux, que la haine contre la tyrannie turque les anime, que vos troupes, marchant à leur tête, les rendront invincibles.

Pour les Vénitiens, ils joueront votre jeu, mais quand vous aurez gagné la partie.

Si l'Égypte a secoué le joug de Moustapha, je ne doute pas que votre majesté n'ait quelque part à cette révolution; celle qui a pu faire venir des flottes de la Néva dans le Péloponèse aura bien envoyé un habile négociateur dans le pays des pyramides. La mer Noire doit être couverte de vos saïques; ainsi Stamboul peut ne recevoir de vivres ni de l'Égypte, ni de la Grèce, ni du Voncara d'Enghis. Vous assaillez ce vaste empire depuis Colchos jusqu'à Memphis. Voilà mes idées; elles sont moins grandes que ce que votre majesté a fait jusqu'ici. Le revers annoncé de la Valachie m'ôte le sommeil, sans m'ôter l'espérance: le roman des chars de Cyrus me plaît toujours, dans un terrain sec comme les plaines d'Andrinople et le voisinage de Stamboul.

Je ne trouve point que les tableaux génevois soient trop chers, je trouve seulement votre majesté impériale généreuse; mais j'oserais désirer cent capitaines de plus, au lieu de cent tableaux. Je voudrais que tout fût employé à vous faire triompher, et que vous achevassiez votre code, plus beau que celui de Justinien, dans la ville où il le signa. Si votre majesté veut me rendre la santé et prolonger ma vie, je la conjure de vouloir bien me faire parvenir quelque bonne nouvelle qui ne plaira pas à frère Ganganelli, mais qui réjouira beaucoup le capucin de Ferney, tout prêt à étrangler les Turcs avec son cordon.

Je redouble mes vœux; mon âme est aux pieds de votre majesté impériale.

XLIII

DE L'IMPÉRATRICE

Le 9/20 mai 1770

Monsieur, vos deux lettres, la première du 10, et la seconde du 14 d'avril, me sont parvenues l'une après l'autre, avec leurs incluses. Tout de suite j'ai commandé deux chars selon le dessin et la description que vous avez bien voulu m'envoyer, et dont je vous suis bien obligée. J'en ferai faire l'épreuve en ma présence, bien entendu qu'ils ne feront mal à personne dans ce moment-là. Nos militaires conviennent que ces chars feraient leur effet contre des troupes rangées: ils ajoutent que la façon d'agir des Turcs, dans la campagne passée, était d'entourer nos troupes en se dispersant, et qu'il n'y avait jamais un escadron ou un bataillon ensemble. Les janissaires seuls choisissaient des endroits couverts, comme bois, chemins creux, etc., pour attaquer par troupes, et alors les canons font leur effet. En plusieurs occasions nos soldats les ont reçus à coups de baïonnette, et les ont fait rétrograder.

Vous avez raison, monsieur, l'église grecque voit jusqu'ici partout le dos des musulmans, et même en Morée. Quoique je n'aie point encore de nouvelles directes de ma flotte, cependant les nouvelles publiques répètent tant qu'elle s'est emparée du Péloponèse, qu'à la fin il faudra bien croire qu'il en est quelque chose. La moitié de la flotte n'y était point encore, lorsque la descente s'est faite.

Soyez assuré, monsieur, que je fais un cas infini de votre amitié, et des témoignages réitérés que vous m'en donnez. Je suis très sensible encore à la part que vous prenez à cette guerre, qui finira comme elle pourra. Nous aurons affaire à Moustapha de près ou de loin, comme la Providence le jugera à propos.

Quoi qu'il en soit, je vous prie d'être persuadé que Caterine II ne cessera jamais d'avoir une estime et une considération particulière pour l'illustre ermite de Ferney.

XLIV

DE L'IMPÉRATRICE

Le 16/27 mai 1770

Monsieur, un courrier parti de devant Coron en Morée, de la part du comte Féodor Orlof, m'a apporté l'agréable nouvelle qu'après que ma flotte eut abordé, le 17 février, à Porto-Vitello, mes troupes se joignirent aux Grecs, qui désiraient de recouvrer leur liberté. Ils se partagèrent en deux corps, dont l'un prit le nom de légion orientale de Sparte; et le second, celui de légion du nord de Sparte. La première s'empara, dans peu de jours, de Passava, de Berdoni, et de Misistra, qui est l'ancienne Sparte. La seconde s'en alla prendre Calamata, Léontari, et Arcadie. Ils firent quatre mille prisonniers Turcs dans ces différentes places, qui se rendirent après quelque défense; celle de Misistra surtout fut plus sérieuse que les autres.

La plupart des villes de la Morée sont assiégées. La flotte s'était portée de Porto-Vitello à Coron; mais cette dernière ville n'était point prise encore le 29 de mars, jour du départ du courrier. Cependant on en attendait si bien la réduction dans peu, qu'on avait déjà dépêché trois vaisseaux pour s'emparer de Navarin. Le 28, on avait reçu la nouvelle, devant Coron, d'une affaire qui s'était passée entre les Grecs et les Turcs, au passage de l'isthme de Corinthe. Le commandant turc a été fait prisonnier en cette occasion.

Je me hâte de vous donner ces bonnes nouvelles, monsieur, parce que je sais qu'elles vous feront plaisir, et que cela est bien authentique, puisqu'elles me viennent directement. Je m'acquitte aussi par là de la promesse que je vous ai faite de vous communiquer les nouvelles aussitôt que je les aurais reçues. Soyez assuré, monsieur, de l'invariabilité de mes sentiments.

CATERINE

Voilà la Grèce au point de redevenir libre, mais elle est bien loin encore d'être ce qu'elle a été: cependant on entend avec plaisir nommer ces lieux, dont on nous a tant rebattu les oreilles dans notre jeunesse.

XLV

DE L'IMPÉRATRICE

A ma maison de campagne de Czarskozélo, le 26 mai/6 juin 1770

Monsieur, je me hâte de répondre à votre lettre du 18 mai, que j'ai reçue hier au soir, parce que je vous vois en peine. Les vicissitudes que les adhérents de Moustapha répandent que mon armée doit avoir essuyés, la perte de la Valachie, sont des contes dont je n'ai senti d'autre chagrin que celui de vous voir appréhender que cela ne soit vrai. Dieu merci, rien de tout cela n'existe. Je vous ai mandé, la poste passée, les nouvelles que j'ai reçues de la Morée, qui, pour premier début, paraissent assez satisfesantes. J'espère que par votre intercession la sainte Vierge n'abandonnera pas les fidèles.

Dormez tranquillement, monsieur; les affaires de votre favorite (après ce que vous me dites, et l'amitié que vous ne cessez de me témoigner, je prends hardiment ce titre) vont un train très honnête: elle-même en est contente, et ne craint les Turcs ni par terre ni par mer.

Cette flotte turque, dont on fait tant de bruit, est merveilleusement équipée! Faute de matelots, on a mis sur les vaisseaux de guerre les jardiniers du sérail.

Après avoir bien bataillé, viendra la paix, temps pendant lequel j'espère achever mon code.

Adieu, monsieur; portez-vous bien, et soyez assuré qu'on ne saurait ajouter à la sensibilité que j'ai pour toutes les marques d'amitié que vous me donnez. Rien aussi n'égale l'estime que j'en fais.

CATERINE

XLVI

DE VOLTAIRE

A Ferney, 4 juillet 1770

Madame, j'ai reçu la lettre dont votre majesté impériale m'honore, en date du 27 mai. Je vous admire en tout; mon admiration est stérile, mais elle voudrait vous servir: encore une fois je ne suis pas du métier, mais je parierais ma vie que dans une plaine ces chars armés, soutenus par vos troupes, détruiraient tout bataillon ou tout escadron ennemi qui marcherait régulièrement; vos officiers en conviennent: le cas peut arriver. Il est difficile que dans une bataille tous les corps turcs attaquent en désordre, dispersés, et voltigeant vers les flancs de votre armée; mais s'ils combattent d'une manière si irrégulière, en sauvages sans discipline, vous n'aurez pas besoin des chars de Tomyris; il suffira de leur ignorance et de leur emportement pour les faire battre comme vous les avez toujours battus.

Je ne conçois pas comment votre majesté n'est pas encore maîtresse de Brahilof et de Bender, au moment que je vous écris; mais peut-être ces deux places sont-elles prises, et nous n'en avons pas encore la nouvelle.

Les gazettes me font toujours une peine égale à mon attachement; je crains que les Turcs ne soient en force dans le Péloponèse.

Je n'entends plus parler de la révolution prétendue arrivée en Égypte; tout cela m'inquiète pour mes chers Grecs et pour vos armées victorieuses, qui ne me sont pas moins chères.

La France envoie une flotte contre Tunis; j'aimerais encore mieux qu'elle envoyât trente vaisseaux de ligne contre Constantinople.

Votre entreprise sur la Grèce est sans contredit la plus belle manœuvre qu'on ait fait depuis deux mille ans; mais il faut qu'elle réussisse pleinement: ce n'est pas assez qu'elle vous fasse un honneur infini. *Où est le profit, là est la gloire,* disait notre roi Louis XI, qui ne vous égalait en rien.

Je donnerais tout ce que j'ai au monde pour voir votre majesté impériale sur le sopha de Moustapha. Son palais est assez vilain, ses jardins aussi; vous auriez bientôt fait de cette prison le lieu le plus délicieux de la terre. Daignez, je vous en conjure, me dire si vous espérez y parvenir. Il me semble qu'il ne faudrait qu'une bataille; elle serait décisive.

Je ne reviens point de ma surprise. Votre majesté est obligée de diriger des armées en Valachie, en Pologne, dans la Bessarabie, dans la Géorgie; et elle trouve encore du temps pour daigner m'écrire: je suis stupéfait et confus, autant que reconnaissant. Daignez toujours agréer mon profond respect et mon enthousiasme pour votre majesté impériale.

Le très vieux ermite de Ferney

XLVII

DE VOLTAIRE

A Ferney, 20 juillet 1770

Madame, votre lettre du 6 juin, que je soupçonne être du nouveau style, me fait voir que votre majesté impériale prend quelque pitié de ma passion pour elle. Vous me donnez des consolations, mais aussi vous me donnez quelques craintes, afin de tenir votre adorateur en haleine. Mes consolations sont vos victoires, et ma crainte est que votre majesté ne fasse la paix l'hiver prochain.

Je crois que les nouvelles de la Grèce nous viennent quelquefois un peu plus tôt par la voie de Marseille, qu'elles n'arrivent à votre majesté par les courriers. Selon ces nouvelles, les Turcs ont été quatre fois battus, et tout le Péloponèse est à vous.

Si Ali-Bey s'est en effet emparé de l'Egypte, comme on le dit, voilà deux grandes cornes arrachées au croissant des Turcs; et l'étoile du nord est certainement beaucoup plus puissante que leur lune. Pourquoi donc faire la paix, quand on peut pousser si loin ses conquêtes?

Votre majesté me dira que je ne pense pas assez en philosophe, et que la paix est le plus grand des biens. Personne n'est plus convaincu que moi de cette vérité; mais permettez-moi de désirer très fortement que cette paix soit signée de votre main dans Constantinople. Je suis persuadé que si vous gagnez une bataille un peu honnête en-deçà ou en-delà du Danube, vos troupes pourront marcher droit à la capitale.

Les Vénitiens doivent certainement profiter de l'occasion; ils ont des vaisseaux et quelques troupes. Lorsqu'ils prirent la Morée, ils n'étaient appuyés que par la diversion de l'empereur en Hongrie: ils ont aujourd'hui une protection bien plus puissante; il me paraît que ce n'est pas le temps d'hésiter.

Moustapha doit vous demander pardon, et les Vénitiens doivent vous demander les lois.

Ma crainte est encore que les princes chrétiens, ou soi-disant tels, ne soient jaloux de l'étoile du nord: ce sont des secrets dans lesquels il ne m'est pas permis de pénétrer.

Je crains encore que vos finances ne soient dérangées par vos victoires mêmes; mais je crois celles de Moustapha plus en désordre par ses défaites. On dit que votre majesté fait un emprunt chez les Hollandais; le padisha turc ne pourra emprunter chez personne, et c'est encore un avantage que votre majesté a sur lui.

Je passe de mes craintes à mes consolations. Si vous faites la paix, je suis bien sûr qu'elle sera très glorieuse, que vous conserverez la Moldavie, la Valachie, Azof, et la navigation sur la mer Noire, au moins jusqu'à Trébisonde. Mais que deviendront mes pauvres Grecs? que deviendront ces nouvelles légions de Sparte? Vous renouvellerez, sans doute, les jeux isthmiques, dans lesquels les Romains assurèrent aux Grecs leur liberté par un décret public; et ce sera l'action la plus glorieuse de votre vie. Mais comment maintenir la force de ce décret, s'il ne reste des troupes en Grèce? Je voudrais encore que le cours du Danube et que la navigation sur ce fleuve vous appartinssent le long de la Valachie, de la Moldavie, et même de la Bessarabie. Je ne sais si j'en demande trop, ou si je n'en demande pas assez: ce sera à vous de décider, et de faire frapper une médaille qui éternisera vos succès et vos bienfaits. Alors Tomyris se changera en Solon, et achèvera ses lois tout à son aise. Ces lois seront le plus beau monument de l'Europe et de l'Asie; car, dans tous les autres états, elles sont faites après coup, comme on calfate des vaisseaux qui ont des voies d'eau; elles sont innombrables, parce qu'elles sont faites sur des besoins toujours renaissants; elles sont contradictoires, attendu que ces besoins ont toujours changé; elles sont très mal rédigées, parce qu'elles ont presque toujours été écrites par des pédants, sous des gouvernements barbares. Elles ressemblent à nos villes bâties irrégulièrement au hasard, mêlées de palais et de chaumières, dans des rues étroites et tortueuses.

Enfin, que votre majesté donne des lois à deux mille lieues de pays, après avoir donné sur les oreilles à Moustapha!

Voilà les consolations du vieux ermite qui, jusqu'à son dernier moment, sera pénétré pour vous du plus profond respect, de l'admiration la plus juste, et d'un dévouement sans bornes pour votre majesté impériale.

XLVIII

DE L'IMPÉRATRICE

A Pétersbourg, le 10/21 juillet 1770

Monsieur, en réponse à votre lettre et à vos questions du 4 juillet, je vous annonce que, selon vos souhaits, le comte Romanzof, qui commande mon armée en Moldavie, a remporté la victoire la plus complète sur nos ennemis, le 7 de ce mois, à douze lieues environ du Danube. Notre droite était appuyée au Pruth. Le camp turc était retranché de quatre retranchements qui furent tous emportés à la pointe du jour, la baïonnette à la main. Le carnage dura quatre heures, après lesquelles mes troupes se trouvèrent maîtresses du champ de bataille, du camp des Turcs, de trente canons de fonte, d'une grande quantité de provisions de bouche et de munitions de guerre, et de beaucoup de prisonniers.

Notre perte n'est point considérable: il n'y a pas même eu un officier de marque blessé ou tué. Au départ du courrier on poursuivait encore les fuyards. L'armée turque était de quatre-vingt mille hommes, commandés par le kan de Crimée et par trois bachas.

Le comte Romanzof me marque qu'il a fait chanter le *Te Deum* dans la propre tente du kan de Crimée, qui doit être la plus belle des tentes possibles. Le siége de Bender doit être commencé dans ce moment, et puis nous verrons.

Je ne vous entretiendrais pas de tous ces faits de guerre, si vous ne m'aviez paru désirer d'en être informé.

Soyez persuadé du cas que je fais de votre amitié; j'y répondrai toujours avec empressement, quelque affaire que j'aie.

CATERINE

XLIX

DE L'IMPÉRATRICE

Le 22 juillet/2 auguste 1770

Monsieur, je vous ai mandé, il y a dix jours, que le comte Romanzof avait battu le kan de Crimée, combiné avec un corps considérable de Turcs; qu'on leur avait pris tentes, artillerie, etc., sur la petite rivière nommée Larga: j'ai le plaisir aujourd'hui de vous informer qu'hier au soir un courrier du comte m'a apporté la nouvelle que mon armée a remporté, le jour même que je vous écrivis (le 21 juillet), une victoire complète sur celle du seigneur Moustapha, commandée par le visir Ali-Bey, par l'aga des janissaires, et par sept ou huit bachas. Ils ont été forcés dans leurs retranchements: leur artillerie, au nombre de cent trente canons, leur camp, leurs bagages, les munitions en tout genre, sont tombés entre nos mains. Leur perte est considérable; la nôtre, si modeste que je crains d'en faire mention, afin que le fait ne paraisse fabuleux. Cependant le combat a duré cinq heures.

Le comte de Romanzof, que je viens de faire maréchal, pour cette victoire, me mande que, telle que les anciens Romains, mon armée ne demande jamais combien il y a d'ennemis, mais seulement où sont-ils? Cette fois-ci les Turcs étaient au nombre de cent cinquante mille, retranchés sur les hauteurs que baigne le Kogul, ruisseau à vingt-cinq werstes du Danube, ayant Ismaïlof derrière eux.

Mais, monsieur, mes nouvelles ne se bornent pas là: j'ai des avis certains, quoiqu'ils ne soient pas directs, que ma flotte a battu celle des Turcs devant Napoli de Romanie, et qu'elle a dispersé les vaisseaux ennemis qu'elle n'a pas coulés à fond.

Le siége de Bender a été ouvert encore le 21 juillet. Le prince Prosorofski a fait un butin immense en bestiaux de toute espèce, entre Oczakof et Bender. Ma flotte d'Azof croît en grandeur et en espérance en face du seigneur Moustapha.

Je ne puis rien vous dire de Brahilof, sinon que c'est un vieux château sur le bord du Danube, que le général Renne avait pris le jour même de la bataille du Pruth, année 1711.

Il ne dépend que des Grecs de faire revivre la Grèce. J'ai fait mon possible pour orner les cartes géographiques de la communication de Corinthe à Moscou. Je ne sais ce qui en sera.

Pour vous faire rire, je vous dirai que le sultan a eu recours aux prophètes, aux sorciers, aux devins, et aux fous, qui passent pour saints chez les musulmans. Ils lui ont prédit que le 21 serait un jour extrêmement fortuné pour l'empire ottoman. Tout de suite sa hautesse a envoyé un courrier au visir, pour lui dire de passer le Danube ce jour-là, et de profiter de l'heureuse constellation. Nous verrons un peu si les revers pourront ramener ce prince à la raison, et s'ils ne le désabuseront pas des tromperies et des mensonges.

Vos chers Grecs ont donné dans plusieurs occasions des preuves de leur ancien courage, et l'esprit ne leur manque pas.

Adieu, monsieur; portez-vous bien: continuez-moi votre amitié, et soyez assuré de la mienne. CATERINE

L

DE VOLTAIRE

A Ferney, 11 auguste 1770

Madame, chaque lettre dont votre majesté impériale m'honore me guérit de la fièvre que me donnent les nouvelles de Paris. On prétendait que vos troupes avaient eu partout de grands désavantages; qu'elles avaient évacué entièrement la Morée et la Valachie; que la peste s'était mise dans vos armées; que tous les revers avaient succédé à vos succès: votre majesté est mon médecin; elle me rend une pleine santé. Je ne manque pas d'écrire sur-le-champ l'état des choses, dès que j'en suis instruit; j'allonge les visages de ceux qui attristaient le mien.

Daignez donc, madame, avoir la bonté de me conserver cette santé que vous m'avez rendue; il ne faut pas abandonner son malade dans sa convalescence.

J'ai encore de petits ressentiments de fièvre, quand je vois que les Vénitiens ne se décident pas, que les Géorgiens n'ont pas formé une armée, et qu'on n'a nulle nouvelle positive de la révolution de l'Égypte.

Il y a un Brahilof, un Bender, qui me causent encore des insomnies; je vois dans mes rêves leurs garnisons prisonnières de guerre, et je me réveille en sursaut.

Votre majesté dira que je suis un malade bien impatient, et que les Turcs sont beaucoup plus malades que moi. Sans mes principes d'humanité, je dirais que je voudrais les voir tous exterminés, ou du moins chassés si loin qu'ils ne revinssent jamais.

Nous autres Français, madame, nous valons mieux qu'eux: nous disons prodigieusement de sottises, nous en fesons beaucoup, mais tout cela passe bien vite; on ne s'en souvient plus au bout de huit jours. La gaîté de la nation semble inaltérable. On apprend à Paris le tremblement de terre qui a bouleversé trente lieues de pays à Saint-Domingue; on dit: C'est dommage; et on va à l'opéra. Les affaires les plus sérieuses sont tournées en ridicule.

Nous sommes actuellement dans la plus belle saison du monde:

voilà un temps charmant pour battre les Turcs. Est-ce que ces barbares-là attaqueront toujours comme des houssards? ne se présenteront-ils jamais bien serrés, pour être enfilés par quelques uns de mes chars babyloniques?

Je voudrais du moins avoir contribué à vous tuer quelques Turcs; on dit que pour un chrétien c'est une œuvre fort agréable à Dieu. Cela ne va pas à mes maximes de tolérance; mais les hommes sont pétris de contradictions: et d'ailleurs votre majesté me tourne la tête.

Encore une fois, madame, quelques nouvelles, par charité, de cinq ou six villes prises et de cinq ou six combats gagnés, quand ce ne serait que pour faire taire l'envie.

Je me mets aux pieds de votre majesté impériale, avec le plus profond respect et la plus vive impatience. *L'ermite de Ferney*

LI

DE L'IMPÉRATRICE

Le 9/20 auguste 1770

Monsieur, vous me dites, dans votre lettre du 20 de juillet, que je vous donne des craintes pour vous tenir en haleine, et que mes victoires sont vos consolations: voici une petite dose de ces dernières que j'ai à vous donner.

Je viens de recevoir un courrier, qui m'a apporté les suites de la bataille de Kogul. Mes troupes se sont avancées sur le Danube, et ont pris poste sur le bord de ce fleuve, vis-à-vis d'Isacki. Le visir et l'aga des janissaires se sont sauvés sur l'autre bord; mais le reste, qui a voulu les imiter, a été tué, noyé, et dispersé. Il a fait abattre le pont, et près de deux mille janissaires ont été faits prisonniers. Vingt canons, cinq mille chevaux, un butin immense, et une grande quantité de vivres de toute espèce, sont tombés entre nos mains. Les Tartares ont envoyé sur-le-champ prier le maréchal comte de Romanzof de les laisser passer en Crimée: il leur a fait répondre qu'il exigeait leur hommage, et il a envoyé un corps considérable sur la gauche, vers Ismaïlof, pour leur faire une douce violence.

Il y a longtemps que nous savons qu'ils ne demandent pas mieux.

Vous ne voulez point de paix, monsieur; soyez tranquille, jusqu'ici on n'en entend point parler. Je conviens avec vous que c'est une bonne chose que la paix: lorsqu'elle existait, je croyais que c'était le *non plus ultrà* du bonheur: me voilà depuis près de deux ans en guerre, je vois que l'on s'accoutume à tout. La guerre, en vérité, a des moments bien bons. Je lui trouve un grand défaut, c'est qu'on n'y aime point son prochain comme soi-même. J'étais accoutumée à penser qu'il n'est pas honnête de faire du mal aux gens; je me console cependant un peu aujourd'hui, en disant à Moustapha: *Tu l'as voulu, George Dandin!* Et après cette réflexion, je suis à mon aise comme ci-devant.

Les grands événements ne m'ont jamais déplu, et les conquêtes ne m'ont jamais tentée. Je ne vois point aussi que le moment de la paix soit bien proche. Il est plaisant qu'on fasse accroire aux Turcs que nous ne pourrons point soutenir longtemps la guerre. Si la passion n'inspirait ces gens-là, comment pourraient-ils avoir oublié que Pierre-le-Grand soutint, pendant trente ans, la guerre, tantôt contre ces mêmes Turcs, tantôt contre les Suédois, les Polonais, les Persans, sans que l'empire en fût réduit à l'extrémité? Au contraire, la Russie est toujours sortie de chacune de ces guerres plus florissante qu'auparavant; et ce sont les guerres qui ont mis l'industrie en branle. Chaque guerre chez nous a été la mère de quelque nouvelle ressource, qui donnait plus de vivacité au commerce et à la circulation.

Votre projet de paix, monsieur, me paraît ressembler un peu au partage du lion de la fable; vous gardez tout pour votre favorite. Il ne faut point exclure de cette paix les légions de Sparte; nous parlerons après des jeux isthmiques.

Au moment que j'allais finir cette lettre, je reçois la nouvelle de la prise d'Ismaïlof, avec quelques circonstances assez singulières.

Le visir, avant de passer le Danube, harangua ses troupes, et leur dit qu'il était impossible de résister plus longtemps aux Russes; que lui visir se voyait dans la nécessité de passer de l'autre côté du Danube; qu'il leur enverrait autant de bâtiments qu'il pourrait pour les sauver; mais qu'en cas qu'il ne pût effectuer sa promesse, si les troupes russes venaient à les attaquer, il leur conseillait de mettre bas les armes, et qu'il les assurait que l'impératrice de Russie les ferait traiter avec humanité; que tout ce qu'on leur avait fait accroire jusqu'ici des Russes avait été imaginé par les ennemis des deux empires.

Dès que mes troupes se présentèrent devant Ismaïlof, les Turcs en sortirent, et ceux qui y restèrent mirent bas les armes. La capitulation de la ville fut faite dans une demi-heure. On y prit quarante-huit canons, et des magasins considérables de toute espèce. On compte, depuis le 21 jusqu'au 27 juillet, c'est-à-dire depuis la bataille de Kogul, près de huit mille prisonniers; et depuis l'année passée, nous avons pris à l'ennemi près de cinq cents canons.

Le comte Romanzof a envoyé un corps à droite vers votre Brahilof, qui sera pris, selon votre intention, et un autre à gauche qui doit s'emparer de Kilia.

Eh bien! monsieur, êtes-vous content? Je vous prie de l'être autant de mon amitié que je le suis de la vôtre.

CATERINE

LII

DE VOLTAIRE

A Ferney, 28 auguste 1770

Madame, mes craintes sont dissipées, malgré tous les efforts des dissidents de Pologne et des gazetiers des autres pays; votre victoire complète, remportée sur les Ottomans auprès du Pruth, est une terrible réponse.

Que votre majesté impériale me permette de lui témoigner l'excès de ma joie. Je ne suis plus en peine de la Grèce, sur laquelle on me donnait tant d'alarmes. Je vous crois toujours maîtresse de Navarin et de plusieurs autres places. Il n'est pas croyable que vos troupes aient évacué ce pays, comme on le dit, lorsque vous battez les Turcs sur mer comme sur terre; et quand même la division de vos forces vous obligerait de différer ou même d'abandonner la conquête de la Grèce, ce serait toujours une entreprise qui vous comblerait de gloire. Je maintiens qu'il ne s'est rien fait de si grand depuis Annibal; et cet Annibal, qui fut enfin contraint de retourner en Afrique, n'en a pas moins de réputation. Quand vous n'auriez réussi qu'à porter la terreur aux portes de Constantinople, à mener vos troupes jusqu'auprès de Corinthe, et à peupler vos états d'un grand nombre de familles grecques, vous auriez eu encore un grand avantage; mais votre dernière victoire me fait tout espérer.

Si vous voulez pousser vos conquêtes, vous les étendrez, je pense, où il vous plaira; et si vous voulez la paix, vous la dicterez. Pour moi, je veux toujours que votre majesté aille se faire couronner à Constantinople. Pardonnez-moi cette opiniâtreté; elle est presque aussi forte que celle avec laquelle je suis attaché à votre personne et à votre gloire: et puisque vous êtes devenue ma passion dominante, je me flatte que votre majesté impériale daignera toujours recevoir avec bonté le profond respect et le dévouement inviolable du vieux ermite de Ferney.

LIII

DE L'IMPÉRATRICE

Le 18/29 auguste 1770

Monsieur, au risque de vous importuner trop souvent, il faut que je vous dise qu'hier je reçus la nouvelle que le général-major, comte Tottleben, a pris aux Turcs les deux forts situés au-delà du mont Caucase, nommés Schéripan et Bagdat. Il tient bloqués le fort et la ville de Cotatis, en langue du pays Koutai, sur le Phase, qui tombe dans la mer Noire. Mes troupes ne sont plus qu'à soixante werstes de cette mer. L'ancienne Trébisonde est à leur gauche. Salomon, prince d'Immirette, agit de concert avec le comte. L'épouse de ce prince vint dans le camp russe, et pria le général de permettre qu'à la prise de Bagdat, elle pût jouir de l'honneur d'entrer dans la ville la première. Vous jugez bien qu'elle ne fut point refusée.

Ce Bagdat n'est ni aussi beau, ni aussi grand que celui des *Mille et une Nuits*. Ne trouvez-vous pas, monsieur, Moustapha bien accommodé, et les gazettes bien menteuses?

J'oubliais de vous dire qu'avant la prise de ces villes, le prince Héraclius a battu les Turcs sous Acalziké.

Je me recommande à votre amitié et à vos prières: on n'en saurait faire un plus grand cas qu'en fait votre favorite,

CATERINE

LIV

DE VOLTAIRE

A Ferney, 5 septembre 1770

Madame, j'étais si plein des victoires de votre majesté impériale, et si bouffi d'enthousiasme et de gloire, que j'oubliai de vous envoyer les vers que le roi de Prusse m'écrivait sur votre respectable personne, et sur le peu respectable Moustapha; voici ces vers:

> Si monsieur le mamamouchi
> Ne s'était point mêlé des troubles de Pologne,
> Il n'aurait point avec vergogne
> Vu ses spahis mis en hachi;
> Et de certaine impératrice
> (Qui vaut seule deux empereurs)
> Reçu pour prix de son caprice
> Des leçons qui devraient rabaisser ses hauteurs.
> Vous voyez comme elle s'acquitte
> De tant de devoirs importants:
> J'admire avec le vieil ermite
> Ses immenses projets, ses exploits éclatants:
> Quand on possède son mérite,
> On peut se passer d'assistants.

Je n'ai pas l'honneur de penser comme les têtes couronnées. Je crois fermement que cent mille hommes de troupes auxiliaires en Grèce et sur le Danube n'auraient fait nul mal. Il valait mieux, dans votre situation, être secourue que louée. Votre gloire en a augmenté, mais les conquêtes ont été retardées.

Les dernières lettres de Venise disent que, dans une émeute populaire, les fidèles musulmans se sont déchaînés contre tous les Francs, qu'ils ont tué l'ambassadeur de France, et presque tous ses domestiques; que l'ambassadeur d'Angleterre n'a pu échapper à la fureur du peuple qu'en se déguisant en matelot; que le baile de Venise s'est longtemps défendu dans sa maison; et qu'à la fin le grand-seigneur lui a envoyé une garde de mille hommes.

Si ces nouvelles étaient vraies (ce que je ne veux pas croire), quels princes de l'Europe n'armeraient pas sur-le-champ pour venger le droit des gens? Vous seule le soutenez, madame: aussi vous seule jouirez d'une gloire immortelle.

Que votre majesté impériale me permette de me mettre à ses pieds. *Le vieil ermite de Ferney*

LV

DE L'IMPÉRATRICE

A Pétersbourg, 31 auguste/11 septembre 1770

Monsieur, quoique cette fois-ci, en réponse à votre lettre du 11 d'auguste, je n'aie point à vous donner de grands faits de guerre, j'espère ne pas nuire à votre convalescence en vous disant qu'après la prise d'Ismaïlof, les Tartares du Bourjak et de Belgorod se sont séparés de la Porte. Ils ont envoyé des délégués aux deux généraux de mes armées pour capituler, et se sont rangés ensuite sous la protection de la Russie. Ils ont donné des otages, et ont prêté serment, sur l'Alcoran, de ne plus seconder les Turcs ni le kan de Crimée, et de ne point reconnaître le kan, à moins qu'il ne se soumette aux mêmes conditions, c'est-à-dire de vivre tranquille sous la protection de la Russie, et de se détacher de la Porte. On ne sait pas ce qu'est devenu ce kan. Cependant il y a apparence que, sinon lui, du moins une grande partie de son monde, embrassera le même parti.

Les Tartares, dès le commencement de cette guerre, la regardaient comme injuste; ils n'avaient aucun sujet de plainte; le commerce, interrompu avec l'Ukraine, leur causait une perte plus réelle, qu'ils ne pouvaient espérer d'avantages par les rapines.

Les musulmans disent que les deux dernières batailles leur coûtent près de quarante mille hommes: cela fait horreur, j'en conviens; mais quand il s'agit de coups, il vaut mieux battre que d'être battu.

Je n'oserais, d'après cela, vous demander, monsieur, si vous êtes content, parce que, quelque amitié que vous ayez pour moi, je suis persuadée que vous ne sauriez voir le malheur de tant d'hommes sans en ressentir de la peine. J'espère pourtant que cette même amitié vous consolera du malheur des Turcs: vous serez tolérant et humain, et il n'y aura aucune contradiction dans vos sentiments. Il est impossible que vous aimiez les ennemis des arts.

Conservez-moi, je vous prie, votre amitié, et soyez assuré que j'y suis très sensible.

CATERINE

P.S. Il faut que je vous parle d'un phenomene nouveau: un grand nombre de déserteurs turcs viennent à notre armée. On prétend que c'est une chose dont il n'y a jamais eu d'exemple. Ces déserteurs assurent qu'ils sont mieux traités chez nous, qu'ils ne le sont chez eux.

LVI

DE VOLTAIRE

A Ferney, 14 septembre 1770

Madame, nous savions, par Venise et par Marseille, la nouvelle de vos deux victoires navales, remportées à Napoli de Romanie et à Scio. Je reçois dans l'instant, aux acclamations de cent mille bouches, le détail que votre majesté impériale daigne me faire de la victoire de M. le maréchal de Romanzof sur le visir Ali-Bey, et sur tant de bachas suivis de cent cinquante mille hommes.

Si je meurs des maladies qui m'accablent, je mourrai à demi content, puisque Moustapha est à demi détrôné. Je lui sais bon gré de consulter à la fois des prophètes et des fous. Ces gens-là ont été, de tout temps, de la même espèce; la seule différence est que les prophètes ont été des fous plus dangereux. Les rigides musulmans en admettent quatre cent quarante mille, en comptant tous les héros de l'ancien Testament: cela ferait une armée beaucoup plus forte que celle d'Ali-Beg ou Ali-Bey.

Je vois plus que jamais que les chars de Cyrus sont fort inutiles à vos troupes victorieuses. Si elles rencontrent Ali-Bey une seconde fois, elles le battront infailliblement; mais il faut traverser le Danube en présence d'une armée qui est encore nombreuse. Il n'y a rien que je ne croie M. le comte de Romanzof capable de faire; mais osera-t-on tenter ce passage, après lequel il faudrait absolument ou prendre Constantinople, ou n'avoir point de retraite? Je lève les mains au ciel, je fais des vœux, et je me tais.

Ceux qui souhaitaient des revers à votre majesté seront bien confondus. Eh! pourquoi lui souhaiter des disgrâces, dans le temps qu'elle venge l'Europe? Ce sont apparemment des gens qui ne veulent pas qu'on parle grec; car si vous étiez souveraine de Constantinople, votre majesté établirait bien vite une belle académie grecque. On vous ferait une Cateriniade; les Zeuxis et les Phidias couvriraient la terre de vos images; la chute de l'empire ottoman serait célébrée en grec; Athènes serait une de vos capitales; la langue grecque deviendrait la langue universelle; tous les négociants de la mer Égée demanderaient des passeports grecs à votre majesté.

Je n'aime point les Vénitiens, qui attendent si tard à se faire Grecs. Je suis aussi un peu fâché contre cet Ali d'Égypte, qui ne remue pas plus qu'une momie. Mais enfin, je n'ai point à me plaindre; deux victoires sur mer et deux victoires sur terre sont des faveurs bien honnêtes dont je remercie votre majesté impériale du fond de mon cœur. Je chante des *Te Deum* dans mon lit, et un *De profundis* pour Moustapha.

Que votre majesté impériale soit toujours aussi heureuse qu'elle mérite de l'être, et qu'elle daigne agréer le profond respect, la joie, et l'attachement inviolable du vieil ermite des Alpes.

LVII

DE L'IMPÉRATRICE

Le 10/21 septembre 1770

Monsieur, vous m'avez dit, dans votre dernière lettre, que je devais vous mander la prise d'une demi-douzaine de villes: je pense vous avoir déjà dit la nouvelle de la prise d'Ismaïlof sur le Danube; j'y ajoute aujourd'hui celle de la forteresse de Kilia-Nova. Après plusieurs jours de tranchée ouverte, la garnison turque, de cinq mille hommes, a été renvoyée sur l'autre rive de la rivière.

Les lettres de Malte m'ont apporté la confirmation du grand combat naval donné dans le canal de Scio; et le lendemain de cette action ma flotte a réduit en cendres trente-trois vaisseaux ennemis, qui s'étaient retirés dans le port de Liberno en Asie.

J'espère, monsieur, que vous ne serez pas fâché d'apprendre que ceux qui prennent plaisir à nous faire battre sur le papier, sont bien loin de leur compte. Je vous prie de me conserver votre amitié, et d'être assuré, etc.

CATERINE

LVIII

DE VOLTAIRE

A Ferney, 21 septembre 1770

Madame, vive l'auguste, l'adorable Catherine! Vivent ses troupes victorieuses! Sa lettre du 20 auguste, nouveau style, est du plus beau style dont on ait jamais écrit. L'armée d'Alexandre forcera enfin les Athéniens à dire du bien d'elle. L'envie est contrainte d'admirer.

Votre majesté a bien raison; la guerre est très utile à un pays, quand on la fait avec succès sur les frontières. La nation devient alors plus industrieuse, plus active, comme plus terrible. Les Turcs sont battus de tous côtés chez eux, et chaque victoire augmente encore le courage et l'espérance de vos troupes. Les échos ont dit à nos Alpes que, tandis que le visir repasse le

Danube en désordre, le général Tottleben a vaincu un corps considérable de Turcs vers Erzerom, et s'est même emparé de cette ville.

Si la chose est vraie, il me semble que votre majesté ne peut hésiter à suivre sa destinée, qui l'appelle à si haute voix. La plus grande des révolutions est commencée; votre génie l'achèvera. J'ai dit, il y a longtemps, que si jamais l'empire turc est détruit, ce sera par la Russie; mon auguste impératrice accomplira ma prédiction. Je ne crains plus la paix, après la lettre dont elle m'honore.

Un grand monarque m'avait mandé que non seulement votre majesté ferait la paix, mais qu'elle la ferait avec modération; je ne vois pas pourquoi tant se modérer avec ce Moustapha, qui ne se modérerait point s'il était vainqueur.

Quand je parlais de paix, en la redoutant, quand je disais que vous en dicteriez les conditions, j'étais bien loin d'imaginer que votre majesté abandonnerait ces braves Spartiates. Dieu me préserve de l'en soupçonner! mais, après tant de victoires, il ne s'agit pas d'obtenir leur grâce auprès de leur vilain maître: il est temps qu'ils n'aient d'autre maître que ma protectrice, ou plutôt qu'ils soient libres sous ses drapeaux.

J'ai craint quelque temps que votre armée ne passât le Danube, et ne s'exposât à quelques revers. J'ai cru le Danube très difficile à traverser en présence des Turcs, et la retraite plus difficile; mais à présent tout me paraît aisé; la terreur s'est emparée d'eux, et cette terreur combat pour vous. Je suis persuadé que dix mille de vos soldats battraient cinquante mille osmanlis.

Je ne suis pas surpris que votre âme, faite pour toutes les grandes choses, prenne goût à une pareille guerre. Je crois vos troupes de débarquement revenues en Grèce, et votre flotte de la mer Noire menaçant les environs de Constantinople. Si cette révolution de l'Egypte, dont on m'avait tant flatté, pouvait s'effectuer, je croirais l'empire turc détruit pour jamais.

Il me semble qu'il a manqué aux Vénitiens la première des qualités en politique, la hardiesse. La finesse n'a jamais réussi à personne dans les grandes choses; elle n'est bonne que pour les moines.

Mais devant qui osé-je me livrer à mes idées? Je parle au génie tutélaire du Nord; je dois me taire, imposer silence à mon enthousiasme, et rester dans les bornes du profond respect et de l'attachement qui me met aux pieds de votre majesté impériale, pour le peu que j'ai à vivre. *L'ermite de Ferney*

LIX

DE L'IMPÉRATRICE

A Pétersbourg, le 16/27 septembre 1770

Monsieur, que de choses j'ai à vous dire aujourd'hui! je ne sais par où commencer.

Ma flotte, non pas sous le commandement de mes amiraux, mais sous celui du comte Alexis Orlof, après avoir battu la flotte ennemie, l'a brûlée tout entière dans le port de Chesme, anciennement Clazomène. J'en ai reçu, il y a trois jours, la nouvelle directe. Près de cent vaisseaux de toute espèce ont été réduits en cendres. Je n'ose dire le nombre des musulmans qui ont péri: on le fait monter jusqu'à vingt mille.

Un conseil général de guerre avait terminé la désunion des deux amiraux, en déférant le commandement au général des troupes de terre, qui se trouvait sur cette flotte, et qui au reste était leur ancien dans le service. Le résultat fut unanimement approuvé de tous, et dès ce moment l'union fut rétablie. Je l'ai toujours dit, les héros sont nés pour les grands événements.

La flotte turque fut poursuivie depuis Napoli de Romanie, où elle avait été déjà harcelée à deux reprises, jusqu'à Scio. Le comte Orlof savait qu'un renfort était parti de Constantinople; il crut qu'il préviendrait la jonction, en attaquant l'ennemi sans perte de temps. Arrivé dans le canal de Scio, il vit que cette jonction s'était faite. Il se trouvait avec neuf vaisseaux de haut-bord en présence de seize vaisseaux de ligne ottomans: le nombre des frégates et autres bâtiments était encore plus inégal. Il ne balança pas, et trouva la disposition des esprits telle, qu'il n'y eut qu'un avis, qui fut de vaincre ou de mourir. Le combat commença: le comte Orlof se tint au centre; l'amiral Spiridof, qui avait à son bord le comte Féodor-Orlof, commanda l'avant-garde; le contre-amiral Elphinston l'arrière-garde.

L'ordre de bataille des Turcs était tel qu'une de leurs ailes se trouvait appuyée contre une île pierreuse, et l'autre à des bas-fonds, de façon qu'ils ne pouvaient être tournés.

Le feu fut terrible de part et d'autre pendant plusieurs heures; les vaisseaux s'approchèrent de si près, que le feu de la mousqueterie se joignit à celui des canons. Le vaisseau de l'amiral Spiridof avait affaire à trois vaisseaux de guerre et un chebec turcs. Il accrocha malgré cela le capitan pacha, qui portait quatre-vingt-dix canons; il y jeta tant de grenades et de matières combustibles que le feu prit au vaisseau, se communiqua au nôtre, et tous deux sautèrent en l'air, un moment après que l'amiral Spiridof et le comte Féodor-Orlof, avec environ quatre-vingt-dix personnes, en furent descendus.

Le comte Alexis, voyant, dans le plus fort du combat, les vaisseaux amiraux voler en l'air, crut son frère péri. Il sentit alors qu'il était homme; il s'évanouit: mais un moment après, reprenant ses esprits, il ordonna de lever toutes les voiles, et se jeta avec ses vaisseaux entre les ennemis. A l'instant de la victoire, un officier lui apporta la nouvelle que son frère et l'amiral étaient vivants; il dit qu'il ne saurait décrire ce qu'il sentit en ce moment, le plus heureux de sa vie. Le reste de la flotte turque se jeta sans ordre ni règle dans le port de Chesme.

Le lendemain fut employé à préparer les brûlots, et à canonner l'ennemi dans le port; à quoi celui-ci répondit. Mais dans la nuit les brûlots furent lâchés, et firent si bien leur devoir, qu'en moins de six heures la flotte turque fut consumée tout entière. La terre et l'onde tremblaient, dit-on, de la grande quantité de vaisseaux ennemis qui sautaient en l'air. On l'a senti jusqu'à Smyrne, qui est à douze lieues de Chesme.

Les nôtres, pendant cet incendie, tirèrent du port un vaisseau turc de soixante canons, qui se trouvait sous le vent, et qui, par cette raison, n'avait pas été consumé. Ils s'emparèrent ensuite d'une batterie que les Turcs avaient abandonnée.

La guerre est une vilaine chose, monsieur! Le comte Orlof me dit que le lendemain de l'incendie de la flotte, il vit avec effroi que l'eau du port de Chesme, qui n'est pas fort grand, était teinte de sang, tant il y était péri de Turcs.

Cette lettre, monsieur, servira de réponse à la vôtre du 26 d'auguste, où vos alarmes à notre sujet commençaient déjà à se dissiper. J'espère qu'à présent vous n'en avez plus. Mes affaires, ce me semble, vont assez bien. Pour ce qui regarde la prise de Constantinople, je ne la crois pas si prochaine. Cependant il ne faut, dit-on, désespérer de rien. Je commence à croire que cela dépend plus de Moustapha que de tout autre. Ce prince s'y est si bien pris jusqu'ici, que s'il continue dans l'opiniâtreté que ses amis lui inspirent, il exposera son empire à de très grands dangers. Il a oublié son rôle d'agresseur.

Adieu, monsieur; portez-vous bien. Si des combats gagnés peuvent vous plaire, vous devez être bien content de nous. Soyez assuré de l'estime et de la considération que je vous porte.

CATERINE

LX

DE VOLTAIRE

A Ferney, 2 octobre 1770

Madame, je ne vis pas dans le dix-huitième siècle, je me trouve transporté dans les Alpes du temps de la fondation de Babylone. Je vois une héroïne de la maison d'Ascanie, portée sur le trône des Roxelans, qui triomphe sur le Scirus, sur le Phase, sur le Pont-Euxin, sur la mer Égée, sur les rives du Danube. M. d'Alembert, qui est actuellement à Ferney, est dans le même enthousiasme que moi, et la seule différence est qu'il l'exprime mieux. Nous haïssons également Moustapha; nous ne cherchons parmi les arbustes de nos montagnes que des lauriers, pour en orner le portrait de votre majesté impériale; mais nous n'en trouvons point. Tous les naturalistes disent qu'on n'en trouve plus qu'en Russie.

Après la lettre du 29 auguste, dont votre majesté impériale m'honore, nous nous attendons fermement que votre armée victorieuse aura passé le Danube; que le visir aura été battu *iterum* vers Andrinople; que la ville de ce méchant Constantin, qui a été baptisé si tard, aura ouvert ses portes; que les dames du sérail auront été tirées d'esclavage; que la flotte de la mer Égée aura donné la main à la flotte du Pont-Euxin; que Moustapha sera parti pour Damas ou pour Alep, etc., etc., etc.

Vous aviez bien raison, madame, de dire, au commencement de cette guerre, que ceux qui vous l'avaient suscitée travaillaient à votre gloire: certainement votre majesté leur a une grande obligation.

Nous ne laissons pas d'avoir de la gloire aussi. Il y a dans Paris de très jolis carrosses à la nouvelle mode, et on a inventé des surtouts pour le dessert qui sont de très bon goût: on a même exécuté depuis peu un motet à grands chœurs, qui a fait beaucoup de bruit, du moins dans la salle où l'on chantait; enfin nous avons une danseuse dont on dit des merveilles.

Malgré nos triomphes, l'âme de M. d'Alembert et la mienne volent aux Dardanelles, au Danube, à la mer Noire, à Bender, en Crimée, et surtout à Pétersbourg: c'est là qu'elles sont aux pieds de votre majesté, pénétrées d'admiration, de respect, de joie, et remplies de l'espérance de lui écrire à Stamboul.

De votre majesté impériale, l'adorateur de latrie, VOLTAIRE, enseveli dans Ferney, et criant: *Gloire dans les hauts!*

LXI

DE L'IMPÉRATRICE

Ce 28 septembre/9 octobre 1770

Monsieur, vous aimez les belles âmes: voyez comme celle du comte Alexis Orlof s'est peinte dans la réponse qu'il a faite aux consuls chrétiens de Smyrne! Je suis persuadée que vous serez content de lui (l'imprimé ci-joint la contient). Ai-je tort, quand je dis que ces Orlof sont nés pour les grandes choses?

Vous me demandez, dans votre lettre du 21 septembre, si le général Tottleben s'est emparé d'Erzerom. Je vous ai informé, je pense, que sa dernière conquête était la ville de Cotatis. On ne va pas si vite en guerre, parce qu'il faut faire deux repas par jour, et que, pour que cela se fasse, il faut avoir ou trouver de quoi.

Je veux sincèrement la paix, non parce que les ressources me manquent pour faire la guerre, mais parce que je hais l'effusion du sang humain. Si M. Moustapha fait de l'opiniâtre, j'espère qu'il nous trouvera l'année qui vient partout où nous pourrons le persuader qu'il vaut mieux céder aux circonstances pour sauver son empire que de pousser l'entêtement jusqu'à l'extrémité.

Les Grecs, les Spartiates ont bien dégénéré; ils aiment la rapine mieux que la liberté. Ils sont à jamais perdus s'ils ne profitent point des dispositions et des conseils du héros que je leur ai envoyé. Je ne parle point des Vénitiens: je trouve qu'il n'y a que le pape et le roi de Sardaigne qui aient du mérite en Italie.

Soyez assuré, monsieur, qu'on ne saurait sentir plus de satisfaction que j'en ressens chaque fois que je reçois de vos lettres; elles contiennent tant de témoignages de votre amitié, que je ne puis que vous en être très obligée.

CATERINE

P.S. Dans ce moment on vient de m'apporter la nouvelle que Belgorod, en turc *Akkermann*, sur le Dniester, s'est rendu le 26 septembre par capitulation. Bientôt, je pense, vous entendrez parler de votre Brahilof.

LXII

DE VOLTAIRE

A Ferney, 12 octobre 1770

Madame, la lettre de votre majesté impériale, du 11 septembre, me confirme dans ma joie continue, mais sans redoublement. Je suis persuadé que si Moustapha, son visir Azem, et son mufti, étaient informés de l'intérêt que je prends à eux, ils m'en remercieraient en me fesant empaler.

Béni soit leur Allah, si en effet Ali est roi d'Égypte; mais cette nouvelle grâce de la Providence, en faveur de Moustapha, me paraît bien douteuse. Nous le saurions à Marseille, qui envoie continuellement des vaisseaux au port d'Alexandrie; nous en aurions eu des nouvelles certaines par Venise; personne n'en parle. On ne se fait pas roi d'Égypte incognito. J'ose dire plus: votre majesté aurait déjà, dans ce pays de Pharaon et de Moïse, quelque bon Israélite qui encouragerait la révolution au nom du Seigneur, et qui vous en rendrait compte. Je me borne donc à faire les plus tendres vœux pour que mon cher Moustapha soit chassé à jamais des bords du Nil et de ceux du Danube.

Que votre majesté me permette seulement de plaindre ces pauvres Grecs, qui ont le malheur d'appartenir encore à des gens qui parlent turc. Ce sont de petites mortifications que j'éprouve au milieu des plaisirs que me donnent toutes vos victoires. C'est bien assez qu'en aussi peu de temps vous soyez maîtresse absolue de la Moldavie, de la Valachie, de presque toute la Bessarabie, des deux rivages de la mer Noire, d'un côté vers Azof, et de l'autre vers le Caucase.

Quand votre majesté fesait ses belles lois, dont la première était la tolérance, elle ne se doutait pas qu'une aussi bonne chrétienne deviendrait la protectrice des circoncis du Budziak, tous descendants en droite ligne de Tamerlan et de Gengiskan. Mais puisque vous êtes tous enfants de Noé (quoiqu'il n'ait jamais été connu de personne, excepté des Juifs), il est clair que vous êtes tous cousins, et que vous devez vous supporter les uns les autres. Cette tolérance de votre majesté pour messieurs les Tartares bessarabes engagera sans doute l'invincible Moustapha à vous demander la paix. Mais que deviendra ma pauvre Grèce? Aurai-je la douleur de voir les enfants du galant Alcibiade obéir à d'autres qu'à Catherine-la-Grande?

Je remets toujours, madame, au premier congrès, les intérêts des jeux olympiques et du théâtre d'Athènes entre vos mains; mais j'aime mieux m'en rapporter à une bataille qu'à une assemblée de plénipotentiaires. Vous êtes si bien servie par MM. les comtes Orlof et par M. le maréchal de Romanzof, que, malgré mon humeur pacifique, je préfère sans contredit des victoires nouvelles à un accommodement.

Je suis un peu pressé, je l'avoue, parce que, étant fort vieux et malade, je veux jouir au plus tôt. Pour peu que vous tardiez à vous asseoir sur le trône de Stamboul, il n'y aura pas moyen que je sois témoin de ce petit triomphe.

Que votre majesté impériale daigne toujours agréer le profond respect, et la reconnaissance, et les desirs honnêtes du vieil ermite de Ferney.

LXIII

DE L'IMPÉRATRICE

Le 7/18 octobre 1770

Monsieur, l'arrivée du prince Henri de Prusse à Pétersbourg a été suivie de la prise de Bender, que je vous annonce. L'un et l'autre m'a empêché de répondre à vos trois lettres, que j'ai reçues consécutivement. Les nouvelles publiques assurent aussi que le comte Orlof s'est emparé de Lemnos. Nous voilà entièrement dans le pays des fables: je crains qu'avec le temps cette guerre ne paraisse fabuleuse elle-même.

Si le mamamouchi ne fait pas la paix cet hiver, je ne réponds point de ce qui lui arrivera l'année prochaine. Encore un peu de ce bonheur dont nous avons vu des essais, et l'histoire des Turcs pourra fournir un nouveau sujet de tragédie pour les siècles futurs.

Vous direz, monsieur, que depuis le succès de cette campagne je suis dans les grands airs; mais c'est que, depuis que j'ai du bonheur, l'Europe me trouve beaucoup d'esprit. Cependant à quarante ans on n'augmente guère, devant le Seigneur, en esprit et en beauté.

Je pense effectivement avec vous que bientôt il sera temps que j'aille étudier le grec dans quelque université: en attendant, on traduit Homère en russe; c'est toujours quelque chose, pour commencer. Nous verrons, d'après les circonstances, s'il sera nécessaire d'aller plus loin. L'esprit du peuple turc se range de notre côté; ils disent que leur sultan est insensé d'exposer son empire à tant de revers, et que les conseils de ses amis deviendront funestes aux musulmans.

Adieu, monsieur; portez-vous bien, et priez Dieu pour nous.

CATERINE

LXIV

DE VOLTAIRE

A Ferney, 25 octobre 1770

Madame, Clazomène était autrefois une très belle ville: Alexandre l'augmenta; les Turcs l'ont dévastée; mais sous votre empire, elle redeviendrait florissante.

La lettre de votre majesté impériale, du 16/27 septembre, me fait tressaillir de joie et frémir d'horreur. Tous ces comtes Orlof sont des héros, et je vous vois la plus heureuse ainsi que la première princesse de l'univers. Je plains beaucoup M. le prince de Koslofsky. Comment ne pleurerais-je pas celui qui m'a apporté le portrait de mon héroïne? mais enfin il est mort en vous servant.

Quel fruit tirera à la fin votre majesté impériale de tout ce carnage dont Moustapha est la seule cause, et dont il doit être aussi las qu'intimidé? Il faut que ce prince soit ensorcelé, si de son sopha il ne demande pas la paix à votre trône.

Les Anglais et les Espagnols sont prêts à se faire la guerre dans les deux mondes, pour une petite île déserte; mais votre majesté combat à présent pour l'empire d'Orient.

On mande de Marseille qu'Ali-Bey s'est donné en effet en Égypte un pouvoir dont le padisha Moustapha ne peut plus le priver; mais qu'il n'a pas entièrement rompu avec la Porte ottomane. Cependant je persiste toujours à croire que les provisions ne peuvent plus venir d'Égypte à Constantinople devant votre flotte victorieuse.

Je crois votre majesté impériale maîtresse de la mer Noire; ainsi je ne vois que la Natolie qui puisse fournir des vivres et des secours à la capitale de votre ennemi.

Je n'en sais certainement pas assez pour oser examiner seulement si votre armée peut passer ou non le Danube; il ne m'appartient que de faire des souhaits. Le bruit se répand que le prince Repnin et le général Bawer ont traversé ce fleuve avec des troupes légères pour reconnaître les Turcs et les inquiéter. Je m'en rapporte à la prudence et au zèle de vos généraux; mais j'ose être presque sûr que les Turcs ne tiendront pas devant vos troupes. Quand une fois la terreur s'est emparée d'une nation, elle ne fait qu'augmenter, à moins que le temps ne la rassure. Jamais les conquérants du pays que les Turcs occupent aujourd'hui n'ont donné à leurs ennemis le temps de respirer.

Je vois que votre majesté les imite parfaitement: il n'y a point d'ailleurs de saisons pour vos soldats; ils peuvent prendre Bender en octobre, et marcher vers Andrinople en novembre.

Plus vos succès sont grands, plus mon étonnement redouble qu'on ne les ait pas secondés, et que la race des Turcs ne soit pas déjà chassée de l'Europe.

Je pense que les plus grands princes se trompent souvent en politique beaucoup plus que les particuliers dans leurs affaires de famille. Ils aiment fort leurs intérêts, ils les entendent; et, par une fatalité trop commune, ils ne les suivent presque jamais.

Quoi qu'il en soit, voici le temps de la plus belle et de la plus noble révolution, depuis les conquêtes des premiers califes. Si cette révolution ne vous est pas réservée, elle ne l'est à personne. Je serais très affligé que votre majesté ne retirât de tant de travaux que de la gloire. Votre âme forte et généreuse me dira que c'est beaucoup, et moi je prendrai la liberté de répondre qu'après tant de sang et de tresors prodigués, il faut encore quelque autre chose: les rayons de la gloire des souverains, dans de pareilles circonstances, se comptent par le nombre des provinces qu'ils acquièrent.

Pardon de mes inutiles réflexions. Votre majesté les excusera, puisque le cœur les dicte, et vous vous en direz plus en deux mots que je ne vous en dirais en cent pages.

Que votre majesté impériale daigne agréer avec sa bonté ordinaire ma joie de vos succès, mon admiration pour messieurs les comtes Orlof, pour vos généraux et vos braves troupes, mes vœux pour des succès encore plus grands, mon profond respect, mon enthousiasme, et mon attachement inviolable.

Le vieil ermite

LXV

DE VOLTAIRE

A Ferney, 6 novembre 1770

Madame, si Bender est pris l'épée à la main, comme on le dit, j'en rends de très humbles actions de grâces à votre majesté impériale; car, dans mon lit, où je suis malade, je n'ai d'autre plaisir que celui de vos victoires, et chacune de vos conquêtes est mon restaurant.

On confirme encore de Marseille qu'Ali-Bey est roi d'Égypte, et qu'il s'est emparé d'Alexandrie, où il établit déjà un commerce considérable avec toutes les nations trafiquantes. Plaise à la Vierge Marie, à qui Ali-Bey ne croit point du tout, que tout cela soit exactement vrai!

Ce qui me fait une peine extrême, c'est que vos troupes victorieuses ne sont point encore dans Andrinople. Votre majesté dira que je suis un vieillard bien impétueux, que rien ne peut me satisfaire; que vous avez beau, pour me faire plaisir, battre Moustapha tous les jours, que je ne serai content que lorsque vous serez sur les bords de l'Euphrate. Eh bien! madame, cela est vrai. La Mésopotamie est un pays admirable; on peut s'y faire transporter en litière, ce qu'on ne peut pas faire à Pétersbourg vers le mois de novembre. Monseigneur le prince Henri y est bien! Oui; mais c'est un héros, quoiqu'il ne soit pas un géant: il est juste qu'il voie l'héroïne du nord, car il est aussi aimable qu'il est grand général.

Au reste, madame, je suppose qu'Ali-Bey garde l'Égypte en dépôt à votre majesté impériale; car ma passion veut encore vous donner l'Égypte, afin que votre académie des sciences, dont j'ai l'honneur d'être, connaisse bien les antiquités de ce pays-là; et c'est ce que probablement on ne fera jamais sous un Ali-Bey.

On dit que la peste est à Constantinople. Il faut que Moustapha ait fait le dénombrement de son peuple; car Dieu, d'ordinaire, envoie la peste aux rois qui ont voulu savoir leur compte. Il en coûta soixante et dix mille Juifs au bon roi David, et il n'y avait pas grande perte. J'espère que votre majesté chassera bientôt de Stamboul la peste et les Turcs.

Je me mets aux pieds de votre majesté impériale, du fond de mon désert et de mon néant, avec le plus profond respect, et une passion qui ne fait que croître et embellir.

LXVI

DE VOLTAIRE

A Ferney, 20 novembre 1770

Madame, votre majesté impériale l'avait bien prévu, vos ennemis n'ont servi qu'à votre gloire; et, de quelque manière que vous finissiez cette grande guerre, votre gloire ne sera point passagère. Victorieuse et législatrice à la fois, vous avez assuré l'immortalité à votre nom. Je suis un peu affligé, en qualité de Français, d'entendre dire que c'est un chevalier de Tott qui fortifie les Dardanelles. Quoi! c'est ainsi que finissent les Français qui ont commencé autrefois la première croisade! Que dirait Godefroi de Bouillon, si cette nouvelle pouvait parvenir jusqu'à lui, dans le pays où l'on ne reçoit de nouvelles de personne?

On parle toujours de peste en Allemagne; on la craint, on exige partout des billets de santé; et l'on ne songe pas que, si on avait aidé votre majesté à chasser cette année les Turcs de l'Europe, on aurait pour jamais chassé la peste avec eux. On oublie les plus grands, les plus véritables intérêts, pour un intérêt chimérique, pour une politique qui me paraît bien déraisonnable. Il me semble que l'on fait bien des fautes de plus d'un côté: c'est le sort de la plupart des ministères.

On se prépare à la guerre en France, et on espère la paix, dont on a le plus grand besoin. Il serait trop ridicule qu'on éprouvât le plus grand des fléaux pour une méchante île inhabitée; il ne faut jamais faire la guerre qu'avec l'extrême probabilité d'y gagner beaucoup. Puisse la guerre contre Moustapha finir par le détrôner, ou du moins par l'appauvrir pour trente ans! Puisse votre majesté impériale jouir d'un triomphe très durable, et pacifier la Pologne après avoir écrasé la Turquie!

Vous avez deux voisins qui font des vers, le roi de Prusse et le roi de la Chine; Frédéric en a déjà fait pour vous, j'en attends de Kien-Long.

Je me mets à vos pieds victorieux et plus blancs que ceux de Moustapha, avec le plus profond respect et la plus grande passion.

LXVII

DE VOLTAIRE

A Ferney, 26 novembre 1770

Madame, il faut vouloir ce qu'on ne peut empêcher. Je vois qu'on obligera ce gros Moustapha à vous demander la paix; mais, au nom de Jésus-Christ notre sauveur, faites-la-lui payer bien cher. Quand votre majesté impériale sera devenue son amie, je l'appellerai sa hautesse. On a débité qu'il voyait familièrement l'ambassadeur d'Angleterre deux fois par semaine, et qu'il lui parlait en italien; j'ai bien de la peine à le croire; les Turcs apprennent l'arabe tout au plus. Je connais des souveraines fort supérieures en tout aux Moustapha, qui parlent plusieurs langues en perfection; mais pour le padisha de Stamboul, je doute fort qu'il ait ce mérite, et qu'il ait chez lui une académie.

On dit aussi qu'il va confier ses armées invincibles à son frère, ce qui contredit un peu les desseins pacifiques qu'on lui attribue; mais son frère en sait-il plus que lui? et puisqu'il est padisha, pourquoi ne commande-t-il pas ses armées lui-même?

Je m'imagine qu'il tremblerait de peur devant l'un des quatre Orlof, qui valent mieux que les quatre fils Aymon, et qui sont des héros plus réels. Je plains beaucoup plus l'anarchie polonaise que l'insolence ottomane: toutes les deux sont dans la détresse qu'elles méritent. Vive le roi de la Chine, qui fait des vers, et qui est en paix avec tout le monde!

J'avoue à votre majesté que je déteste le gouvernement papal; je le trouve ridicule et abominable; il a abruti et ensanglanté la moitié de l'Europe pendant trop de siècles. Mais le Ganganelli, qui règne aujourd'hui, est un homme d'esprit, qui sent apparemment combien il est honteux de laisser la ville de Constantin à des barbares, ennemis de tous les arts; et qu'il faut préférer des Grecs, quoique schismatiques, à des mahométans.

Le roi de Sardaigne, qui a des droits à l'île de Chypre, n'aime point ces barbares. Mais, encore une fois, je ne comprends pas l'indifférence des Vénitiens, qui pouvaient reprendre Candie en trois mois; encore moins l'impératrice-reine, à qui Belgrade, la Bosnie, et la Servie étaient ouvertes. On est devenu bien modéré avec les Turcs, et bien honnête. Pardon, madame, de mes réflexions; mais vous avez daigné m'accoutumer à dire ce que je pense, et on pardonne tout aux grandes passions.

LXVIII

DE L'IMPÉRATRICE

A Pétersbourg, le 2/13 décembre 1770

Monsieur, les répétitions deviennent ennuyeuses. Je vous ai si souvent mandé telle ou telle ville prise, les Turcs battus, etc.! Pour amuser, il faut, dit-on, de la diversité: eh bien! apprenez que votre cher Brahilof a été assiégé, qu'on a donné un assaut, que cet assaut a été repoussé, et le siége levé.

Le comte de Romanzof s'est fâché: il a envoyé une seconde fois le général-major Glébof, avec un renfort, vers ce Brahilof. Vous croirez peut-être que les Turcs, encouragés par la levée du siége, se sont défendus comme des lions? point du tout. A la seconde approche de nos troupes, ils ont abandonné la place, le canon, et les magasins qui y étaient. M. Glébof y est entré et s'y est établi. Un autre corps est allé réoccuper la Valachie.

J'ai reçu avant-hier la nouvelle que Bucharest, la capitale de cette principauté, a été prise le 15 de novembre, après un petit combat avec la garnison turque.

Mais ce qui va vraiment vous divertir, parceque vous souhaitiez que le Danube fût franchi, c'est que le maréchal Romanzof envoya, dans le même temps, de l'autre côté du fleuve quelques centaines de chasseurs et des troupes légères qui partirent d'Ismaïlof sur des bateaux, et s'emparèrent du fort de Soulthcha, qui est à quinze werstes de l'endroit où le visir était campé. Ils envoyèrent la garnison dans l'autre monde, emmenèrent plusieurs prisonniers, et treize pièces de canon; ils enclouèrent le reste, et revinrent heureusement à Kilia. Le visir, ayant appris cette petite incartade, leva son camp, et s'en fut avec son monde à Babadaki.

Voilà où nous en sommes, et, s'il plaît à Moustapha, nous continuerons, quoique, pour le bien de l'humanité, il serait bien temps que ce seigneur-là se rangeât à la raison.

M. Tottleben est allé attaquer Potis sur la mer Noire. Il ne dit pas grand bien des successeurs de Mithridate; mais en revanche il trouve le climat de l'ancienne Ibérie le plus beau du monde.

Les dernières lettres d'Italie disent ma dernière escadre à Mahon. Si le sultan ne se ravise, je lui en enverrai encore une demi-douzaine: on dirait qu'il y prend plaisir.

La maladie présente des Anglais ne saurait être guérie que par une guerre: ils sont trop riches et désunis: une guerre les appauvrira, et réunira les esprits. Aussi la nation la veut-elle, mais la cour n'en veut qu'au gouverneur de Buénos-Ayres.

Vous voyez, monsieur, que je réponds à plusieurs de vos lettres par celle-ci. Les fêtes auxquelles le séjour du prince Henri de Prusse, qui part aujourd'hui pour voir Moscou, a donné lieu, ont un peu dérangé mon exactitude à vous répondre. Je lui en ai donné plusieurs qui ont paru lui plaire: il faut que je vous conte la dernière.

C'était une mascarade à laquelle il se trouva trois mille six cents personnes. A l'heure du souper, entrée d'Apollon, des *quatre Saisons*, et des *douze Mois* de l'année; c'était des enfants de huit à dix ans, choisis dans les instituts d'éducation que j'ai établis pour les nobles des deux sexes. Apollon, par un petit discours, invita la compagnie de se rendre dans le salon préparé par les Saisons, puis il ordonna à sa suite de présenter leurs dons à ceux à qui ils étaient destinés.

Ces enfants s'acquittèrent au mieux de ce qu'ils avaient à dire et à faire. Vous trouverez ci-joint leurs petits compliments, qui, il est vrai, ne sont que des enfantillages.

Les cent vingt personnes qui devaient souper dans la salle

des *Saisons* s'y rendirent. Elle était ovale, et contenait douze niches, dans chacune desquelles il y avait une table pour dix personnes. Chaque niche représentait un mois de l'année, et l'appartement était orné en conséquence. Sur les niches on avait pratiqué une galerie qui régnait autour de la salle, et sur laquelle il y avait, outre la foule des masques, quatre orchestres.

Lorsqu'on fut placé à table, les quatre Saisons, qui avaient suivi Apollon, se mirent à danser un ballet avec leur suite: ensuite arriva Diane et ses nymphes. Lorsque le ballet fut fini, la musique, composée par Traïetto pour cette fête, se fit entendre, et les masques entrèrent. A la fin du souper, Apollon vint dire qu'il priait la compagnie de se rendre au spectacle qu'il avait préparé. Dans un appartement attenant à la salle, on avait dressé un théâtre, où ces mêmes enfants jouèrent la petite comédie de *l'Oracle*, après laquelle l'assemblée trouva tant de plaisir à la danse, qu'on ne se retira qu'à cinq heures du matin. Toute cette fête avait été préparée avec tant de mystère, qu'on ignorait qu'il y eût autre chose qu'un bal masqué. Vingt et un appartements étaient remplis de masques: la salle des Saisons avait dix-neuf toises de long, et elle était large à proportion.

Je pense qu'Ali-Bey ne pourra que trouver son compte dans la continuation de la guerre. On dit que les chrétiens et les Turcs sont très contents de lui, qu'il est tolérant, brave, et juste.

Ne trouvez-vous pas singulière cette frénésie qui a pris à toute l'Europe de voir la peste partout, et les précautions prises en conséquence, tandis qu'elle n'est qu'à Constantinople, où elle n'a jamais cessé? J'ai pris mes précautions aussi. On parfume tout le monde jusqu'à étouffer, et cependant il est très douteux que cette contagion ait passé le Danube.

Adieu, monsieur; portez-vous bien, et continuez-moi votre amitié; personne n'en connaît mieux le prix que moi.

CATERINE

LXIX

DE VOLTAIRE

A Ferney, 22 décembre 1770

Madame, ma passion commence à être un peu malheureuse. Je ne sais plus de nouvelles ni de votre majesté impériale ni de mon ennemi Moustapha. Tout ce que je puis faire cette fois-ci, c'est de vous ennuyer de mon petit commerce avec le roi de la Chine votre voisin.

Je me suis imaginé que les pluies du mois de décembre, la crainte de la peste, et celle de la famine, pourraient suspendre le cours de vos conquêtes, et que votre majesté aurait peut-être le temps de s'amuser d'une espèce de petite *Encyclopédie* nouvelle, qui paraît devers le mont Jura. Il y est parlé de votre très admirable personne, dès la page 17 du premier tome, à propos de l'*alphabet*. Il faut que l'auteur soit bien plein de vous, puisqu'il vous met partout où il peut.

Je ne sais pas quel est cet auteur, mais sans doute c'est un homme à qui vous avez marqué de la bonté, et qui doit parler de votre majesté au mot *Reconnaissance*.

Il y a, dit-on, en France, des gens qui trouvent cela mauvais; mais l'univers entier devrait le trouver bon, et si j'étais un peu votre victime, j'en serais bien glorieux.

Il n'y a encore que trois volumes d'imprimés. On les a envoyés, par les voitures publiques, à votre surintendant des postes, avec l'adresse de votre majesté impériale.

Je prends la liberté de vous parler d'une fabrique de montres établie à Ferney, et de vous offrir ses services lorsque votre majesté, en accordant la paix à Moustapha, voudra lui faire la faveur de lui envoyer une montre avec son portrait. Il pourra trembler, mais aussi il pourra être attendri. En un mot, ma fabrique de montres est à votre service; si j'étais jeune, je la conduirais moi-même à Saratof.

Le roi de Prusse prétend qu'Ali-Bey n'est point du tout roi d'Égypte; c'est encore une raison pour faire la paix avec cette maudite puissance ottomane, dont tant de gens prennent le parti. Je mourrai certainement de douleur de ne vous pas voir sur le trône de Constantinople. Je sais bien que la douleur ne fait mourir que dans les romans; mais aussi vous m'avez inspiré une passion un peu romanesque, et il faut qu'avec une impératrice telle que vous, mon roman finisse noblement. J'emporterai avec moi la consolation de vous avoir vue souveraine des deux bords de la mer Noire et de ceux de la mer Égée.

Daignez agréer, malgré toutes mes déclarations, le très profond respect de l'ermite de Ferney.

LXX

DE L'IMPÉRATRICE

Ce 12/23 décembre 1770

Monsieur, jamais mensonge ne fut plus complet que celui de cette prétendue lettre de l'ambassadeur d'Angleterre Murray (datée de Constantinople), où il est dit qu'il voit le padisha deux fois par semaine, et que celui-ci lui parle italien. Aucun ministre étranger ne voit le sultan, que dans les audiences publiques. Moustapha ne sait que le turc, et il est douteux qu'il sache lire et écrire. Ce prince est d'un naturel farouche et sanguinaire: on prétend qu'il est né avec de l'esprit; cela se peut, mais je lui dispute la prudence; il n'en a point marqué dans cette guerre. Son frère est moins imprudent que lui; c'est un dévot. Il lui a déconseillé la guerre, et je ne crois pas qu'on l'envoie jamais commander.

Mais ce qui vous fera rire peut-être, c'est que ces deux princes ont une sœur, qui était la terreur de tous les bachas. Elle avait, avant la guerre, au-delà de soixante ans; elle avait été mariée quinze fois; et lorsqu'elle manquait de mari, le sultan, qui l'aimait beaucoup, lui donnait le choix de tous les bachas de son empire. Or, quand un bacha épouse une princesse de la maison impériale, il est obligé de renvoyer tout son harem. Cette sultane, outre son âge, était méchante, jalouse, capricieuse, et intrigante. Son crédit chez monsieur son frère était sans bornes, et souvent les bachas qu'elle épousait, sans têtes: ce qui n'était point du tout plaisant pour eux; mais cela n'en est pas moins vrai.

Ah! monsieur, vous avez dit tant de belles choses sur la Chine, que je n'ose disputer le mérite des vers du roi de ce pays. Cependant, par les affaires que j'ai avec ce gouvernement, je pourrais fournir des notions qui détruiraient beaucoup de l'opinion qu'on a de leur savoir-vivre, et qui les feraient passer pour des rustres ignorants; mais il ne faut pas nuire à son prochain. Ainsi je me tais, et j'admire les relations des délégués de la *Propagande*, sans les contredire. Au bout du compte, j'ai affaire au gouvernement tartare qui a conquis la Chine, et non pas aux Chinois originaires.

Continuez-moi, monsieur, votre amitié et votre confiance; et soyez assuré que personne ne vous estime plus que moi.

CATERINE

P.S. Les gazettes ont débité que j'avais fait arrêter nombre de personnes de qualité: je dois vous dire qu'il n'en est rien, et qu'âme qui vive, ni grand ni petit, n'a perdu la liberté. Le prince Henri de Prusse m'en est témoin. Je m'en rapporte à lui.

LXXI

DE VOLTAIRE

A Ferney, 22 janvier 1771

Madame,

L'univers admire vos fêtes;
Nos Français en sont confondus:
Et je les admire encor plus
A la suite de vos conquêtes.

Ce qui est encore au-dessus de la magnificence, c'est l'esprit; il n'y a jamais eu de fête imaginée avec plus de génie, mieux ordonnée, plus galante, et plus noble. Nous avons eu à Paris des fusées et une illumination, pour le mariage du dauphin de France et de la fille d'une impératrice. Il n'y a pas un prodigieux effort de génie dans des bouts de chandelles et dans des fusées volantes. Mais, en récompense, il y régnait tant d'ordre, qu'il y eut plus de monde tué et blessé, que vous n'en avez eu dans votre première victoire remportée sur les Turcs.

Il est vrai que j'aurais voulu qu'Apollon eût présenté à votre majesté impériale l'étendard de Mahomet et l'aigrette de héron que le gros Moustapha porte à son gros turban; mais ce sera pour cette année, à la fin de la campagne.

Les choses sont bien changées chez nous. Les croisades furent autrefois commencées en France. Nous sommes à présent les meilleurs amis des infidèles.

La France à l'Église échappe:
Nous avons pris le parti
De secourir le mufti,
Et de dépouiller le pape.

Pour moi, qui suis trop peu de chose pour oser décider entre les églises grecque, latine, et musulmane, je ne m'occupe que de votre gloire dans ma retraite. J'aime mieux vos fêtes que celles de saint Nicolas et de saint Basile, de saint Barjone, surnommé Pierre, et même que celle du Bairam.

Si j'ai pour sainte Catherine
Un peu plus de dévotion,
C'est parceque mon héroïne
Descend jusqu'à porter son nom.

Passe pour Hercule, voilà un digne saint celui-là; aussi est-il le patron d'un comte Orlof, et de tous les quatre. On dit qu'un de ces saints vient de faire encore une de ces actions qu'on ne trouve pas dans la *Légende*; qu'ayant pris un vaisseau turc où étaient les meubles et les domestiques d'un bacha, il les a renvoyés à leur maître. Non seulement vos courtisans sont les maîtres des Turcs dans l'art de la guerre, mais ils leur apprennent à être polis; voilà du véritable héroïsme, et c'est vous qui l'inspirez.

Vous voilà, madame, à mon avis, la première puissance de l'univers; car je vous mets sans difficulté au-dessus du roi de la Chine, votre proche voisin, quoiqu'il fasse des vers, et que je lui aie écrit une épître qu'il ne lira pas. Que votre majesté impériale jouisse long-temps de sa gloire et de son bonheur!

Sans les soixante-dix-huit ans qui me talonnent, Apollon

m'est témoin que je n'aurais pas établi une colonie d'horlogers dans mon village. Elle serait actuellement vers Astracan, où je l'aurais conduite; elle ne travaillerait que pour votre majesté.

Ma colonie fait réellement d'excellents ouvrages; elle vous en fera parvenir quelques uns incessamment, et vous verrez qu'on ne peut travailler mieux ni à meilleur compte. Vous dépensez trop en canons et en vaisseaux, pour ne pas joindre à vos magnificences une juste économie, qui est au fond la source de la grandeur.

Vivez, régnez, madame, pour la gloire de la Russie, et pour l'exemple du monde.

Que votre majesté impériale daigne conserver ses bontés à son admirateur et à son sujet par le cœur. Je reçois dans ce moment la lettre dont votre majesté impériale m'honore, du 12 décembre, vieux style. Je me doutais bien que la lettre de l'ambassadeur d'Angleterre en Turquie était de l'imagination d'un pensionnaire de nos gazetiers. Je remercie plus que jamais vos bontés, qui me fournissent de quoi faire taire nos badauds welches.

Quoi! ce brutal de Sardanapale turc veut encore faire une campagne! Ah! madame, Dieu soit béni! il ne vous faudra qu'une seule victoire sur le chemin d'Andrinople pour détrôner cet homme indigne du trône, et que j'ai entendu vanter par quelques uns de nos Welches comme un génie. Mais où ira-t-il? Voilà un Ali-Bey ou Beg qui ne le recevra pas dans le pays d'Osiris; voilà un bacha d'Acre qui se révolte. Il y a une destinée; la vôtre est sensible. Votre empire est dans la vigueur de son accroissement, et celui de Moustapha dans sa décadence; le chevalier de Tott ne le sauvera pas de sa ruine.

Je me mets aux pieds de votre majesté impériale, plein de joie et d'espérance, avec le plus profond respect, et la reconnaissance la plus vive. *L'ermite de Ferney*

LXXII

DE L'IMPÉRATRICE

A Pétersbourg, 12/23 janvier 1771

Monsieur, si vous vous trouvez malheureux lorsque Moustapha n'est pas battu coup sur coup, les mois d'hiver ne peuvent que vous donner de l'humeur. Cependant, j'ai reçu la consolante nouvelle que Creigova en Valachie, sur la rivière Olta, a été occupé par mes troupes dans le courant du mois dernier.

Il me semble que vous devriez être content de l'année 1770, et qu'il n'y a pas encore de quoi coqueter avec le roi de la Chine mon voisin, à qui, malgré ses vers et votre passion naissante (n'allez pas vous en fâcher), je dispute à peu près le sens commun. Vous direz que c'est jalousie toute pure de ma part; point du tout: je ne troquerai point mon nez à la romaine contre sa face large et plate; je n'ai aucune prétention à son talent de faire de mauvais vers: je n'aime à lire que les vôtres.

L'épître à mon rival est charmante; j'en ai d'abord fait part au prince Henri de Prusse, à qui elle a fait un égal plaisir. Mais si le destin veut que j'aie un rival auprès de vous, au nom de la vierge Marie, que ce ne soit point le roi de la Chine, contre qui j'ai une dent. Prenez plutôt monseigneur Ali-Bey d'Égypte, qui est tolérant, juste, affable, humain. Il est parfois un peu pillard; mais il faut passer quelques défauts à son prochain. Les lampes d'or de la Mecque l'ont tenté: eh bien! il en saura faire un bon usage. Il en reviendra de la besogne à Moustapha *gazi*, qui ne sait faire ni la paix ni la guerre.

Vous direz peut-être que je cherche à gêner vos goûts, et que l'inclination ne se commande point: je ne prétends pas vous gêner, je vous présente seulement une pétition ou remontrance en faveur d'Ali d'Égypte, contre le nez camus et les mauvais vers de mon sot voisin, avec lequel, Dieu merci, je n'ai plus de démêlés.

J'ai reçu vos livres, monsieur; je les dévore; je vous en suis bien redevable, et aussi pour la page 17. Je serais au désespoir si cela fesait tort à l'auteur dans sa patrie. Ce seigneur, qui m'avait prise en grippe, n'a plus de voix au chapitre; peut-être ses successeurs distingueront-ils mieux les affaires d'avec les passions personnelles, du moins faut-il l'espérer pour le bien des affaires. Je vous prie instamment de me faire tenir la suite de votre *Encyclopédie*, lorsqu'elle paraîtra.

Dites-moi si vous avez reçu la volumineuse description de la fête que j'ai donnée au prince de Prusse. Il y a six jours qu'il nous a quittés; il a paru se plaire ici plus que l'abbé Chappe, qui, courant la poste dans un traîneau bien fermé, a tout vu en Russie.

Pour ce qui regarde la manufacture de Ferney, je vous ai déjà écrit de nous envoyer des montres de toute espèce, pour quelques milliers de roubles: je les prendrai toutes.

Le roi de Prusse a beau dire, Ali-Bey est souverain maître de l'Égypte. Si je vais à Stamboul, je le prierai d'y venir, afin que vous puissiez le voir de vos yeux. Et comme je ne doute point que vous ne me fassiez le plaisir d'accepter la place de patriarche, vous aurez la consolation d'administrer le sacrement de baptême à Ali-Bey, par immersion ou autrement.

Jusque-là, monsieur, vous voudrez bien ne point mourir de douleur de ce que je ne suis pas encore dans Constantinople. Quelle est la pièce qui finit avant le troisième acte? quel est le roman qui abandonne son héros à moitié chemin, en quartier d'hiver au bord d'une rivière?

Je suis toujours avec beaucoup d'amitié la plus sincère de vos amies.

CATERINE

LXXIII

DE VOLTAIRE

9 février 1771

Madame, on dit qu'enfin Moustapha se résout à demander grâce, qu'il commence à concevoir que votre majesté impériale est quelque chose sur le globe, et que l'étoile du nord est plus forte que son croissant.

Je ne sais si le chevalier de Tott sera le médiateur de la paix. Je me flatte que du moins sa hautesse paiera les frais du procès que sa petitesse vous a intenté si mal à propos; et qu'il se défera de sa belle coutume de loger aux Sept-Tours les ministres des puissances auxquelles il fait la guerre, coutume qui devrait armer l'Europe contre lui.

Votre majesté va reprendre ses habits de législatrice, après avoir quitté sa robe d'amazone; elle n'aura pas de peine à pacifier la Pologne; enfin mon étoile du nord sera bien plus brillante que nos soleils du midi.

Je suis toujours fâché que mon étoile n'établisse pas son zénith directement sur le canal de la mer Noire; mais enfin si la paix est écrite dans le ciel, il faut bien que votre belle et auguste main la signe: je me soumets aux ordres du destin. C'est une autre sacrée majesté qui de tout temps a mené les majestés de ce bas monde.

Elle vient d'envoyer le duc de Choiseul, et le duc de Praslin, et le parlement de Paris à la campagne, au milieu de l'hiver. Elle a fait un cordelier pape. Elle va ôter au pauvre Ali-Bey l'espérance d'être pharaon en Égypte, et pourrait bien le réduire à l'état que Joseph prédit au grand-panetier de Pharaon.

Le destin fait de ces tours-là tous les jours sans y songer; les bons chrétiens comme vous, madame, disent que c'est la Providence, et je le dis aussi pour vous faire ma cour.

Cependant, si votre majesté est prédestinée à ne point convenir des articles avec le divan, je supplie votre Providence de faire passer le Danube à vos troupes victorieuses, et de donner des fêtes à M. le prince Henri, dans l'Atméidan.

Je murmure un peu contre ce destin, qui m'a donné soixante et dix-sept ans, et une santé si faible, avec une passion si violente de voir la cour de mon héroïne, garnie de ses héros.

J'ai le malheur de me mettre de loin à ses pieds avec le plus profond respect. *L'ermite de Ferney*

P.S. J'ai écrit une lettre en vers au roi de Danemarck, dans laquelle se trouve le nom de votre majesté impériale; mais je n'ose vous l'envoyer sans votre permission.

LXXIV

DE VOLTAIRE

A Ferney, 12 mars 1771

Madame, vous êtes bénie par-dessus toutes les impératrices et par-dessus toutes les femmes. On m'assure qu'un gros corps de vos troupes a passé le Danube; que le peu qui restait en Valachie, de mes ennemis les Turcs, a été exterminé; que vos vaisseaux bloquent les Dardanelles, et qu'enfin je pourrai me faire transporter en litière à Constantinople vers la fin d'octobre, si je suis en vie.

Il est vrai que le visir français, qui n'est plus visir, n'avait à se reprocher que son peu de coquetterie avec votre majesté impériale. Il était d'autant plus coupable en cela, qu'il est d'ailleurs très galant, et qu'il aime les actions nobles, généreuses, et hardies. Je ne l'ai pas reconnu à ce procédé; j'ai eu avec lui de grandes disputes. Je n'ai jamais cédé; je lui ai toujours mandé que je vous serais fidèle, que vous seriez triomphante, et que son Moustapha n'était qu'un gros bœuf appelé *sultan*. Mes disputes avec lui n'ont point altéré la bienveillance qu'il m'a toujours témoignée; et actuellement qu'il est malheureux, je lui suis attaché plus que jamais; comme je suis plus que jamais *catherinien*, contre ceux qui sont assez malavisés pour être *moustaphites*.

Votre majesté impériale aura, dans le nouveau roi de Suède, un voisin qui est en tout fort au-dessus de son âge, et qui joint beaucoup d'esprit et de grâces à de grandes connaissances. Les voisins ne sont pas toujours amis intimes; mais celui-ci, jusqu'à présent, paraît digne d'être le vôtre. Je ne crois pas qu'il fasse encore des vers comme Kien-Long, mais il paraît valoir beaucoup mieux que votre voisin oriental.

Ma colonie aura l'honneur d'envoyer, avant un mois, quelques montres, puisque votre majesté daigne le permettre; elle est à vos pieds ainsi que moi.

Mon imagination ne s'occupe à présent que du Danube, de la mer Noire, d'Andrinople, de l'Archipel, et de la figure que fera Moustapha avec son eunuque noir dans son harem.

Je supplie votre majesté impériale de bien agréer le profond respect, la reconnaissance, et l'enthousiasme du vieil ermite de Ferney.

LXXV

DE L'IMPÉRATRICE

A Pétersbourg, 3/14 mars 1771

Monsieur, en lisant vos *Questions sur l'Encyclopédie*, je répétais ce que j'ai dit mille fois: qu'avant vous personne n'écrivit comme vous, et qu'il est très douteux qu'après vous quelqu'un vous égale jamais. C'est dans ces réflexions que me trouvèrent vos deux dernières lettres, du 22 de janvier et du 5 de février.

Vous jugez bien, monsieur, du plaisir qu'elles m'ont fait. Vos vers et votre prose ne seront jamais surpassés: je les regarde comme le *non plus ultra* de la littérature française, et je m'y tiens. Quand on vous a lu, l'on veut vous relire encore, et l'on est dégoûté des autres lectures.

Puisque la fête que j'ai donnée au prince Henri a eu votre approbation, je vais la croire belle: avant celle-là je lui en avais donné une à la campagne, où les bouts de chandelles et les fusées ne furent pas épargnés. Il n'y eut personne de blessé; les précautions avaient été bien prises. L'horrible désastre arrivé à Paris l'an passé nous a rendus prudents. Outre cela, je ne me souviens pas d'avoir vu depuis long-temps un carnaval plus animé: depuis le mois d'octobre jusqu'au mois de février il n'y a eu que fêtes, danses, spectacles, etc.

Je ne sais si c'est la campagne passée qui me l'a fait paraître tel, ou si véritablement la joie régnait parmi nous. J'apprends qu'il n'en est pas de même ailleurs, quoiqu'on y jouisse de la douceur d'une paix non interrompue depuis huit ans. J'espère que ce n'est pas la part chrétienne qu'on prend aux malheurs des infidèles qui en est la cause; ce sentiment serait indigne de la postérité des premiers croisés.

Il n'y a pas longtemps que vous aviez en France un nouveau saint Bernard, qui prêchait une croisade contre nous autres, sans, je crois, qu'il sût bien au juste lui-même pour quel objet.

Mais ce saint Bernard s'est trompé dans ses prophéties, comme le premier. Rien n'est arrivé de ce qu'il avait prédit: il n'a fait qu'aigrir les esprits. Si c'était là son but, il faut avouer qu'il a réussi. Ce but cependant ne paraît pas digne d'un aussi grand saint.

Vous, monsieur, qui êtes si bon catholique, persuadez à ceux de votre croyance que l'Église grecque, sous Caterine II, n'en veut point à l'Église latine, ni à aucune autre, et qu'elle ne fait que se défendre.

Avouez, monsieur, que cette guerre a fait briller nos guerriers. Le comte Alexis Orlof ne cesse de faire des actions honorables: il vient d'envoyer quatre-vingt-six prisonniers algériens et salétins au grand-maître de Malte, en le priant de les faire échanger, à Alger, contre des esclaves chrétiens. Il y a bien longtemps qu'aucun chevalier de Saint-Jean de Jérusalem n'a délivré autant de chrétiens des mains des infidèles.

Avez-vous lu, monsieur, la lettre de ce comte aux consuls européens de Smyrne, qui intercédaient auprès de lui pour qu'il épargnât cette ville après la défaite de la flotte turque? Vous me parlez du renvoi qu'il a fait d'un vaisseau turc où étaient les meubles, les domestiques, etc., d'un bacha; voici le fait:

Peu de jours après la bataille navale de Chesme, un trésorier de la Porte revenait du Caire sur un vaisseau, avec ses femmes, ses enfants, et tout son bien, et s'en allait à Constantinople: il apprit en chemin la fausse nouvelle que la flotte turque avait battu la nôtre; il se hâta de descendre à terre pour porter le premier cette nouvelle au sultan. Pendant qu'il courait à toute bride à Stamboul, un de nos vaisseaux amena son navire au comte Orlof, qui défendit sévèrement que personne entrât dans la chambre des femmes, et qu'on touchât à la charge du vaisseau. Il se fit amener la plus jeune des filles du Turc, âgée de six ans, et lui fit présent d'une bague de diamants et de quelques fourrures, et la renvoya, avec toute sa famille et leurs biens, à Constantinople.

Voilà ce qui a été imprimé à peu près dans les gazettes. Mais, ce qui ne l'a pas été jusqu'ici, c'est que le comte Romanzof ayant envoyé un officier au camp du visir, cet officier fut mené d'abord au kiaga du visir; le kiaga lui dit, après les premiers compliments: "Y a-t-il quelqu'un des comtes Orlof à l'armée?" L'officier lui répondit que non. Le Turc lui demanda avec empressement: "Où sont-ils donc?" Le major lui dit que deux servaient sur la flotte, et que les trois autres étaient à Pétersbourg. "Eh bien! répliqua le Turc, sachez que leur nom m'est en vénération, et que nous sommes tous étonnés de ce que nous voyons. C'est envers moi surtout que leur générosité s'est signalée. Je suis ce Turc qui doit ses femmes, ses enfants, ses biens, au comte Orlof. Je ne puis jamais m'acquitter envers eux; mais si pendant ma vie je puis leur rendre service, je le compterai pour un bonheur." Il ajouta beaucoup d'autres protestations, et dit entre autres choses que le visir connaissait sa reconnaissance, et l'approuvait. En disant ces paroles, les larmes coulaient de ses yeux.

Voilà donc les Turcs touchés jusqu'aux larmes de la générosité des Russes de la religion grecque. Le tableau de cette action du comte Orlof pourra faire un jour, dans ma galerie, le pendant de celui de Scipion.

Les sujets de mon voisin le roi de la Chine, depuis que celui-ci a commencé à lever quelques entraves injustes, commercent avec les miens. Ils ont échangé pour trois millions de roubles d'effets, les premiers quatre mois que ce commerce a été ouvert.

Les fabriques royales de mon voisin sont occupées à faire des tapisseries pour moi, tandis que mon voisin demande du blé et des moutons.

Vous me parlez souvent de votre âge, monsieur; mais quel qu'il soit, vos ouvrages sont toujours les mêmes; témoin cette *Encyclopédie* remplie de choses nouvelles. Il ne faut que la lire, pour voir que votre génie est dans toute sa force; à votre égard, les accidents attribués à l'âge deviennent préjugés.

Je suis très curieuse de voir les ouvrages de vos horlogers: si vous alliez établir une colonie à Astracan, je chercherais un prétexte pour vous y aller voir. A propos d'Astracan, je vous dirai que le climat de Taganrock est, sans comparaison, plus beau et plus sain que celui d'Astracan. Tous ceux qui en reviennent disent qu'on ne saurait assez louer cet endroit, sur lequel, à l'imitation de la vieille dont il est parlé dans Candide, je vais vous conter une anecdote.

Après la première prise d'Azof par Pierre-le-Grand, ce prince voulut avoir un port sur cette mer, et il choisit Taganrock. Ce port fut construit. Ensuite il balança long-temps s'il bâtirait Pétersbourg sur la Baltique, ou une ville à Taganrock. Enfin les circonstances le décidèrent pour la Baltique. Nous n'y avons pas gagné du côté du climat: il n'y a presque point d'hiver là-bas, tandis que le nôtre est très long.

Les Welches, monsieur, qui vantent le génie de Moustapha, vantent-ils aussi ses prouesses? Pendant cette guerre, je n'en connais d'autres, sinon qu'il a fait couper la tête à quelques visirs, et qu'il n'a pu contenir la populace de Constantinople, qui a roué de coups, sous ses yeux, les ambassadeurs des principales puissances de l'Europe, lorsque le mien était renfermé aux Sept-Tours: l'internonce de Vienne est mort de ses blessures. Si ce sont là des traits de génie, je prie le ciel de m'en priver à jamais, et de le réserver tout entier pour Moustapha et le chevalier Tott son soutien. Ce dernier sera étranglé à son tour: le visir Mahomet l'a bien été, quoiqu'il eût sauvé la vie au sultan, et qu'il fût le beau-fils de ce prince.

La paix n'est pas si prochaine que les papiers publics l'ont débité. La troisième campagne est inévitable, et monsieur Ali-Bey aura encore gagné du temps pour s'affermir. Au bout du compte, s'il ne réussit pas, *il ira passer le carnaval à Venise* avec vos exilés.

Je vous prie, monsieur, de m'envoyer l'épître que vous avez adressée au jeune roi de Danemarck, et dont vous me parlez: je ne veux pas perdre une seule ligne de ce que vous écrivez. Jugez par là du plaisir que j'ai à lire vos ouvrages, du cas que j'en fais, et de l'estime et de l'amitié que j'ai pour le saint ermite de Ferney, qui me nomme sa favorite: vous voyez que j'en prends les airs.

LXXVI

DE L'IMPÉRATRICE

Le 5/16 mars 1771

Monsieur, j'ai reçuvos deux lettres du 14 et 27 février, presque en même temps. Vous désirez que je vous dise un mot sur les grossièretés et les sottises des Chinois, dont j'ai fait mention dans une de mes lettres: nous sommes voisins, comme vous le savez; nos lisières, de part et d'autre, sont bordées de peuples pasteurs, tartares, et païens. Ces peuplades sont très portées au brigandage. Ils s'enlèvent (souvent par représailles) des troupeaux, et même du monde. Ces querelles sont terminées par des commissaires envoyés sur les frontières.

Messieurs les Chinois sont si grands chicaneurs, que c'est la mer à boire de finir même des misères avec eux; et, plus d'une fois, il est arrivé que, n'ayant plus rien à demander, ils exigeaient les os des morts; non pour leur rendre des honneurs, mais uniquement pour chicaner.

Des misères pareilles leur ont servi de prétexte pour interrompre le commerce pendant dix années; je dis de prétexte, parce que la vraie raison était que sa majesté chinoise avait donné en monopole, à un de ses ministres, le commerce avec la Russie. Les Chinois et les Russes s'en plaignaient également; et comme tout commerce naturel est très difficile à gêner, les deux nations échangeaient leurs marchandises là où il n'y avait point de douane établie, et préféraient la nécessité aux risques.

Lorsque d'ici on leur écrivait l'état des choses, on recevait, en réponse, de très amples cahiers de prose mal arrangée, où l'esprit philosophique et la politesse ne se fesaient pas même entrevoir, et qui, d'un bout à l'autre, n'étaient qu'un tissu d'ignorance et de barbarie. On leur a dit ici qu'on n'avait garde d'adopter leur style, parce qu'en Europe et en Asie ce style passait pour impoli.

Je sais qu'on peut répondre à cela que les Tartares, qui ont fait la conquête de la Chine, ne valent pas les anciens Chinois; je le veux croire: mais toujours cela prouve que les conquérants n'ont point adopté la politesse des conquis; et ceux-ci courent risque d'être entraînés par les mœurs dominantes.

Je viens à présent à l'article LOIS, que vous avez bien voulu me communiquer, et qui est si flatteur pour moi. Assurément, monsieur, sans la guerre que le sultan m'a injustement déclarée, une grande partie de ce que vous dites serait fait; mais, pour le présent, on ne peut parvenir encore qu'à faire des projets pour les différentes branches du grand arbre de la législation, d'après mes principes, qui sont imprimés, et que vous connaissez. Nous sommes fort occupés à nous battre; et cela nous donne trop de distraction pour mettre toute l'application convenable à cet immense ouvrage.

J'aime mieux vos vers, monsieur, qu'un corps de troupes auxiliaires: celles-ci pourraient tourner le dos dans un moment décisif. Vos vers feront les délices de la postérité, qui ne sera que l'écho de vos contemporains: ceux que vous m'avez envoyés s'impriment dans la mémoire, et le feu qui y règne est étonnant; il me donne l'enthousiasme de prophétiser: vous vivrez deux cents ans.

On espère volontiers ce que l'on souhaite: accomplissez, s'il vous plaît, ma prophétie; c'est la première que je fais.

CATERINE

LXXVII

DE L'IMPÉRATRICE

Ce 31 mars/11 avril 1771

Monsieur, vos bénédictions me feront prospérer, malgré le grand froid, la guerre, Moustapha, et son eunuque noir.

L'on vous a dit vrai, monsieur; un détachement de l'armée du comte Romanzof a passé le Danube, et a causé beaucoup d'effroi sur l'autre rive. Il est vrai encore que vos ennemis les Turcs ont été chassés de la Valachie; il ne leur reste qu'un seul endroit de ce côté-ci du Danube, nommé Turno. Il y a eu un combat très vif à Gorgora: deux mille musulmans y ont mordu la poussière, et quatre mille au moins ont été noyés dans le Danube; après quoi le château, qui est situé sur une île de ce fleuve, s'est rendu, par capitulation, au comte Olitz.

Le sultan, très fâché de ces nouvelles pertes, et ne sachant apparemment à qui s'en prendre, a envoyé chercher la tête du hospodar *in partibus* qu'il fit l'année passée. Celui-ci, soit dit en passant, a trouvé la Valachie presque entière entre nos mains.

On me confirme de toutes parts le bien que vous me dites du nouveau roi de Suède: proche parent, proche voisin, il faut espérer que nous vivrons en paix.

Tout se prépare pour vous satisfaire et donner de la besogne au sultan. Le comte Orlof, qui était venu ici pour un moment, est reparti pour Livourne avec son prince Dolgorouky: ils s'embarqueront pour Paros; les troupes y campent, et entre autres un gros détachement du régiment des gardes Préobrajensky.

On ne saurait ajouter, monsieur, aux sentiments d'estime et d'amitié que j'ai pour vous.

CATERINE

LXXVIII

DE VOLTAIRE

A Ferney, 30 avril 1771

Madame, j'envoie à votre majesté impériale, selon ses ordres, l'épître au roi de Danemarck. Il me paraît qu'elle ne vaut pas celle que j'ai adressée à l'héroïne du Nord. Il semble que j'aie proportionné mon peu de force à la grandeur du sujet. Car, bien que le roi de Danemarck fasse aussi le bonheur de ses peuples, bien qu'il ait tiré des coups de canon contre les pirates d'Alger, il n'a point humilié l'orgueil ottoman, il n'a point triomphé de Moustapha; il n'a pas encore joint le goût des lettres à la gloire des conquêtes.

A l'égard des Welches qui sont à l'occident de l'Allemagne, et vis-à-vis l'Angleterre, ils ne font actuellement nulle conquête depuis qu'ils ont perdu la fertile contrée du Canada; ils font toujours beaucoup de livres, sans qu'il y en ait un seul de bon; ils ont de mauvaise musique, et point d'argent. Les parlements du royaume, qui se croyaient le parlement d'Angleterre, à cause de l'équivoque du nom, bataillent contre le gouvernement à coups de brochures; les théâtres retentissent de mauvaises pièces qu'on applaudit; et tout cela compose le premier peuple de l'univers, la première cour de l'univers, les premiers singes de l'univers. Ils ont une guerre civile par écrit, qui ne ressemble pas mal à la guerre civile des rats et des grenouilles.

Je ne sais si le chevalier de Tott sera le premier canonnier de l'univers, mais je me flatte que le trône ottoman, pour lequel j'ai très peu d'inclination, ne sera pas le premier trône.

J'entends dire dans mes déserts que l'ouverture de la campagne est déjà signalée par une de vos victoires. Je supplie votre majesté impériale de daigner m'instruire si je dois commander ma litière, cette année ou l'année prochaine, pour m'aller promener sur le Bosphore.

Ma colonie travaille en attendant, et profite des bontés de votre majesté; elle compte faire partir dans huit jours trois ou quatre petites caisses de montres, depuis la valeur d'environ huit louis jusqu'à celle de quatre-vingts. Il y en a en diamants avec votre portrait, peint par un excellent peintre; toutes les montres sont bonnes et bien réglées. On a travaillé avec le zèle qu'on doit avoir quand il faut vous servir; tous les prix sont d'un grand tiers meilleur marché qu'en Angleterre; et cependant rien n'est épargné.

Nous souhaitons tous bien ardemment, dans mon canton, que toutes les heures de ces montres vous soient favorables, et que Moustapha passe toujours de mauvais quarts d'heure.

Que l'héroïne du nord daigne toujours agréer le profond respect et la reconnaissance du vieux malade du mont Jura.

LXXIX

DE VOLTAIRE

A Ferney, 6 mai 1771

Madame, je me ferai donc porter en litière à Taganrock, puisque le climat est si doux; mais je crois que l'air de votre cour serait beaucoup plus sain pour moi. J'aurai le plaisir de ne mourir ni à la grecque ni à la romaine. Votre majesté impériale permet que chacun s'embarque pour l'autre monde selon sa fantaisie. On ne me proposera point de billet de confession.

Mais je n'irai point à Nipchou; ce n'est pas là qu'on rencontre des Chinois de bonne compagnie; ils sont tous occupés dans Pékin à transcrire les vers du roi de la Chine en trente-deux caractères.

Je soupçonne vos chers voisins orientaux d'être fort peu instruits, très vains, et un peu fripons; mais vos autres voisins les

Turcs sont plus ignorants et plus vains. On les dit moins fripons, parce qu'ils sont plus riches.

Je crois que vos troupes battraient plus aisément encore les suivants de Confucius que ceux de Mahomet.

Je mets à vos pieds le quatrième et le cinquième tome des *Questions sur l'Encyclopédie*; je ne puis m'empêcher d'y parler de temps de mon gros Moustapha; et, tandis que vos braves troupes prennent des villes et chassent les janissaires, je prends la liberté de donner quelques croquignoles à leur maître, en me couvrant de votre égide.

Je suis persuadé que le grand poëte Kien-long n'aurait pas violé le droit des gens dans la personne de votre ministre. On dit que le grand sultan le tient toujours prisonnier, comme s'il l'avait pris à la guerre. J'espère qu'il sera délivré à la première bataille.

Mon étonnement est toujours que les princes et les républiques de la religion de Christ souffrent tranquillement les affronts que leurs ambassadeurs essuient à la Porte ottomane, eux qui sont souvent si pointilleux sur ce qu'on appelle le point d'honneur.

Je fais toujours des vœux pour Ali-Bey; mais je ne sais pas plus de nouvelles de l'Égypte que n'en savaient les Hébreux, qui en ont raconté tant de merveilleuses choses.

Comme on allait faire le petit paquet des *Questions* d'un ignorant *sur l'Encyclopédie*, mes colons de Ferney, qui se regardent comme appartenant à votre majesté impériale, sont arrivés avec deux caisses de leurs montres; je les ai trouvées si grosses que je n'ai pas osé les faire partir toutes deux à la fois. J'ai mis les *Questions encyclopédiques* dans la caisse qui partira demain par les voitures publiques.

Je l'ai envoyée au bureau des coches de Suisse, avec cette simple adresse:

A sa majesté impériale, l'impératrice de Russie.

A ce nom, tout doit respecter la caisse, et il n'y a point de confédéré polonais qui ose y toucher. Votre majesté est trop bonne, trop indulgente, et, en vérité, trop magnifique, de daigner tant dépenser en bagatelles par pure bienfesance, lorsqu'elle dépense si prodigieusement en canons, en vaisseaux, et en victoires.

Il me semble que si vos Tartaro-Chinois de Nipchou avaient du bon sens, ils achèteraient des montres communes qu'ils revendraient ensuite dans tout leur empire avec avantage. Les Gènevois ont un comptoir à Kanton, et y gagnent considérablement. Ne pourrait-on pas en établir un sur votre frontière? Ma colonie fournirait des montres d'argent du prix de douze à treize roubles, des montres d'or qui ne passeraient pas trente à quarante roubles, et elle répondrait d'en fournir pour deux cent mille roubles par an, s'il était nécessaire.

Mais il paraît que les Chinois sont trop soupçonneux et trop soupçonnables, pour qu'on entame avec eux un grand commerce, qui demande de la générosité et de la franchise.

Quoi qu'il en soit, je ne suis que le canal par lequel passent ces envois et ces propositions.

J'admire autant votre grandeur d'âme, que je chéris vos succès et vos conquêtes.

Je suis aux pieds de votre majesté impériale avec le plus profond respect et la plus inviolable reconnaissance.

P.S. Je rouvre mon paquet pour dire à votre majesté impériale que je reçois dans l'instant, de Paris, un livre *in*-4° intitulé, *Manifeste de la République confedérée de Pologne, du* 15 *novembre* 1769; la date de l'édition est de 1770.

On croirait, à la beauté des caractères, qu'il vient de l'imprimerie royale de Paris: cet ouvrage ne mérite pourtant pas les honneurs du Louvre. Voici ce qui se trouvé à la page 5: "La sublime Porte, notre bonne voisine et fidèle alliée, excitée par les traités qui la lient à la république, et par l'intérêt même qui l'attache à la conservation de nos droits, a pris les armes en notre faveur; tout nous invite donc à réunir nos forces pour nous opposer à la chute de notre sainte religion."

Ne voilà-t-il pas une conclusion bien plaisante? nous avons obtenu, à force d'intrigues, que les mahométans fissent insolemment la guerre la plus injuste; donc nous devons prévenir la chute de la sainte Église catholique, dont tout le monde se moque, mais que personne ne veut détruire, du moins à présent.

Je pense que c'est un bedeau d'une paroisse de Paris qui a écrit cette belle apologie. Votre majesté la connaît sans doute. Elle a fait beaucoup d'impression sur le ministère de France.

On impute à vos troupes, dans cet écrit, pages 240 et 241, des cruautés qui, si elles étaient vraies, seraient capables de soulever tous les esprits.

Ce manifeste se répand dans toute l'Europe. Votre majesté y répondra par des victoires, et par des générosités, qui rendent la victoire encore plus respectable.

LXXX

DE VOLTAIRE

A Ferney, 15 mai 1771

Madame, il faut vous dire d'abord que j'ai eu l'honneur d'avoir dans mon ermitage madame la princesse Daschkof. Dès qu'elle est entrée dans le salon, elle a reconnu votre portrait en *mezzo-tinto*, fait à la navette sur un satin, entouré d'une guirlande de fleurs. Votre majesté impériale l'a dû recevoir du sieur Lasalle; c'est un chef-d'œuvre des arts que l'on exerce dans la ville de Lyon, et qu'on cultivera bientôt à Pétersbourg, ou dans Andrinople ou dans Stamboul, si les choses vont du même train.

Il faut qu'il y ait quelque vertu secrète dans votre image; car je vis les yeux de madame la princesse Daschkof fort humides en regardant cette étoffe. Elle me parla quatre heures de suite de votre majesté impériale, et je crus qu'elle ne m'avait parlé que quatre minutes.

Je tiens d'elle le sermon de l'archevêque de Twer, Platon, prononcé devant le tombeau de Pierre-le-Grand, le lendemain que votre majesté eut reçu la nouvelle de la destruction entière de la flotte turque par la vôtre. Ce discours, adressé au fondateur de Pétersbourg et de vos flottes, est à mon gré un des plus beaux monuments qui soient dans le monde. Je ne crois pas que jamais aucun orateur ait eu un sujet aussi heureux. Le Platon des Grecs n'en traita point de pareil. Je regarde cette cérémonie auguste comme le plus beau jour de votre vie: je dis de votre vie passée, car je compte bien que vous en aurez de plus beaux encore.

Puisque vous avez déjà un Platon a Pétersbourg, j'espère que MM. les comtes Orlof vont former des Miltiades et des Thémistocles en Grèce.

J'ai l'honneur, madame, d'envoyer à votre majesté impériale la traduction d'un sermon lithuanien, en échange de votre sermon platonicien: c'est une réponse modeste aux mensonges un peu grossiers et ridicules que les confédérés de Pologne ont fait imprimer à Paris.

C'est un grand bonheur d'avoir des ennemis qui ne savent pas mentir avec esprit. Ces pauvres gens ont dit dans leur manifeste que vos troupes n'osaient regarder les Turcs en face. Ils ont raison, elles n'ont presque jamais vu que leur dos.

Je ne sais pas quel sermon les Autrichiens vont prêcher en Hongrie. C'est peut-être la paix, c'est peut-être une croisade. On nous conte que le sultan Ali-Bey est demeuré court dans un de ses sermons en Syrie, et qu'il a presque perdu la parole. Je n'en crois rien: vous le rendez plus éloquent que jamais. Moustapha sera prêché à droite et à gauche; il finira par se confesser à l'évêque Platon, et par avouer qu'il est un gros cochon, qui a grommelé contre mon auguste héroïne fort mal à propos. J'ai toujours l'honneur de haïr son croissant, autant que j'ai d'attachement, de respect, et de reconnaissance, pour la brillante étoile du nord. *Le vieil ermite de Ferney*

LXXXI

DE VOLTAIRE

25 mai 1771

Madame, j'ai actuellement dans mon ermitage un de vos sujets de votre royaume de Cazan, c'est M. Polianski. Je n'ai jamais vu tant de politesse, de circonspection, et de reconnaissance, pour les bontés de votre majesté impériale: on dit qu'Attila était originaire de Cazan; si la chose est vraie, il se peut fort bien que le fléau de Dieu ait été un très aimable homme; je n'en doute pas même, puisque Honoria, la sœur d'un sot empereur, Valentinien III, devint amoureuse de lui, et voulut à toute force l'épouser.

La cour du roi d'Espagne admire la générosité de M. le comte Alexis Orlof, et la reconnaissance du bacha. Pour la cour de Versailles, elle n'est occupée que des tracasseries des cours de justice.

Pendant que ces pauvretés welches amusent sérieusement l'oisiveté de toute la France, peut-être dans ce moment votre flotte détruit celle des Turcs, peut-être vos troupes ont-elles passé le Danube.

On dit cependant que votre majesté impériale, à qui le Turc a déjà rendu M. Obreskof, est en train d'écouter des propositions de paix; pour moi, je crois qu'elle n'est en train que de vaincre.

Je me mets à ses pieds avec le plus profond respect et la plus tendre reconnaissance. *Le vieil ermite de Ferney*

LXXXII

DE L'IMPÉRATRICE

Ce 20/31 mai 1771

Monsieur, les puissances du Nord vous ont sans doute beaucoup d'obligation pour les belles épîtres que vous leur avez adressées; je trouve la mienne admirable; chacun de mes jeunes confrères, j'en suis sûre, en dira autant de la sienne. Je suis très fâchée de ne pouvoir nous donner en revanche que de la mauvaise prose. De ma vie je n'ai su faire ni vers, ni musique, mais je ne suis point privée du sentiment qui fait admirer les productions du génie.

La description que vous me faites du premier peuple de l'univers ne donnera d'envie à aucun autre sur l'état présent des Welches. Ils crient beaucoup en ce moment, sans, ce me semble, savoir pourquoi: on dit que c'est la mode, et qu'à Paris elle tient souvent lieu de raison. On veut un parlement, on en a un; la cour a exilé les membres qui composaient l'ancien, et personne ne dispute au roi le pouvoir d'exiler ceux qui ont encouru sa disgrâce.

Ces membres, il faut l'avouer, étaient devenus tracassiers, et rendaient l'état anarchique. Il paraît que tout le bruit qu'on a fait ne mène à rien, et qu'il y a beaucoup plus de grands mots que de principes fondés sur des autorités dans tous les écrits du parti opposé à la cour. Il est vrai aussi qu'il est difficile de juger de l'état des choses à la distance d'où je les vois.

Apparemment que les Turcs ne font pas grand fond sur les canons du sieur Tott, puisqu'ils ont enfin relâché mon résident, lequel, si on en peut croire les discours du ministre de la Porte, doit se trouver à présent sur le territoire autrichien.

Y a-t-il un exemple dans l'histoire que les Turcs aient relâché, au milieu de la guerre, le ministre d'une puissance qu'ils avaient offensée par une telle enfreinte du droit des gens? On croirait que le comte Romanzof et le comte Orlof leur ont appris à vivre.

Voilà un pas vers la paix; mais elle n'est pas faite pour cela. L'ouverture de la campagne nous a été très favorable, comme on vous l'a dit, monsieur. Le général-major Weismann a passé le Danube à deux reprises: la première avec sept cents, la seconde avec deux mille hommes. Il a défait un corps de six mille Turcs, s'est emparé d'Isacki, où il a brûlé les magasins ennemis, le pont que l'on commençait à construire, les frégates, les galères, et les bateaux qu'il n'a pu emmener avec lui: il a fait un grand butin, et beaucoup de prisonniers, outre cinquante-un canons de bronze, dont il a encloué la moitié. Il est revenu sur cette rive-ci, sans que personne l'en empêchât, quoique le visir, avec soixante mille hommes, ne fût qu'à six heures du chemin d'Isacki.

Si la paix ne se fait pas cette année, vous pourrez commander votre litière. N'oubliez pas, monsieur, d'y faire mettre une pendule de votre fabrique de Ferney; nous la placerons dans Sainte-Sophie, et elle fournira aux futurs antiquaires le sujet de quelques savantes dissertations.

CATERINE

LXXXIII

DE L'IMPÉRATRICE

Le 24 mai/4 juin 1771

Monsieur, si vous vous faites porter en litière à Taganrock, comme votre lettre du 6 de mai me l'annonce, vous ne pourrez éviter Pétersbourg. Je ne sais si l'air de ma cour vous conviendrait, et si huit mois d'hiver vous rendraient la santé. Il est vrai que, si vous aimez à être au lit, le froid vous en fournirait un prétexte spécieux; mais vous n'auriez nul besoin de prétexte: vous ne seriez point gêné, je vous assure, et j'ose dire qu'il n'y a guère d'endroits où on le soit moins. A l'égard des billets de confession, nous en ignorons jusqu'au nom. Nous compterions pour un ennui mortel de parler de ces disputes rebattues, et sur lesquelles on prescrit le silence par édit dans d'autres pays. Nous laissons volontiers croire à chacun ce qui lui plaît. Tous les Chinois de bonne compagnie planteraient là le roi de la Chine et ses vers, pour se rendre à Nipchou, si vous y veniez, et ils ne feraient que leur devoir en rendant hommage au premier lettré de notre siècle.

Le croiriez-vous, monsieur? mes voisins orientaux, tels que vous les décrivez, sont les meilleurs voisins possibles; je l'ai toujours dit, et la guerre présente m'a confirmée dans cette opinion.

J'attends, avec une impatience que je n'ai que pour vos ouvrages, le quatrième et le cinquième tome des *Questions sur l'Encyclopédie*. Je vous en remercie d'avance. Continuez, je vous prie, à m'envoyer vos excellentes productions, et battons Moustapha. Les croquignoles que vous lui donnez devraient le rendre sage; il en est temps.

Je vous ai mandé, dans ma précédente, qu'il y a apparence que mon résident est relâché. Les princes et les républiques chrétiennes sont eux-mêmes la cause des affronts que leurs ambassadeurs essuient à Constantinople; ils en font trop accroire à ces barbus: se montrer ou intrigants ou rampants n'est pas le moyen de se faire estimer. Voilà la règle à peu près que l'Europe a suivie, et c'est aussi ce qui a gâté ces barbares. Le roi Guillaume d'Angleterre disait qu'*il n'y a point d'honneur à garder avec les Turcs.*

Les Italiens ont traité leurs prisonniers de guerre avec dureté, mais ils ont donné l'exemple de la souplesse envers la Porte.

Les nouvelles d'Ali-Bey portent qu'il fait des progrès en Syrie, et qui alarment d'autant plus le sultan qu'il n'a que peu de troupes à lui opposer.

Je connais le manifeste *in*-4° dont vous me parlez. Le duc de Choiseul, qui n'était pas prévenu en notre faveur, l'avait fait supprimer à cause de son absurdité, et des calomnies ridicules qu'il contenait: vous pouvez juger par là du mérite de la pièce. Les cruautés qu'on y reproche à mes troupes sont des mensonges pitoyables. C'est aux Turcs qu'il faut demander des nouvelles de l'humanité des troupes russes pendant cette guerre. La populace même de Constantinople et tout l'empire turc en ont été si affectés, qu'ils attribuent toutes nos victoires à la bénédiction du ciel, obtenue par l'humanité avec laquelle on en a usé avec eux en toute occasion.

D'ailleurs ce n'est pas aux brigands de Pologne à parler sur cette matière; ce sont eux qui commettent tous les jours des férocités épouvantables envers tous ceux qui ne se joignent pas à leur clique pour piller et brûler leur propre pays.

Vous voudrez bien, monsieur, que je vous remercie particulièrement pour le ton d'amitié et d'intérêt qui règne en général dans votre dernière lettre. J'en suis bien reconnaissante, et véritablement touchée. Continuez-moi votre amitié, et soyez assuré que la mienne vous est sincèrement acquise.

CATERINE

LXXXIV

DE VOLTAIRE

A Ferney, 19 juin 1771

Madame, sur la nouvelle d'une paix prochaine entre votre majesté impériale et sa hautesse Moustapha, j'ai renoncé à tous mes projets de guerre et de destruction, et je me suis mis à relire votre *Instruction* pour le code de vos lois. Cette lecture m'a fait encore plus d'effet que les premières. Je regarde cet écrit comme le plus beau monument du siècle. Il vous donnera plus de gloire que dix batailles sur les bords du Danube, car enfin c'est votre ouvrage; votre génie l'a conçu, votre belle main l'a écrit; et ce n'est pas votre main qui a tué des Turcs. Je supplie votre majesté, si elle fait la paix, de garder Taganrock, que vous dites être un si beau climat, afin que je puisse m'y aller établir pour y achever ma vie, sans voir toujours des neiges comme au mont Jura. Pourvu qu'on soit à l'abri du vent du nord à Taganrock, je suis content.

J'apprends dans ce moment que ma colonie vient de faire partir encore une énorme caisse de montres. J'ai extrêmement grondé ces pauvres artistes; ils ont trop abusé de vos bontés; l'émulation les a fait aller trop loin. Au lieu d'envoyer des montres pour trois ou quatre milliers de roubles tout au plus, comme je le leur avais expressément recommandé, ils en ont envoyé pour environ huit mille: cela est très indiscret. Je ne crois pas que votre majesté ait intention de donner tant de montres aux Turcs, quoiqu'ils les aiment beaucoup: mais voici, madame, ce que vous pouvez faire. Il y en a de très belles avec votre portrait, et aucune n'est chère. Vous pouvez en prendre pour trois à quatre mille roubles, qui serviront à faire vos présents, composés de montres depuis environ quinze roubles jusqu'à quarante ou cinquante; le reste pourrait être abandonné à vos marchands, qui pourraient y trouver un très grand profit.

Je prends la liberté surtout de vous prier, madame, de ne point faire payer sur-le-champ la somme de trente-neuf mille deux cent trente-huit livres de France, à quoi se monte le total des deux envois. Vous devez d'ailleurs faire des dépenses si énormes, qu'il faut absolument mettre un frein à votre générosité. Quand on ferait attendre un an mes colons pour la moitié de ce qu'ils ont fourni, je les tiendrais trop heureux, et je me chargerais bien de leur faire prendre patience.

Au reste ils m'assurent, et plusieurs connaisseurs m'ont dit que tous ces ouvrages sont à beaucoup meilleur marché qu'à Genève, et à plus d'un grand tiers au-dessous du prix de Londres et de Paris. On dit même qu'ils seraient vendus à Pétersbourg le double de la facture qu'on trouvera dans les caisses, ce qui est aisé à faire examiner par des hommes intelligents.

Si votre majesté était contente de ces envois et des prix, mes fabricants disent qu'ils exécuteraient tout ce que vous leur feriez commander. Ce serait un détachement de la colonie de Saratof, établi à Ferney, en attendant que je le menasse à Taganrock. J'aurais mieux aimé qu'ils vous eussent envoyé quelques carillons pour Sainte-Sophie, ou pour la mosquée d'Achmet; mais, puisque vous n'avez pas voulu cette fois-ci vous emparer du Bosphore, le grand-turc et son grand-visir seront trop honorés de recevoir de vous des montres avec votre portrait, et d'apprendre à vous respecter toutes les heures de la journée.

Pour moi, madame, je consacre à votre majesté impériale toutes les heures qui me restent à vivre. Je me mets à vos pieds avec le plus profond respect et l'attachement le plus inviolable.

Le vieux malade du mont Jura

LXXXV

DE L'IMPÉRATRICE

[Juin] 1771

Monsieur, Après une bataille aussi signalée que celle de Tchesmé, la première victoire navale que la flotte de l'empire de Russie ait gagnée depuis 900 ans, il parut bien naturel de rendre au fondateur de cette marine, dans la ville qu'il avait bâtie, un hommage de la reconnaissance publique. Le lendemain donc du Te Deum, chanté dans l'église où cet empereur est inhumé, on a célébré en grande cérémonie, selon le rite de la vraie église catholique grecque, un service pour le repos de son âme. Mais avant qu'il commençât, l'évêque de Tver prononça le sermon que la princesse Dachkof vous a donné, à l'honneur de l'âme et du génie de Pierre I. Il n'y eut personne qui ne donnât ce jour-là des marques de sensibilité et de reconnaissance pour la mémoire de ce grand homme. Et nous sortîmes tous de l'église très contents les uns des autres. J'ai regretté seulement que l'étendard de l'empire Ottoman que les nôtres avaient arraché de-dessus le vaisseau amiral turc, ait volé en l'air avec notre navire l'Eustache, ce qui m'a privé du plaisir de l'étendre de mes mains ce jour-là au pied de la tombe de Pierre-le-Grand.

Je ne connais les ouvrages du sieur Lasalle que par ce que vous venez de m'en dire.—Si mon portrait, qui est dans votre salon, me ressemble, il doit vous exprimer ma sensibilité pour l'amitié que vous voulez bien me marquer. Votre conversation de quatre heures avec la princesse Dachkof sur mon sujet m'en est une nouvelle preuve. Le sermon prêché à Sainte-Toloranski, que vous m'avez envoyé, est admirable; il n'y a rien de comparable à vos écrits et à la gaieté qui y règne. Ces sermons-là n'ennuient pas.

Vous trouvez donc mes ennemis bien sots; cependant une grande partie de l'Europe a beaucoup de peine à se persuader que Moustapha et les prétendus confédérés, ses amis, soient aussi dépourvus de sens commun qu'ils le sont en effet. J'espère que la postérité, dégagée de passions, me fera justice de ces gens-là, et vos écrits n'y contribueront pas peu. La cour de Vienne et le roi de Prusse par leurs bons offices ont porté les Turcs, après avoir été bien battus, à mettre le sieur Obreskof en liberté, ce qui achemine la paix, qui cependant n'aura pas lieu, à ce qu'il paraît, avant que cette campagne soit terminée.

Lorsque je répondais à votre lettre du 15 mai, j'ai reçu celle du 25 mai où vous me parlez de monsieur Polianski que je fais voyager. C'est un jeune officier qui s'est distingué par son intégrité en Sibérie, où il a réparti dans deux cercles, par ordre du gouverneur, une capitation unique, au lieu des vexations qui se commettaient anciennement, au grand contentement de tous les payants, dont le nombre passait les quatorze mille âmes. Le gouverneur me l'ayant fortement recommandé et trouvant en lui, joint à ses autres qualités, un grand désir de s'instruire, je l'ai envoyé dans les pays étrangers, compatriote d'Attila; mais dans l'impossibilité de l'imiter, je lui souhaite au moins une princesse Honoria pareille à celle que vous citez, sœur ou fille de quelque souverain bien sot, n'importe, pourvu qu'elle ait une bonne dot, car monsieur Polianski n'est pas riche; ne pourriez-vous point lui en procurer une?

L'envoyé d'Espagne m'a dit hier, en me notifiant le décès d'un infant mort de la petite vérole, que le roi d'Espagne avait déclaré que se ferait inoculer qui voudrait, mais que jamais il ne le permettrait à sa famille, quoique l'impératrice-reine lui en eût donné l'exemple. Ne trouvez-vous pas extraordinaire qu'un roi, de gaieté de cœur, livre toute sa famille à la mort? Sa majesté catholique se fait, je pense, saigner par précaution: eh bien, s'il raisonne conséquemment, pourquoi ne pas préserver sa famille de la plus horrible des maladies par un moyen aisé et qui en vérité est moins douloureux qu'une saignée? Je suis persuadée que le grand inquisiteur se ferait inoculer aussi pour plaire au roi d'Espagne, qui l'en recompenserait par quelque grosse abbaye, ce qui vaut bien quelque grain de petite vérole.

Je n'ai rien à redire aux amusements présents de messieurs les Welches, parce que je trouve que tout est au mieux dans le meilleur des mondes possibles. Je vous prie de me continuer votre souvenir et d'être assuré des sentiments que j'ai pour vous.

C'est aujourd'hui que l'armée commandée par le général prince Dolgorouki se présente devant Pérécop; vous lui sou haitez bonheur, n'est-ce pas?

LXXXVI

DE VOLTAIRE

A Ferney, 4 juillet 1771

Républiques, grands potentats,
Qui craignîtes que Catherine
N'achevât bientôt la ruine
Du plus pesant des Moustaphas:
Vous, qui du moins ne voulez pas
Seconder son ardeur divine,
Je n'irai point dans vos états;
Je ne veux voir que les climats
Honorés par mon héroïne.

Votre majesté impériale doit être bien persuadée que mon projet est de passer l'été à Pétersbourg, avant d'aller jouir des douceurs de l'hiver à Taganrock. Elle daigne me dire, dans sa lettre du 23 mai, que je pourrais avoir bien froid pendant huit mois; mais, madame, avez-vous comme nous cent vingt milles de montagnes de glaces éternelles, sur lesquelles un aigle et un vautour n'oseraient voler? Voilà pourtant ce qui forme la frontière de cette belle Italie; voilà ce que M. le comte de Schouvalof a vu, ce que tous vos voyageurs ont vu, et ce qui fait ma perspective vis-à-vis mes fenêtres. Il est vrai que l'éloignement est assez grand pour que le froid en soit diminué; et il faut avouer qu'on mange des petits pois peut-être un peu plus tard auprès de Pétersbourg que dans nos vallées; mais ma passion, madame, augmente tous les jours tellement, que je commence à croire que votre climat est plus beau que celui de Naples.

Je me flatte que votre majesté doit avoir reçu actuellement les quatrième et cinquième tomes du questionneur.

Si je questionnais le chevalier de Boufflers, je lui demanderais comment il a été assez follet pour aller chez ces malheureux confédérés, qui manquent de tout, et surtout de raison, plutôt que d'aller faire sa cour à celle qui va les mettre à la raison.

Je supplie votre majesté de le prendre prisonnier de guerre; il vous amusera beaucoup; rien n'est si singulier que lui, et quelquefois si aimable. Il vous fera des chansons; il vous dessinera; il vous peindra, non pas si bien que mes colons de Ferney vous ont peinte sur leurs montres, mais il vous barbouillera. Le voilà donc, ainsi que M. de Tott, protecteur de Moustapha et de l'Alcoran. Pour moi, madame, je suis fidèle à l'Église grecque, d'autant plus que vos belles mains tiennent en quelque façon l'encensoir, et qu'on peut vous regarder comme le patriarche de toutes les Russies.

Si votre majesté impériale a une correspondance suivie avec Ali-Beg ou Ali-Bey, j'implore votre protection auprès de lui. J'ai une petite grâce à lui demander; c'est de faire rebâtir le temple de Jérusalem, et d'y rappeler tous les Juifs, qui lui paieront un gros tribut, et qui feront de lui un très grand seigneur; il faut qu'il ait toute la Syrie jusqu'à Alep, et que, depuis Alep jusqu'au Danube, tout le reste soit à vous, à moins que vous n'aimiez mieux faire la paix cette année, pour redevenir législatrice et donner des fêtes.

Le malheureux manifeste des confédérés n'a pas fait grande fortune en France. Tous les gens sensés conviennent que la Pologne sera toujours le plus malheureux pays de l'Europe, tant que l'anarchie y règnera. J'ai un petit démon familier qui m'a dit tout bas à l'oreille qu'en humiliant d'une main l'orgueil ottoman, vous pacifieriez la Pologne de l'autre. En vérité, madame, vous voilà la première personne de l'univers, sans contredit; je n'en excepte pas votre voisin Kien-long, tout poëte qu'il est. Comment faites-vous après cela pour n'être pas d'une fierté insupportable? Comment daignez-vous descendre à écrire à un vieux radoteur comme moi?

Vous avez la bonté de me demander à qui on a adressé les caisses de montres: à vous, madame, point d'autre adresse qu'*à sa majesté impériale*, le tout recommandé aux soins de monsieur le gouverneur de Riga et de monsieur le directeur-général de vos postes.

Je réitère à votre majesté que je suis très indigné contre mes colons, qui ont abusé de vos bontés, malgré mes déclarations expresses; et je la supplie encore une fois très instamment de les faire attendre tant qu'il lui conviendra, et de ne se point gêner pour eux.

Il est vrai que cette colonie se perfectionne tous les jours; votre nom seul lui porte bonheur. Ces artistes viennent de faire des montres d'un travail admirable. Vous y êtes gravée en or, ce sont des ouvrages parfaits; ils sont destinés, je crois, pour l'Allemagne.

Je ne m'attendais pas que mon village, caché au pied des Alpes, et qui ne contenait qu'environ quarante misérables quand j'y arrivai, travaillerait un jour pour le vaste empire de Russie, et pour celle qui fait la gloire de cet empire.

Je me mets à vos pieds, et je me sens tout glorieux d'exister encore dans le beau siècle que vous avez fait naître.

Que votre majesté impériale agrée plus que le profond respect du très vieux et très passionné Welche du mont Jura.

LXXXVII

DE L'IMPÉRATRICE

26 juin/7 juillet 1771

Monsieur, le 14 juin Moustapha reçut une nouvelle croquignole: le prince Dolgorouky, à la tête de son armée, força les lignes de Pérécop, et entra dans la Crimée. Le kan, avec cinquante mille Tartares et sept mille Turcs, la défendait: ils prirent la fuite lorsqu'ils apprirent qu'un autre corps détaché allait les couper; et au départ du courrier, les députés de la forteresse de Pérécop étaient dans notre camp, pour régler leur accord. J'attends de moment en moment la nouvelle de la réduction de cette place.

L'amiral Sinevin est parti de Taganrock, et se promène présentement sur la mer d'Azof, peut-être aussi plus loin; je ne puis vous dire au juste, vu que cela dépend du temps, de la mer, et des vents.

Voilà, monsieur, tout ce que j'ai à vous dire pour le présent. Je me recommande à vos prières et à votre amitié.

CATERINE

LXXXVIII

DE VOLTAIRE

A Ferney, 10 juillet 1771

Madame, votre majesté impériale trouvera que le vieux des montagnes écrit trop souvent; mais mon cœur est trop plein, il faut que mes sentiments débordent sur le papier.

J'avais lu, dans une critique assez vive du grand ouvrage de l'abbé Chappe, que dans une contrée de l'occident, appelée le pays des Welches, le gouvernement avait défendu l'entrée du meilleur livre et du plus respectable que nous ayons; qu'en un mot il n'était pas permis de faire passer à la douane des pensées, l'Instruction sublime et sage, signée *Caterine*; je ne pouvais le croire. Cette extravagance barbare me semblait trop absurde. J'ai écrit à un commis des feuilles de papier: j'ai su de lui que rien n'est plus vrai. Voici le fait; un libraire de

Hollande imprime cette Instruction, qui doit être celle de tous les rois et de tous les tribunaux du monde; il en dépêche à Paris une balle de deux mille exemplaires. On donne le livre à examiner à un cuistre, censeur des livres, comme si c'était un livre ordinaire, comme si un polisson de Paris était juge des ordres d'une souveraine, et de quelle souveraine! Ce maroufle imbécile trouve des propositions téméraires, malsonnantes, offensives d'une oreille welche; il le déclare à la chancellerie comme un livre dangereux, comme un livre de philosophie; on le renvoie en Hollande sans autre examen.

Et je suis encore chez les Welches! et je respire leur atmosphère! et il faut que je parle leur langue! Non, on n'aurait pas commis cette insolence imbécile dans l'empire de Moustapha; et je suis persuadé que Kien-long ferait mandarin du premier degré le lettré qui traduirait votre Instruction en bon chinois.

Madame, il est vrai que je ne suis qu'à un mille de la frontière des Welches, mais je ne veux point mourir parmi eux. Ce dernier coup me conduira dans le climat tempéré de Taganrock.

Avant de faire partir ma lettre, je relis l'Instruction.

"Il faut qu'un gouvernement soit tel qu'un citoyen ne puisse pas craindre un autre citoyen; mais que tous craignent les lois.

Il ne faut défendre par les lois que ce qui peut être nuisible à chacun en particulier, ou à la société en général, etc."

Sont-ce donc ces maximes divines que les Welches n'ont pas voulu recevoir? Ils méritent...ils méritent...ils méritent... tout ce qu'ils ont.

Je demande pardon à votre majesté impériale, je suis trop en colère; les vieillards doivent être moins impétueux. Si je vais me fâcher à la fois contre la Turquie et contre la Welcherie, cela est capable de suffoquer ce pauvre cacochyme, qui se met, en toussant, aux pieds de votre majesté impériale.

LXXXIX

DE L'IMPÉRATRICE

Le 16/27 juillet 1771

Monsieur, je crois vous avoir mandé la prise des lignes de Pérécop par assaut, et la fuite du kan de Crimée à la tête de soixante mille hommes, et la réduction du fort d'Orka, qui s'est rendu par accord le 14 juin. Après cela, mon armée entra sur trois colonnes en Crimée; celle de la droite s'empara de Koslof, port sur la mer Noire; celle du milieu, que commandait le prince Dolgorouky en personne, marcha vers Karasbasar, où il reçut une députation des chefs des ordres de la Crimée, qui proposèrent une capitulation pour toute la presqu'île. Mais, comme leurs députés tardèrent à revenir, le prince Dolgorouky s'avança vers Caffa, autre port sur la mer Noire. Là, il attaqua le camp turc, dans lequel il y avait vingt-cinq mille combattants, qui s'enfuirent sur les vaisseaux qui les avaient amenés. Le sérasquier Ibrahim pacha, étant resté presque seul, envoya pour capituler; mais le prince lui fit dire qu'il devait se rendre prisonnier de guerre, ce qu'il fit.

Nos troupes entrèrent donc dans Caffa, tambour battant, le 29 juin. En attendant, la colonne gauche avait traversé la langue de terre qui est entre la mer d'Azof et la Crimée, d'où l'on envoya un détachement, qui s'empara de Kertz et de Yenikale, ce qui se fit tout de suite: de façon que notre flotte d'Azof, qui se tenait dans le détroit, prête à le passer, doit être à l'heure qu'il est à Caffa. Le prince Dolgorouky m'écrit qu'à la vue du port il y a trois pavillons russes qui croisent.

Je me hâte de vous mander ces bonnes nouvelles que j'ai reçues ce matin, sachant la part que vous y prendrez. Vous excuserez aussi, en faveur de ces nouvelles, le peu d'ordre que j'ai mis dans cette lettre, que je vous écris fort à la hâte.

Il ne reste à l'ennemi, dans la Crimée, que deux ou trois méchants petits forts: les places de conséquence sont emportées, et je dois recevoir incessamment la capitulation signée par les Tartares.

Si après cela, monsieur, le sultan n'en a pas assez, on pourra lui en donner encore, et d'une autre espèce.

Soyez assuré de mon amitié et de l'estime distinguée que j'ai pour vous.

CATERINE

XC

DE VOLTAIRE

A Ferney, 30 juillet 1771

Madame, est-il vrai que vous ayez pris toute la Crimée? Votre majesté impériale daignait me mander, par sa lettre du 10 juin, que M. le prince Dolgorouky était devant Pérécop ou Précop. La déesse aux cent bouches, qui arrive tous les jours du nord au midi, et qui depuis long-temps n'apporte que des sottises du midi au nord, débite que la Crimée entière est sous votre puissance, et qu'elle ne s'est pas fait beaucoup prier.

C'est du moins une consolation d'avoir le royaume de Thoas, où la belle Iphigénie fut si long-temps religieuse, et où son frère Oreste vint voler une statue, au lieu de se faire exorciser.

Mais si, après avoir pris cette Chersonèse taurique, vous accordez la paix à Moustapha, que deviendra ma pauvre Grèce, que deviendra ce beau pays de Démosthène et de Sophocle? J'abandonne volontiers Jérusalem aux musulmans; ces barbares sont faits pour le pays d'Ézéchiel, d'Élie, et de Caïphe. Mais je serai toujours douloureusement affligé de voir le théâtre d'Athènes changé en potagers, et le lycée en écuries. Je m'intéressais fort au sultan Ali-Bey; je me fesais un plaisir de le voir négocier avec vous du haut d'une pyramide; faudra-t-il que je renonce à toutes mes belles illusions? Il est bien dur pour moi que vous n'ayez conquis que la Moldavie, la Valachie, la Bessarabie, la Scythie, le pays des Amazones, et celui de Médée; cela fait environ quatre cents lieues; ces bagatelles-là ne me suffisent pas.

Je comptais bien que vous feriez rebâtir Troie, et que votre majesté impériale se promènerait en bateau sur les bords du Scamandre. Je vois qu'il faut que je modère mes désirs, puisque vous modérez les vôtres.

Je suis devenu aveugle, mais j'entends toujours la trompette qui m'annonce vos victoires, et je me dis: Si tu ne peux jouir du bonheur de la voir, tu auras au moins celui d'entendre parler d'elle tous les moments de ta vie.

Si votre majesté impériale garde la Chersonèse, comme je le

crois, elle ajoutera un nouveau chapitre à son code, en faveur des musulmans qui habitent cette contrée. Son église grecque, la seule catholique et la seule véritable, sans doute, n'y fera pas beaucoup de conversions; mais elle pourra y établir un grand commerce. Il y en avait un autrefois entre cette Scythie et la Grèce. Apollon même fit présent au Tartare Abaris d'une flèche qui le portait d'un bout du monde à l'autre, à la manière de nos sorciers. Si j'avais cette flèche, je serais aujourd'hui à Pétersbourg, au lieu de présenter sottement, du pied des Alpes, mon profond respect et mon attachement inviolable à la souveraine d'Azof, de Caffa, et de mon cœur. *Le vieux malade*

XCI

DE L'IMPÉRATRICE

Le 22 juillet/2 auguste 1771

Monsieur, je ne saurais mieux répondre à vos deux lettres, du 19 juin et 6 juillet, qu'en vous mandant que Taman et trois autres petites villes, savoir Temruk, Achaï, et Alton, situées sur une grande île qui forme l'autre côté du détroit de la mer d'Azof, dans la mer Noire, se sont rendues à mes troupes dans les premiers jours de juillet. Cet exemple a été suivi par plus de deux cent mille Tartares, qui demeurent dans ces îles et en terre ferme.

L'amiral Sinevin, qui est sorti du canal avec sa flottille, a donné la chasse à quatorze bâtiments ennemis pour s'amuser; un brouillard cependant les a sauvés de ses griffes.

N'est-il pas vrai que voilà bien des matériaux pour corriger et augmenter les cartes géographiques? Dans cette guerre, on a entendu nommer des endroits dont on n'avait jamais ouï parler auparavant, et que les géographes disaient déserts. N'est-il pas vrai aussi que nous fesons des conquêtes comme quatre? Vous me direz qu'il ne faut pas beaucoup d'esprit pour s'emparer de villes abandonnées. Voilà aussi peut-être la raison qui m'empêche d'être, comme vous dites, d'une fierté insupportable.

A propos de fierté, j'ai envie de vous faire sur ce point ma confession générale. J'ai eu de grands succès durant cette guerre; je m'en suis réjouie très naturellement; j'ai dit: La Russie sera bien connue par cette guerre; on verra que cette nation est infatigable, qu'elle possède des hommes d'un mérite éminent, et qui ont toutes les qualités qui forment les héros; on verra qu'elle ne manque point de ressources, et qu'elle peut se défendre, et faire la guerre avec vigueur lorsqu'elle est injustement attaquée.

Toute pleine de ces idées, je n'ai jamais fait réflexion à Caterine, qui, à quarante-deux ans, ne saurait croître ni de corps ni d'esprit, mais qui, par l'ordre naturel des choses, doit rester et restera comme elle est. Ses affaires vont-elles bien, elle dit tant mieux; si elles allaient moins bien, elle emploierait toutes ses facultés à les remettre dans la meilleure des lisières possibles.

Voilà mon ambition, et je n'en ai point d'autre; ce que je vous dis est vrai. J'irai plus loin: je vous dirai que, pour épargner le sang humain, je souhaite sincèrement la paix; mais cette paix est très éloignée encore, quoique les Turcs, par d'autres motifs, la désirent ardemment. Ces gens-là ne savent pas la faire.

Je souhaite également la pacification des querelles déraisonnables de la Pologne. J'ai affaire là à des têtes écervelées, dont chacune, au lieu de contribuer à la paix commune, y nuit au contraire par caprice et par légèreté. Mon ambassadeur a publié une déclaration qui devrait leur ouvrir les yeux; mais il est à présumer qu'ils s'exposeront plutôt à la dernière extrémité, que de prendre incessamment un parti sage et convenable. Les tourbillons de Descartes n'existèrent jamais qu'en Pologne. Là, chaque tête est un tourbillon, qui tourne sans cesse sur lui-même; le hasard seul l'arrête, et jamais la raison ou le jugement.

Je n'ai point encore reçu ni vos *Questions*, ni vos montres de Ferney: je ne doute pas que l'ouvrage de vos fabricants ne soit parfait, puisqu'ils travaillent sous vos yeux.

Ne grondez pas vos colons de m'avoir envoyé un surplus de montres; cette dépense ne me ruinera pas. Il serait bien malheureux pour moi si j'étais réduite à n'avoir pas, à point nommé, d'aussi petites sommes, chaque fois qu'il me les faut. Ne jugez point, je vous prie, de nos finances par celles des autres états de l'Europe ruinés; vous me feriez tort. Quoique nous ayons la guerre depuis trois ans, nous bâtissons, et tout le reste va comme en pleine paix. Il y a deux ans qu'aucun nouvel impôt n'a été créé; la guerre présentement a son état fixé; une fois réglé, il ne dérange en rien les autres parties. Si nous prenons encore un ou deux Caffa, la guerre est payée.

Je serai contente de moi toutes les fois que j'aurai votre approbation, monsieur. J'ai relu aussi mes Instructions pour le code, il y a quelques semaines, parce que je croyais alors la paix plus prochaine qu'elle ne l'est, et j'ai trouvé que j'avais raison en l'écrivant. J'avoue que ce code, pour lequel beaucoup de matériaux se préparent, et d'autres sont déjà prêts, me donnera encore bien de la tablature, avant qu'il parvienne au degré de perfection où je souhaite de le voir; mais il n'importe, il faut qu'il s'achève, quoique Taganrock ait la mer au midi et des hauteurs au nord.

Cependant vos projets sur cette place ne pourront avoir lieu avant que la paix n'ait assuré ses environs contre toute appréhension du côté de la terre et de la mer; car, jusqu'à la prise de la Crimée, c'était la place frontière vis-à-vis les Tartares. Peut-être m'amènera-t-on dans peu le kan de Crimée en personne. J'apprends dans ce moment qu'il n'a pas passé la mer avec les Turcs, mais qu'il est resté dans les montagnes, avec une très petite suite, à peu près comme le prétendant en Écosse, après la défaite de Culloden. S'il me vient, nous travaillerons à le dégourdir cet hiver; et pour me venger de lui, je le ferai danser, et il ira à la comédie française.

Adieu, monsieur; continuez-moi votre amitié, et soyez assuré des sentiments que j'ai pour vous.

CATERINE

P.S. J'allais fermer cette lettre, lorsque je reçois la vôtre, du 10 juillet, dans laquelle vous me mandez l'aventure arrivée à mon *Instruction* en France. Je savais cette anecdote, et même l'appendice, en conséquence de l'ordre du duc de Choiseul. J'avoue que j'en ai ri quand je l'ai lu dans les gazettes, et j'ai trouvé que j'étais assez vengée.

L'incendie arrivé à Pétersbourg a consumé en tout cent quarante maisons, selon les rapports de la police, parmi lesquelles il y en avait une vingtaine bâties en pierre; le reste n'était que des baraques de bois. Le grand vent avait porté la flamme et les tisons de tous côtés, ce qui renouvela l'incendie le lendemain, et lui donna un air surnaturel; mais il n'est pas douteux que le grand vent et l'excessive chaleur ont causé tout ce mal, qui sera bientôt réparé. Chez nous, on construit avec plus de célérité que dans aucun autre pays de l'Europe. En 1762, il y eut un incendie deux fois aussi considérable, qui consuma un grand quartier bâti en bois; il fut reconstruit en briques en moins de trois ans.

XCII

DE VOLTAIRE

7 auguste 1771

Madame, est-il bien vrai, suis-je assez heureux pour qu'on ne m'ait pas trompé? Quinze mille Turcs tués ou faits prisonniers auprès du Danube, et cela dans le même temps que les troupes de votre majesté impériale entrent dans Pérécop! Cette nouvelle vient de Vienne; puis-je y compter? mon bonheur est-il certain?

Je veux aussi, madame, vous vanter les exploits de ma patrie. Nous avons depuis quelque temps une danseuse excellente à l'opéra de Paris. On dit qu'elle a de très beaux bras. Le dernier opéra-comique n'a pas eu un grand succès; mais on en prépare un qui fera l'admiration de l'*univers*; il sera exécuté dans la première ville de l'*univers*, par les meilleurs acteurs de l'*univers*.

Notre contrôleur-général, qui n'a pas l'argent de l'*univers* dans ses coffres, fait des opérations qui lui attirent des remontrances et quelques malédictions.

Notre flotte se prépare à voguer de Paris à Saint-Cloud.

Nous avons un régiment dont on a fait la revue; les politiques en présagent un grand événement.

On prétend qu'on a vu un détachement de jésuites vers Avignon, mais qu'il a été dissipé par un corps de jansénistes, qui était fort supérieur; il n'y a eu personne de tué: mais on dit qu'il y aura plus de quatre convulsionnaires d'excommuniés.

Je ne manquerai pas, madame, si votre majesté impériale le

juge à propos, de lui rendre compte de la suite de ces grandes révolutions.

Pendant que nous fesons des choses si mémorables, votre majesté s'amuse à prendre des provinces en terre ferme, à dominer sur la mer de l'Archipel et sur la mer Noire, à battre des armées turques. Voilà ce que c'est que de n'avoir rien à faire, et de n'avoir qu'un petit état à gouverner.

Je n'en suis pas moins attaché à votre majesté impériale avec un profond respect et un inviolable dévouement, qui ne finira qu'avec ma vie. *Le vieux malade de Ferney*

XCIII

DE L'IMPÉRATRICE

Le 14/25 auguste 1771

Monsieur, je vois par le contenu de votre lettre du 30 juillet, qu'alors vous n'aviez point encore reçu mes lettres, qui vous annonçaient la soumission de toute la Crimée. Elle a fait son accord avec le prince Dolgorouki. Aujourd'hui j'ai reçu un courrier, qui m'annonce que les ambassadeurs tartares sont en chemin pour me demander la confirmation du kan qu'ils ont élu à la place de Sélim Ghérai, trop attaché intérieurement aux Turcs, parce qu'il avait des possessions personnelles en Romélie. Les Mourza lui ont persuadé de s'en aller, et lui ont fourni à cet effet quelques esquifs. Je m'en vais donc faire distribuer des sabres, des aigrettes, des kaftans, et j'aurai un faux air de Moustapha.

Ces Tartares ont fait quelques efforts pour secouer l'oppression ottomane; d'ailleurs, nous n'en aurions pas eu aussi bon marché. Je défierais à présent Oreste de voler une statue en Crimée: il n'y a pas l'ombre des beaux-arts chez ces gens-là; mais ils n'en conservent pas moins le goût de prendre ce qui ne leur appartient pas.

Laissez faire sultan Ali-Bey: vous verrez qu'il deviendra joli garçon, après avoir pris Damas le 6 juin. Si votre chère Grèce, qui ne sait que faire des vœux, agissait avec autant de vigueur que le seigneur des pyramides, le théâtre d'Athènes cesserait bientôt d'être un potager, et le lycée une écurie. Mais si cette guerre continue, mon jardin de Czarskozélo ressemblera bientôt à un jeu de quilles, car à chaque action d'éclat j'y fais élever quelque monument. La bataille de Kogul, où dix-sept mille combattants en battirent cent cinquante mille, y a produit un obélisque, avec une inscription qui ne contient que le fait et le nom du général: la bataille navale de Tchesme a fait naître, dans une très grande pièce d'eau, une colonne rostrale: la prise de la Crimée y sera perpétuée par une grosse colonne; la descente dans la Morée, et la prise de Sparte, par une autre.

Tout cela est fait des plus beaux marbres qu'on puisse voir, et que les Italiens même admirent. Ces marbres se trouvent les uns sur les bords du lac Ladoga, les autres à Caterinimbourg, en Sibérie, et nous les employons comme vous voyez: il y en a presque de toutes couleurs.

Outre cela, derrière mon jardin, dans un bois, j'ai imaginé de faire bâtir un temple de mémoire, auquel on arrivera par un arc de triomphe. Tous les faits importants de la guerre présente y seront gravés sur des médaillons, avec des inscriptions simples et courtes en langue du pays, avec la date et les noms de ceux qui les ont effectués. J'ai un excellent architecte italien, qui fait les plans de ce bâtiment, qui, j'espère, sera beau, de bon goût, et fera l'histoire de cette guerre. Cette idée m'amuse beaucoup, et je crois que vous ne la trouverez point déplacée.

Jusqu'à ce que je sache que la promenade que vous me proposez sur le Scamandre soit plus agréable que celle de la belle Néva, vous voudrez bien que je préfère cette dernière. Je m'en trouve si bien! Je renonce aussi à la réédification de Troie; j'ai à rebâtir ici tout un faubourg, qu'un incendie a ruiné ce printemps.

Je vous prie, monsieur, d'être persuadé de ma sensibilité pour toutes les choses obligeantes et heureuses que vous me dites: rien ne me fait plus de plaisir que les marques de votre amitié. Je regrette de ne pouvoir être sorcière, j'emploierais mon art à vous rendre la vue et la santé.

CATERINE

XCIV

DE VOLTAIRE

A Ferney, 31 auguste 1771

Madame, j'ose dire que votre majesté impériale me devait la lettre dont elle m'honore, du 16 juillet. J'avais besoin de cette douce consolation, après deux détestables gazettes consécutives, dans lesquelles on disait que les troupes de notre invincible sultan Moustapha étaient partout pleinement victorieuses. Je ne conçois pas ce qu'on gagne à débiter de si impudents mensonges, qui ne peuvent séduire les peuples que cinq ou six jours. Quand on trompe les hommes, il faut les tromper longtemps, comme on a fait à Rome. Il n'en est pas de même en fait d'exploits militaires.

Je présume que tous les Tartares de Crimée sont actuellement vos sujets. Je vous vois marcher de conquête en conquête: on m'assure que vos troupes, véritablement victorieuses, ont passé le Danube, et que vous avez cent vaisseaux dans les mers de l'Archipel.

Je bénis Dieu d'être né pour voir cette grande révolution. Personne ne s'attendait, lorsque Pierre-le-Grand était de mon temps à Sardam, qu'un jour votre majesté impériale dominerait sur la mer Noire, sur l'Archipel, et sur le Danube.

On m'assure que mon cher Ali-Bey a pris Damas, et qu'il a mis le siége devant Alep, afin d'essayer jusqu'où l'invincible Moustapha peut porter la vertu de la résignation. Si cela est vrai, comme je le souhaite du fond de mon cœur, jamais la patience d'un sultan n'a été plus exercée. Mais il faut que cet invincible héros soit un homme bien opiniâtre, pour ne pas vous demander la paix à genoux.

Nous avons eu un roi, nommé Louis XI, qui disait: "*Quand orgueil marche devant, dommage marche derrière.*" Moustapha ne s'est pas souvenu de cette maxime: il vous avait ordonné de vider la Podolie; vous avez fort mal obéi. J'ose me flatter à la fin que vous lui ordonnerez de vider Constantinople, et qu'il vous obéira.

Si vous daignez encore, madame, trouver dans tout ce fracas

quelques moments pour lire mes rêveries, les quatrième et cinquième volumes des *Questions sur l'Encyclopédie* doivent être actuellement entre vos belles mains. Voici, en attendant, une feuille du tome septième, qui n'est pas encore mise au net. L'auteur a pris la liberté de dire un petit mot de votre majesté à la page 356.

Je me mets à vos pieds, je les baise beaucoup plus respectueusement que ceux du pape: il se croit le premier personnage du monde; Moustapha croyait aussi l'être, mais je sais bien à qui ce nom est dû.

Que ma souveraine agrée le profond respect de sa vieille créature.

XCV

DE L'IMPÉRATRICE

Le 4/15 septembre 1771

Monsieur, vous me demandez s'il est vrai que dans le temps même que mes troupes entrèrent dans Pérécop, il y a eu sur le Danube une action au désavantage des Turcs; je vous répondrai qu'on n'a donné cet été, du côté du Danube, qu'un seul combat, où le lieutenant-général, prince Repnin, a battu avec son corps détaché un corps de Turcs qui s'était avancé après que le commandant de Giurgi leur eut rendu cette place, à peu près comme Lauterbourg passa aux Autrichiens lorsque M. de Noailles commandait l'armée française, après la mort de l'empereur Charles VI. Le prince Repnin étant tombé malade, le lieutenant-général Essen a voulu reprendre Giurgi, mais il a été repoussé à l'assaut. Cependant, quoi qu'en disent les gazettes, Bucharest est toujours entre nos mains, avec toutes les places de la rive du Danube, depuis Giurgi jusqu'à la mer Noire.

Je ne porte aucune envie aux exploits que vous me mandez de votre patrie. Si les beaux bras de la belle danseuse de l'opéra de Paris, et l'opéra-comique, qui fait l'admiration de l'univers, consolent la France de la destruction de ses parlements et des nouveaux impôts, après huit ans de paix, il faut convenir que voilà des services essentiels qu'ils ont rendus au gouvernement.

Mais lorsque ces impôts auront été perçus, les coffres du roi seront-ils remplis, et l'état libéré?

Vous me dites, monsieur, que votre flotte se prépare à voguer de Paris à Saint-Cloud: je vous donnerai nouvelles pour nouvelles. La mienne est venue d'Azof à Caffa. A Constantinople on est très affligé de la perte de la Crimée: pour les dissiper, il faudrait leur envoyer l'opéra-comique; et les marionnettes aux mutins de Pologne, au lieu de cette foule d'officiers français qu'on envoie s'y perdre. Ceux de mes troupes qui aiment le spectacle peuvent assister aux drames de M. Soumarokof à Tobolsk, où il y a de fort bons acteurs.

Adieu, monsieur; combattons les méchants, qui ne veulent point rester en repos, et battons-les puisqu'ils le désirent. Aimez-moi, et portez-vous bien.

CATERINE

XCVI

DE VOLTAIRE

17 septembre 1771

Madame, me trompé-je cette fois-ci? Une flotte tout entière de mes amis les Turcs, réduite en cendres dans le port de Lemnos! le comte Alexis Orlof, maître de cette île! c'est ce qu'on me mande de Venise. Ces nouvelles retentissent dans les échos des Alpes, et nous répétons les noms de votre majesté impériale et du comte Orlof. Il me semble que c'est à peu près dans le même temps qu'une autre flotte turque fut consumée dans cette mer, l'année passée; voilà un bel anniversaire. On voit bien que Lemnos était en effet l'île de Vulcain; ce dieu brûle vos ennemis.

Ah, Moustapha! Moustapha! Eh bien! votre hautesse se jouera-t-elle encore à mon impératrice? lui ordonnerez-vous de vider sans délai la Podolie? trouverez-vous fort impertinent qu'elle n'ait pas obéi aux ordres de votre sublime Porte? mettrez-vous encore ses ministres en prison? voilà mon auguste souveraine en possession de votre Tartarie-Crimée, maîtresse de tous vos états au-delà du Danube, maîtresse de toute votre mer Noire. Vous n'êtes point galant, Moustapha; vous deviez venir lui faire la cour, et baiser ses belles mains, au lieu de lui faire la guerre. Croyez-moi, demandez-lui très humblement pardon; c'est ce que vous avez de mieux à faire.

Savez-vous bien, monsieur Moustapha, que mon héroïne, occupée continuellement à vous battre, trouve encore le temps de m'écrire des lettres pleines d'esprit et de grâces? vous douteriez-vous, par hasard, de ce que signifient ces mots, *grâces* et *esprit*? Elle a daigné me mander, du 22 juillet–2 auguste, qu'on lui aurait l'obligation d'une carte géographique de la Crimée, on n'en a jamais eu de passables jusqu'à présent; vous n'êtes pas géographes, vous autres Turcs: vous possédez un beau pays, mais vous ne le connaissez pas. Mon impératrice vous le fera connaître.

Savez-vous seulement où était le paradis terrestre? Moi, je le sais. Il est partout où est Catherine II; prosternez-vous avec moi à ses pieds.

Donné à Ferney, le 3 de la lune de Schéval.

XCVII

DE VOLTAIRE

A Ferney, 2 octobre 1771

Seigneur Moustapha, je demande pardon à votre hautesse du dernier compliment que je vous ai fait sur votre flotte, prétendue brûlée par ces braves Orlof; ce qui est vraisemblable n'est pas toujours vrai. On m'avait mal informé; mais vous avez encore de plus fausses idées, que je n'ai de fausses nouvelles.

Vous vous êtes plus lourdement trompé que moi, quand vous avez commencé cette guerre contre ma belle impératrice. Vous êtes bien payé d'avoir été un ignorant qui, du fond de votre sérail, ne saviez point à qui vous aviez affaire! Plus vous étiez ignorant, et plus vous étiez orgueilleux. C'est une grande leçon pour tous les rois. Il y a près de trois ans que je vous prédis malheur. Mes prédictions se sont accomplies; et, quant à votre flotte brûlée, ce qui est différé n'est pas perdu. Comptez sur MM. les comtes Orlof.

D'ailleurs il est bien plus agréable de vous prendre la Crimée, que de vous brûler quelques vaisseaux. Ne soyez plus si glorieux, mon bon Moustapha. Il est vrai que mon impératrice vous donne une place dans son temple de mémoire; mais vous y serez placé, comme les rois vaincus l'étaient au Capitole.

On m'écrit que vous entendez enfin raison, et que vous demandez la paix. Je ne sais si vous êtes assez raisonnable pour faire cette démarche, et si on m'a trompé sur cette affaire comme sur votre flotte.

J'ignore encore s'il est vrai que vos troupes aient battu mon cher ami Ali-Bey, en Syrie. J'ai peur que ce petit succès ne vous enivre; mais, prenez-y garde, les Russes ne ressemblent pas aux Égyptiens; ils vous donnent sur les oreilles depuis trois ans, et vous les frotteront encore, si vous persistez à ne pas demander pardon à l'auguste Catherine. J'ai été très fâché que vous l'ayez forcée d'interrompre son beau code de lois, pour vous battre. Elle aurait mieux aimé être Thémis que Bellone; mais, grâce à vous, elle est montée au temple de la gloire par tous les chemins. Restez dans votre temple de l'orgueil et de l'oisiveté, et croyez que je serai toujours tout à vous.

L'ermite de Ferney

Je prends la liberté d'envoyer ma lettre à sa majesté impériale de Russie, qui ne manquera pas de vous la faire rendre.

XCVIII

DE L'IMPÉRATRICE

A Pétersbourg, 6/17 octobre 1771

Monsieur, j'ai à vous fournir un petit supplément à l'article FANATISME, qui ne figurera pas mal aussi dans celui des CONTRADICTIONS, que j'ai lu avec la plus grande satisfaction dans le livre des *Questions sur l'Encyclopédie*. Voici de quoi il s'agit.

Il y a des maladies à Moscou: ce sont des fièvres pourprées, des fièvres malignes, des fièvres chaudes avec taches et sans taches, qui emportent beaucoup de monde, malgré toutes les précautions qu'on a prises. Le grand-maître comte Orlof m'a demandé en grâce d'y aller, pour voir sur les lieux quels seraient les arrangements les plus convenables à prendre pour arrêter ce mal. J'ai consenti à cette action si belle et si zélée de sa part, non sans sentir une vive peine sur le danger qu'il va courir.

A peine était-il en chemin depuis vingt-quatre heures, que le maréchal Soltikof m'écrivit la catastrophe suivante, qui s'est passée à Moscou du 15 au 16 septembre, vieux style.

L'archevêque de cette ville, nommé Ambroise, homme d'esprit et de mérite, ayant appris qu'il y avait depuis quelques jours une grande affluence de populace devant une image qu'on prétendait qui guérissait les malades (lesquels expiraient aux pieds de la sainte Vierge), et qu'on y portait beaucoup d'argent, envoya mettre son sceau sur cette caisse, pour l'employer ensuite à quelques œuvres pieuses; arrangement économique, que chaque évêque est très en droit de faire dans son diocèse. Il est à supposer qu'il avait intention d'ôter cette image, comme cela s'est pratiqué plus d'une fois, et que ceci n'était qu'un préambule. Effectivement, cette foule de monde rassemblée dans un temps d'épidémie ne pouvait que l'augmenter. Mais voici ce qui arriva.

Une partie de cette populace se mit à crier, "*L'archevêque veut voler le trésor de la sainte Vierge; il faut le tuer*". L'autre prit parti pour l'archevêque. Des paroles ils en vinrent aux coups. La police voulut les séparer, mais la police ordinaire n'y put suffire. Moscou est un monde, non une ville. Les plus furieux se mirent à courir vers le Krémelin; ils enfoncèrent les portes du couvent où réside l'archevêque; ils pillèrent ce couvent, s'enivrèrent dans les caves, où beaucoup de marchands tiennent leurs vins; et n'ayant point trouvé celui qu'ils cherchaient, une partie s'en alla vers le couvent nommé Donskoi, d'où ils tirèrent ce respectable vieillard, qu'ils massacrèrent inhumainement; l'autre resta à se battre, en partageant le butin.

Enfin le lieutenant-général Jérapkin arriva avec une trentaine de soldats, qui les obligèrent bien vite à se retirer. Les plus mutins furent pris. En vérité, ce fameux dix-huitième siècle a bien là de quoi se glorifier! nous voilà devenus bien sages! Mais ce n'est pas à vous qu'il faut parler sur cette matière: vous connaissez trop les hommes pour vous étonner des contradictions et des extravagances dont ils sont capables. Il suffit de lire vos *Questions sur l'Encyclopédie*, pour être persuadé de la profonde connaissance que vous avez de l'esprit et du cœur des humains.

Je vous dois mille remercîments, monsieur, de la mention que vous voulez bien faire de moi dans divers endroits de ce dictionnaire très utile et très agréable: je suis étonnée d'y trouver souvent mon nom, à la fin d'une page où je l'attendais le moins.

J'espère que vous aurez reçu, à l'heure qu'il est, la lettre-de-change pour le paiement des fabricants qui m'ont envoyé leurs montres.

La nouvelle du combat naval donné à Lemnos est fausse. Le comte Alexis Orlof était encore à Paros le 24 juillet, et la flotte turque n'ose montrer ses beaux yeux en-deçà des Dardanelles. Votre lettre au sujet de ce combat est unique. Je sens, comme je le dois, les marques d'amitié qu'il vous plaît de me donner, et je vous ai les plus grandes obligations pour vos charmantes lettres.

J'ai trouvé, monsieur, dans les *Questions sur l'Encyclopédie* si remplies de choses aussi excellentes que nouvelles, à l'article ÉCONOMIE PUBLIQUE, page 61 de la cinquième partie, ces paroles: "Donnez à la Sibérie et au Kamtschatka réunis, qui font quatre fois l'étendue de l'Allemagne, un Cyrus pour souverain, un Solon pour législateur, un duc de Sulli, un Colbert pour surintendant des finances, un duc de Choiseul pour ministre de la guerre et de la paix, un Anson pour amiral; ils y mourront de faim avec tout leur génie".

Je vous abandonne tout le pays de la Sibérie et du Kamtschatka, qui est situé au-delà du soixante-troisième degré; en revanche je plaide chez vous la cause de tout le terrain qui se trouve entre le soixante-troisième et le quarante-cinquième degré: il manque d'hommes en proportion de son étendue, de vins aussi. Non seulement il est cultivable, mais même très fertile. Les blés y viennent en si grande abondance, qu'outre la consommation des habitants, il y a des brasseries immenses d'eau-de-vie; et il en reste encore assez pour en mener par terre en hiver, et par les rivières en été, jusqu'à Archangel, d'où on l'envoie dans les pays étrangers. Et peut-être en a-t-on mangé dans plus d'un endroit, en disant que les blés ne mûrissent jamais en Sibérie.

Les animaux domestiques, le gibier, les poissons, se trouvent en grande abondance dans ces climats; et il y en a d'espèce excellente qu'on ignore dans les autres pays de l'Europe.

Généralement les productions de la nature, en Sibérie, sont d'une richesse extraordinaire: témoin la grande quantité de mines de fer, de cuivre, d'or, et d'argent, les carrières d'agates de toutes couleurs, de jaspe, de cristaux, de marbre, de talc, etc., etc., qu'on y trouve.

Il y a des districts entiers couverts de cèdres d'une épaisseur extraordinaire, aussi beaux que ceux du mont Liban, et des fruitiers sauvages de beaucoup d'espèces différentes.

Si vous êtes curieux, monsieur, de voir des productions de la Sibérie, je vous en enverrai des collections de différentes espèces, qui ne sont communes qu'en Sibérie, et rares partout ailleurs. Mais une chose qui démontre, je pense, que le monde est un peu plus vieux que nos nourrices ne nous le disent, c'est qu'on trouve dans le nord de la Sibérie, à plusieurs toises sous terre, des ossements d'éléphants, qui, depuis fort long-temps, n'habitent plus ces contrées.

Les savants, plutôt que de convenir de l'antiquité de notre globe, ont dit que c'était de l'ivoire fossile; mais ils ont beau dire, les fossiles ne croissent point en forme d'éléphant très complet.

Ayant plaidé ainsi devant vous la cause de la Sibérie, je vous laisse le jugement du procès, et me retire, en vous réitérant les assurances de la plus haute considération, et de l'amitié et de l'estime la plus sincère.

CATERINE

XCIX

DE VOLTAIRE

A Ferney, 18 octobre 1771

Madame, je n'écris point par cette poste à Moustapha; permettez-moi de donner la préférence à votre majesté impériale;

il n'y a pas moyen de parler à ce gros cochon, quand on peut s'adresser à l'héroïne du siècle.

J'ai le cœur navré de voir qu'il y a de mes compatriotes parmi ces fous de confédérés. Nos Welches n'ont jamais été trop sages, mais du moins ils passaient pour galants; et je ne sais rien de si grossier que de porter les armes contre vous. Cela est contre toutes les lois de la chevalerie. Il est bien honteux et bien fou qu'une trentaine de blancs-becs de mon pays aient l'impertinence de vous aller faire la guerre, tandis que deux cent mille Tartares quittent Moustapha pour vous servir. Ce sont les Tartares qui sont polis, et les Français sont devenus des Scythes. Daignez observer, madame, que je ne suis point Welche; je suis Suisse, et si j'étais plus jeune, je me ferais Russe.

Votre majesté impériale m'a bien consolé par sa lettre du 4 septembre; elle a daigné m'apprendre le véritable état des affaires vers le Danube. La France, ma voisine, retentissait des plus fausses nouvelles; mais je reste toujours dans ma surprise que Moustapha ne demande point la paix. Est-ce qu'il aurait quelques succès contre mon cher Ali-Bey?

Ah! madame, qu'une paix glorieuse serait belle, après toutes vos victoires!

Tandis que vous avez la bonté de perdre quelques moments à lire le quatrième et le cinquième volume des *Questions*, le questionneur a fait partir le sixième et le septième; mais il a bien peur de ne pouvoir continuer. Il n'en peut plus, il est bien malade; et voilà pourquoi il désirait que votre majesté allât bien vite à Constantinople, car assurément il n'a pas le temps d'attendre.

Ma colonie est à vos pieds; je voudrais qu'elle pût envoyer des montres à la Chine, par vos caravanes; mais elle est beaucoup plus glorieuse d'en avoir envoyé à Pétersbourg. Votre majesté impériale est trop bonne; je suis toujours étonné de tout ce que vous faites. Il me semble que le roi de Prusse en est tout aussi surpris et presque aussi aise que moi. Rien n'égale l'admiration pour votre personne, la reconnaissance, et le profond respect du vieux malade de Ferney.

C

DE VOLTAIRE

A Ferney, 2 novembre 1771

Madame, j'aime toujours mieux prendre la liberté d'écrire à mon héroïne qu'à Moustapha, qui n'est point du tout mon héros. J'aurais, à la vérité, beaucoup de plaisir à lui rire au nez, sur la belle reprise de Giurgi, ou Giorgiova, et sur la défaite totale de ce terrible Oginski.

J'ai bien peur qu'on n'ait trouvé quelques uns de nos Welches parmi leurs prisonniers: *Que diable allaient-ils faire dans cette galère?*

Apparemment que votre majesté impériale avait donné le mot à mon cher Ali-Bey, pour qu'il reprît Damas et la sainte Jérusalem, pendant que votre majesté reprendrait Giorgiova. Si cette aventure de Damas est vraie, je n'ai plus d'inquiétude que pour le sérail de mon cher Moustapha. On me flatte que M. le comte Alexis Orlof est maître de Négrepont; cela me donne des espérances pour Athènes, à laquelle je suis toujours attaché, en faveur de Sophocle, d'Euripide, de Ménandre, et du vieil Anacréon mon confrère, quoique les Athéniens soient devenus les plus pauvres poltrons du continent. Mais d'où vient que Raguse, l'ancienne Épidaure (à ce qu'on dit), laquelle appartint si long-temps à l'empire d'orient, c'est-à-dire au vôtre, se met-elle sous la protection de l'empire d'occident? Y a-t-il donc d'autre protection à présent que celle de mon héroïne? Que font les *savii grandi* de Venise? Pourquoi ne reprennent-ils pas le royaume de Minos, pendant que les braves Orlof prennent le royaume de Philoctète? C'est qu'il n'y a actuellement rien de grand dans l'Europe que mon auguste Catherine II, à qui j'ai voué mes derniers soupirs.

J'étais bien malade; la nouvelle de Giorgiova m'a ressuscité pour quelque temps, et je respire encore avec le plus profond respect et la plus vive reconnaissance pour votre majesté impériale.

Le vieux malade de Ferney

CI

DE VOLTAIRE

12 novembre 1771

Madame, les malheurs ne pouvaient arriver à votre majesté impériale ni par vos braves troupes, ni par votre sublime et sage administration; vous ne pouviez souffrir que par les fléaux qui ont de tout temps désolé la nature humaine. La maladie contagieuse qui afflige Moscou et ses environs est venue, dit-on, de vos victoires mêmes. On débite que cette contagion a été apportée par des dépouilles de quelques Turcs vers la mer Noire. Moustapha ne pouvait donner que la peste, dont son beau pays est toujours attaqué. C'était assurément une raison de plus pour tous les princes vos voisins de se joindre à vous, et d'exterminer sous vos auspices les deux grands fléaux de la terre, la peste et les Turcs. Je me souviens qu'en 1718 nous arrêtâmes la peste à Marseille; je ne doute pas que votre majesté impériale ne prenne encore de meilleures mesures que celles qui furent prises alors par notre gouvernement. L'air ne porte point cette contagion, le froid la diminue, et vos soins maternels la dissiperont; l'infâme négligence des Turcs augmenterait votre prévoyance, si quelque chose pouvait l'augmenter.

On parle d'une disette qui se fait sentir dans votre armée navale. Mais je ne la crois pas, puisque c'est un des braves comtes Orlof qui la commande. C'en serait trop que d'éprouver à la fois les trois faveurs dont le prophète Gad en donna une à choisir à votre petit prétendu confrère David, pour avoir fait le dénombrement de sa chétive province.

J'éprouve aussi des fléaux dans mes villages; le malheur se fourre dans les trous de souris, comme il marche la tête levée dans les grands empires. Ma colonie d'horlogers a essuyé des persécutions, mais je les ai tirés d'affaire à force d'argent, et j'espère toujours qu'ils pourront vous servir à établir un commerce utile entre vos états et la Chine. En vérité j'aurais mieux aimé les faire travailler sur les bords du Volga que sur ceux du lac de Genève.

Chassez à jamais la peste et les Ottomans au-delà du Danube;

et recevez, madame, avec votre bonté ordinaire, le profond respect et l'attachement inviolable du vieil ermite de Ferney pour votre majesté impériale.

CII

DE VOLTAIRE

A Ferney, 18 novembre 1771

Madame, je vois, par la lettre dont votre majesté impériale m'honore du 6 octobre, vieux style, que vous êtes née pour instruire les hommes autant que pour les gouverner.

La populace sera difficilement instruite; mais tous ceux qui auront reçu une éducation seulement tolérable profiteront de plus en plus des lumières que vous répandez. Il est triste que l'archevêque de Moscou ait été le martyr de la *bonne Vierge*; les barbares imbéciles, superstitieux, et ivrognes, qui l'ont tué, méritent sans doute un châtiment qui fasse impression sur ces têtes de buffles. Je suis persuadé que, depuis la mort du fils de la *sainte Vierge*, il n'y a presque point eu de jour où quelqu'un n'ait été assassiné à son occasion; et à l'égard des assassinats en front de bandière, dont le fils et la mère ont été le prétexte, ils sont en grand nombre et trop connus. Le meurtre de l'archevêque est bien punissable; je trouve celui du chevalier de La Barre plus horrible, parce qu'il a été commis de sang-froid, par des hommes qui devaient avoir du sens commun et de l'humanité.

Je rends grâces à la nature de ce que la maladie épidémique de Moscou n'est point la peste. Ce mot effrayait nos pays méridionaux. Chacun débitait des contes funestes. Les mensonges imprimés qui courent tous les jours sur votre empire font bien voir comment l'histoire était écrite autrefois. Si le roi d'Égypte avait perdu une douzaine de chevaux, on disait que l'*Ange exterminateur* était venu tuer tous les quadrupèdes du pays.

M. le grand-maître Orlof est un ange *consolateur*, il a fait une action héroïque. Je conçois qu'elle a dû bien émouvoir votre cœur partagé entre la crainte et l'admiration; mais vous devez être moins surprise qu'une autre: les grandes actions sont de votre compétence. Je remercie votre majesté impériale de tout ce qu'elle daigne m'apprendre sur la Sibérie méridionale; elle m'en dit plus en dix lignes que l'abbé Chappe dans un *in-folio*. Si vous le permettez, cela entrera dans un supplément aux *Questions*, qu'on prépare à présent au mont Krapack. J'avoue que je suis fort étonné des squelettes d'éléphants trouvés dans le nord de la Sibérie. Je crois difficilement à l'ivoire fossile, et j'ai aussi beaucoup de peine à croire à de véritables dents d'éléphants enterrés trente pieds sous les glaces; mais je crois la nature capable de tout, et il se pourrait bien faire (en expliquant les choses respectueusement) que l'Adam des Hébreux, connu jadis d'eux seuls, fût de très fraîche date: six mille ans sont en effet bien peu de chose.

Votre majesté, qui m'a déjà donné tant de marques de bonté, veut m'envoyer quelques productions de la Sibérie. J'oserais lui demander de la graine de ces beaux cèdres, qui n'ont pas de peine à surpasser ceux du Liban, car le Liban n'en a presque plus; je les planterais dans mon ermitage, où il fait quelquefois presque aussi froid qu'en Sibérie. Je sais bien que je ne les verrai pas croître; mais la postérité les verra, et elle dira: Voilà les bienfaits de celle qui érigea le temple de Mémoire.

Les artistes de Ferney ont reçu l'argent que votre majesté a eu la bonté de leur envoyer. Ils sont à vos pieds comme moi. Je ne me souvenais pas de vous avoir parlé d'une pendule; mais si vous en voulez, vous en aurez incessamment: votre majesté n'aurait qu'à fixer le prix, je lui réponds qu'elle serait bien servie, et à bon compte. Ce n'est peut-être pas le temps de proposer un commerce de pendules et de montres avec la Chine; mais votre universalité fait tout à la fois. C'est là, selon mon avis, la vraie grandeur, la vraie puissance.

Les Gènevois ont bien établi un petit commerce de montres à Kanton; votre majesté pourrait en établir un dans l'endroit où les Russes commercent avec les Chinois. Un homme de confiance pourrait envoyer de Pétersbourg à Ferney les ordres auxquels on se conformerait; mais j'ai bien peur que ce plan ne tienne un peu de la proposition des chars de guerre de Cyrus. Vous avez très bien battu les Turcs sans le secours de ces beaux chars de guerre à la nouvelle mode.

Je me flatte qu'à présent le comte Alexis Orlof leur a pris le Nègrepont sans aucun char: il ne vous faut que des chars de triomphe. Je me mets de loin derrière eux, et je crie *io trionfo* d'une voix très faible et très cassée, mais qui part d'un cœur pénétré de tout ce que votre majesté impériale peut inspirer à l'ermite, etc.

CIII

DE L'IMPÉRATRICE

A Pétersbourg, 18/29 novembre 1771

Monsieur, pour faire tenir votre lettre au seigneur Moustapha, le maréchal Romanzof a envoyé, le mois passé, le général-major Veismann au-delà du Danube. Après avoir fait sauter en l'air deux petits forts qui barraient son chemin, il a marché vers Balada, où le grand-visir était campé; il a pris cette place, a battu les troupes du visir, s'est emparé du canon fondu l'an passé par M. Tott à Constantinople; ensuite il est entré poliment dans le camp du visir pour le voir et lui parler, mais il ne l'y a pas trouvé.

Nos troupes légères se sont portées jusqu'au mont Hémus, sans rencontrer à qui s'adresser. Alors M. Veismann, croyant sa commission achevée, retourna vers Isacki, qu'il rasa. Pendant ce temps-là, un autre général-major a pris les forts de Matelina et de Girsova; et le lieutenant-général Essen s'amusait à battre quarante mille Turcs, commandés par Moussou-Ouglou, ci-devant visir, qui s'était avancé en Valachie.

Après la défaite de Moussou, Giurgi fut repris. Les deux rives du Danube, depuis cet endroit jusqu'à la mer Noire, sont présentement nettoyées de Turcs, comme une maison hollandaise l'est de la poussière. Tout ceci s'est passé du 20 au 27 octobre, vieux style.

Consolez-vous, monsieur; votre cher Ali-Bey est maître de Damas. Mais quelle honte pour vos compatriotes, pour cette noblesse française si remplie d'honneur, de courage, et de générosité, de se trouver parmi les bandits de Pologne, qui font serment, devant des images miraculeuses, d'assassiner leur roi, quand ils ne savent pas combattre! Si après ce coup M. de Vioménil et ses compagnons ne quittent pas ces gens-là, que faudra-t-il penser?

Nous avons ici présentement le halga sultan, frère du kan indépendant de la Crimée, par la grâce de Dieu et des armes de la Russie: c'est un jeune homme de vingt-cinq ans, plein d'esprit et du désir de s'instruire.

J'ai à vous dire que les maladies à Moscou sont réduites, par les soins infatigables du comte Orlof, à un dixième de ce qu'elles étaient. Ses frères ont fait le diable à quatre dans l'Archipel: ils ont partagé leur flotte en deux: l'aîné a fait plusieurs descentes depuis le cap Matapan jusqu'à Lemnos, a enlevé à l'ennemi des magasins et des bâtiments, et a détruit ce qu'il n'a pu emporter; le cadet en a fait autant sur les côtes d'Asie et d'Afrique; mais sa maladie, très sérieuse, l'a obligé de revenir à Livourne.

Si ces nouvelles, monsieur, peuvent vous rendre la santé, elles auront un nouveau mérite à mes yeux, parce qu'on ne saurait s'intéresser plus vivement que je le fais à tout ce qui vous regarde.

Dites-moi, je vous prie, si l'édition de *l'Encyclopédie* qu'on fait à Genève est avouée par les auteurs de la première; les éditeurs nouveaux m'ont demandé des mémoires sur la Russie pour les y insérer.

CIV

DE VOLTAIRE

A Ferney, 3 décembre 1771

Madame, voilà sans doute une belle action que les confédérés ont faite. Je ne doute pas que le révérend père Ravaillac et le révérend père Poignardini n'aient été les confesseurs de ces messieurs, et qu'ils ne les aient munis du pain des forts, comme le dit le révérend père Strada, en parlant du bienheureux Balthasar Gérard, assassin du prince d'Orange. Du moins votre pauvre archevêque de Moscou n'a été tué que par des gueux ivres, par une populace effrénée que la raison ne peut jamais gouverner, et qu'il faut emmuseler comme des ours; mais le roi de Pologne a été trahi, assailli, frappé par des gentilshommes qui parlent latin, qui lui avaient juré obéissance.

On dit qu'on a imprimé dans les états de votre majesté impériale une relation de cette conspiration étonnante. Oserais-je vous supplier de daigner m'en faire parvenir un exemplaire? Il pourrait me servir en temps et lieu, supposé que j'aie encore quelque temps à vivre. J'avoue que j'ai la faiblesse d'aimer la vie, quand ce ne serait que pour voir l'estampe de votre temple de Mémoire, et celle de votre statue érigée vis-à-vis celle de Pierre-le-Grand.

Nous sommes inondés de tant de nouvelles que je n'en crois aucune. La renommée est une déesse qui n'acquiert le sens commun qu'avec le temps; encore même ne l'acquiert-elle pas toujours. L'histoire la plus vraie est mêlée de mensonges, comme l'or dans la mine est souillé par des métaux étrangers; mais les grandes actions, les grands monuments, restent à la postérité. La gloire se dégage des lambeaux dont on la couvre, et paraît à la fin dans toute sa splendeur. Heureux l'écrivain qui donnera dans un siècle l'histoire de Catherine II!

Nous avons toujours dans notre voisinage un comte Orlof, en Suisse, avec sa famille; tandis que les autres vous servent sur terre et sur mer. M. Polianski nous fait l'honneur de venir quelquefois à Ferney; il nous enchante par tout ce qu'il nous dit de la magnificence de votre cour, de votre affabilité, de votre travail assidu, de la multiplicité des grandes choses que vous faites en vous jouant. Enfin il me met au désespoir d'avoir près de quatre-vingts ans, et de ne pouvoir être témoin de tout cela. M. Polianski a un désir extrême de voir l'Italie, où il apprendrait plus à servir votre majesté impériale que dans le voisinage de la Suisse et de Genève; il attend sur cela vos ordres et vos bontés depuis long-temps. C'est un très bon esprit et un très bon homme, dont le cœur est véritablement attaché à votre majesté.

Nous voici dans un temps, madame, où il n'y a pas moyen de prendre de nouvelles provinces à mon cher ami Moustapha. J'en suis fâché; mais je le prie d'attendre au printemps.

Je renouvelle mes vœux pourla constante prospérité de vos

armes, pour votre santé, pour votre gloire, pour vos plaisirs. Je me mets aux pieds de votre majesté impériale avec la plus sensible reconnaissance et le plus profond respect.

Le vieux malade de Ferney

CV

DE L'IMPÉRATRICE

Ce 3/14 décembre 1771

Monsieur, je viens de recevoir votre lettre du 18 novembre. Grâce aux arrangements pris par le comte Orlof à Moscou, il n'y avait, le 28 de ce même mois, que deux personnes de mortes, dans cette ville, de la contagion dont vos pays méridionaux ont si grand effroi, et avec raison. Mais il y a encore des malades; les médecins assurent que les deux tiers en réchapperont. Ce qu'il y a de singulier, c'est qu'aucune personne de qualité n'en a été attaquée, et qu'il est mort plus de femmes que d'hommes. Dans les corps disséqués, on a trouvé que le sang s'était réfugié dans le cœur et les poumons; qu'il n'y en avait pas une goutte dans les veines; que tous les remèdes étaient mortels, hors ceux qui provoquaient la sueur.

Je vous enverrai incessamment des noix de cèdre de Sibérie; j'ai fait écrire au gouverneur de m'en envoyer de toutes fraîches. Vous les aurez vers le printemps.

Les contes de l'abbé Chappe ne méritent guère de croyance. Je ne l'ai jamais vu; et cependant il prétend dans son livre avoir mesuré, dit-on, des bouts de bougie dans ma chambre, où il n'a jamais mis le pied. Ceci est un fait.

Votre lettre me tire d'inquiétude au sujet de l'argent des montres, puisqu'enfin il est arrivé. Pour ce qui regarde le commerce des montres à la Chine, je crois qu'il ne serait pas impossible d'y parvenir en s'adressant à quelque comptoir d'ici, qui trouvera bien le moyen de les faire parvenir à la frontière de la Chine; car, quoi qu'en disent certains écrivains, la couronne ne fait plus ce commerce.

Les tableaux que j'ai fait acheter en Hollande, de la collection de Braamcamp, ont tous péri sur les côtes de Finlande. Il faudra s'en passer. J'ai eu du guignon cette année; en pareil cas, il n'y a d'autre ressource que de s'en consoler.

Je vous ai mandé les nouvelles que j'ai reçues de mes armées de terre et de mer: il ne me reste donc en ce moment, monsieur, que de vous renouveler tous les sentiments que vous me connaissez.

CATERINE

CVI

DE VOLTAIRE

A Ferney, 16 décembre 1771

Madame, j'importune votre majesté impériale de mes félicitations et de mes battements de main: on n'a jamais fait avec elle. Une ville n'est pas plutôt prise, qu'une autre est rendue. A peine les Turcs sont-ils battus sur la rive gauche du Danube, qu'ils sont défaits sur la rive droite; si on leur prend cent canons à Giorgiova, on leur en prend cent cinquante dans une bataille. Voilà du moins ce qu'on me dit, et ce qui me comble de joie.

J'espère, par-dessus tout cela, que l'attentat des confédérés sera pour vous un nouveau sujet de gloire.

Votre majesté me permettrait-elle de joindre à ce petit billet une requête de mes colons? Vous vous souvenez que vous trouvâtes dans leurs caisses plus de montres qu'ils n'en avaient spécifié dans leur facture. Les artistes qui, par l'oubli de leur facture, n'ont pas été compris dans le paiement ordonné par votre majesté, se jettent à vos pieds; ce sont des gens dont toute la fortune est dans leurs doigts. Il ne s'agit que de deux cent quarante-sept roubles, à ce que je crois.

Il y a un de mes artistes qui fait des montres en bagues, à répétition, à secondes, quart et demiquart, et à carillon. C'est un prodige bien singulier; mais ces bagatelles difficiles ne sont pas dignes de l'héroïne qui venge l'Europe de l'insolence des Turcs, malgré une partie de l'Europe.

Le roi de Prusse s'est amusé à faire un poëme épique contre les confédérés. Je crois que M. l'abbé d'Oliva paiera les frais de l'impression.

Que votre majesté impériale daigne agréer le profond respect, l'attachement, l'admiration, la reconnaissance du vieux malade de Ferney.

CVII

DE VOLTAIRE

A Ferney, 1er janvier 1772

Madame, je souhaite à votre majesté impériale, pour l'année 1772, non pas augmentation de gloire, car il n'y a plus moyen, mais augmentation de croquignoles sur le nez de Moustapha et de ses visirs, quelques victoires nouvelles, votre quartier-général à Andrinople, et la paix.

La lettre de votre majesté impériale, du 18 novembre, vieux style, peut me faire vivre encore pour le moins cette année bissextile. Si vous aviez pris la mode des anciens Romains en tout, vos lettres seraient toujours farcies de lauriers. Je voudrais que le frère du nouveau Thoas de la Tauride pût voyager dans nos climats, et que je pusse l'entendre. Je serais bien charmé d'apprendre à nos Welches qu'il y a un bel-esprit dans le pays où Iphigénie égorgeait, en qualité de religieuse, tous les étrangers en l'honneur d'une vilaine statue de bois, toute semblable à Notre-Dame miraculeuse de Czenstokova.

Je ne sais encore, madame, si c'était la vraie peste qui s'était emparée de Moscou; mais elle est dans notre voisinage. Elle a envoyé devant Dieu cinq cent cinquante personnes à Crémone en un jour, à ce que dit la renommée. Pour peu qu'elle ait duré huit jours, il n'y a plus personne dans cette ville. On prétend qu'elle est venue de la foire de Sinigaglia, pays appartenant à mon saint-père le pape, sur la côte de la mer Adriatique. Les papes ne pouvant plus détrôner les princes, leur envoient ce fléau de Dieu pour les amener à résipiscence. Mais la peste étant venue par le voisinage de Notre-Dame-de-Lorette, elle pourra bien passer par Rome. Il serait triste que le grand-inquisiteur et le sacré collége eussent le charbon.

Le fait est que Genève, ma voisine, tremble de tout son cœur, attendu qu'elle a plus de commerce avec Crémone qu'avec

Rome; mais sûrement les processions des catholiques auront purifié l'air avant que la peste vienne à Ferney, qui est tout au beau milieu des hérétiques.

Une autre peste est celle des confédérés de Pologne; je me flatte que votre majesté impériale les guérira de leur maladie contagieuse. Nos chevaliers welches, qui ont été porter leur inquiétude et leur curiosité chez les Sarmates, doivent mourir de faim s'ils ne meurent pas du charbon. Voilà une plaisante croisade qu'ils ont été faire. Cela ne servira pas à faire valoir la prudence et la galanterie de ma chère nation.

Votre majesté me demande si les auteurs de l'*Encyclopédie* avouent l'édition de Genève: ils la souffrent, mais ils n'en sont pas les maîtres. Elle devait se faire à Paris; notre inquisition ne l'a pas permis. Les libraires de Paris se sont associés avec ceux de Genève pour cet ouvrage, qui ne sera fait de plusieurs années. Ils en sont les maîtres, et ils font travailler des auteurs à tant la feuille, comme je fais travailler mes manœuvres dans mon jardin, à tant la toise. Ils ont fait écrire à M. le prince Gallitzin à La Haye, et lui ont demandé sa protection pour obtenir des suppléments; ils ont raison: les articles de Russie donneront du lustre à leur édition, en dépit des canons fondus par M. de Tott. Ce M. de Tott, au reste, est un homme de beaucoup d'esprit; c'est dommage qu'il ait pris le parti de Moustapha.

Je suis fâché qu'Ali-Bey, le prince Héraclius, le prince Alexandre, ne connaissent point les fêtes de nos remparts, nos admirables opéra-comiques, notre fax-hall perfectionné, et qu'ils ne sachent pas danser le menuet proprement.

Je me mets aux pieds de votre majesté impériale pour l'année 1772, dont je compte voir le premier jour, car elle commence aujourd'hui, et personne n'est sûr du second.

Votre admirateur et votre très humble et très passionné serviteur, *Le vieux malade de Ferney*

La peste de Crémone vient de cesser; on dit que ce n'est rien; peut-être demain recommencera-t-elle.

CVIII

DE VOLTAIRE

A Ferney, 14 janvier 1772

Madame, quoi ! votre âme, partagée entre la Crimée, la Moldavie, la Valachie, la Pologne, la Bulgarie, occupée à rosser le grave Moustapha, et à faire occuper une douzaine d'îles dans l'Archipel par vos Argonautes, daigne s'abaisser jusqu'à être en peine si les horlogers de mon village ont reçu l'argent de leurs montres? Vous êtes comme Tamerlan qui, le jour de la bataille d'Ancyre, ne put s'endormir jusqu'à ce que son nain eût soupé.

J'ai mandé cependant à votre majesté impériale qu'ils avaient tous été très bien payés, excepté trois ou quatre pauvres diables dont on avait oublié la facture. Ma lettre est du mois de novembre. Je me flatte qu'elle n'a pas été interceptée par M. Pulawski. En tout cas, il aura vu qu'une impératrice qui entre dans les plus petits détails comme dans les plus grands est une personne qui mérite quelques considérations et quelques ménagements.

Je me souviens même de vous avoir proposé, dans une de mes lettres, un commerce de montres avec le roi de la Chine, ce qui serait plus convenable qu'un commerce de vers, tout grand poëte qu'il est.

Le roi de Prusse, qui a fait un poëme contre les confédérés, et qui fait assurément mieux des vers que tous les Chinois ensemble, peut lui envoyer ses écrits, mais moi je ne lui enverrai que des montres.

J'avouerai même que, malgré la guerre, mon village a fait partir des caisses de montres pour Constantinople; ainsi me voilà en correspondance à la fois avec les battants et les battus.

Je ne sais pas encore si Moustapha a acheté de nos montres: mais je sais qu'il n'a pas trouvé avec vous l'heure du berger, et que vous lui faites passer de très mauvais quarts d'heure. On dit qu'il a fait pendre un évêque grec qui avait pris votre parti. Je vous recommande le mufti à la première occasion.

Permettez-moi de dire à votre majesté que vous êtes incompréhensible. A peine la mer Baltique a-t-elle englouti pour soixante mille écus de tableau, que vous fesiez venir pour vous de la Hollande, que vous en faites venir de France pour quatre cent cinquante mille livres. Vous achetez encore mille raretés en Italie. Mais, en conscience, où prenez-vous tout cet argent? Est-ce que vous auriez pillé le trésor de Moustapha, sans que les gazettes en eussent parlé? Nos Français sont en pleine paix, et nous n'avons pas le sou. Dieu nous préserve de la guerre! Il y a quatre ans qu'on recommande à nos charités les soldats et les officiers français pris par les troupes de l'empereur de Maroc. Il y a un an qu'une petite frégate du roi, établie sur le lac de Genève, à quatre pas de mon village, fut confisquée pour dettes, dans un port de Savoie: je sauvai l'honneur de notre marine en rachetant la frégate; le ministère ne me l'a point payée. Si vous avez le courage de Tomyris, il faut que je vous soupçonne d'avoir les trésors de Crésus, supposé pourtant que Crésus fût aussi riche qu'on le dit; car je me défie toujours des exagérations de l'antiquité, à commencer par Salomon, qui possédait environ six milliards de roubles, et qui n'avait pas d'ouvriers chez lui pour bâtir son temple de bois.

Je n'ai pas répondu sur-le-champ aux deux dernières lettres dont votre majesté impériale m'a honoré, parce que les neiges dont je suis entouré me tuent. Voilà pourquoi je voulais m'établir sur quelque côte méridionale du Bosphore de Thrace; mais vous n'avez pas voulu encore aller jusque-là, et j'en suis bien fâché.

Je me mets à vos pieds; permettez-moi de les baiser en toute humilité, et même vos mains, qu'on dit que vous avez les plus belles du monde. C'est à Moustapha de venir les baiser avec autant d'humilité que moi. *Le vieux malade de Ferney*

CIX

DE L'IMPÉRATRICE

Le 30 janvier/10 février 1772

Monsieur, vous me demandez un exemplaire imprimé de l'attentat des révérends pères poignardins confédérés pour l'amour de Dieu; mais il n'y a point eu de relation de cette détestable scène imprimée ici. J'ai ordonné de remettre à M. Polianski, votre protégé, l'argent pour son voyage d'Italie; j'espère qu'il l'aura reçu à l'heure qu'il est, de même que vos colons, auxquels j'ai dit d'envoyer deux cent quarante-sept roubles qui manquent au compte qui leur a été payé ci-devant.

Dans une de vos lettres vous me souhaitez, entre autres belles choses que votre amitié pour moi vous inspire, une augmentation de plaisirs: je vais vous parler d'une sorte de plaisir bien intéressant pour moi, et sur lequel je vous prie de me donner vos conseils.

Vous savez, car rien ne vous échappe, que cinq cents demoiselles sont élevées dans une maison ci-devant destinée à trois cents épouses de notre Seigneur. Ces demoiselles, je dois l'avouer, surpassent notre attente: elles font des progrès étonnants, et tout le monde convient qu'elles deviennent aussi aimables qu'elles sont remplies de connaissances utiles à la société. Elles sont de mœurs irréprochables, sans avoir cependant l'austérité minutieuse des recluses. Depuis deux hivers on a commencé à leur faire jouer des tragédies et des comédies; elles s'en acquittent mieux que ceux qui en font profession ici: mais j'avoue qu'il n'y a que très peu de pièces qui leur conviennent, parce que leurs supérieurs veulent éviter de leur en faire jouer qui remuassent trop tôt les passions. Il y a trop d'amour, dit-on, dans la plupart des pièces françaises, et les meilleurs auteurs même ont été souvent gênés par ce goût ou caractère national. En faire composer, cela est impossible; ce ne sont pas là des ouvrages de commande, c'est le fruit du génie. Des pièces mauvaises et insipides nous gâteraient le goût. Comment faire donc? je n'en sais rien, et j'ai recours à vous. Faut-il ne choisir que des scènes? mais cela est beaucoup moins intéressant, à mon avis, que des pièces suivies.

Personne ne saurait mieux en juger que vous, monsieur; aidez-moi, je vous prie, de vos conseils.

J'allais finir cette lettre, lorsque je reçois la vôtre du 14 janvier. Je vois à regret que je n'ai point répondu à quatre de vos lettres: cette dernière est écrite avec tant de vivacité et de chaleur, qu'il semble que chaque nouvelle année vous rajeunit. Je fais des vœux pour que votre santé se rétablisse dans le cours de celle-ci.

Plusieurs de nos officiers, que vous avez eu la complaisance d'admettre à Ferney, sont revenus enchantés et de vous, et de l'accueil que vous leur avez fait. En vérité, monsieur, vous me donnez des preuves bien sensibles de votre amitié; vous l'étendez jusqu'à nos jeunes gens, avides de vous voir et de vous entendre: je crains qu'ils n'abusent de votre complaisance. Vous direz peut-être que je ne sais ce que je veux et ce que je dis, et que le comte Théodore Orlof a été à Genève sans entrer à Ferney; mais j'ai bien grondé le comte Théodore de n'être point allé vous voir, au lieu de passer quatorze heures à Genève: et, s'il faut tout dire, c'est une mauvaise honte qui l'a retenu. Il prétend qu'il ne s'explique pas en français avec assez de facilité. A cela je lui ai répondu qu'un des principaux mobiles de la bataille de Tchesme était dispensé de savoir exactement la grammaire française, et que l'intérêt que M. de Voltaire veut bien prendre à tout ce qui regarde la Russie, et l'amitié qu'il me marque, me fait supposer que peut-être il n'aurait point eu de regret (quoiqu'il n'aime pas le carnage) d'entendre les détails de la prise de la Morée, et des deux journées mémorables du 24 et 26 juin 1770, de la bouche même d'un officier-général aussi aimable qu'il est brave; et qu'il lui aurait pardonné de ne pas s'expliquer exactement dans une langue étrangère que bien des naturels commencent à ignorer, s'il en faut juger par tant d'ouvrages insipides et mal écrits qu'on imprime tous les jours.

Vous vous étonnez de mes emplettes de tableaux: je ferais mieux peut-être d'en acheter moins, mais des occasions perdues ne se retrouvent plus. Mes deniers d'ailleurs ne sont pas confondus avec ceux de l'état; et avec de l'ordre on vient à bout de bien des choses. Je parle par expérience.

Je m'aperçois que ma lettre devient trop longue. Je finis en vous priant de me continuer votre amitié, et d'être persuadé que, si la paix n'a point lieu, je ferai tout mon possible pour vous donner le plaisir de voir Moustapha encore mieux accommodé qu'il ne l'a été ci-devant. J'espère que tous les bons chrétiens s'en réjouiront avec nous, et que, de façon ou d'autre, ceux qui ne le sont point se rangeront à la raison, par des démonstrations aussi convaincantes que deux et deux font quatre.

CX

DE VOLTAIRE

A Ferney, 12 février 1772

Madame, j'ai peur que votre majesté impériale ne soit bien lasse des lettres d'un vieux raisonneur suisse, qui ne peut vous servir à rien, qui n'a pour vous qu'un zèle inutile, qui déteste cordialement Moustapha, qui n'aime point du tout les confédérés polaques, et qui se borne à crier, dans son désert, aux truites du lac de Genève: Chantons Catherine II.

Il m'est tombé entre les mains une petite pièce de vers d'un jeune Courlandais ou Courlandois qui est venu dans mon ermitage, et que j'aime beaucoup, parce qu'il pense comme moi. Il m'a dit qu'il n'osait pas mettre à vos pieds ce rogaton; mais que, puisque j'avais la hardiesse de vous ennuyer quelquefois en prose, il ne m'en coûterait pas davantage d'ennuyer votre majesté impériale en vers.

Je cède donc à l'empressement qu'a ce bon Courlandais de vous faire bâiller; vous recevrez son ode au milieu de cent paquets qui vous arriveront de la Valachie, des îles de l'Archipel, d'Archangel, et de l'Italie; mais les vers ne veulent être lus que quand on n'a rien à faire; et je ne pense pas que ce soit jamais le cas de votre majesté.

Après tout, elle ne doit pas être surprise qu'un Courlandais fasse des vers, puisque le roi de Prusse et l'empereur de la Chine en font tous les jours. Il est vrai que les vers de l'empereur de la Chine ne sont pas sur les confédérés, mais c'est aux confédérés que le roi de Prusse et mon Courlandais s'adressent.

Au reste, madame, nos nouvellistes disent que, voyant enfin qu'il ne paraissait aucun Godefroi de Bouillon, aucun Renaud, aucun Tancrède pour seconder vos héros, et que personne ne voulait gagner des indulgences plénières en allant reprendre Jérusalem, vous vous amusez à négocier une trêve avec ces vilains Turcs. Tout ce que vous ferez sera bien fait; mais je voudrais qu'ils fussent tous au fond de la mer Égée.

Je ne vous parle point des autres nouvelles qu'on débite; elles me déplairaient beaucoup si elles étaient vraies; mais je ne crois point à cette bavarde qu'on appelle la *Renommée*, je ne crois qu'à la gloire; elle est toujours auprès de vous: elle sait de quoi il s'agit, elle bâtit le temple de Mémoire à Pétersbourg, et je l'encense du fond de ma chaumière.

Je me mets aux pieds de la déesse et de la fondatrice du temple, avec la reconnaissance, le profond respect, et l'attachement que mon cœur lui doit.

CXI

DE VOLTAIRE

A Ferney, 6 mars 1772

Madame, j'ai été sur le point de délivrer pour jamais votre majesté impériale de l'ennui de mes inutiles lettres: et tandis que le roi de Prusse achevait son poëme contre les confédérés; tandis qu'un de nos Français entrait, dit-on, par un trou, comme un blaireau, dans Cracovie; tandis que Moustapha s'obstinait à se faire battre, et que l'aventure de Copenhague étonnait toute l'Europe, je me mourais tout doucement dans mon ermitage, et je partais pour aller saluer ce Pierre-le-Grand, qui prépara tous les prodiges que vous faites, et qui ne se doutait pas qu'ils dussent aller si loin.

Permettez qu'en recouvrant ma faible santé, pour un temps bien court, je mette à vos pieds mes respects et mes chagrins. Ces chagrins sont que des gens de ma nation s'avisent d'aller combattre chez des Sarmates contre un roi légitimement élu, plein de vertu, de sagesse, et de bonté, avec lequel ils n'ont rien à démêler, et qui ne les connaît pas. Cela me paraît le comble de l'absurdité, du ridicule, et de l'injustice.

Mon autre chagrin, c'est que les Grecs soient indignes de la liberté, qu'ils auraient recouvrée s'ils avaient eu le courage de vous seconder. Je ne veux plus lire ni Sophocle, ni Homère, ni Démosthène. Je détesterais jusqu'à la religion grecque, si votre majesté impériale n'était pas à la tête de cette église.

Je vois bien, madame, que vous n'êtes pas iconoclaste, puisque vous achetez tant de tableaux, tandis que Moustapha n'en a pas un. Il y a dans le monde un portrait que je préfère à toute la collection des tableaux dont vous allez embellir votre palais; je l'ai mis sur ma poitrine lorsque j'ai cru mourir, et j'imagine que ce topique m'a conservé un peu de vie. J'emploie le peu qui m'en reste à gémir sur la Pologne, à faire des vœux pour Ali-Bey, à dire des injures à Moustapha, à vous souhaiter une longue file de prospérités, tous les plaisirs possibles, et tous les lauriers, dont vous avez déjà une collection plus grande que celle de vos tableaux.

Que votre majesté impériale daigne agréer, avec sa bonté ordinaire, le profond respect, l'attachement, et les bavarderies de l'ermite du mont Jura.

J'apprends, dans le moment, que mes horlogers de Ferney ont eu la hardiesse d'écrire à votre majesté; je ne doute pas qu'elle ne pardonne à la liberté qu'ils ont prise de la remercier.

CXII

DE VOLTAIRE

A Ferney, 12 mars 1772

Madame, la lettre de votre majesté impériale, du 30 janvier, vieux style, bien ou mal datée, semble m'avoir ranimé, comme vos lettres à vos généraux d'armée semblent devoir faire tomber Moustapha en faiblesse.

L'article de vos cinq cents demoiselles m'intéresse infiniment. Notre Saint-Cyr n'en a pas deux cent cinquante. Je ne sais si vous leur faites jouer des tragédies; tout ce que je sais, c'est que la déclamation, soit tragique, soit comique, me paraît une éducation excellente, qui donne de la grâce à l'esprit et au corps, forme la voix, le maintien, et le goût; on retient cent passages qu'on cite ensuite à propos; cela répand des agréments dans la société, cela fait tous les biens du monde.

Il est vrai que toutes nos pièces roulent sur l'amour: c'est une passion pour laquelle j'ai le plus profond respect; mais je pense, comme votre majesté, qu'il ne faut pas qu'elle se développe de très bonne heure. On pourrait, ce me semble, retrancher de quelques comédies choisies les morceaux les plus dangereux pour de jeunes cœurs, en laissant subsister l'intérêt de la pièce;

il n'y aurait peut-être pas vingt vers à changer dans *le Misanthrope*, et pas quarante lignes dans l'*Avare*.

Si ces demoiselles jouent des tragédies, un jeune homme de mes amis en a fait une depuis peu, dans laquelle on ne peut pas dire que l'amour joue un rôle: ce sont deux espèces de Tartares qui se regardent plutôt comme époux que comme amants; je l'enverrai à votre majesté impériale dès qu'elle sera imprimée. Si elle juge qu'on puisse former un théâtre de nos meilleurs auteurs pour l'éducation de votre Saint-Cyr, je ferai venir de Paris des tragédies et des comédies en feuilles; je les ferai brocher avec des pages blanches, sur lesquelles je ferai écrire les changements nécessaires pour ménager la vertu de vos belles demoiselles. Ce petit travail sera pour moi un amusement et ne nuira pas à ma santé, toute faible qu'elle est. Je serai d'ailleurs soutenu par le plaisir de faire quelque chose qui puisse vous plaire.

Je suppose que votre bataillon de cinq cents filles est un bataillon d'amazones, mais je ne suppose pas qu'elles bannissent les hommes; il faut bien qu'en jouant des pièces de théâtre, la moitié pour le moins de ces jeunes héroïnes fasse des personnages de héros; mais comment feront-elles celui de vieillard dans les comédies? En un mot, j'attends les instructions et les ordres de votre majesté sur tout cela.

Je doute que Moustapha donne une si bonne éducation aux filles de son sérail. Je le crois d'ailleurs, en comique, un fort mauvais plaisant; et, en tragique, je ne le crois pas un Achille.

Ce que j'admire, madame, c'est que vous satisfaites à tout; vous rendez votre cour la plus aimable de l'Europe, dans le temps que vos troupes sont les plus formidables. Ce mélange de grandeur et de grâces, de victoires et de fêtes, me paraît charmant. Tout mon chagrin est d'être dans un âge à ne pouvoir être témoin de tous vos triomphes en tant de genres, et d'être obligé de m'en rapporter à la voix de l'Europe.

J'ai bien un autre chagrin, c'est que mes compatriotes soient dans Cracovie, au lieu d'être à Paris. Je ne peux pas dire que je souhaite qu'ils vous soient présentés avec le grand-visir par quelques uns de vos officiers: cela ne serait pas honnête, et on dit qu'il faut être bon citoyen; j'attends le dénouement de cette affaire, et celui de la pièce que l'on joue actuellement en Danemarck.

Le vieux malade se met aux pieds de votre majesté impériale avec le profond respect et l'attachement qu'il conservera jusqu'au dernier moment de sa vie.

CXIII

DE L'IMPÉRATRICE

Le 19/30 mars 1772

Monsieur, j'ai reçu successivement vos deux lettres du 12 février et du 6 mars. Je n'y ai pas répondu plus tôt à cause d'une blessure que je me suis faite par maladresse à la main droite, ce qui m'a empêchée d'écrire pendant quelques semaines; à peine pouvais-je signer.

Votre dernière lettre m'a vraiment alarmée sur l'état où vous avez été; j'espère que celle-ci vous trouvera rétabli. L'ode de M. Dastec n'est point l'ouvrage d'un malade. Si les hommes pouvaient devenir sages, il y a long-temps que vous les auriez rendus tels. Oh! que j'aime vos écrits! il n'y a rien de mieux selon moi. Si ces fous de confédérés étaient des êtres capables de raison, vous les auriez persuadés, vous les auriez ramenés au droit sens; mais je sais un remède qui les guérira. J'en ai un aussi pour les petits-maîtres sans aveu qui abandonnent Paris, pour venir servir de précepteurs à des brigands. Ce dernier remède vient en Sibérie; ils le prendront sur les lieux. Ces secrets sont efficaces, et ne sont point d'un charlatan.

Si la guerre continue, il ne nous restera guère plus que Byzance à prendre, et, en vérité, je commence à croire que cela n'est pas impossible; mais il faut être sage, et dire avec ceux qui le sont que la paix vaut mieux que la plus belle guerre du monde. Tout cela dépend du seigneur Moustapha. Je suis prête à l'une comme à l'autre: et, quoiqu'on vous dise que la Russie est sur les dents, n'en croyez rien; elle n'a pas encore touché à mille ressources que d'autres puissances ont épuisées, même en temps de paix. De trois ans, elle n'a imposé aucune nouvelle taxe: non que cela ne fût fesable, mais parce que nous avons suffisamment ce qu'il nous faut.

Je sais que les chansonniers de Paris ont débité que j'avais fait enrôler le huitième homme: c'est un mensonge grossier, et qui n'a pas le sens commun. Apparemment qu'il y a chez vous des gens qui aiment à se tromper; il faut leur laisser ce plaisir, parce que tout est au mieux dans ce meilleur des mondes possibles, selon le docteur Pangloss.

Les procédés de M. Tronchin envers moi sont les plus honnêtes du monde. Je suis comme l'impératrice Théodora, j'aime les images, mais il faut qu'elles soient bien peintes. Elle les baisait, c'est ce que je ne fais pas; il pensa lui en arriver malheur.

J'ai reçu la lettre de vos horlogers. Je vous envoie ces noisettes, qui contiennent le germe de l'arbre qu'on appelle cèdre de Sibérie. Vous pouvez les faire planter en terre; ils ne sont rien moins que délicats. Si vous en voulez plus que ce paquet n'en contient, je vous en enverrai.

Recevez mes remerciements de toutes les amitiés que vous me témoignez, et soyez assuré de toute mon estime.

CATERINE

CXIV

DE L'IMPÉRATRICE

Le 23 mars/3 avril 1772

Monsieur, votre lettre du 12 mars m'a causé un contentement bien grand. Rien ne saurait arriver de plus heureux à notre communauté que ce que vous me proposez. Nos demoiselles jouent la comédie et la tragédie: elles ont donné *Zaïre* l'année passée, et pendant ce carnaval elles ont représenté *Zémire*, tragédie russe, et la meilleure de M. Soumarocof, dont vous aurez entendu parler. Ah! monsieur, vous m'obligerez infiniment si vous entreprenez en faveur de ces aimables enfants le travail que vous nommez un amusement, et qui coûterait tant de peine à tout autre. Vous me donnerez par-là une marque bien sensible de cette amitié dont je fais un cas si distingué.

D'ailleurs ces demoiselles, je dois l'avouer, sont charmantes, et tous ceux qui les voient l'avouent aussi. Il y en a de quatorze à quinze ans. Si vous les voyiez, je suis persuadée qu'elles s'attireraient votre approbation. J'ai été plus d'une fois tentée de vous envoyer quelques uns des billets que j'ai reçus d'elles, et qui assurément n'ont pas été composés par leurs maîtres; ils sont trop naturels et trop enfantins. On y voit répandus sur chaque ligne l'innocence, l'agrément, et la gaieté de leur esprit.

Je ne sais si ce bataillon de filles, comme vous le nommez, produira des amazones; mais nous sommes très éloignés, je vous l'avoue, d'en faire des religieuses, et de les rendre étiques à force de brailler la nuit à l'église, comme cela se pratique à Saint-Cyr. Nous les élevons, au contraire, pour les rendre les délices des familles où elles entreront; nous ne les voulons ni prudes ni coquettes; mais aimables, et en état d'élever leurs enfants, d'avoir soin de leur maison.

Voici comment on s'y prend pour distribuer les rôles des pièces de théâtre: on leur dit qu'une telle pièce sera jouée, et on leur demande qui veut jouer tel rôle; il arrive souvent qu'une chambrée entière apprend ce rôle; après quoi on choisit celle qui s'en acquitte le mieux. Celles qui jouent les rôles d'hommes portent, dans les comédies, une espèce de frac long, que nous appelons la mode de ce pays-là. Dans la tragédie, il est aisé d'habiller nos héros convenablement, et pour la pièce, et pour leur état. Les vieillards sont les rôles les plus difficiles et les moins bien rendus: une grande perruque et un bâton ne rident point l'adolescence; ces rôles ont été un peu froids jusqu'ici. Nous avons eu ce carnaval un petit-maître charmant, un Blaise original, une dame de Croupillac admirable, deux soubrettes et un Avocat patelin à ravir, et un Jasmin très intelligent.

Je ne sais pas comment Moustapha pense sur l'article de la comédie; mais il y a quelques années, il donna au monde le spectacle de ses défaites, sans pouvoir se résoudre à changer de rôle. Nous avons ici le kalga sultan, frère du kan, très indépendant, de la Crimée, par la grâce de Dieu et les armes de la Russie. Ce jeune prince tartare est d'un caractère doux; il a de l'esprit, il fait des vers arabes; il ne manque aucun de nos spectacles; il s'y plaît; il va à ma communauté les dimanches après-dîner (lorsqu'il est permis d'y entrer) pendant deux heures, pour voir danser les demoiselles. Vous direz que c'est mener le loup au bercail; mais ne vous effarouchez point: voici comme on s'y prend.

Il y a une très grande salle, dans laquelle on a placé un double rang de balustrades; les enfants dansent dans l'intérieur; le monde est rangé autour des balustrades: et c'est l'unique occasion que les parents ont de voir nos demoiselles, auxquelles il n'est point permis de sortir de douze ans de la maison.

N'ayez pas peur, monsieur; vos Parisiens, qui sont à Cracovie, ne me feront pas grand mal; ils jouent une mauvaise farce, qui finira comme les comédies italiennes.

Il est à appréhender que cette malheureuse histoire du Danemarck ne soit pas la seule qui s'y passe. Je crois avoir répondu, monsieur, à toutes vos questions. Donnez-moi au plus tôt des nouvelles satisfesantes sur votre santé, et soyez persuadé que je suis toujours la même

CATERINE

CXV

DE VOLTAIRE

29 mai 1772

Madame, le vieux malade de Ferney a reçu presque en même temps de votre majesté impériale les deux lettres dont elle l'a honoré; l'une en date du 19 mars, et l'autre, du 5 avril, avec le paquet contenant les fruits du cèdre du Liban, que les dix tribus, chassées par le bon Salmanazar, ont sans doute transplanté en Sibérie.

Votre majesté me comble toujours de faveurs. Je vais semer ces petites fèves, dès que la saison le permettra. Ces cèdres-là ombrageront peut-être un jour des Génevois; mais, du moins, ils n'auront pas sous leurs ombrages des rendez-vous de confédérés sarmates.

J'ai enfin eu l'honneur de voir un des cinq Orlof; les héros qu'on appelle les fils Aymon ne sont qu'au nombre de quatre, ceux-ci sont cinq. J'ai vu celui qui ne se mêle de rien, et qui est philosophe: il m'a étonné, et mes regrets ont redoublé de n'avoir pu jouir de l'honneur de voir les quatre autres; mais votre majesté sait que je mourrai avec un regret bien plus cuisant.

Nos extravagants de chevaliers errants, qui ont couru sans mission, vers la zone glaciale, combattre pour le *liberum veto*, méritent assurément toute votre indignation; mais les dévots à Notre-Dame de Czenstokova sont cent fois plus coupables. Du moins, nos don Quichotte welches ne peuvent se reprocher ni bassesse, ni fanatisme: ils ont été très mal instruits, très imprudents, et très injustes.

J'étais moi-même bien mal instruit, ou plutôt aussi aveugle des yeux de l'âme que de ceux du corps, de ne pas comprendre ce que le roi de Prusse m'écrivait, il y a environ un an: "Vous verrez un dénouement auquel personne ne s'attend". J'avais toujours mon Moustapha en tête; ma chimère sur les frontières de ma Suisse était que, grâce à mon héroïne, il n'y eût plus de Turcs en Turquie. Elle prenait dès ce temps-là même un parti encore plus noble et plus utile, celui de détruire l'anarchie en Pologne, en rendant à chacun ce que chacun croit lui appartenir, et en commençant par elle-même.

Mais qui sait si, après avoir exécuté ce grand projet, elle n'achèvera pas l'autre, et si un jour elle n'aura pas trois capitales, Pétersbourg, Moscou, et Byzance? Cette Byzance est plus agréablement située que les deux autres. Il en sera de votre séjour sur le Bosphore de Thrace comme de mes cèdres du Liban; je ne les verrai pas, mais au moins mes héritiers les verront.

Je ne verrai pas non plus votre Saint-Cyr, qui est fort au-dessus de notre Saint-Cyr. Nos demoiselles seront très dévotes et très honnêtes, mais les vôtres joindront à ces deux bonnes qualités, celle de jouer la comédie, comme elles fesaient autrefois chez nous. L'article de la barbe vous embarrasse; mais si Esther n'avait point de barbe, Mardochée en avait. On prétend même que, lorsque la Mardochée, ornée d'une très courte barbe blonde, vint un jour répéter son rôle avec Esther, tête-à-tête dans sa chambre, cette Esther, tout étonnée, lui dit: Eh! mon Dieu! ma sœur, pourquoi avez-vous mis votre barbe à votre menton? Quoi qu'il en soit, votre majesté impériale allie à merveille le temporel et le spirituel. Elle envoie d'un côté des plénipotentiaires et de l'autre des troupes victorieuses; ainsi elle donnera la paix à main armée; on ne la donne guère autrement.

Enfin je triomphe aussi dans mon coin. J'ai toujours soutenu contre mes contradicteurs opiniâtres que vous viendriez à bout de tout. Il semble que votre courage avait passé dans ma tête. Aucun de mes anti-raisonneurs ne m'a intimidé pendant quatre ans. J'ai enfin gagné obscurément ma gageure, quand vous êtes montée au faîte de la gloire et de la félicité, et quand Moustapha, Kien-long, Ganganelli, et le grand-lama, ne peuvent vous disputer d'être la première personne de notre globe. Cela me rend bien fier.

Mais je n'en suis ni plus ni moins attaché à votre majesté impériale avec le respect que tout le monde vous doit comme moi. *Le vieux malade*

CXVI

DE L'IMPÉRATRICE

A Pétershoff, 25 juin/6 juillet 1772

Monsieur, je vois avec plaisir, par votre lettre du 29 mai, que mes noisettes de cèdres vous sont parvenues: vous les sèmerez à Ferney; j'en ai fait autant ce printemps à Czarskozélo. Ce nom vous paraîtra peut-être un peu dur à prononcer; cependant c'est un endroit que je trouve délicieux, parce que j'y plante et que j'y sème. La baronne de Thunder-ten-tronk trouvait bien son château le plus beau des châteaux possibles. Mes cèdres sont déjà de la hauteur du petit doigt; que sont les vôtres? J'aime à la folie présentement les jardins à l'anglaise, les lignes courbes, les pentes douces, les étangs en forme de lacs, les archipels en terre ferme, et j'ai un profond mépris pour les lignes droites, les allées jumelles. Je hais les fontaines qui donnent la torture à l'eau pour lui faire prendre un cours contraire à sa nature; les statues sont reléguées dans les galeries, les vestibules, etc.; en un mot, l'anglomanie domine dans ma plantomanie.

C'est au milieu de ces occupations que j'attends tranquillement la paix. Mes ambassadeurs sont à Yassi depuis six semaines, et l'armistice pour le Danube, la Crimée, la Géorgie, et la mer Noire, a été signé le 19 de mai, vieux style, à Giurgevo. Les plénipotentiaires turcs sont en chemin au-delà du Danube; leurs équipages, faute de chevaux, sont traînés par la race du dieu Apis. A la fin de chaque campagne, j'ai fait proposer la paix à ces messieurs; ils ne se sont plus apparemment crus en sûreté derrière le mont Hémus, puisque cette fois ils ont parlementé tout de bon. Nous verrons s'ils sont assez sensés pour faire la paix à temps.

Les chalands de la vierge de Czenstokova se cacheront sous le froc de saint François, et ils auront tout le temps de méditer un grand miracle par l'intercession de cette dame. Vos petits-maîtres prisonniers retourneront chez eux débiter avec suffisance, dans les ruelles de Paris, que les Russes sont des barbares qui ne savent pas faire la guerre.

Ma communauté, qui n'est point barbare, se recommande à vos soins. Ne nous oubliez point, je vous en prie. Moi, de mon côté, je vous promets de faire de mon mieux, afin de continuer à donner le tort à ceux qui, contre votre opinion, ont soutenu pendant quatre ans que je succomberais.

Soyez assuré que je suis bien sensible à tous les témoignages d'amitié que vous me donnez. Mon amitié et mon estime pour vous ne finiront qu'avec ma vie.

CATERINE

CXVII

DE VOLTAIRE

A Ferney, 31 juillet 1772

Madame, il y a bien long-temps que je n'ai osé importuner votre majesté impériale de mes inutiles lettres. J'ai présumé que vous étiez dans le commerce le plus vif avec Moustapha et les confédérés de Pologne. Vous les rangez tous à leur devoir, et ils doivent vous remercier tous de leur donner, à quelque prix que ce soit, la paix dont ils avaient très grand besoin.

Votre majesté a peut-être cru que je la boudais, parce qu'elle n'a pas fait le voyage de Stamboul et d'Athènes, comme je l'espérais. J'en suis affligé, il est vrai; mais je ne peux être fâché contre vous, et d'ailleurs si votre majesté ne va pas sur le Bosphore, elle ira du moins faire un tour vers la Vistule. Quelque chose qui arrive, Moustapha a toujours le mérite d'avoir contribué, pour sa part, à votre grandeur, s'il vous a empêchée de continuer votre beau code; et Pallas la guerrière, après l'avoir bien battu, va redevenir Minerve la législatrice.

Il n'y a plus que ce pauvre Ali-Bey qui soit à plaindre; on le dit battu et en fuite: c'est dommage. Je le croyais paisible possesseur du beau pays où l'on adorait autrefois les chats et les chiens; mais, comme vous êtes plus voisine de la Prusse que de l'Égypte, je pense que vous vous consolez du petit malheur arrivé à mon cher Ali-Bey. Je présume aussi que votre majesté n'a point fait faire le voyage de Sibérie à nos étourdis de Français qui ont été en Pologne où ils n'avaient que faire. Puisqu'ils aimaient à voyager, il fallait qu'ils vinssent vous admirer à Pétersbourg; cela eût été plus sensé, plus décent, et beaucoup plus agréable. Pour moi, c'est ainsi que j'en userais si je n'étais pas octogénaire. J'estime fort Notre-Dame de Czenstokova; mais j'aurais donné, dans mon pèlerinage, la préférence à Notre-Dame de Pétersbourg. Je n'ai plus qu'un souffle de vie, je l'emploierai à vous invoquer, en mourant, comme ma sainte, et la plus sainte assurément que le nord ait jamais portée.

Le vieux malade de Ferney se met à vos pieds avec le plus profond respect et une reconnaissance qui ne finira qu'avec sa vie.

CXVIII

DE VOLTAIRE

A Ferney, 21 auguste 1772

Madame, je ne cesse d'admirer celle qui, ayant tous les jours à écrire en Turquie, à la Chine, en Pologne, trouve encore du temps pour daigner écrire au vieux malade du mont Jura. Il y a long-temps que je sais que vous avez plusieurs âmes, en dépit des théologiens, qui aujourd'hui n'en admettent qu'une. Mais enfin votre majesté impériale n'a pas plusieurs mains droites; elle n'a qu'une langue pour dicter, et la journée n'a que vingt-quatre heures pour vous, ainsi que pour les Turcs, qui ne savent ni lire ni écrire; en un mot, vous m'étonnez toujours, quoique je me sois promis depuis long-temps de n'être plus étonné de rien.

Je ne suis pas même étonné que mes cèdres n'aient point germé, tandis que ceux de votre majesté sont déjà de quelques lignes hors de terre. Il n'est pas juste que la nature me traite aussi bien que vous. Si vous plantiez des lauriers au mois de janvier, je suis sûr qu'ils vous donneraient au mois de juin de quoi mettre autour de votre tête.

Je ne sais pas s'il est vrai que les dames de Cracovie fassent bâtir en France un château pour nos officiers. Je doute que les Polonaises aient assez d'argent de reste pour payer ce monument. Ce château pourrait bien être celui d'Armide, ou quelque château en Espagne.

Ce qui doit paraître plus fabuleux à nos Français, et qui cependant est très vrai, à ce qu'on m'assure, c'est que votre majesté, après quatre ans de guerre, et par conséquent de dépenses prodigieuses, augmente la paie de ses armées d'un cinquième. Notre ministre des finances doit tomber à la renverse en apprenant cette nouvelle.

Je me flatte que Falconet en dira deux mots sur la base de votre statue; je me flatte encore que ce cinquième sera pris dans les bourses que mon cher Moustapha sera obligé de vous payer, pour les frais du procès qu'il vous a intenté si maladroitement.

Je vous annonce aujourd'hui un gentilhomme flamand, jeune, brave, instruit, sachant plusieurs langues, voulant absolument apprendre le russe, et être à votre service; de plus, bon musicien: il s'appelle le baron de Pellemberg. Ayant su que je devais avoir l'honneur de vous écrire, il s'est offert pour courrier, et le voilà parti; il en sera ce qu'il pourra; tout ce que je sais, c'est qu'il en viendra bien d'autres, et que je voudrais bien être du nombre.

Voici le temps, madame, où vous devez jouir de vos beaux jardins qui, grâce à votre bon goût, ne sont point symétrisés. Puissent tous les cèdres du Liban y croître avec les palmes!

Le vieux malade de Ferney se met aux pieds de votre majesté impériale, avec le plus profond respect et la plus sensible reconnaissance.

CXIX

DE VOLTAIRE

A Ferney, 28 auguste 1772

Madame, pardon; mais, non seulement votre majesté impériale me protége, elle m'instruit; elle a bien voulu me défaire de quelques erreurs françaises sur la Sibérie; elle me permet les questions.

Je prends donc la liberté de lui demander s'il est vrai qu'il y ait en Sibérie une espèce de héron tout blanc, avec les ailes et la queue couleur de feu, et surtout s'il est vrai que, par la paix du Pruth, Pierre-le-Grand se soit obligé à envoyer tous les ans un de ces oiseaux avec un collier de diamants à la Porte ottomane. Nos livres disent que cet oiseau s'appelle, chez vous, *kratsshot*, et chez les Turcs, *chungar*.

Je doute fort, madame, que votre majesté impériale paie désormais un tribut de chungar et de diamants au seigneur Moustapha. Les gazettes disent qu'elle achète un diamant d'environ trois millions à Amsterdam; j'espère que Moustapha paiera ce brillant en signant le traité de paix, s'il sait écrire.

Votre extrême indulgence m'a accoutumé à la hardiesse de questionner une impératrice: cela n'est pas ordinaire; mais, en vérité, il n'y a rien de si extraordinaire dans le monde entier que votre majesté, aux pieds de laquelle se met, avec le plus profond respect, *Le vieux malade de Ferney*

CXX

DE L'IMPÉRATRICE

Le 1/12 septembre 1772

Monsieur, j'ai à vous annoncer, en réponse à votre lettre du 21 d'auguste, que je vais commencer avec Moustapha une nouvelle correspondance à coups de canon. Il lui a plu d'ordonner à ses plénipotentiaires de rompre le congrès de Fokschan; la trève finit avec lui. C'est apparemment l'âme qui a ce département-là qui vous a dit cette nouvelle. Je vous prie de m'instruire de ce que font les autres âmes que vous me donnez, tandis que je pense à Moustapha. Il m'a toujours paru que je n'avais à la fois qu'une seule idée. J'espère au moins que messieurs les théologiens me feront un compliment en cérémonie au premier concile œcuménique où je présiderai, pour avoir soutenu leur opinion en cette occasion.

Je crois qu'il faut ranger le château que les dames polonaises prétendent bâtir aux officiers français engagés au service des prétendus confédérés, au nombre de beaucoup d'autres bâtiments pareils, élevés dans l'imagination de l'une et l'autre nation depuis plusieurs années, et qui se sont évaporés en particules si subtiles, que personne ne les a pu apercevoir. Il n'y a pas jusqu'aux miracles de la Dame de Czenstokova qui n'aient eu ce sort, depuis que les moines de ce couvent se trouvent en compagnie d'un beau régiment d'infanterie russe, lequel occupe maintenant cette forteresse.

On ne vous a point trompé, monsieur, lorsqu'on vous a dit que j'ai augmenté, ce printemps, d'un cinquième la paie de tous mes officiers militaires, depuis le maréchal jusqu'à l'enseigne. J'ai acheté en même temps la collection de tableaux de feu M. de Crozat, et je suis en marché d'un diamant de la grosseur d'un œuf.

Il est vrai qu'en augmentant ainsi ma dépense, d'un autre côté mes possessions se sont aussi accrues un peu, par un accord fait entre la cour de Vienne, le roi de Prusse, et moi. Nous n'avons point trouvé d'autre moyen de garantir nos frontières des incursions des prétendus confédérés, commandés par des officiers français, que de les étendre.

A propos, que dites-vous de la révolution de Suède? Voilà une nation qui perd, en moins d'un quart d'heure, sa forme de gouvernement et sa liberté. Les états, entourés de troupes et de canons, ont délibéré vingt minutes sur cinquante-sept points qu'ils ont signés, comme de raison. Je ne sais si cette violence est douce; mais je vous garantis la Suède sans liberté, et son roi aussi despotique que celui de France, et cela, deux mois après que le souverain et la nation s'étaient juré réciproquement la stricte conservation de leurs droits.

Le père Adam ne trouve-t-il pas que voilà bien des consciences en danger?

Adieu, monsieur; souvenez-vous de moi en bien, et soyez assuré du sensible plaisir que me font vos lettres. Vous pourriez m'en faire un plus grand encore, ce serait de vous bien porter en dépit de vos années.

CATERINE

CXXI

DE VOLTAIRE

Septembre 1772

Madame, votre rhinocéros n'est pas ce qui me surprend; il se peut très bien que quelque Indien ait amené autrefois un rhinocéros en Sibérie, comme on en a conduit en France et en Hollande. Si Annibal fit passer les Alpes à travers les neiges à des éléphants, votre Sibérie peut avoir vu autrefois les mêmes tentatives, et les os de ces animaux peuvent s'être conservés dans les sables. Je ne crois pas que la position de l'équateur ait jamais changé; mais je crois que le monde est bien vieux.

Ce qui m'étonne davantage, c'est votre inconnu, qui fait des comédies dignes de Molière; et, pour dire encore plus, dignes de faire rire votre majesté impériale; car les majestés rient rarement, quoiqu'elles aient besoin de rire. Si un génie tel que le vôtre trouve des comédies plaisantes, elles le sont sans doute. J'ai demandé à votre majesté des cèdres de Sibérie, j'ose lui demander à présent une comédie de Pétersbourg. Il serait aisé d'en faire une traduction. Je suis né trop tôt pour apprendre la langue de votre empire. Si les Grecs avaient été dignes de ce que vous avez fait pour eux, la langue grecque serait aujourd'hui la langue universelle; mais la langue russe pourrait bien prendre sa place. Je sais qu'il y a beaucoup de plaisanteries dont le sel n'est convenable qu'aux temps et aux lieux, mais il y en a aussi qui sont de tous pays, et ce sont sans contredit les meilleures. Je suis sûr qu'il y en a beaucoup de cette espèce dans la comédie qui vous a plu davantage; c'est celle-là dont je prends la liberté de demander la traduction. Il est assez beau, ce me semble, de faire traduire une pièce de théâtre, quand on joue un si grand rôle sur le théâtre de l'univers. Je ne demanderai jamais une traduction à Moustapha, encore moins à Pulauski.

Le dernier acte de votre grande tragédie paraît bien beau; le théâtre ne sera pas ensanglanté, et la gloire fera le dénouement.

CXXII

DE VOLTAIRE

1er octobre 1772

Comment se peut-il faire qu'il y ait encore chez nos Welches de prétendus raisonneurs et de prétendus politiques qui osent dire que "Pierre le Grand a tout épuisé pour former une armée, une flotte et un port, et que ses successeurs achèveront de tout ruiner pour soutenir l'ostentation de ces vains établisements"? Ce sont les propres paroles de la page 204 d'un nouveau livre intitulé: *Histoire philosophique et politique des établissements et du commerce des Européens aux Indes.* Il y a d'ailleurs de très-bonnes choses dans ce livre; mais cette sottise est pillée de ce fou de Jean-Jacques Rousseau, qui s'est avisé de juger souverainement tous les rois du haut de son grenier.

Il me semble que tous vos succès auraient dû apprendre à tous les législateurs à être un peu plus réservés dans leurs discours: quand on étonne tous les sages, on doit confondre tous les sots.

Que Votre Majesté Impériale daigne conserver ses bontés à son vieux malade de Ferney.

CXXIII

DE L'IMPÉRATRICE

Le 6/17 octobre 1772

Monsieur, je ne vous dispute point la possibilité de la venue des rhinocéros et des éléphants des Indes en Sibérie: cela se peut. Je ne vous ai envoyé le récit de notre savant que comme un simple objet de curiosité, et nullement pour appuyer mon opinion. Je vous avoue que j'aimerais que l'équateur changeât de position: l'idée riante que dans vingt mille ans la Sibérie, au lieu de glaces, pourra être couverte d'orangers et de citronniers, me fait plaisir dès à présent.

Dès que la traduction de la comédie russe qui nous a fait

le plus rire sera achevée, elle prendra le chemin de Ferney. Vous direz peut-être, après l'avoir lue, qu'il est plus aisé de me faire rire que les autres majestés, et vous aurez raison: le fond de mon caractère est extrêmement gai.

On trouve ici que l'auteur anonyme de ces nouvelles comédies russes, quoiqu'il annonce du talent, a de grands défauts; qu'il ne connaît point le théâtre, que ses intrigues sont faibles, mais qu'il n'en est pas de même des caractères qu'il trace; que ceux-ci sont soutenus et pris dans la nature qu'il a devant les yeux; qu'il a des saillies, qu'il fait rire, que sa morale est pure, et qu'il connaît bien sa nation: mais je ne sais si tout cela soutiendra la traduction.

En vous parlant de comédies, permettez, monsieur, que je rappelle à votre mémoire la promesse que vous avez bien voulu me faire, il y a près d'un an, d'accommoder quelques bonnes pièces de théâtre pour mes instituts d'éducation. Je ne vous parle point aujourd'hui de la grande tragédie de la guerre, du congrès rompu, du congrès renoué, de la trève prolongée; j'espère vous mander dans peu la fin de tout ceci. Vous serez un des premiers instruits de la signature du traité définitif; après quoi nous nous réjouirons.

Je suis, comme je serai toujours, monsieur, avec l'estime et la considération la plus distinguée,

CATERINE

CXXIV

DE VOLTAIRE

2 novembre 1772

Madame, il me paraît, par votre dépêche du 12 septembre, qu'il y a une de vos âmes qui fait plus de miracles que Notre-Dame de Czenstokova, nom très difficile à prononcer. Votre majesté impériale m'avouera que la *Santa-Casa di Loretta* est beaucoup plus douce à l'oreille, et qu'elle est bien plus miraculeuse, puisqu'elle est mille fois plus riche que votre *sainte Vierge* polonaise. Du moins les musulmans n'ont pas de semblables superstitions, car leur sainte maison de la Mecque, ou Mecca, est beaucoup plus ancienne que le mahométisme, et même que le judaïsme. Les musulmans n'adorent point, comme nous autres, une foule de saints, dont la plupart n'ont point existé, et parmi lesquels il n'y en a pas quatre peut-être avec qui vous eussiez daigné souper.

Mais aussi voilà tout ce que vos Turcs ont de bon. Je suis très content, puisque mon impératrice reprend l'habitude de leur donner sur les oreilles.

Je remercie de tout mon cœur votre majesté de vous être avancée vers le midi; je vois bien qu'à la fin je serai en état de faire le voyage que j'ai projeté depuis long-temps; vous accourcissez ma route de jour en jour. Voilà trois belles et bonnes têtes dans un bonnet: la vôtre, celle de l'empereur des Romains, et celle du roi de Prusse.

Le dernier m'a envoyé sa belle médaille de *regno redintegrato*. Ce mot de *redintegrato* est singulier, j'aurais autant aimé *novo*. Le *redintegrato* conviendrait mieux à l'empereur des Romains, s'il voulait monter à cheval avec vous, et reprendre une partie de ce qui appartenait autrefois, si légitimement, par usurpation, au trône des Césars, à condition que vous prendriez tout le reste, qui ne vous appartint jamais, toujours en allant vers le midi, pour la facilité de mon voyage.

Il y a environ quatre ans que je prêche cette petite croisade. Quelques esprits creux, comme moi, prétendent que le temps approche où sainte Marie-Thérèse, de concert avec sainte Catherine, exaucera mes ferventes prières; ils disent que rien n'est plus aisé que de prendre en une campagne la Bosnie, la Servie, et de vous donner la main à Andrinople. Ce serait un spectacle charmant de voir deux impératrices tirer les deux oreilles à Moustapha, et le renvoyer en Asie.

Certainement, disent-ils, puisque ces deux braves dames se sont si bien entendues pour changer la face de la Pologne, elles s'entendront encore mieux pour changer celle de la Turquie.

Voici le temps des grandes révolutions, voici un nouvel univers créé, d'Archangel au Borysthène; il ne faut pas s'arrêter en si beau chemin. Les étendards portés de vos belles mains sur le tombeau de Pierre-le-Grand, par ma foi moins grand que vous, doivent être suivis de l'étendard du grand prophète.

Alors je demanderai une seconde fois la protection de votre majesté impériale pour ma colonie, qui fournira de montres votre empire, et les coiffures de blondes aux dames de vos palais.

Quant à la révolution de Suède, j'ai bien peur qu'elle ne cause un jour quelque petit embarras; mais la cour de France n'aura de long-temps assez d'argent pour seconder les bonnes intentions qu'on pourrait avoir avec le temps dans cette partie du nord, qui n'est pas la plus fertile, à moins qu'on ne vous vende le diamant nommé le *pitt* ou *le régent*; mais il n'est gros que comme un œuf de pigeon, et le vôtre est plus gros qu'un œuf de poule.

Je me mets à vos pieds avec l'enthousiasme d'un jeune homme de vingt ans, et les rêveries d'un vieillard de près de quatre-vingts.

CXXV

DE L'IMPÉRATRICE

Le 11/22 novembre 1772

Monsieur, j'ai reçu votre lettre du 2 de novembre, lorsque je répondais à une belle et longue lettre que M. d'Alembert m'écrit après un silence de cinq ou six ans, et dans laquelle il réclame, au nom des philosophes et de la philosophie, les Français faits prisonniers en différents endroits de la Pologne. Le billet ci-joint contient ma réponse.

Je suis fâchée que la calomnie ait induit les philosophes en erreur. M. de Moustapha revient de la sienne; il fait travailler de très bonne foi, à Bucharest, son reis-effendi au rétablissement de la paix, après quoi il pourra renouveler les pèlerinages de la Mecque, que le seigneur Ali-Bey avait un peu dérangés depuis sa levée de bouclier. Je ne sais pas jusqu'où les Turcs poussent le respect pour leurs saints; mais je suis témoin oculaire qu'ils en ont. Voici le fait:

Lors de mon voyage sur le Volga, je descendis de ma galère à vingt verstes plus bas que la ville de Casan, pour voir les ruines de l'ancienne Bulgar, que Tamerlan avait bâtie pour son petit-fils. J'y trouvai en effet sept à huit maisons de pierre, et autant de minarets construits très solidement. Je m'approchai d'une masure, près de laquelle se tenaient une quarantaine de Tartares. Le gouverneur de la province me dit que cet endroit était un lieu de dévotion pour ces gens-là, et que ceux que je voyais y étaient venus en pèlerinage. Je voulus savoir en quoi consistait cette dévotion; pour cet effet, je m'adressai à un de ces Tartares, dont la physionomie me parut prévenante: il me fit signe qu'il n'entendait pas le russe et se mit à courir pour appeler un homme qui se tenait à quelques pas de là. Cet homme s'approcha, et je lui demandai qui il était. C'était un iman qui parlait assez bien notre langage: il me dit que dans cette masure avait habité un homme d'une vie sainte, qu'ils venaient de fort loin pour faire leurs prières sur son tombeau, lequel était près de là. Ce qu'il me conta me fit conclure que c'était assez l'équivalent du culte de nos saints.

C'est le roi de Suède qui donnera lieu au moyen de raccourcir votre voyage, s'il s'empare de la Norvége, comme on le débite. La guerre pourrait bien devenir général par cette escapade politique. Si la France n'a pas d'argent, l'Espagne en a suffisamment; et il faut avouer qu'il n'y a rien de plus commode qu'un autre paie pour nous.

Adieu, monsieur; conservez-moi votre amitié. Je vous souhaite de tout mon cœur les années de l'Anglais Jean Kings, qui a vécu jusqu'à cent soixante-neuf ans. Le bel âge!

CATERINE

CXXVI

DE VOLTAIRE

1er décembre 1772

Madame, j'avoue qu'il est assez singulier qu'en donnant la paix aux Turcs, et des lois à la Pologne, on me donne aussi une traduction d'une comédie. Je vois bien qu'il y a certaines âmes qui ne sont pas embarrassées de leur universalité; je n'en suis pas moins fâché contre votre majesté impériale de l'église grecque, et contre la majesté impériale de l'église romaine, qui pouvaient souffleter toutes deux, de leurs mains blanches, la majesté de Moustapha, rendre la liberté à toutes les dames du sérail, et rebénir Sainte-Sophie. Je ne vous pardonnerai jamais, mesdames, de ne vous être pas entendues pour faire ce beau coup. On aurait cessé à jamais de parler de Clorinde et d'Armide; il ne serait plus question de Goffredo. Il valait certainement mieux prendre Constantinople qu'une vilaine ville de Jérusalem; le Bosphore vaut mieux que le torrent de Cédron. J'ai essuyé là une mortification terrible; mais enfin je m'en console par la gloire que vous avez acquise, et par tout le solide attaché à votre gloire, et même encore par l'espérance que ce qui est différé n'est pas perdu.

Oserai-je, madame, tout fâché que je suis contre vous, demander une grâce à votre majesté impériale? Elle ne regarde ni Moustapha ni son grand-visir: c'est pour un ingénieur de mon pays, qui est, comme moi, moitié Français, moitié Suisse. C'est un bon physicien, qui fait actuellement dans nos Alpes des expériences sur la glace; car nous avons des glaces ici tout comme à Pétersbourg. Cet ingénieur se nomme Aubry; il est peu connu, mais il mérite de l'être. Ce serait une nouvelle grâce dont j'aurais une obligation infinie à votre majesté, si elle daignait lui faire accorder une patente d'associé à votre illustre académie. Il est vrai que nous n'avons pas de glace à présent, ce qui est fort rare, mais nous en aurons incessamment.

Je demande très humblement pardon de ma hardiesse; votre indulgence m'a depuis long-temps accoutumé à de telles libertés.

C'est une chose bien ridicule et bien commune que tous les bruits qui courent dans la bavarde ville de Paris, sur votre congrès de Fokschan et sur tout ce qui peut y avoir quelque rapport. Les rois sont comme les dieux; les peuples en font mille contes, et les dieux boivent leur nectar sans se mettre en peine de la théologie des chétifs mortels. Je suis, par exemple, très sûr que vous ne vous souciez point du tout de la colère où je suis que vous n'alliez point passer l'hiver sur le Bosphore. Je suis tout aussi sûr que je mourrai inconsolable de ne m'être point jeté à vos pieds à Pétersbourg; mon cœur y est, si mon corps n'y est pas. Ce pauvre corps de près de quatre-vingts ans n'en peut plus, et ce cœur est pénétré pour votre majesté impériale du plus profond respect et de la plus sensible reconnaissance.

CXXVII

DE VOLTAIRE

A Ferney, 11 décembre 1772

Madame, votre oiseau qu'on appelle *flamant*, ressemble assez aux caricatures que mon ami M. Huber a faites de moi; il m'a donné le cou et les jambes, et même un peu de la physionomie de ce prétendu héron blanc. Je me doutais bien que jamais Pierre-le-Grand n'avait payé un pareil tribut au seigneur de Stamboul.

On doit assurément un tribut de louanges à votre majesté impériale, pour vos beaux établissements de garçons et de filles. Je ne sais pas pourquoi on ose encore parler de Lycurgue et de ses Lacédémoniens, qui n'ont jamais rien fait de grand, qui n'ont laissé aucun monument, qui n'ont point cultivé les arts, qui sont depuis si long-temps esclaves des barbares que vous avez vaincus pendant quatre années de suite.

La lettre qui est venue dans le paquet de la part de M. de Betzky est bien précieuse; je la crois de notre Falconet; mais ce que votre majesté impériale a daigné m'écrire sur votre institution du *plus que Saint-Cyr*, est bien au-dessus de la lettre imprimée de Falconet, qui pourtant est bonne.

Étant né trop tôt, et ne pouvant être témoin de tout ce que fait ma grande impératrice, j'ai saisi l'occasion de lui envoyer ce jeune baron de Pellemberg, qui est un tiers d'allemand, un tiers de flamand, et un tiers d'espagnol, et qui voulait changer ces trois tiers pour une totalité russe. Je ne le connais, madame, que par son enthousiasme pour votre personne unique; je ne l'ai vu qu'en passant: il m'a demandé une lettre, j'ai pris la liberté de la lui donner, comme j'en donnerai, si vous le permettez, à quiconque voudra faire le pèlerinage de Pétersbourg par pure dévotion pour sainte Catherine II.

On me dit une triste nouvelle pour moi, que ce Polianski, que votre majesté impériale a fait voyager, et dont j'ai tant aimé et estimé le caractère, s'est noyé dans la Néva, en revenant à Pétersbourg; si cela est, j'en suis extrêmement affligé. Il y aura toujours des malheurs particuliers, mais vous faites le bonheur public. Le mien est dans les lettres dont vous m'honorez. J'attends la comédie; je la ferai jouer dans ma petite colonie le jour que je ferai un feu de joie pour la paix de Fokschan ou de Bucharest, supposé que vous gardiez par cette paix trois ou quatre provinces, et l'empire de la mer Noire. Mais je proteste toujours contre toute paix qui ne vous donnera pas Stamboul. Ce Stamboul était l'objet de mes vœux, comme sainte Catherine II l'objet de mon culte. Puisse ma sainte goûter toutes les sortes de plaisirs comme elle a toute sorte de gloire!

Le vieux malade de Ferney, qui n'a ni gloire, ni plaisir

CXXVIII

DE VOLTAIRE

Le 3 janvier 1773

Madame, je serais bien fâché qu'on ne fût pas philosophe vers la Norvége. Cette équipée me paraîtrait fort prématurée; elle pourrait fournir quelques nouveaux lauriers à votre couronne; mais ils sont un peu secs dans cette partie du monde, et je les aimais mieux vers le Danube.

Ma philosophie pacifique prend la liberté de présenter à votre majesté impériale une consultation. Sous Pierre-le-Grand, votre académie demandait des lumières, et on a recours aux siennes sous Catherine-la-Grande.

C'est un ingénieur un peu Suisse comme moi, qui cherche à prévenir les ravages que font continuellement les eaux dans les branches de nos Alpes. Il a jugé que vous vous connaissez encore mieux en glace que nous. Il est vrai pourtant qu'avec notre quarante-sixième degré, et la douceur inouïe de notre présent hiver, nous éprouvons quelquefois des froids aussi cruels que les vôtres. J'ai imaginé de faire passer cette consultation par vos très belles mains, dont on m'a tant parlé, et que mon extrême jeunesse et mon respect me défendent de baiser.

Cet ingénieur, nommé Aubry, mourra d'ailleurs de la jaunisse, s'il n'est pas associé de l'académie: j'ai l'honneur d'en être depuis long-temps: de qui emploierai-je la protection, si ce n'est de notre souveraine!

M. Polianski m'apprend qu'il n'est point noyé, comme on l'avait dit; qu'au contraire il est dans le port, et que votre majesté l'a fait secrétaire de l'académie. Je présume que vous pourrez avoir la bonté de lui donner la consultation. Nous avons assez près de nous Notre-Dame-des-Neiges, que j'aurais pu employer dans cette affaire qui la regarde; mais je ne prie jamais que Notre-Dame de Pétersbourg, dont je baise les pieds en toute humilité avec la plus sincère dévotion.

CXXIX

DE VOLTAIRE

A Ferney, 13 février 1773

Madame, ce qui m'a principalement étonné de vos deux comédies russes, c'est que le dialogue est toujours vrai et toujours naturel, ce qui est à mon avis un des premiers mérites dans l'art de la comédie; mais un mérite bien rare, c'est de cultiver ainsi tous les arts, lorsque celui de la guerre occupait toute la nation. Je vois que les Russes ont bien de l'esprit et du bon esprit; votre majesté impériale n'était pas faite pour gouverner des sots; c'est ce qui m'a toujours fait penser que la nature l'avait destinée à régner sur la Grèce. J'en reviens toujours à mon premier roman; vous finirez par là. Il arrivera que dans dix ans Moustapha se brouillera avec vous, il vous chicanera sur la Crimée, et vous lui prendrez Byzance. Vous voilà tout accoutumée à des partages; l'empire turc sera partagé, et vous ferez jouer l'*Œdipe* de Sophocle dans Athènes.

Je me borne à me réjouir de voir que les dissidents, pour lesquels je m'étais tant intéressé, aient enfin gagné leur procès. J'espère même que les sociniens auront bientôt en Lithuanie quelque conventicule public, où Dieu le père ne partagera plus avec personne le trône qu'il occupa tout seul jusqu'au concile de Nicée. Il est bien plaisant que les Juifs, qui ont crucifié le *logos*, aient tant de synagogues chez les Polonais, et que ceux qui diffèrent d'opinions avec la cour romaine sur le *logos* ne puissent avoir un trou pour fourrer leurs têtes.

J'aurai bientôt quelque chose à mettre aux pieds de votre majesté impériale sur les horreurs de toutes ces disputes ecclésiastiques: c'est là mon objet; je ne m'en écarte point; c'est la tolérance que je veux, c'est la religion que je prêche, et vous êtes à la tête du synode dans lequel je ne suis qu'un simple moine. Si ma strangurie m'emporte, vous n'en recevrez pas moins ma bagatelle.

Nous avons actuellement l'honneur d'avoir autant de neiges et de glaces que vous. Un corps aussi faible que le mien n'y peut pas résister. Bienheureux sont les enfants de Rurick! encore plus heureux les Lapons et leurs rangifères, qui ne peuvent vivre que dans leur climat! Cela me prouve que la nature a fait chaque espèce pour sa gaîne, et qu'elle a mis des Samoïèdes au septentrion, comme des Nègres au midi, sans que les uns soient venus des autres.

Je vous avais bien dit que je radotais, madame: vivez heureuse et comblée de gloire, sans oublier les plaisirs; cela n'est pas si radoteur.

Je me mets aux pieds de votre majesté impériale, avec le plus profond respect et le plus sincère attachement.

Le vieux malade de Ferney

CXXX

DE L'IMPÉRATRICE

A Pétersbourg, le 20 février/3 mars 1773

Monsieur, j'espère qu'il n'est plus question de la colère que vous aviez, le premier décembre, contre les majestés impériales de l'église grecque et romaine.

Le prince Orlof, qui aime la physique expérimentale, et qui naturellement est doué d'une perspicacité particulière sur toutes ces matières-là, est peut-être celui qui a fait la plus curieuse de toutes les expériences sur la glace. La voici:

Il a fait creuser en automne les fondements d'une porte cochère, et pendant les plus fortes gelées de l'hiver, il a fait remplir d'eau ces fondements, afin qu'elle s'y convertît en glace. Lorsqu'ils furent remplis à la hauteur convenable, on les garantit soigneusement des rayons du soleil, et au printemps on éleva dessus une porte cochère voûtée en briques et très solide. Elle existe depuis quatre ans, et elle existera, je crois, jusqu'à ce qu'on l'abatte. Il est bon de remarquer que le terrain sur lequel cette porte est bâtie est marécageux, et que la glace tient lieu du pilotis qu'on aurait été obligé d'employer à son défaut.

L'expérience de la bombe remplie d'eau, et exposée à la gelée, a été faite en ma présence; elle a crevé en moins d'une heure avec beaucoup de fracas.

Quand on vous a dit que la gelée élève des maisons hors de terre, on aurait dû ajouter que cela arrive à de mauvaises baraques de bois, mais jamais à des maisons de pierres. Il est vrai que des murs de jardin assez minces, et dont les fondements sont mal assis, ont été levés de terre et renversés peu à peu par la gelée. Les pilotis que la glace peut accrocher se soulèvent aussi à la longue.

Si les Turcs continuent de suivre les bons conseils de leurs soi-disant amis, vous pouvez être sûr que vos souhaits de nous voir sur le Bosphore seront bien près de leur accomplissement, et cela viendra peut-être fort à propos pour votre convalescence; car j'espère que vous vous êtes défait de cette vilaine fièvre continue que vous m'annoncez, et dont jamais je ne me serais doutée en voyant la gaieté qui règne dans vos lettres.

Je lis présentement les œuvres d'Algarotti. Il prétend que tous les arts et toutes les sciences sont nés en Grèce. Dites-moi, je vous prie, cela est-il bien vrai? Pour de l'esprit, ils en ont encore, et du plus délié; mais ils sont si abattus qu'il n'y a plus de nerf chez eux. Cependant je commence à croire qu'à la longue on pourrait les aguerrir: témoin cette nouvelle victoire de Patras remportée sur les Turcs après la fin du second armistice. Le comte Alexis me mande qu'il y en a qui se sont admirablement comportés.

Il y a eu aussi quelque chose de pareil sur les côtes d'Égypte, dont je n'ai point encore les détails; et c'était encore un capitaine grec qui commandait. Votre baron Pellemberg est à l'armée. M. Polianski est secrétaire de l'académie des beaux-arts. Il n'est pas noyé, quoi qu'il passe souvent la Néva en carrosse; mais chez nous il n'y a pas de danger à cela en hiver.

Je suis bien aise d'apprendre que mes deux comédies ne vous ont pas paru tout à fait mauvaises. J'attends avec impatience le nouvel écrit que vous me promettez; mais j'en ai encore plus de vous savoir rétabli.

Soyez assuré, monsieur, de mon extrême sensibilité pour tout ce que vous me dites d'obligeant et de flatteur. Je fais des vœux sincères pour votre conservation, et suis toujours avec l'amitié et tous les sentiments que vous me connaissez.

CATERINE

CXXXI

DE VOLTAIRE

A Ferney, 25 mars 1773

Madame, permettez qu'un de vos sujets, qui demeure entre les Alpes et le mont Jura, et qui vient de ressusciter pour quelques jours, après cinquante-deux accès de fièvre, dise quelques nouvelles de l'autre monde à votre majesté impériale. J'ai trouvé sur les bords du Styx les Tomyris, les Sémiramis, les Penthésilée, les Élisabeth d'Angleterre: elles m'ont toutes dit qu'elles n'approchaient pas de la véritable Catherine, de cette seule Catherine qui attirera les regards de la postérité; mais elles m'ont appris que vous n'étiez pas au bout de vos travaux, et qu'il fallait que vous prissiez encore la peine de bien battre mon cher Moustapha.

Le roi de Prusse me paraît croire que vos négociations sont rompues avec ce gros musulman; mais les choses peuvent changer d'un moment à l'autre, en fait de négociations comme en fait de guerre. J'attends très humblement de la destinée et de votre génie le débrouillement de tout ce chaos où la terre est plongée, de Dantzick aux embouchures du Danube, bien persuadé que, quand la lumière succédera à ces ténèbres, il en résultera pour vous de l'avantage et de la gloire.

Si votre guerre recommence, je n'en verrai pas la fin, par la raison que je serai probablement mort avant que vous ayez gagné cinq ou six batailles contre les Turcs.

Je me suis borné, dans ma dernière lettre, à demander la protection de votre majesté impériale, pour savoir quelles précautions on prend dans votre zone illustre et glaciale, pour assurer les levées des terres et des murailles contre les efforts de la glace; je me suis restreint à la physique, les affaires politiques ne sont pas de ma compétence.

On dit que, parmi les Français, il y a des Welches qui sont grands amis de Moustapha, et qui se trémoussent pour embarrasser mon impératrice; je ne veux point le croire; je ne suis qu'un pauvre Suisse qui se défie de tous les bruits qui courent, et qui est incrédule comme Thomas Didyme l'apôtre. Mais je crois fermement à votre gloire, à votre magnificence, à la supériorité que vous avez acquise sur le reste du monde depuis que vous gouvernez, à votre génie noble et mâle: j'ose croire aussi à vos bontés pour moi. Je me mets aux pieds de votre majesté impériale pour le peu de temps que j'ai encore à vivre: agréez le profond respect et le sincère attachement du vieux malade de Ferney.

CXXXII

DE VOLTAIRE

20 avril 1773

Madame, c'est à présent plus que jamais que votre majesté impériale est mon héroïne, et fort au-dessus de la majesté. Comment! au milieu de vos négociations avec Moustapha, au milieu de vos nouveaux préparatifs pour le bien battre, quand la moitié de votre génie doit être vers la Pologne, et l'autre vers Bucharest, il vous reste encore un autre génie qui en sait plus que les membres de votre académie des sciences, et qui daigne donner à mon ingénieur les leçons qu'il attendait d'eux! Combien avez-vous donc de génies? ayez la bonté de me faire cette confidence. Je ne vous demande pas de me dire si vous irez assiéger Andrinople, fort aisé à prendre, tandis que les troupes autrichiennes s'empareront de la Servie et de la Bosnie. Ces secrets-là ne sont pas plus de ma compétence que le renvoi de nos chevaliers errants. Je me borne à rire quand je lis dans une de vos lettres que vous voulez les garder quelque temps dans vos états pour qu'ils enseignent les belles manières dans vos provinces.

Le portail voûté, élevé sur la glace, et subsistant sur elle depuis quatre ans, me paraît un des miracles de votre règne; mais c'est aussi un miracle de votre climat. Je doute fort qu'on pût, dans nos cantons, élever un monument pareil; pour la bombe remplie d'eau, je pense qu'elle crèverait par une forte gelée, tout comme à Pétersbourg.

On dit que le thermomètre d'esprit-de-vin a été de cinquante degrés au-dessous de la congélation, cette année, dans votre résidence; nous péririons, nous autres Suisses, si jamais le thermomètre descendait chez nous à vingt: notre plus grand froid est à quinze et seize, et cette année il n'a pas atteint jusqu'à dix.

Je me flatte bien que vos bombes crèveront désormais sur les têtes des Turcs, et que M. le prince Orlof bâtira des arcs de triomphe non pas sur la glace, mais dans l'Atmeidan de Stamboul; et c'est alors que vous ferez naître en Grèce des Phidias comme des Miltiades.

Je crois qu'Algarotti se trompe, s'il dit que les Grecs inventèrent les arts. Ils en perfectionnèrent quelques uns, et encore assez tard.

Il y avait d'ailleurs un vieux proverbe que les Chaldéens avaient instruit l'Égypte, et que l'Égypte avait enseigné la Grèce.

Les Grecs avaient été civilisés si tard, qu'ils furent obligés d'apprendre l'alphabet de Tyr, quand les Phéniciens vinrent commercer chez eux et y bâtir des villes. Ces Grecs se servaient auparavant de l'écriture symbolique des Égyptiens.

Une autre preuve de l'esprit peu inventif des Grecs, c'est que leurs premiers philosophes allaient s'instruire dans l'Inde, et que Pythagore même y apprit la géométrie.

C'est ainsi, madame, que des philosophes étrangers viennent déjà prendre des leçons à Pétersbourg. Le grand homme qui prépara les voies dans lesquelles vous marchez, et qui fut le précurseur de votre gloire, disait avec grande raison que les arts fesaient le tour du monde, et circulaient comme le sang dans nos veines. Votre majesté impériale paraît aujourd'hui forcée de cultiver l'art de la guerre, mais vous ne négligez point les autres.

Je ne croyais pas, il y a un mois, habiter encore le globe que vous étonnez. Je rends grâce à la nature, qui a peut-être voulu que je vécusse jusqu'au temps où vous serez établie dans la patrie d'Orphée et de Mars, c'est-à-dire dans quelques mois; mais ne me faites pas attendre plus long-temps. Il faut absolument que je parte pour le néant. Je mourrai en vous conservant le culte que j'ai voué à votre majesté impériale. Que l'immortelle Catherine daigne toujours agréer mon profond respect, et conserver ses bontés au vieux malade de Ferney, qui l'idolâtre malgré son respect.

CXXXIII

DE L'IMPÉRATRICE

A Pétershof, ce 19/30 juin 1773

Monsieur, je prends la plume pour vous donner avis que le maréchal de Romanzof a passé le Danube avec son armée le 11 juin v. st. Le général baron Weissmann lui nettoya le chemin en culbutant, le premier, un corps de douze mille Turcs. Les lieutenants-généraux Stoupichin et Potemkin en firent autant de leur côté. Ceux-ci eurent affaire à dix-huit ou vingt mille musulmans, dont ils envoyèrent bon nombre dans l'autre monde, pour en porter la nouvelle à ces dames polies, de la part desquelles vous m'avez dit tant de choses flatteuses, après les cinquante-deux accès de fièvre dont vous vous êtes, à mon très grand contentement, tiré aussi heureusement qu'un jeune homme de vingt ans.

Chaque corps turc nous a laissé son camp, son artillerie, ses bagages. Voilà donc notre cher Moustapha en train d'être joliment tapé de nouveau, après avoir négocié et rompu deux congrès consécutifs, et avoir joui de divers armistices pendant près d'un an. Cet honnête homme-là ne sait point profiter des circonstances. Il n'est pas douteux que vous serez témoin oculaire de la fin de cette guerre. J'espère que le passage du

Danube y contribuera; il nous donnera la joie de rendre le sultan plus traitable, et nous laisserons bavarder les Welches. Leurs nouvelles méritent bien peu d'attention: ils ont débité que j'avais demandé trente mille Tartares au kan, et qu'il me les avait refusés. Je n'ai jamais pensé à pareille absurdité, et je doute fort que M. de Saint-Priest l'ait mandé à sa cour, comme on l'assure; parce qu'ordinairement les ambassadeurs sont réputés avoir au moins le sens commun.

Le froid qu'on a senti ici cet hiver a été moindre que celui de la Sibérie, qu'on fait monter à un degré fabuleux, surtout à Irkutska. Je suis tentée de n'y pas ajouter plus de foi qu'aux sentiments d'Algarotti sur la Grèce. Vous m'avez tirée d'erreur en quatre mots: me voilà convaincue que ce n'est pas en Grèce que les arts ont été inventés. J'en suis fâchée pourtant, car j'aime les Grecs, malgré tous leurs défauts.

Portez-vous bien, conservez-moi votre amitié, et soyez assuré de tous mes sentiments pour vous. Réjouissons-nous ensemble du passage du Danube: il ne sera pas si célèbre que celui du Rhin par Louis XIV, mais il est plus rare, les Russes ne l'ayant franchi de huit cents ans, à ce que disent nos antiquaires.

CXXXIV

DE VOLTAIRE

A Ferney, 10 auguste 1773

Madame, il faudrait que les jours eussent à Pétersbourg plus de vingt-quatre heures, pour que votre majesté impériale eût seulement le temps de lire tout ce qu'on lui écrit de l'Europe et de l'Asie. Pour la fatigue de répondre à tout cela, je ne la conçois pas.

Je voulais, moi chétif, moi mourant, prendre la liberté de vous écrire touchant les fausses nouvelles qu'on nous débite sur votre guerre renouvelée avec ce Moustapha, de vous parler du mariage de monseigneur votre fils, du voyage de madame la princesse de Darmstadt, qui est, après vous, ce que l'Allemagne a vu naître de plus parfait; j'allais même jusqu'à vous dire que Diderot, qui n'est pas welche, est le plus heureux des

Français, puisqu'il va à votre cour. Je voulais vous parler des dernières volontés d'Helvétius, dont on dédie l'ouvrage posthume à votre majesté. Je poussais mon indiscrétion jusqu'à vous dire que je ne suis point du tout de son avis sur le fond de son livre. Il prétend que tous les esprits sont nés égaux; rien n'est plus ridicule. Quelle différence entre certaine souveraine et ce Moustapha, qui a fait demander à M. de Saint-Priest si l'Angleterre est une île?

Je voulais être assez hardi pour parler à fond du passage du Danube. Je voulais demander si Falconnet-Phidias placera la statue de Catherine II, la seule vraie Catherine, ou sur une des Dardanelles, ou dans l'Atmeidan de Stamboul; mais considérant qu'elle n'a pas un moment à perdre, et craignant de l'importuner, je n'écris rien.

Je me borne à lever les mains vers l'étoile du nord; je suis de la religion des sabbéens: ils adoraient une étoile.

Le vieux malade de Ferney

CXXXV

DE VOLTAIRE

A Ferney, 12 auguste 1773

Madame, que votre majesté impériale me laisse d'abord baiser votre lettre de Petershof, du 19 juin de votre chronologie grecque, qui n'est pas meilleure que la nôtre; mais, de quelque manière que nous supputions les temps, vous comptez vos jours par des victoires; vous savez combien elles me sont chères. Il me semble que c'est moi qui ai passé le Danube. Je monte à cheval dans mes rêves, et je vais le grand galop à Andrinople. Je ne cesserai de vous dire qu'il me paraît bien étonnant, bien inconséquent, bien triste, bien mal de toute façon, que vos amis, l'impératrice-reine, et l'empereur des Romains, et le héros du Brandebourg, ne fassent pas le voyage de Constantinople avec vous. Ce serait un amusement de trois ou quatre mois tout au plus, après quoi vous vous arrangeriez ensemble, comme vous vous êtes arrangés en Pologne.

Je demande bien pardon à votre majesté; mais cette partie de plaisir sur la Propontide me paraît si naturelle, si facile, si agréable, si convenable, que je suis toujours stupéfait que les trois puissances aient manqué une si belle fête. Vous me direz, madame, que je pourrai jouir de cette satisfaction avec le temps; mais permettez-moi de vous représenter que je suis très pressé, que je n'ai que deux jours à vivre, et que je veux absolument voir cette aventure avant de mourir. L'auguste Catherine ne peut-elle pas dire amicalement à l'auguste Marie-Thérèse: "Ma chère Marie, songez donc que les Turcs sont venus deux fois assiéger Vienne; songez que vous laissez passer la plus belle occasion qui se soit présentée depuis *Ortogul* ou *Ortogrul*, et que, si on laisse respirer les ennemis du saint nom chrétien et de tous les beaux-arts, ces maudits Turcs deviendront peut-être plus formidables que jamais. Le chevalier de Tott, qui a beaucoup de génie, quoiqu'il ne soit point ingénieur, fortifiera toutes leurs places sur la mer Égée et sur le Pont-Euxin, quoique Moustapha et son grand-visir ignorent que ces deux petites mers se soient jamais appelées Pont-Euxin et mer Égée. Les janissaires et les levantis se disciplineront. Voilà notre ami Ali-Bey mort, Moustapha va être maître absolu de ce beau pays de l'Égypte qui adorait autrefois des chats, et qui ne connaît point saint Jean Népomucène.

Profitons d'un moment favorable qui reste encore; Russes, Autrichiens, Prussiens, fondons sur ces ennemis de l'Église grecque et latine. Nous accorderons au roi de Prusse, qui ne se soucie d'aucune église, une ou deux provinces de plus, et allons souper à Constantinople".

Certainement l'auguste Catherine fera un discours plus éloquent et plus pathétique; mais y a-t-il rien de plus raisonnable et de plus plausible? cela ne vaut-il pas mieux que mes chars de Cyrus? Hélas! l'idée de cette croisade ne réussira pas mieux que celle de mes chars; vous ferez la paix, madame, après avoir bien battu les Turcs; vous aurez quelques avantages de plus, mais les Turcs continueront d'enfermer les femmes, et d'être les amis des Welches, tout galants que sont ces Welches.

Je ne suis donc qu'à moitié satisfait.

Mais ce n'est pas à moitié que je suis l'adorateur de votre

majesté impériale, c'est avec la fureur de l'enthousiasme; qu'elle pardonne ma rage à mon profond respect.

Le vieux malade de Ferney

CXXXVI

DE L'IMPÉRATRICE

Le 15/26 septembre 1773

Monsieur, je vais satisfaire aux demandes que vous ne m'avez point faites, mais que vous m'indiquez dans votre lettre du 10 auguste; je répondrai aussi à celle du 12 de ce mois, que j'ai reçue en même temps. Cela vous annonce une dépêche longue à faire bâiller, en réponse à vos charmantes, mais très courtes lettres; jetez la mienne au feu si vous voulez; mais souvenez-vous que l'ennui est de mon métier, et qu'il se trouve ordinairement à la suite des rois. Pour le raccourcir donc, j'entre en matière.

M. de Romanzof, au lieu d'établir ses foyers dans l'Atmeidan de Stamboul, selon vos souhaits, a jugé à propos de rebrousser chemin, parce que, dit-il, il n'a pas trouvé à dîner aux environs de Silistrie, et que la marmite du visir était encore à Schiumla. Cela se peut, mais il devait prévoir au moins qu'il devait dîner sans compter sur son hôte. Je range ce fait parmi les fautes d'orthographe, et je m'en console par la conversation de madame la landgrave de Darmstadt, qui est douée d'une âme forte et mâle, d'un esprit élevé et cultivé. La quatrième de ses filles va épouser mon fils; la cérémonie des noces est fixée au 29 septembre, vieux style.

Comme chef de l'église grecque, je ne puis vous laisser ignorer la conversion de cette princesse, opérée par les soins, le zèle, et la persuasion de l'évêque Platon, qui l'a réunie au giron de l'église catholique-universelle-grecque, seule vraie croyante établie en Orient. Réjouissez-vous de notre joie, et que cela vous serve de consolation dans un temps où votre église latine est affligée, divisée, et occupée de l'extinction mémorable de la compagnie de Jésus.

A la suite du prince héréditaire de Darmstadt, j'ai eu le plaisir de voir arriver M. Grimm. Sa conversation est un délice pour moi; mais nous avons encore tant de choses à nous dire, que jusqu'ici nos entretiens ont eu plus de chaleur que d'ordre et de suite. Nous avons beaucoup parlé de vous. Je lui ai dit, ce que vous avez oublié peut-être, que vos ouvrages m'avaient accoutumée à penser.

J'attendais Diderot d'un moment à l'autre; mais je viens d'apprendre, à mon grand regret, qu'il est tombé malade à Duisbourg. L'*Histoire politique et philosophique du commerce des Indes* me donne une très grande aversion pour les conquérants du Nouveau-Monde, et m'a empêchée, jusqu'à ce moment, de lire l'ouvrage posthume d'Helvétius. Je n'en ai pas d'idée; mais il est bien difficile d'imaginer que Pierre-le-Sauvage, portefaix dans les rues de Londres, dont j'ai le tableau peint par le fils de Phidias-Falconet, soit né avec les mêmes facultés des premiers hommes de ce siècle.

Je n'oserais citer le seigneur Moustapha, mon ennemi et le vôtre, parce que M. de Saint-Priest, qui a vécu à Paris, et qui par conséquent a de l'esprit comme quatre, prétend qu'il en a prodigieusement. Mais, à propos de Moustapha, j'ai à vous dire que Lameri, votre protégé, a débuté, dans le tragique, par Orosmane, et, dans le comique, par le rôle du fils du Père de famille, avec un égal succès.

Je vous rends mille grâces de la belle harangue que vous me composez pour inviter les cours coopérantes dans les affaires de Pologne à souper au sérail. Je l'emploierai volontiers; mais je sais d'avance que la dame à qui vous voulez que je l'adresse a un chérubin indomptable, assis sur le trépied de la politique, et qui, par sa lenteur et l'obscurité de ses oracles, détruirait l'effet des plus belles harangues du monde, quelque grandes que fussent les vérités qu'elles pussent contenir. D'ailleurs, il y a des gens qui n'aiment que ce qu'ils ont inventé, et qui sacrifient tout aux idées reçues.

Je souhaite sans doute la paix, et pour y parvenir il ne me reste qu'à faire la guerre aussi long-temps que les choses resteront en cet état: vous aurez au moins l'espérance de voir finir la captivité des dames turques.

C'est avec tous les sentiments que vous me connaissez, et avec la plus vive reconnaissance de tout ce que votre amitié vous dicte pour moi, que je ne cesserai de vous souhaiter l'âge de Mathusalem, ou du moins celui de cet Anglais qui fut gai et bien portant jusqu'à cent soixante-seize ans. Imitez-le, vous qui êtes inimitable.

CATERINE

CXXXVII

DE VOLTAIRE

A Ferney, 1er novembre 1773

Madame, je vois par la lettre du 26 septembre, dont votre majesté impériale m'honore, que Diderot est tombé malade sur les frontières de la Hollande. Je me flatte qu'il est actuellement à vos pieds; vous avez plus d'un Français enthousiaste de votre gloire. S'il y en a quelques uns qui sont pour Moustapha, j'ose croire que ceux qui sont dévots à sainte Catherine valent bien ceux qui se sont faits Turcs. Il est vrai que Diderot et moi nous n'entrons point dans des villes par un trou, comme des étourdis; nous ne nous fesons point prendre prisonniers, comme des sots; nous ne nous mêlons point de l'artillerie où nous n'entendons rien. Nous sommes des missionnaires laïques qui prêchons le culte de sainte Catherine, et nous pouvons nous vanter que notre église est assez universelle.

J'avoue, à ma honte, que j'ai échoué dans le projet de ma croisade. J'aurais voulu que madame la grande-duchesse eût été rebaptisée dans l'église de Sainte-Sophie, en présence du prophète Grimm, et que votre auguste alliée eût établi des tribunaux de chasteté tant qu'elle aurait voulu dans la Bosnie et dans la Servie. Pierre l'ermite était pour le moins aussi chimérique que moi, et cependant il réussit; mais aussi il faut considérer qu'il était moine; la grâce de Dieu l'assistait, et elle m'a manqué tout net. Si je n'ai point la grâce, j'ai du moins la raison en ma faveur.

Sérieusement, madame, il me paraît absurde qu'on ait eu un si beau coup à faire et qu'on l'ait manqué; je suis persuadé que la postérité s'en étonnera. N'ai-je pas entendu dire qu'avant la campagne du Pruth un ambassadeur demandant à Pierre Ier où il prétendait établir le siége de son empire, il répondit: *A Constantinople?* Sur ce pied-là, je disais: Catherine-la-Grande, ayant réparé si bien le malheur de Pierre-le-Grand, accomplira sans doute son dessein; et l'auguste Marie-Thérèse, dont la capitale a été assiégée deux fois par les Turcs, contribuera de tout son pouvoir à cette sainte entreprise. Je me suis trompé en tout; elle a pardonné aux Turcs en bonne chrétienne; et le roi de Prusse, roi des calvinistes, a été le seul prince qui ait protégé les jésuites, lorsque le bon homme saint Pierre a exterminé le bon homme Ignace: que peut dire à cela le prophète Grimm?

Il faut que M. de Saint-Priest ait bien raison, et que Moustapha ait un esprit bien supérieur, puisqu'il a su engager les meilleurs chrétiens du monde dans ses intérêts, et réunir à la fois en sa faveur les Français et les Allemands.

Le roi de Prusse dit toujours que vous battrez Moustapha toute seule; que vous n'avez besoin de personne, je le veux croire; mais vos états ne sont pas tous aussi peuplés qu'ils sont immenses; le temps, la fatigue, et les combats, diminuent les armées, et avant que la population soit proportionnée à l'étendue des terres, il faut des siècles. C'est là ce qui fait ma peine; je vois que le temps est toujours trop court pour les grandes âmes. Ce n'est pas à un barbouilleur inutile qu'il faut de longues années, c'est à une héroïne née pour changer la face du monde. Elle est encore dans la fleur de son âge; je voudrais que Dieu lui envoyât des lettres-patentes contre-signées Mathusalem, pour mettre ses états au point où elle les veut. On dit que des corps de Turcs ont été bien battus; c'est une grande consolation pour Pierre l'ermite.

Je me mets aux pieds de votre majesté impériale avec le plus profond respect et l'attachement le plus inviolable.

CXXXVIII

DE VOLTAIRE

A Ferney, 30 décembre 1773

Madame, le roi de Prusse me fait l'honneur de me mander, du 10 décembre, que votre armée a battu celle du grand-visir, et que Silistrie est prise. Il ajoute que le grand-visir s'est enfui à Andrinople avec le grand étendard de Mahomet.

Je suppose qu'un roi n'est jamais trompé quand il écrit des nouvelles; et, dans cette supposition, je suis près de mourir de joie, au lieu de mourir de vieillesse, comme on me l'annonçait tout à l'heure avant que je reçusse la lettre du roi de Prusse.

Mort ou vif, il est bien fâcheux d'être si loin des merveilles de votre règne, et M. Diderot est un heureux homme; mais aussi il mérite son bonheur. Pour moi, j'expire dans le désespoir de n'avoir pu voir mon héroïne qui sera celle du monde entier, et de n'avoir pu lui présenter mon très profond et très inutile respect.

CXXXIX

DE L'IMPÉRATRICE

Le 27 décembre 1773/7 janvier 1774

Monsieur, le philosophe Diderot, dont la santé est encore chancelante, restera avec nous jusqu'au mois de février, qu'il retournera dans sa patrie; Grimm pense aussi partir vers ce temps-là. Je les vois très souvent, et nos conversations ne finissent pas. Ils pourront vous dire, monsieur, le cas que je fais de Henri IV, de *la Henriade*, et de l'auteur de tant d'autres écrits qui ont illustré notre siècle.

Je ne sais s'ils s'ennuient beaucoup à Pétersbourg; mais, pour moi, je leur parlerais toute ma vie sans m'en lasser. Je trouve à Diderot une imagination intarissable, et je le range parmi les hommes les plus extraordinaires qui aient existé. S'il n'aime pas Moustapha, comme vous me le mandez, au moins je suis sûre qu'il ne lui veut point de mal; la bonté de son cœur ne le lui permettrait pas, malgré l'énergie de son esprit et le penchant que je lui vois de faire incliner la balance de mon côté.

Eh bien! monsieur, il faut se consoler de ce que le projet de votre croisade a échoué, et supposer que vous avez eu affaire à de bonnes âmes auxquelles on ne peut accorder cependant l'énergie de Diderot.

Comme chef de l'église grecque, je ne puis en bonne foi vous laisser dans l'erreur sans vous reprendre. Vous auriez voulu que la grande-duchesse eût été rebaptisée dans Sainte-Sophie. Rebaptisée dites-vous? Ah! monsieur, l'église grecque ne rebaptise point; elle regarde comme très bon et très authentique tout baptême administré dans les autres communions chrétiennes. La grande-duchesse, après avoir prononcé en langue russe la profession de foi orthodoxe, a été reçue dans le sein de l'église au moyen de quelques signes de croix, avec de l'huile odoriférante qu'on lui a administrée en grande cérémonie; ce qui chez vous, comme chez nous, s'appelle confirmation. A cette occasion, on impose un nom; mais sur ce dernier point nous sommes plus chiches que vous, qui en donnez par douzaine; ici on n'en prend qu'un seul, et cela nous suffit.

Vous ayant mis au fait de ces choses importantes, je continue de répondre à votre lettre du 1er novembre. Vous saurez à présent, monsieur, qu'un corps détaché de notre armée, après avoir passé le Danube au mois d'octobre, battit un corps de Turcs très considérable, et fit prisonnier un bacha à trois queues qui le commandait.

Cet événement aurait pu avoir des suites, mais le fait est (chose dont vous ne serez pas content peut-être) qu'il n'en eut pas; de sorte que Moustapha et moi, nous nous trouvons à peu près dans la situation où nous étions il y a six mois, à cela près qu'il est attaqué d'un asthme, et que je me porte bien. Il se peut que ce sultan soit un esprit supérieur, mais il n'en est pas moins battu pour cela depuis cinq ans, malgré les conseils de M. de Saint-Priest et les instructions du chevalier Tott, qui se tuera à force de fondre des canons et d'exercer des canonniers. Il a beau être vêtu de caftans et d'hermines, l'artillerie turque n'en sera pas meilleure et mieux servie; mais toutes ces choses sont des enfantillages auxquels on donne beaucoup plus d'importance qu'ils ne méritent. Je ne sais où j'ai lu que ces tours d'esprit sont naturels aux Welches.

Adieu, monsieur; portez-vous bien, et soyez assuré que personne ne fait plus de cas de votre amitié que moi.

CXL

DE L'IMPÉRATRICE

A Pétersbourg, le 8/19 janvier 1774

Monsieur, je pense que les nouvelles que le roi de Prusse vous a données de la défaite du visir et de la prise de Silistrie, lui sont venues de Pologne, le pays, après la France, où l'on débite les plus fausses. Je m'attends à voir les oisifs fort occupés d'un voleur de grand chemin qui pille le gouvernement d'Orembourg, et qui tantôt, pour effrayer les paysans, prend le nom de Pierre III, et tantôt celui de son employé. Cette vaste province n'est pas peuplée à proportion de sa grandeur; la partie montagneuse est occupée par des Tartares, nommés Baschkis, pillards depuis la création du monde. Le pays plat est habité par tous les vauriens dont la Russie a jugé à propos de se défaire depuis quarante ans, ainsi que l'on a fait à peu près dans les colonies de l'Amérique pour les pourvoir d'hommes.

Le général Bibikof est allé avec un corps de troupes pour rétablir la tranquillité là où elle est troublée. A son arrivée à Casan, qui est à sept cents verstes (ou cent lieues d'Allemagne) d'Orembourg, la noblesse de ce royaume vint lui offrir de se joindre à ses troupes, avec quatre mille hommes bien armés, bien montés, et entretenus à leurs dépens. Il accepta leur offre. Cette troupe seule est plus qu'en état de remettre l'ordre dans le gouvernement limitrophe.

Vous jugez bien que cette incartade de l'espèce humaine ne dérange en rien le plaisir que j'ai de m'entretenir avec Diderot. C'est une tête bien extraordinaire que la sienne; la trempe de son cœur devrait être celle de tous les hommes; mais enfin, comme tout est au mieux dans ce meilleur des mondes possibles, et que les choses ne sauraient changer, il faut les laisser aller leur train, et ne pas se garnir le cerveau de prétentions inutiles. La mienne sera toujours de vous témoigner ma reconnaissance pour toutes les marques d'amitié que vous me donnez.

CATERINE

CXLI

DE VOLTAIRE

2 février 1774

Madame, la lettre du 19 janvier, dont votre majesté impériale m'honore, m'a transporté en esprit à Orembourg, et m'a fait connaître M. Pugatschef; c'est apparemment le chevalier de Tott qui a fait jouer cette farce; mais nous ne sommes plus au temps des Démétrius, et telle pièce de théâtre qui réussissait il y a deux cents ans, est sifflée aujourd'hui. Si quelque prétendu Inca venait au Pérou se dire fils ou petit-fils du soleil, je doute qu'il fût reconnu pour tel, quand même il serait annoncé par des jésuites, et quand ils feraient valoir des prophéties en sa faveur.

Votre majesté ne paraît pas trop inquiète de l'équipée de M. Pugatschef. Je croyais que la province d'Orembourg était le plus agréable pays de votre empire, que les Persans y avaient apporté tous leurs trésors pendant leurs guerres civiles, qu'on ne songeait qu'à s'y réjouir; et il se trouve que c'est un pays barbare, rempli de vagabonds et de scélérats. Vos rayons ne peuvent pas pénétrer partout en même temps: un empire de deux mille lieues en longitude ne se police qu'à la longue. Cela me confirme dans mon idée de l'antiquité du monde. J'en demande pardon à la Genèse, mais j'ai toujours pensé qu'il a fallu cinq ou six mille ans avant que la horde juive sût lire et écrire; et je soupçonne qu'Hercule et Thésée n'auraient pas été reçus dans votre académie de Pétersbourg. Un jour viendra que la ville d'Orembourg sera plus peuplée que Pékin, et qu'on y jouera des opéra-comiques.

En attendant, je me flatte que vous vous amuserez, madame, à battre le nouveau sultan, ou que vous lui dicterez des conditions de paix, telles que les anciens Romains en imposaient aux anciens rois de Syrie. Cependant, chargée du poids immense de la guerre contre un vaste empire, et du gouvernement de votre empire, encore plus vaste, voyant tout, fesant tout par vous-même, vous trouvez encore du temps pour converser avec notre philosophe Diderot, comme si vous étiez désœuvrée.

Je n'ai jamais eu la consolation de voir cet homme unique; il est la seconde personne de ce monde avec qui j'aurais voulu m'entretenir: il me parlerait de votre majesté: majesté! ce n'est pas cela que je veux dire, c'est de votre supériorité sur les êtres pensants: car je compte les autres êtres pour rien. Je vous demande donc, madame, votre protection auprès de lui. Ne peut-il pas se détourner d'une cinquantaine de verstes, pour venir me prolonger la vie en me contant ce qu'il a vu et entendu à Pétersbourg?

S'il ne vient pas sur le bord du lac de Genève, j'irai, moi, me faire enterrer sur le bord du lac Ladoga; il faut que je voie votre nouvelle création, je suis las de toutes les autres.

Je me mets à vos pieds avec adoration de latrie.

CXLII

DE L'IMPÉRATRICE

?mars-avril 1774

Monsieur, les gazettes seules font beaucoup de bruit du brigand Pugatschef, lequel n'est en relation directe ni indirecte avec M. de Tott. Je fais autant de cas des canons fondus par l'un, que des entreprises de l'autre. M. de Pugatschef et M. de Tott ont cependant cela de commun, que le premier file tous les jours sa corde de chanvre, et que l'autre s'expose à chaque instant au cordon de soie.

Diderot est parti pour retourner à Paris. Nos conversations ont été très fréquentes; et sa visite m'a fait un très grand plaisir. On ne rencontre pas souvent de tels hommes. Il a eu de la peine à nous quitter; le seul attachement à sa famille l'a séparé de nous. Je lui manderai le désir que vous avez de le voir. Il s'arrêtera quelque temps à La Haye. Cette lettre répond à la vôtre du 4 mars, vieux style. Je n'ai pour le présent rien d'intéressant à vous mander; mais je ne laisserai pas de vous répéter les sentiments d'estime, d'amitié et de considération que vous m'avez inspirés depuis long-temps.

CATERINE

CXLIII

DE VOLTAIRE

A Ferney, 7 mai 1774

Madame!

Je suis un téméraire, je demande une grâce à Votre Majesté Impériale. Ce n'est pas pour un Turc, ce n'est pas pour un cannonier Welche au service de la Sublime Porte, ce n'est pas pour un des gueux qui suivent Pugatchew, ni pour un prêtre ultramontain, ni pour un petit-maître Welche, c'est, Madame, pour un de Vos sujets qui est venu dans mon petit établissement de Ferney passer quatre mois. Il a employé ces quatre mois à apprendre le français, et dès qu'il l'a su, il m'est venu dire: je suis Livonien, marchand de profession, tolérant de religion. J'ai essuyé des pertes, dans mon commerce; je dois de l'argent et on m'en doit. Je voudrais obtenir un sauf conduit de sa Majesté Impériale pour deux ans, comment faut-il s'y prendre?

Je lui ai répondu: il faut que Vous présentiez un placet très court et très net à Sa Majesté Bienfesante, conçu en ces termes.

Michel Rose, natif de Riga, supplie très humblement Sa Majesté Impériale de daigner ordonner qu'il lui soit envoyé un sauf conduit à Lubek chez Messieurs Gansplan banquiers.

Aussitôt je l'ai fait partir pour Lubek, où je voudrais bien aller avec lui, attendu que Lubek est sur le chemin de Pétersbourg, mais je suis condamné à mourir à Ferney en fesant des vœux pour que les Turcs soient bien battus, pour que les canons de M-r le Baron de Tott crévent et pour que M-r Pugatschew soit incessamment pendu.

Je me traine aux pieds de Votre Majesté comme je peux avec tout le respect, tout l'attachement, toute la reconnaissance, tous les sentimens possibles. *Le vieux malade de Ferney*

V.

CXLIV

DE VOLTAIRE

9 auguste 1774

Madame, je suis positivement en disgrâce à votre cour. Votre majesté impériale m'a planté là pour Diderot, ou pour Grimm, ou pour quelque autre favori: vous n'avez eu aucun égard pour ma vieillesse; passe encore si votre majesté était une coquette française; mais comment une impératrice victorieuse et législatrice peut-elle être si volage?

Je me suis brouillé pour vous avec tous les Turcs, et même encore avec M. le marquis Pugatschef; et votre oubli est la récompense que j'en reçois. Voilà qui est fait, je n'aimerai plus d'impératrice de ma vie.

Je songe cependant que j'aurais bien pu mériter ma disgrâce. Je suis un petit vieillard indiscret, qui me suis laissé toucher par les prières d'un de vos sujets nommé Rose, Livonien de nation, marchand de profession, déiste de religion, qui est venu apprendre la langue française à Ferney; peut-être n'a-t-il pu mériter vos bontés que j'osais réclamer pour lui.

Je m'accuse encore de vous avoir ennuyée par le moyen d'un Français dont j'ai oublié le nom, qui se vantait de courir à Pétersbourg pour être utile à votre majesté, et qui, sans doute, a été fort inutile.

Enfin, je me cherche des crimes pour justifier votre indifférence. Je vois bien qu'il n'y a point de passion qui ne finisse. Cette idée me ferait mourir de dépit, si je n'étais tout près de mourir de vieillesse.

Que votre majesté, madame, daigne donc recevoir cette lettre comme ma dernière volonté, comme mon testament.

Signé votre admirateur, votre délaissé, votre vieux Russe de Ferney.

CXLV

DE L'IMPÉRATRICE

Le 15/24 auguste 1774

Monsieur, quoique très plaisamment vous pretendiez être en disgrâce à ma cour, je vous déclare que vous ne l'êtes point: je ne vous ai planté là ni pour Diderot, ni pour Grimm, ni pour tel autre favori. Je vous révère tout comme par le passé; et quoi qu'on vous dise de moi, je ne suis ni volage, ni inconstante.

Le marquis de Pugatschef m'a donné du fil à retordre cette année; j'ai été obligée, pendant plus de six semaines, de m'occuper de cette affaire avec une attention non interrompue, et puis, vous me grondez, et vous me dites que, de votre vie, vous ne voulez plus aimer d'impératrice. Cependant il me semble que pour avoir fait une si jolie paix avec les Turcs, vos ennemis et les miens, je méritais de votre part quelque indulgence, et point de haine.

Malgré mes occupations, je n'ai point oublié l'affaire de Rose le Livonien, votre protégé. Son sauf-conduit n'a pu être expédié à Lubeck comme vous le désiriez, parce que Rose, outre ses dettes, s'est sauvé de prison, et qu'il a emporté quelques milliers de roubles à différentes personnes: il serait remis tout de suite en prison, malgré les sauf-conduits, qui ne sont guère en usage chez nous. Je n'ai point reçu d'autres lettres depuis plusieurs mois que celle au sujet de ce Rose; et par conséquent, je n'ai aucune connaissance du Français dont vous me parlez dans votre lettre du 9 de ce mois.

Mais en vérité, monsieur, j'aurais envie de me plaindre à mon tour des déclarations d'extinction de passion que vous me faites, si je ne voyais, à travers votre dépit, tout l'intérêt que l'amitié vous inspire encore pour moi.

Vivez, monsieur, et raccommodons-nous; car aussi bien il n'y a pas de quoi nous brouiller: j'espère bien que dans un codicille en ma faveur, vous rétracterez ce prétendu testament si peu galant. Vous êtes bon Russe, et vous ne sauriez être l'ennemi de

CATERINE

CXLVI

DE VOLTAIRE

A Ferney, ce 6 octobre 1774

Madame,

L'amour fit le serment, l'amour l'a violé.

Je pardonne à votre majesté impériale, et je rentre dans vos chaînes. Ni le grand-turc ni moi, nous ne gagnerions rien à être en colère contre vous; mais je mettrais, si j'osais, une condition au pardon que j'accorde si bénignement à votre majesté; ce serait de savoir si le marquis de Pugatschef est agent ou instrument. Je n'ai pas l'impertinence de vous demander son secret; je ne crois pas le marquis instrument d'Achmet IV, qui choisissait si mal les siens, et qui, probablement, n'avait rien de bon à choisir. Pugatschef ne servait pas le pape Ganganelli, qui est allé trouver saint Pierre, avec un passe-port de saint Ignace. Il n'était aux gages, ni du roi de la Chine, ni du roi de Perse, ni du grand-mogol. Je dirais donc avec circonspection à ce Pugatschef: Monsieur, êtes-vous maître ou valet? agissez-vous pour votre compte ou pour celui d'un autre? Je ne vous demande pas qui vous emploie, mais seulement si vous êtes employé: quoi qu'il en soit, monsieur le marquis, j'estime que vous finirez par être pendu: vous le méritez bien, car vous êtes non seulement coupable envers mon auguste impératrice, qui vous ferait peut-être grâce, mais vous l'êtes envers tout l'empire, qui ne vous pardonnera pas. Laissez-moi maintenant reprendre le fil de mon discours avec votre souveraine.

Madame, quoi! dans le temps que vous êtes occupé du sultan, du grand-visir, de son armée détruite, de vos triomphes, de votre paix si glorieuse et si utile, de vos grands établissements, et même de Pugatschef, vous baissez les yeux sur le Livonien Rose! vous avez deviné que c'est un escroc, un fripon! votre majesté clairvoyante a très bien deviné, et j'étais un imbécile de m'être laissé séduire par sa face rebondie.

Je ne puis, cette année, grossir la foule des Européans et des Asiatiques qui viennent contempler l'admirable autocratrice, victorieuse, pacificatrice. La saison est trop avancée; mais je demande à votre majesté la permission de venir me mettre à ses pieds l'année prochaine, ou dans deux ans ou dans dix. Pourquoi n'aurai-je pas le plaisir de me faire enterrer dans quelque coin de Pétersbourg, d'où de pusse vous voir passer et repasser sous vos arcs de triomphes, couronnée de lauriers et d'oliviers?

En attendant, je me mets à vos pieds, de mon trou de Ferney, en regardant votre portrait avec des yeux toujours étonnés, et un cœur toujours plein de transport. *Le vieux malade*

CXLVII

DE VOLTAIRE

A Ferney, 19 octobre 1774

Madame, mon impertinence ne fatigue pas aujourd'hui votre majesté impériale pour la large face du Livonien Rose, ni pour celle de l'avocat Duménil, qui voulait vous aider à faire des lois, *par le conseil de son parrain*. Il s'agit aujourd'hui d'un jeune gentilhomme, bon géomètre, bon ingénieur, ayant des mœurs et du courage; il se nomme de Murnan: sa famille est de la province où je suis. Il est fortement recommandé à M. Euler, que vous honorez de votre protection. Tous ses maîtres rendent de lui le témoignage le plus avantageux.

Votre majesté ne doit point être surprise qu'il désire passionnément d'entrer à votre service. Tout ce qui doit affliger ce jeune officier, c'est que vous ayez sitôt accordé la paix au sultan; car il aurait bien voulu lever le plan de Constantinople, et contrecarrer le chevalier de Tott.

Il ne m'appartient pas d'oser vous présenter personne; mais enfin votre majesté ne peut m'empêcher d'être jaloux de tous ceux qui ont vingt-cinq ans, qui peuvent aller sur la Néva et sur le Bosphore, qui peuvent vous servir de la tête et de la main, et qui seront prédestinés, si, par hasard, ils sont tués à votre service. Il est bien dur de vivre au coin de son feu en pareil cas.

Je me mets tristement aux pieds de votre majesté impériale, comme un vieux Suisse inutile.

CXLVIII

DE L'IMPÉRATRICE

Le 22 octobre/2 novembre 1774

Volontiers, monsieur, je satisferai votre curiosité sur le compte de Pugatschef: ce me sera d'autant plus aisé qu'il y a un mois qu'il est pris, ou, pour parler plus exactement, qu'il a été lié et garrotté par ses propres gens, dans la plaine inhabitée entre le Volga et le Jaïck, où il avait été chassé par les troupes envoyées contre eux de toutes parts. Privés de nourriture et de moyens pour se ravitailler, ses compagnons, excédés d'ailleurs des cruautés qu'il commettait, et espérant obtenir leur pardon, le livrèrent au commandant de la forteresse du Jaïck, qui l'envoya à Sinbirsk, au général comte Panin. Il est présentement en chemin, pour être conduit à Moscou. Amené devant le comte Panin, il avoua naïvement dans son premier interrogatoire qu'il était cosaque du Don, nomma l'endroit de sa naissance, dit qu'il était marié à la fille d'un cosaque du Don, qu'il avait trois enfants; que, dans ces troubles, il avait épousé une autre femme, que ses frères et ses neveux servaient dans la première armée, que lui-même avait servi les deux premières campagnes contre la Porte, etc.

Comme le général Panin a beaucoup de Cosaques du Don avec lui, et que les troupes de cette nation n'ont jamais mordu à l'hameçon de ce brigand, tout ceci fut bientôt vérifié par les compatriotes de Pugatschef. Il ne sait ni lire ni écrire, mais c'est un homme extrêmement hardi et déterminé. Jusqu'ici il n'y a pas la moindre trace qu'il ait été l'instrument de quelque puissance, ni qu'il ait suivi l'inspiration de qui que ce soit. Il est à supposer que M. Pugatschef est maître brigand, et non valet d'âme qui vive.

Je crois qu'après Tamerlan, il n'y en a guère eu qui ait plus détruit l'espèce humaine. D'abord il fesait pendre, sans rémission ni autre forme de procès, toutes les races nobles, hommes, femmes, et enfants, tous les officiers, tous les soldats qu'il pouvait attraper: nul endroit où il a passé n'a été épargné: il pillait et saccageait ceux-mêmes qui, pour éviter ses cruautés, cherchaient à se le rendre favorable par une bonne réception: personne n'était devant lui à l'abri du pillage, de la violence et du meurtre.

Mais ce qui montre bien jusqu'où l'homme se flatte, c'est qu'il ose concevoir quelque espérance. Il s'imagine qu'à cause de son courage je pourrais lui faire grâce, et qu'il ferait oublier ses crimes passés par ses services futurs. S'il n'avait offensé que moi, son raisonnement pourrait être juste, et je lui pardonnerais; mais cette cause est celle de l'empire, qui a ses lois.

Vous voyez par là, monsieur, que Duménil, avocat, dont je n'ai jamais entendu parler, malgré les avis de son parrain, est venu trop tard pour législater. M. La Rivière même, qui nous supposait, il y a six ans, marcher à quatre pattes, et qui très poliment s'était donné la peine de venir de la Martinique pour nous dresser sur nos pieds de derrière, n'était plus à temps.

Quant au baisemain des prêtres sur lequel vous me questionnez, je vous dirai que c'est un usage de l'église grecque, établi, je pense, presque avec elle. Depuis dix ou douze ans, les prêtres commencent à retirer leurs mains, les uns par politesse, les autres par humilité. Ainsi, ne vous gendarmez pas trop contre un ancien usage qui s'abolit peu à peu.

Je ne sais pas aussi si vous trouveriez beaucoup à me gronder sur ce que, dès ma quatorzième année, je me suis conformée à cet usage établi. En tout cas, je ne serais pas la seule qui mériterais de l'être. Si vous venez ici, et si vous vous y faites prêtre, je vous demanderai votre bénédiction; et quand vous me l'aurez donnée, je baiserai de bon cœur cette main qui a écrit tant de belles choses, et tant de vérités utiles. Mais, pour que vous sachiez où me trouver, je vous avertis que cet hiver je m'en vais à Moscou. Adieu, portez-vous bien.

CATERINE

CXLIX

DE VOLTAIRE

A Ferney, 16 décembre 1774

Madame, c'était donc un diable d'homme que ce marquis de Pugatschef? et il faut que le divan soit bien bête pour ne lui avoir pas envoyé quelque argent. Il ne savait donc pas plus écrire que Gengis-kan et Tamerlan? Il y a eu même, dit-on, des gens qui ont fondé des religions, sans pouvoir seulement signer leur nom. Tout cela n'est pas à l'honneur de la nature humaine: ce qui lui fait honneur, c'est votre magnanimité. Votre majesté impériale donne de grands exemples, qui sont déjà suivis par le prince votre fils. Il vient de donner une pension à un jeune homme de mes amis, nommé M. de La Harpe, qu'il ne connaît que par son mérite trop méconnu en France. De tels bienfaits, répandus à propos, enflent la bouche de la renommée, et passent à la postérité.

Je crois que votre majesté, qui sait lire et écrire, va reprendre le bel ouvrage de sa législation, quoiqu'elle n'ait plus auprès d'elle le pauvre Solon, nommé La Rivière, qui était venu vous donner des leçons, et qu'elle n'ait pas encore pour premier ministre cet avocat sans cause nommé Duménil, qui vient enseigner la coutume de Paris à Pétersbourg, de la part de son parrain.

Vous serez réduite à donner des lois sans le secours de ces deux grands personnages; mais je vous conjure, madame, d'insérer dans votre code une loi expresse qui n'accorde la permission de baiser les mains des prêtres qu'à leurs maîtresses. Il est vrai que Jésus-Christ se laisse baiser les jambes par Madeleine, mais ni nos prêtres ni les vôtres n'ont rien de commun avec Jésus-Christ.

J'avoue qu'en Italie et en Espagne les dames baisent la main d'un jacobin ou d'un cordelier, et que ces marauds-là prennent beaucoup de liberté avec nos femmes. Je voudrais que les dames de Pétersbourg fussent un peu plus fières. Si j'étais femme à Pétersbourg, jeune et jolie, je ne baiserais que les mains de vos braves officiers, qui ont fait fuir les Turcs sur terre et sur mer, et ils me baiseraient tout ce qu'ils voudraient. Jamais on ne pourrait me résoudre à baiser la main d'un moine, qui est souvent très malpropre. Je veux consulter sur cette grande question le parrain du sieur Duménil.

En attendant, madame, permettez-moi de baiser la statue de Pierre-le-Grand, et le bas de la robe de Catherine plus grande. Je sais qu'elle a une main plus belle que celle de tous les prêtres de son empire; mais je n'ose baiser que ses pieds, qui sont aussi blancs que les neiges de son pays.

Je la supplie de daigner conserver un peu de bonté pour le vieux radoteur des Alpes.

CL

DE L'IMPÉRATRICE

A Czarskozélo, le 29 décembre 1774/9 janvier 1775

Monsieur, je réponds aujourd'hui à deux de vos lettres. Celle du 19 octobre m'est parvenue par le sieur Murnan, que vous en aviez chargé; votre recommandation l'a fait recevoir à mon service, comme vous l'avez désiré, quoique la guerre soit finie.

Le marquis de Pugatschef, dont vous me parlez encore dans votre lettre du 16 décembre, a vécu en scélérat et va finir en lâche. Il a paru si timide et si faible dans sa prison, qu'on a été obligé de le préparer à sa sentence avec précaution, crainte qu'il ne mourût de peur sur-le-champ.

Dans quelques jours d'ici je pars pour Moscou. C'est là que je reprendrai le grand ouvrage de la législation, privée à la vérité des secours de Solon-la-Rivière, et de la coutume de l'avocat Duménil, dont jusqu'ici je n'ai point entendu parler. Je serais bien aise cependant de faire la connaissance de son parrain; peut-être me fournirait-il un projet pour abolir entièrement l'usage du baisemain des prêtres, contre lequel vous plaidez avez force. Quand vous aurez consulté ce parrain, vous voudrez bien me communiquer son avis; en attendant, vous me permettrez que l'ancienne coutume tombe d'elle-même tout doucement.

Quatre de mes frégates sont arrivées de l'Archipel à Constantinople; l'une d'elles a passé dans la mer Noire pour se rendre dans notre port de Kersch, sans que ce phénomène, le premier, je pense, depuis que le monde existe, ait été précédé d'une comète. Le parrain de M. Duménil sait-il cela? et qu'en dit-il?

Il ne sera peut-être pas fâché d'apprendre un trait de politesse de la part de mon bon frère et ami sultan Abdhul-Achmet, qui, voyant passer mes frégates, du fond de son harem, leur envoya une chaloupe pour les avertir qu'il y avait beaucoup de pierres sous l'eau dans tel endroit du canal, et qu'ils eussent à prendre garde que le courant ne les entraînât de ce côté-là; cela est humain, cela est poli.

Soyez assuré, monsieur, que mes sentiments pour vous sont toujours les mêmes, et que je suis très sensible et très reconnaissante pour tout ce que vous me dites d'agréable, etc.

CATERINE

CLI

DE VOLTAIRE

A Ferney, 28 juin 1775

Madame, pardonnez; voici le fait:

Un très bon peintre, nommé Barrat, arrive chez moi; il me trouve écrivant devant votre portrait; il me peint dans cette attitude, et il a l'audace de vouloir mettre cette fantaisie aux pieds de votre majesté impériale; il l'encadre et la fait partir. Je ne puis que vous supplier de pardonner à la témérité de ce peintre. C'est un homme qui d'ailleurs a le talent de faire en un quart d'heure ce que les autres ne feraient qu'en huit jours. Il peindrait une galerie en moins de temps qu'on y donnerait le bal; il a surtout l'art de faire parfaitement ressembler. Je ne lui connais de défaut que sa témérité de prendre votre majesté impériale pour juge de ses talents. Peut-être aurez-vous l'indulgence de faire placer ce tableau dans quelque coin, et vous direz en passant: Voilà celui qui m'adore pour moi-même, comme les quiétistes adorent Dieu. Vos sujets sont plus heureux que moi, ils vous adorent et vous voient.

J'apprends dans le moment, madame, que votre majesté, qui s'est fait si bien connaître dans la Méditerranée, avait un vice-consul à Cadix, et que ce vice-consul, qui était Allemand, est mort. Il y a un autre Allemand, nommé Jean-Louis Pettremann, demeurant à Cadix, qui servirait très bien votre majesté, si elle n'avait pas disposé de cette place. Il ne m'appartient pas d'oser vous proposer un vice-consul ni un proconsul; je crois que, s'il y avait encore des consuls romains, ils ne tiendraient pas plus devant vous que les grands-visirs.

Daignez, madame, du pinacle de votre gloire, agréer le profond et inutile respect, l'attachement inviolable, et la reconnaissance du vieux malade de Ferney.

CLII

DE VOLTAIRE

A Ferney, 7 juillet 1775

Madame, je suis bien plus téméraire que je ne croyais avec la bienfaitrice de cinquante ou soixante provinces, victorieuse des Moustapha. Elle pardonnera mon impertinence, quand elle verra de quoi il s'agit.

Marc Le Fort, petit-neveu de ce François Le Fort qui rendit quelques services assez importants à la Russie sous les yeux de l'empereur Pierre-le-Grand, représente à l'impératrice Catherine II la très grande, qu'il peut la servir dans le commerce de sa nation à Marseille. Il a séjourné plus de vingt ans dans ce port, et il a été très utile à tous les négociants du Levant.

Si l'intention de sa majesté impériale est que les Russes aient un traité de commerce avec la France, et particulièrement vers la Méditerranée, Marc Le Fort lui offre ses très humbles services.

Il dit que les vaisseaux russes peuvent apporter à Marseille, avec un grand avantage, chanvre, fer, bois, potasse, huile de baleine, et rapporter toutes les denrées de Provence.

Il dit que les Suédois et les Danois font ce commerce, et ont des consuls à Marseille; ces consuls sont Gènevois.

Le petit-neveu du général Le Fort serait un très digne consul de sa majesté impériale.

Voilà donc, madame, en très peu de temps, un vice-consul et un consul que je mets à vos pieds. Cette proposition a je ne sais quel air de l'empire romain; mais, dans le fond de mon cœur, je donne la préférence à l'empire russe.

J'ignore absolument en quels termes est actuellement votre empire avec le petit pays des Welches, qui prétendent toujours être Français; pour moi, j'ai l'honneur d'être un vieux Suisse que vous avez naturalisé votre sujet. Marc Le Fort est un meilleur sujet que moi; nous attendons vos ordres. Le vieux malade de Ferney se met aux pieds de votre majesté impériale: il mourra en invoquant votre nom.

CLIII

DE VOLTAIRE

A Ferney, 18 octobre 1775

Madame, après avoir été étonné et enchanté de vos victoires pendant quatre années de suite, je le suis encore de vos fêtes. J'ai bien de la peine à comprendre comment votre majesté impériale a ordonné à la mer Noire de venir dans une plaine auprès de Moscou. Je vois des vaisseaux sur cette mer, des villes sur les bords, des cocagnes pour un peuple immense, des feux d'artifice, et tous les miracles de l'opéra réunis.

Je savais bien que la très grande Catherine II était la première personne du monde entier; mais je ne savais pas qu'elle fût magicienne.

Puisqu'elle a tant de pouvoir sur tous les éléments, que lui en aurait-il coûté de plus pour m'envoyer la flèche d'Abaris, ou le carrosse du bon homme Élie, afin que je fusse témoin de toutes vos grandeurs et de tous vos plaisirs?

On croit, dans mon pays, que tout cela est un songe. J'en aurais certifié la vérité; j'aurais dit à mes petits compatriotes, qui font les entendus: Messieurs, les fêtes sur la mer Noire sont encore fort peu de chose, en comparaison des établissements pour les orphelins et pour les maisons d'éducation; ces fêtes passent en un jour, mais ces maisons durent tous les siècles.

Je me jette aux pieds de votre majesté impériale, pour lui demander bien humblement pardon d'avoir osé l'interrompre par toutes mes importunités misérables.

Je demande pardon d'avoir laissé partir le tableau d'un peintre de la ville de Lyon.

Je demande pardon d'avoir parlé d'un vice-consul de Cadix, nommé Widellin, et d'un autre qui se présente pour exercer la suprême dignité du vice-consulat.

Je demande pardon d'avoir proposé une autre dignité de consul à Marseille.

J'ai honte de dire qu'il se présentait encore un autre consul à Lyon.

L'empire romain ne donnait jamais que deux consulats à la fois : mais tout le monde veut être consul de Russie. Tous ceux qui entrent chez moi et qui voient votre portrait s'imaginent que j'ai un grand crédit à votre cour. Ils me disent: Faites-nous consuls de cette impératrice qui devrait être souveraine de tout ce globe, mais qui en possède environ un quart. Je tâche de réprimer leur ambition.

Je ferais mieux, madame, de réprimer ma bavarderie. Je sens que j'ennuie la conquérante, la législatrice, la bienfaitrice: il m'est permis de l'adorer, mais il ne m'est pas permis de l'ennuyer à cet excès. Il faut mettre des bornes à mon zèle et à mes témérités, il faut se borner malgré soi au profond respect.

CLIV

DE L'IMPÉRATRICE

A Czarskozélo, 14/25 juin 1776

Monsieur, plus on vit dans ce monde et plus on s'accoutume à voir alternativement les événements heureux céder la place aux plus tristes spectacles, et ceux-ci à leur tour suivis de scènes étonnantes. Les pertes dont vous me parlez, monsieur, m'ont touchée sensiblement en leur temps par toutes les circonstances malheureuses qui les ont accompagnées, aucun secours humain n'ayant pu ni les prévoir, ni les prévenir, ni réussir à sauver tous les deux, ou au moins l'un des deux. La part que vous y prenez, monsieur, m'est une nouvelle preuve des sentiments que vous m'avez toujours témoignés, et pour lesquels je vous ai mille obligations. Nous sommes présentement très occupés à réparer nos pertes. Les réglements que vous me demandez ne sont encore traduits et imprimés qu'en allemand; rien n'est plus difficile que d'avoir une bonne traduction française de quoi que ce soit écrit en russe; cette dernière langue est si riche, si énergique, et souffre tant d'inversions et de compositions de termes, qu'on la manie comme l'on veut; la vôtre est si sage et si pauvre, qu'il faut être vous pour en avoir tiré le parti et l'usage que vous en avez su faire.

Dès que j'aurai une traduction passable, je vous l'enverrai; mais je vous avertis d'avance que cet ouvrage est très sec, très ennuyeux, et que qui y cherchera autre chose que de l'ordre et du sens commun sera trompé. Il n'y a certainement dans tout ce fatras ni esprit ni génie, mais seulement beaucoup d'utilité.

Adieu, monsieur; portez-vous bien, et soyez assuré que rien au monde ne peut changer ma façon de penser à votre égard.

CATERINE

CLV

DE VOLTAIRE

24 janvier 1777

Madame, votre sujet, moitié Suisse, moitié Gaulois, nommé Voltaire, était près de mourir il y a quelques jours: son confesseur catholique-apostolique-romain, c'est-à-dire universel, coureur de Rome, vint pour me préparer au voyage; le malade lui dit: Mon révérend père, Dieu pourrait bien me damner. Et pourquoi cela, vieux bon homme? me dit le prêtre. Hélas! lui répondis-je, c'est qu'on m'a accusé auprès de lui d'être un ingrat. J'ai été comblé des bontés d'une autocratrice qui est une de ses plus belles images dans ce monde, et je ne lui ai point écrit depuis plus d'un an. Qu'est-ce qu'une autocratrice? me dit mon vilain. Eh pardieu! lui dis-je, c'est une impératrice. Vous êtes un grand ignorant; et cette impératrice fait du bien depuis le Kamtschatka jusqu'en Afrique. Oh! si cela est, répartit le prêtre, vous avez bien fait; elle n'a pas de temps à perdre. Il ne faut pas ennuyer une autocratrice-impératrice-bienfaitrice, occupée du soir au matin tantôt à battre les Turcs, tantôt à leur donner la paix, ou bien à couvrir de vaisseaux la mer Noire, et qui s'amuse à faire fleurir onze cent mille lieues carrées de pays. Allez, allez, je vous donne l'absolution.

CLVI

DE L'IMPÉRATRICE

A Pétersbourg, 28 janvier/8 février 1777

Monsieur, j'ai lu cet hiver deux traductions russes nouvellement faites, l'une du Tasse et l'autre d'Homère. On les dit très bonnes; mais j'avoue que votre lettre du 24 janvier, que je viens de recevoir, m'a fait plus de plaisir que le Tasse et Homère. La gaieté et la vivacité qui y règnent me font espérer que votre maladie n'aura aucune suite et que vous passerez très lestement au-delà des cent ans.

Votre souvenir m'est toujours aussi flatteur qu'agréable; mes sentiments pour vous sont toujours invariables.

CLVII

DE L'IMPÉRATRICE

A Pétersbourg, le 20 septembre/1 octobre 1777

Monsieur, pour répondre à vos lettres, il faut que je vous dise premièrement que si vous êtes content du prince Ioussoupof, je dois lui rendre le témoignage qu'il est enchanté de l'accueil que vous avez bien voulu lui faire, et de tout ce que vous avez dit pendant le temps qu'il a eu le plaisir de vous voir.

Secondement, monsieur, je ne puis vous envoyer le recueil de nos lois, parce qu'il n'existe pas encore. L'année 1775, j'ai fait publier des réglements pour le gouvernement des provinces; ceux-ci ne sont traduits qu'en allemand. La pièce qui est à la tête rend raison du pourquoi de ces arrangements; c'est une pièce estimée à cause de la manière concise dont y sont décrits les faits historiques des différentes époques. Je ne crois pas que ces réglements puissent servir aux Treize-Cantons: j'en envoie un exemplaire pour la bibliothèque du château de Ferney.

Notre édifice législatif s'élève peu à peu: l'instruction pour le code en est le fondement: je vous l'ai envoyée il y a dix ans. Vous verrez que ces réglements ne dérogent point aux principes, mais qu'ils en découlent; bientôt ils seront suivis de ceux de finances, de commerce, de police, etc., lesquels nous occupent depuis deux ans; après quoi le code ne sera qu'un ouvrage aisé et facile à rédiger.

Voici l'idée que je m'en fais pour le criminel. Les crimes ne sauraient être en grand nombre; mais de proportionner les peines au crime, cela demande, je crois, un travail à part et beaucoup de réflexions. Je pense que la nature et la force des preuves pourraient être réduites à une forme de demandes très méthodique, très simple, qui éclaircirait le fait. Je suis persuadée, et je l'ai établi, que la meilleure des procédures criminelles et la plus sûre est celle qui fait passer ces sortes de matières par trois instances dans un temps fixé; sans quoi la sûreté personnelle des accusés pourrait être à la merci des passions, de l'ignorance, des balourdises involontaires, et des têtes chaudes.

Voilà des précautions qui pourraient ne pas plaire au soi-disant saint-office; mais la raison a ses droits, contre lesquels il faut que tôt ou tard la sottise et les préjugés viennent échouer.

Je me flatte que la société de Berne approuvera cette façon de penser. Soyez persuadé, monsieur, que la mienne à votre égard n'est soumise à aucune variation.

CATERINE

J'oubliais de vous dire que l'expérience, depuis deux ans, nous confirme que la cour d'équité établie par mes réglements devient le tombeau de la chicane.

CLVIII

DE L'IMPÉRATRICE

A Pétersbourg, 23 novembre/4 décembre 1777

Monsieur, j'ai reçu les trois feuillets imprimés qui accompagnaient votre lettre du 28 octobre. Le sujet que vous proposez est digne de vous: il est à désirer qu'il soit entièrement rempli. Les inquisitions d'état et d'église n'auraient pas besoin du grand fatras de règles et de formes, si les princes étaient instruits ou éclairés. J'attends avec une grande impatience les exemplaires complets que vous me promettez; je vous avoue que ceux de vos écrits me seraient les plus précieux: ils me délasseraient de certains réglements de finance dont la base porte sur ces mots, *Vivre et laisser écrire*. On y travaille depuis deux ans, et je n'en vois pas la fin.

Adieu, monsieur; portez-vous bien, et souvenez-vous quelquefois de moi.

M. de Schouvalof est revenu plus enchanté de vous que jamais.

CLIX

DE VOLTAIRE

A Ferney, 5 décembre 1777

Madame, je reçus hier au soir un des gages de votre immortalité, le code de vos lois en allemand, dont votre majesté impériale daigne me gratifier. J'ai commencé, dès ce matin, à le faire traduire dans la langue des Welches; il le sera en chinois; il le sera dans toutes les langues: ce sera l'évangile de l'univers.

J'avais bien raison de dire, il y a treize ans, que tout nous viendrait de l'étoile du nord.

J'ai pris la liberté d'adresser, il y a quinze jours, à votre majesté, par les chariots de poste d'Allemagne, le *Prix de la justice et de l'humanité*. C'est un petit coup de cloche qui annonce vos bienfaits au genre humain. Nous sommes deux membres de la société de Berne qui avons déposé chacun cinquante louis d'or pour le concurrent qui fera le projet d'un code criminel le plus approchant de vos lois et le plus convenable au pays où nous vivons.

Je voudrais qu'on proposât un prix pour celui qui trouvera la manière la plus prompte et la plus sûre de renvoyer les Turcs dans le pays d'où ils sont venus; mais je crois toujours que ce secret n'est réservé qu'à la première personne du genre humain, qui s'appelle Catherine II. Je me prosterne à ses pieds, et je crie dans mon agonie, *allah*, *allah*, *Catherine rezoul*, *allah*.

O Lord my God, hearken unto me, and instruct me; that I may administer Judgment unto thy People; as thy sacred Laws direct to judge with Righteousness!

THE INSTRUCTIONS

TO THE COMMISSIONERS FOR COMPOSING

A NEW CODE OF LAWS

1. The Christian Law teaches us to do mutual Good to one another, as much as possibly we can.

2. Laying this down as a fundamental Rule prescribed by that Religion, which has taken, or ought to take Root in the Hearts of the whole People; we cannot but suppose, that every honest Man in the Community is, or will be, desirous of seeing his native Country at the very Summit of Happiness, Glory, Safety, and Tranquillity.

3. And that every Individual Citizen in particular must wish to see himself protected by Laws, which should not distress him in his Circumstances, but, on the Contrary, should defend him from all Attempts of others, that are repugnant to this fundamental Rule.

4. In order therefore to proceed to a speedy Execution of what *We* expect from such a general Wish, *We*, fixing the Foundation upon the above first-mentioned Rule, ought to begin with an Inquiry into the natural Situation of this Empire.

5. For those Laws have the greatest Conformity with Nature, whose particular Regulations are best adapted to the Situation and Circumstances of the People, for whom they are instituted.

This natural Situation is described in the three following Chapters.

Chap. I

6. Russia is an European State.

7. This is clearly demonstrated by the following Observations: The Alterations which *Peter the Great* undertook in Russia succeeded with the greater Ease, because the Manners, which prevailed at that Time, and had been introduced amongst us by a Mixture of different Nations, and the Conquest of foreign Territories, were quite unsuitable to the Climate. *Peter the First*, by introducing the Manners and Customs of Europe among the European People in his Dominions, found at that Time such Means as even he himself was not sanguine enough to expect.

Chap. II

8. The Possessions of the Russian Empire extend upon the terrestrial Globe to 32 Degrees of Latitude, and to 165 of Longitude.

9. The Sovereign is absolute; for there is no other Authority but that which centers in his single Person, that can act with a Vigour proportionate to the Extent of such a vast Dominion.

10. The Extent of the Dominion requires an absolute Power to be vested in that Person who rules over it. It is expedient so to be, that the quick Dispatch of Affairs, sent from distant Parts, might make ample Amends for the Delay occasioned by the great Distance of the Places.

11. Every other Form of Government whatsoever would not only have been prejudicial to Russia, but would even have proved its entire Ruin.

12. Another Reason is; That it is better to be subject to the Laws under one Master, than to be subservient to many.

13. What is the true End of Monarchy? Not to deprive People of their natural Liberty; but to correct their Actions, in order to attain the *supreme Good.*

14. The Form of Government, therefore, which best attains this End, and at the same Time sets less Bounds than others to natural Liberty, is that which coincides with the Views and Pur-

poses of rational Creatures, and answers the End, upon which we ought to fix a stedfast Eye in the Regulations of civil Polity.

15. The Intention and the End of Monarchy, is the Glory of the Citizens, of the State, and of the Sovereign.

16. But, from this Glory, a Sense of Liberty arises in a People governed by a Monarch; which may produce in these States as much Energy in transacting the most important Affairs, and may contribute as much to the Happiness of the Subjects, as even Liberty itself.

Chap. III

17. *Of the Safety of the Institutions of Monarchy.*

18. The intermediate Powers, subordinate to, and depending upon the supreme Power, form the essential Part of monarchical Government.

19. *I* have said, that the intermediate Powers, subordinate and depending, proceed from the supreme Power; as in the very Nature of the Thing the Sovereign is the Source of all imperial and civil Power.

20. The Laws, which form the Foundation of the State, send out certain Courts of Judicature, through which, as through smaller Streams, the Power of the Government is poured out, and diffused.

21. The Laws allow these Courts of Judicature to remonstrate, that such or such an Injunction is unconstitutional, and prejudicial, obscure, and impossible to be carried into Execution; and direct, beforehand, to which Injunction one ought to pay Obedience, and in what Manner one ought to conform to it. These Laws undoubtedly constitute the firm and immoveable Basis of every State.

Chap. IV

22. There must be a political Body, to whom the Care and strict Execution of these Laws ought to be confided.

23. This Care, and strict Execution of the Laws, can be nowhere so properly fixed as in certain Courts of Judicature, which

announce to the People the newly-made Laws, and revive those, which are forgotten, or obsolete.

24. And it is the Duty of these Courts of Judicature to examine carefully those Laws which they receive from the Sovereign, and to remonstrate, if they find any Thing in them repugnant to the fundamental Constitution of the State, *&c.* which has been already remarked above in the third Chapter, and twenty-first Article.

25. But if they find nothing in them of that Nature, they enter them in the Code of Laws already established in the State, and publish them to the whole Body of the People.

26. In Russia the Senate is the political Body, to which the Care and due Execution of the Laws is confided.

27. All other Courts of Judicature may, and ought to remonstrate with the same Propriety, to the Senate, and even to the Sovereign himself, as was already mentioned above.

28. Should any One inquire, wherein the Care and due Execution of the Laws consists? I answer, That the Care, and due Execution of the Laws, produces particular Instructions; in consequence of which, the before-mentioned Courts of Judicature, instituted to the End that, by their Care, the Will of the Sovereign might be obeyed in a Manner conformable to the fundamental Laws and Constitution of the State, are obliged to act, in the Discharge of their Duty, according to the Rules prescribed.

29. These Instructions will prevent the People from transgressing the Injunctions of the Sovereign with impunity; but, at the same Time, will protect them from the Insults, and ungovernable Passions of others.

30. For, on the one Hand, they justify the Penalties prepared for those who transgress the Laws; and, on the other, they confirm the Justice of that Refusal to enter Laws repugnant to the good Order of the State, amongst those which are already approved of, or to act by those Laws in the Administration of Justice, and the general Business of the whole Body of the People.

Chap. V

31. *Of the Situation of the People in general.*

32. It is the greatest Happiness for a Man to be so circumstanced, that, if his Passions should prompt him to be mischievous, he should still think it more for his Interest not to give Way to them.

33. The Laws ought to be so framed, as to secure the Safety of every Citizen as much as possible.

34. The Equality of the Citizens consists in this; that they should all be subject to the same Laws.

35. This Equality requires Institutions so well adapted, as to prevent the Rich from oppressing those who are not so wealthy as themselves, and converting all the Charges and Employments intrusted to them as Magistrates only, to their own private Emolument.

36. General or political Liberty does not consist in that licentious Notion, *That a Man may do whatever he pleases.*

37. In a State or Assemblage of People that live together in a Community, where there are Laws, Liberty can only consist *in doing that which every One ought to do*, and *not to be constrained to do that which One ought not to do.*

38. A Man ought to form in his own Mind an exact and clear Idea of what Liberty is. *Liberty is the Right of doing whatsoever the Laws allow:* And if any one Citizen could do what the Laws forbid, there would be no more Liberty; because others would have an equal Power of doing the same.

39. The political Liberty of a Citizen is the Peace of Mind arising from the Consciousness, that every Individual enjoys his peculiar Safety; and in order that the People might attain this Liberty, the Laws ought to be so framed, that no one Citizen should stand in Fear of another; but that all of them should stand in Fear of the same Laws.

Chap. VI

40. *Of Laws in general.*

41. Nothing ought to be forbidden by the Laws, but what may be prejudicial, either to every Individual in particular, or to the whole Community in general.

42. All Actions, which comprehend nothing of this Nature, are in nowise cognizable by the Laws; which are made only with the View of procuring the greatest possible Advantage and Tranquillity to the People, who live under their Protection.

43. To preserve Laws from being violated, they ought to be so good, and so well furnished with all Expedients, tending to procure the greatest possible Good to the People; that every Individual might be fully convinced, that it was his Interest, as well as Duty, to preserve those Laws inviolable.

44. And this is the most exalted Pitch of Perfection which we ought to labour to attain to.

45. Many Things rule over Mankind. Religion, the Climate, Laws, the Maxims received from Government, the Example of past Ages, Manners, and Customs.

46. Hence results a general Sense in the People, similar to these Causes.

47. For Instance, Nature and Climate domineer almost alone over the savage People.

48. Customs govern the Chinese.

49. The Laws tyrannise with savage Ferocity over the Japonese.

50. Manners heretofore took the Lead amongst the Lacedemonians.

51. Maxims of Government, and their ancient Manners bore the Sway at Rome.

52. The different Characters of Nations are blended with Virtues and Vices, with good and bad Qualities.

53. That Composition, or Admixture, might be pronounced happy, from which many and great Blessings spring; though, we

frequently cannot even conjecture the Cause, from whence they should issue.

54. To prove this, I here produce in Evidence different Examples of different Facts. The Spaniards were at all Times remarkably eminent for their Good Faith. History furnishes us with remarkable Instances of their Fidelity in keeping a Pledge intrusted to their Care: They frequently submitted to Death, rather than betray their Trust, and they still retain this Fidelity, for which they were formerly so renowned. All Nations, who trade in Cadiz intrust their Fortunes to the Spaniards; and, hitherto, have had no Reason to repent of their Confidence. But this amazing Quality, blended with their Laziness, forms such a strange Medly, as produces Effects prejudicial to themselves. The other European Nations carry on all that Trade, before their very Eyes, which belongs properly to their Monarchy only.

55. The Character of the Chinese is of a different Complexion, and forms a Contrast which is the very Reverse of that of the Spaniards. The Precariousness of their Lives (arising from the very Nature of their Soil and Climate) produces in them an Activity almost inconceivable; and so immoderate a Fondness for Gain, that no trading Nation can trust them. This known Perfidy of theirs, has preserved to them the sole Trade of Japon. Not one of the European Merchants durst ever venture to engage in the Japon Trade under their Names, though they might have done it with great Ease through their maritime Provinces.

56. By what *I* have here advanced, *I* meant not, in the least, to abridge that infinite Distance which must ever subsist between Vices and Virtues. God forbid! *My* Intention was only to shew, that all the *political* Vices are not moral Vices; and that all the *moral* Vices are not *political* Ones. This Distinction ought to be known and carefully attended to, that in making the Laws nothing may be introduced in them which is contrary to the general Sense of a Nation.

57. The Legislation ought to adapt its Laws to the general Sense of a Nation. We do nothing so well as what we do freely and uncontrouled, and following the natural Bent of our own Inclinations.

58. In order to introduce better Laws, it is essentially necessary to prepare the Minds of the People for their Reception. But that it may never be pleaded in Excuse, that it is impossible to carry even the most useful Affairs into Execution, because the Minds of the People are not yet prepared for it; you must, in that Case, take the Trouble upon yourselves to prepare them; and, by these Means, you will already have done a great Part of the Work.

59. Laws are the peculiar and distinct Institutions of the Legislator; but Manners and Customs are the Institutions of the whole Body of the People.

60. Consequently, if there should be a Necessity of making great Alterations amongst the People for their greater Benefit, that must be corrected by Laws, which has been instituted by Laws, and that must be amended by Custom, which has been introduced by Custom; and it is extreme bad Policy to alter that by Law, which ought to be altered by Custom.

61. There are Means of preventing the Growth of Crimes, and these are the Punishments inflicted by the Laws. At the same Time there are Means for introducing an Alteration in Customs, and these are Examples.

62. Besides, the more a People have an Intercourse with one another, the more easy it is for them to introduce a Change in their Customs.

63. In a Word, every Punishment, which is not inflicted through Necessity, is tyrannical. The Law has not its Source merely from Power. Things indifferent in their Nature, do not come under the Cognizance of the Laws.

Chap. VII

64. *Of the Laws in particular.*

65. Laws carried to the Extremity of Right, are productive of the Extremity of Evil.

66. All Laws, where the Legislation aims at the Extremity of Rigour, may be evaded. It is Moderation which rules a People, and not Excess of Severity.

67. Civil Liberty flourishes, when the Laws deduce every Punishment from the peculiar Nature of every Crime. The Application of Punishment ought not to proceed from the arbitrary Will, or mere Caprice of the Legislator, but from the Nature of the Crime; and it is not the Man, who ought to do Violence to a Man, but the proper Action of the Man himself.

68. Crimes are divisible into four Classes.

69. The first Class of Crimes is that against Religion.

70. The second, against Manners.

71. The third, against the Peace.

72. The fourth, against the Security of the Citizens.

73. The Punishments inflicted upon these ought to flow from the specific Nature of the very Crime.

74. (1*st*) *I* include nothing more under the first Class of Crimes, which affect Religion, but what is a direct and immediate Attack upon it; such as Sacrilege, distinctly and clearly defined by Law: For the Crimes of those who disturb People in the Exercise of Religion, are of the same Nature with those which violate the public Peace and Security, and consequently ought to be referred to those Classes. In order that the Punishment for the above-mentioned Crime of Sacrilege might flow from the Nature of the Thing, it ought to consist in depriving the Offender of those Benefits which we are intitled to by Religion; for Instance, by Expulsion from the Churches, Exclusion from the Society of the Faithful for a limited Time, or for ever, by shunning their Company.

75. And, in general, civil Punishments are also made Use of in Offences of this Nature.

76. (2*d*) In the second Class of Crimes are included those, which are contrary to Good Manners.

77. Such as the Corruption of the Purity of Morals in general, either publick or private; that is, every Procedure contrary to the Regulations; which shew, in what Manner we ought to enjoy the external Conveniencies given to Man by Nature, for his Necessities, Interest, and Satisfaction. The Punishments of these Crimes ought to flow also from the Nature of the Thing.

A Privation of those Advantages, which the Society has annexed to Purity of Morals; pecuniary Penalties, Shame, or Dishonour; a Necessity of absconding; publick Infamy; Expulsion from the City, and the Community; in a Word, all the Punishments depending upon judicial Correction, are sufficient to repress the Presumption, and disorderly Behaviour of both Sexes. In Fact, these Offences do not spring so much from Badness of Heart, as from a certain Forgetfulness, or mean Opinion of one's Self. To this Class belong the Crimes only which are prejudicial to Manners, and not those which at the same Time violate the publick Security; such as carrying off by Force, and Rapes; for they are already classed amongst the Crimes of the fourth Species.

78. (3*d*) The Crimes of the third Class are those which violate the Peace and Tranquillity of the Citizens. The Punishments of them ought also to flow from the very Nature of the Crime, and to bear Relation to this Tranquillity; as for Instance, Imprisonment, Banishment, Corrections, and other Punishments, which reclaim these turbulent People, and bring them back to the established Order. The Crimes against the Peace, *I* confine to those Things only, which consist in a simple Breach of the civil Polity.

79. For those which violate the Peace, and at the same Time directly attack the publick Security, are referred to the fourth Class of Crimes.

(4*th*) The Penalties due to those last Crimes are peculiarly and emphatically termed Capital Punishments. It is a Kind of Retaliation by which the Society deprives that Citizen of his Security, who has deprived, or would deprive another of it. This Punishment is taken from the Nature of the Thing, deduced from Reason, and the Sources of Good and Evil. A Citizen deserves Death, when he has violated the public Security so far as to have taken away, or attempted to take away, the Life of another. Capital Punishment is the Remedy for a distempered Society. If publick Security is violated with respect to Property, Reasons may be produced to prove, that the Offender ought not, in such a Case, to suffer capital Punishment; but that it seems better, and more conformable to Nature, that the Crimes against the publick Security, with respect to Property, should be punished by Privation of Property; and this ought inevitably to have been done, if the Wealth of every One had been common, or equal. But as those who have no Property are always most ready to invade the Property of others, to remedy this Defect, corporal Punishment was obliged to be substituted instead of pecuniary. What *I* have here mentioned is drawn from the Nature of Things, and conduces to the Protection of the Liberty of the Citizens.

Chap. VIII

80. *Of Punishments.*

81. The Love of our Country, Shame, and the Dread of publick Censure, are Motives which restrain, and may deter Mankind from the Commission of a Number of Crimes.

82. The greatest Punishment for a bad Action, under a mild Administration, will be for the Party to be convinced of it. The civil Laws will there correct Vice with the more Ease, and will not be under a Necessity of employing more rigorous Means.

83. In these Governments, the Legislature will apply itself more to prevent Crimes, than to punish them, and should take more Care to instil Good Manners into the Minds of the Citizens, by proper Regulations, than to dispirit them by the Terror of corporal and capital Punishments.

84. In a Word, whatever is termed Punishment in the Law, is, in Fact, nothing but Pain and Suffering.

85. Experience teaches us, that, in those Countries where Punishments are mild, they operate with the same Efficacy upon the Minds of the Citizens, as the most severe in other Places.

86. If a sensible Injury should accrue to a State from some popular Commotion, a violent Administration will be at once for a sudden Remedy, and instead of recurring to the ancient Laws, will inflict some terrible Punishment, in order to crush the growing Evil on the Spot. The Imagination of the People is affected at the Time of this greater Punishment, just as it would have been affected by the least; and when the Dread of this

Punishment gradually wears off, it will be compelled to introduce a severer Punishment upon all Occasions.

87. The People ought not to be driven on by violent Methods, but we ought to make Use of the Means which Nature has given us, with the utmost Care and Caution, in order to conduct them to the End we propose.

88. Examine with Attention the Cause of all Licentiousness; and you will find, that it proceeds from the Neglect of punishing Crimes, not from the Mildness of Punishments. Let us follow Nature, which has given Shame to Man, for his Scourge, and let the greatest Part of the Punishment consist in the Infamy which accompanies the Punishment.

89. And if a Country could be found, where Infamy should not be the Consequence of Punishment; the Reason of this is to be imputed to some tyrannical Government, which inflicted the same Punishments upon the Innocent and the Guilty, without Distinction.

90. And if another Country should be known, where the People are restrained by nothing but the severest Punishments; you must again be assured, that this proceeds from the Violence of the Government, which has ordained those Punishments for the slightest Offences.

91. It happens frequently, that a Legislator, who wants to extirpate an Evil, thinks of nothing but this Method of Cure: His Eyes are fixed on this Object only, and do not foresee the bad Consequences which attend it. When the Evil is once cured, we remark nothing but the Severity of the Legislator; but it leaves a Distemper in the State, arising from this very Severity. The Minds of the People are corrupted, for they are inured to Despotism.

92. The Japonese Histories inform us, on the Subject of Education, that we ought to treat Children with Indulgence; because Correction hardens, and makes them stubborn; and, at the same Time, that Slaves ought not to be used with too much Severity, because they will immediately rebel in their own Defence. By remarking the Spirit, which ought to animate and

govern their *domestick* Polity, could not they from thence have formed their Idea, of what ought to have been infused into the *civil* Polity of their State?

93. One may find, even here, the Means of reclaiming unsettled and rambling Minds back to the right Path, by Maxims of the Law of God, of Philosophy, and of Morality, selected and adapted to their Turn of Mind, and balanced by a due Admixture of Rewards and Punishments; by a just Application of suitable Rules of Honour; by Punishments consisting of Shame, and by perpetuating the Enjoyments of Happiness and sweet Tranquillity. But if there should be any Danger, that Minds, which are so inured to Punishment, as not to be restrained but by the utmost Degree of Severity, and could never be reclaimed by moderate Punishments; in this Case, we ought to act [*observe this with Attention, as a Rule confirmed by the Experience of Facts, on all Occasions where Minds are hardened by the excessive Severity of Punishment*] in a wise, secret, and imperceptible Manner; and, on particular Occasions, to shew Lenity to some, who deserve it, by inflicting moderate Chastisement for their Crimes; and to persevere in this Method, till we gradually attain this end, of mitigating Punishment on all Occasions.

94. It is unjust to punish a Thief, who robs on the High-way, in the same Manner as another, who not only robs, but commits Murder. Every One sees clearly that some Difference ought to be made in their Punishment, for the Sake of the general Safety.

95. There are Countries, where Thieves are unwilling to commit Murder; because they, who only rob, may hope to be transported to their remote Settlements; but they who commit Murder, can, on no pretence whatever, expect that Favour.

96. Good Laws keep strictly a just Medium: They do not always inflict pecuniary, nor always subject Malefactors to corporal Punishment.

All Punishments, by which the human Body might be maimed, ought to be abolished.

Chap. IX

97. *Of the Administration of Justice in general.*

98. The Power of a Judge consists only in a due Execution of the Laws, to the End that no Doubt might arise with respect to the Liberty and Security of the Citizens.

99. For this Reason *Peter the Great* most wisely established the Senate, the Colleges, and the inferior Courts of Judicature; which are to administer Justice in the Name of their Sovereign, and according to the Laws; for this Reason, the Privilege of carrying Appeals to the Sovereign himself was made so difficult: A Law which ought never to be violated.

100. Consequently, there must be Courts of Judicature.

101. These Courts of Judicature make Decisions, and pass Sentences, which ought to be carefully preserved, and publickly known for this Reason, that, in the Courts of Judicature, Justice should be dispensed in the same Manner *this Day*, as it had been *the Day before*; and that the Property and Life of every Citizen should be as surely established, and as firmly secured by them, as the Constitution of the State itself.

102. In a sovereign State, very nice and exact Proofs are required; because, on the Decision of these Courts, not only the Life and Property, but even the Honour of Mankind depends.

103. The Judge ought to enter into the most subtile and minute Particulars of the Cause; so much the more, as the greatest Trust is reposed in him, and as the Affair upon which he decides is of the greatest Consequence. Consequently, we ought not to be surprized to find, in the Laws of these States, so many Rules, Boundaries, and Extensions; which amplify particular Cases, and seem to compose an Art from Reason itself.

104. The Distinction of Employments, Posterity, the Condition of different Ranks of People, established in sovereign States, frequently introduces with it many Divisions in relation to the Nature of Property. But the Laws which relate to the Regulation of this State may still more inlarge the Number of these Divisions.

105. According to this Principle, Wealth is Property, either acquired, or given in Dowry, or inherited from Parents, or Moveables, &c. &c.

106. Every Species of Property is subject to particular Regulations. These are to be strictly adhered to, in order to make a right Disposition of every particular Article; which, by this Method, is still more minutely divided.

107. The more the Number of Processes increase in Courts of Judicature under a Sovereign State, the more the Jurisdiction is overburthened with Decisions; which are some Times repugnant to each other; either because, in the alternate Succession of Judges, some differ in Opinion from others, or because the same Causes are some-times well, some-times ill defended; or finally, because of the innumerable Abuses, which insinuate themselves secretly, and by Degrees, into whatever passes through the Hands of Man.

108. This is a necessary Evil, which the Legislator remedies from time to time, as repugnant to the Nature of a moderate Government.

109. For if any one is obliged to apply to the Courts of Judicature, such Application ought to proceed from the Nature of the Constitution of the State, and not from the Contradiction and Ambiguity of the Laws.

110. In Governments where a Distinction of Persons is introduced, there must likewise be a personal Pre-eminence established by the Laws. The particular Pre-eminence, established by the Laws, which is least burthensome of all to the Community, is this: To be judged before one of the Courts of Judicature, preferably to any other. Hence arise new Difficulties; that is in order to know which Court of Judicature a Man ought to apply to.

111. One frequently hears it said in Europe, that Justice ought to be administered in all Places, in the same Manner as in the Turkish Empire. According to this Sentiment, no Nation under the Sun, but that which is plunged in the grossest Ignorance, could be capable of having a clear Idea of what is essentially necessary to be known by all the Universe.

112. If you examine with Attention all the Formalities of the Law, you will find, without Doubt, many Difficulties present themselves, which a Citizen must go through when he applies to the Law, in order to obtain his Property, or to procure Redress for some Injury he has received. But if you compare these Inconveniencies with the Liberty and Security of the Citizens, you will find them extremely trivial; and you will be convinced, at the same Time, that all the Difficulties, Cavils, and Delays in the Courts of Judicature, are nothing more than the Price, which every Citizen pays for his Liberty.

113. In the Turkish Dominions, where very little Regard is paid to the Property, Life, and Honour of the Subjects, they quickly determine all Disputes in *this*, or *that* Manner. Amongst them the Means of disentangling, and clearing up any knotty Affair, are not in the least attended to, provided the Dispute be but ended. The Basha, enlightened at once, orders the Bastinado on the Soles of the Feet to the Litigants, just as it strikes his Fancy, and then dismisses them.

114. But in States under a moderate Government, where equal Attention is paid to the Life, the Property, and the Honour of the meanest Citizen, no one can lose his Honour or Property, without a long and strict Examination into the Truth. No one can be deprived of Life, unless his Country itself demands it; but even his Country will not take away the Life of any one, without giving him Leave, first, to employ all the Means in his Power to defend it.

115. Where the Honour, Property, Life and Liberty of the Citizens are carefully guarded, these judicial Formalities increase in Proportion.

116. We ought to hear what the Defendant has to say; not only to gain a thorough Information of what he is accused of, but also to enable him to defend himself. He ought therefore either to answer for himself, or chuse any other Person to speak in his Behalf.

117. Some Persons think, that the youngest Counsellor, in every Court of Judicature, according to his Office, might plead for the Defendant; as for Instance, the Ensign in a Company.

Another Advantage would arise from hence, which is the greater Stock of Experience, which the Judges would acquire by that Method, in the Discharge of their Duties.

118. Defence here means nothing more, than a full Remonstrance to the Court of Judicature, of whatever can be urged in favour of the Defendant, in order for his Acquittal.

119. The Laws, which condemn a Man upon the Deposition of one Evidence only, are destructive to Liberty. There was a Law made in the Time of the Heirs of Constantine I, by which the single Evidence of one Man in a high Station is taken for sufficient Proof of the Guilt of the Party accused; and, for this Reason, the Evidence of others, in relation to the very same Affair, are not allowed to be heard. By the Will of this Legislator, the Decision was dispatched in a very quick and very strange Manner. They decided the Affair according to the Figure the Evidence made, and they judged of his Figure according to the Dignity of his Rank.

120. Two Witnesses are absolutely necessary, in order to form a right Judgment: For an Accuser, who affirms, and the Party accused, who denies the Fact, make the Evidence on both Sides equal; for that Reason, a Third is required in order to convict the Defendant; unless other clear collateral Proofs should fix the Credibility of the Evidence in favour of one of them.

121. The Evidence of two Witnesses is esteemed sufficient for Conviction, in every criminal Case whatsoever. The Law believes them, as if they spoke from the Mouth of Truth itself. The following Chapter will evince this more clearly.

122. In the same Manner they decide in almost every State, that every Child conceived in the Time of Wedlock is legitimate: The Law places its whole Confidence in the Mother. This is mentioned here on account of the Obscurity of the Laws in those Cases.

123. The Usage of Torture is contrary to all the Dictates of Nature and Reason; even Mankind itself cries out against it, and demands loudly the total Abolition of it. We see, at this very Time, a People greatly renowned for the Excellence of their civil

Polity, who reject it without any sensible Inconveniencies. It is, therefore, by no Means necessary by its Nature. *We* will explain this more at large here below.

124. There are Laws, which do not allow the Application of Torture, except only in those Cases, where the Prisoner at the Bar refuses to plead, and will neither acknowledge himself innocent nor guilty.

125. To make an Oath too cheap by frequent Practice, is to weaken the Obligation of it, and to destroy its Efficacy. The Kissing of the Cross cannot be used upon any Occasion, but when he, that takes an Oath, has no private Interest of his own to serve; as for Instance, the Judge and the Witnesses.

126. Those who are to be tried for capital Offences, should chuse their own Judges, with the Consent of the Laws; or, at least, should have a Right of rejecting such a Number of them, that those who remain in Court may seem as chosen by the Malefactors themselves.

127. It is likewise just, that some of the Judges should be of the same Rank of Citizenship as the Defendant; that is, his Equals; that he might not think himself fallen into the Hands of such People, as would violently over-rule the Affair to his Prejudice: Of this there are already Instances in the Martial Laws.

128. When the Defendant is condemned, it is not the Judges who inflict the Punishment upon him, but the Law.

129. The Sentence ought to be as clear and distinct as possible; even so far as to preserve the very identical Words of the Law. But if they should include the private Opinion of the Judge, the People will live in Society, without knowing exactly the reciprocal Obligations they lie under to one another in that State.

130. There are many different Ways of passing Sentence. In some Countries they shut up the Judges, and allow them neither meat nor drink, till they are unanimous in their Verdict.

131. There are sovereign States, where the Judges act after the Manner of Jurymen. They consult together, impart their

Minds to one another, moderate their Opinions, so as to conform with the Opinion of others, and strive to agree in their Suffrages.

132. The Judges amongst the Romans allowed no more than the precise Demand, without increasing, diminishing, or moderating it in the least.

133. But their Prætors invented other Forms of Plea for the Plaintiffs Right, which they termed the Right of Good Faith, in which the Manner of determining and pronouncing Sentence was more in the Judges Disposal, who had a Power of deciding as their Conscience directed.

134. For in a false Action for Debt the Plaintiff loses the Cause; and a Penalty ought to be laid upon the Defendant, if he does not acknowledge what he owes, that by these means good Faith might be preserved on both Sides.

135. If Judges, who ought to act according to the Laws, should have a Right to confine a Citizen, who can give Bail, in that Case there would be an End of Liberty, unless he should be put under Confinement, that he might immediately answer a Charge laid against him for such a Crime, as deserves capital Punishment by the Laws. In this Case he is really free; for he is subject to nothing else, but the Power of the Law.

136. But if the legislative Power thinks itself endangered by some secret Conspiracy against the State, or Sovereign, or by some traiterous Correspondence with neighbouring Enemies; in such a Case, the legislative Power allows the executive to take all suspected Citizens into Custody, for a limited Time, who are deprived of their Liberty for that Time; for this Reason only, that it might be preserved inviolate for ever.

137. But it is best to define exactly in the Laws those important Cases, in which a Citizen cannot be admitted to Bail: For the Law, in all Countries, deprives such People of their Liberty, who cannot find sufficient Bail, so long as the common Security, or a Part of it, shall require. In Chapter X this will be treated of more at large.

138. Though all Crimes affect the Community, yet those which affect the Citizens ought to be distinguished from those which still more immediately affect the State, in consideration

of the Union subsisting between the State and the Citizen. The first are termed *proper* or *particular* Crimes, because committed against Individuals; the second are Crimes which affect the Community, or whole Body of the People in general.

139. In some Countries, a Prince placed upon the Throne to see the Law duly executed in every Part of his Dominions, according to the Constitution of the Country, establishes an Officer in every Government, to prosecute Crimes in the Name of the Sovereign; from whence the Name of the Informer is utterly unknown in those Countries. But if ever the People suspect this Avenger of Mankind of abusing the Trust reposed in him, they will then oblige him to declare the Name of his Informer. This Office, established in the Community, watches over the Welfare of the Citizens; the Concealment of the Informer's Name carries on the Business, and the People are quiet. *Peter the Great* has prescribed to the Attorneys to examine, and to determine all Affairs where there is no Witness; and if to this could be still added a Person of Rank, vested with the above-mentioned Office, Informers would be less known amongst us.

140. That Law of Rome is highly blame-worthy, which allowed the Judges to take small Presents, provided they did not annually exceed the Sum of one Hundred Crowns. They to whom we give nothing, demand nothing; but they to whom we give but a Trifle, desire that Instant a little more, and afterwards are hardly to be satisfied. Besides this, it is easier to prove the Truth to him, who, though obliged to take nothing, yet takes a Trifle, than to him who will take more, when he ought to have taken less, and who will always find specious Reasons, and proper Representations sufficient to excuse himself.

141. Among the Roman Laws there is one, which forbids the Confiscation of Property to the Sovereign, except in Cases of *Treason*; and even then, only in the *highest Degree* of that Crime. It would be often extremely prudent to conform to the Spirit of this Law, and to *specify* the *particular* Crimes to which the Confiscation of Property to the Sovereign should *be limited*, and at the same Time no other Part of Property ought to be confiscated to the Sovereign, besides the proper Acquests of the Criminal.

Chap. X

142. *Of the Forms of criminal Courts.*

143. We do not intend here to enter into extensive Inquiries, nor into a subtile Division of every Crime into its respective distinct Species, nor to ascertain which Punishment is best adapted to each. We have already divided them into four Classes; and, by a contrary Procedure, the great Number and Variety of Objects, and the different Circumstances of Time and Place, would oblige us to launch out into an Infinity of trifling Particulars. It will be sufficient here to lay down, 1*st*, The principal *general Rules*, and, 2*dly*, The *Crimes* which are most prejudicial.

144. Q. 1. *From whence have Punishments their Origin, and upon what Right is the Power of Punishing founded?*

145. We may term Laws *the Means* by which People are united together, and protected in Society, and without which, Society would be dissolved and ruined.

146. It was not sufficient to establish these *Means*, which became a *Deposite* to Society: It was requisite, at the same Time, to support them. Punishments were instituted for the Violators of them.

147. Every Punishment is unjust, when it is not essentially necessary to preserve this *Deposite* entire.

148. The first Consequence of these original Rules is this: That the Right of determining the respective Punishment for Crimes appertains solely to the Laws, and that the Legislator, as Representative of the whole Society, and having the entire Power deposited in his own Hands, has the sole Right of making penal Laws. Hence it again follows, that the Judges and Administrations, as being themselves no more than a Part of the Society, cannot with Justice, nor under Pretence of the general Good, inflict a Punishment upon any other Member of the Society, which has not been expressly appointed by the Laws.

149. Another Consequence is, That a Sovereign, who is the Representative, and possesses the whole Power for the Defence of the Community, can, by his own Authority, publish general

penal Laws, to which every Member in the Society is *amenable*; but he ought to abstain from sitting as *Judge himself*, as was mentioned above in the 99th Article. Therefore he ought to appoint *other Persons*, who should judge according to the Laws.

150. The third Consequence is, If the Severity of Punishment should not have been already over-ruled by the beneficent Virtue of Compassion for Mankind, this Consideration alone, *that it is useless*, would suffice to abolish it; which serves for Proof, that it is unjust.

151. The fourth Consequence is, That Judges, in criminal Cases, can have no Right to interpret penal Laws; for this Reason only, that they are not Legislators. Who then should be the lawful Interpreter of them? I answer, the Sovereign, and not the Judge; for the Duty of a Judge consists only in examining closely, whether a Man has, or has not committed such a Fact, contrary to the Law.

152. A Judge, in every criminal Case whatsoever, ought only to form a Judgment in his own Mind by a *Syllogism*, in which the first Proposition lays down the general Law; the second declares, whether the Action in question is conformable to, or repugnant to that Law; and the Conclusion consists either in the Acquittal, or Punishment of the Party accused. If the Judge himself is constrained, by the Obscurity of the Laws, to make more than *one Syllogism* in criminal Cases, then all will be obscure and uncertain.

153. Nothing is so dangerous, as this general Axiom: *The Spirit of the Law ought to be considered, and not the Letter.* This can mean nothing else, but to break down the Fence, which opposes the Torrent of popular Opinions. This is a self-evident Truth, which is not to be controverted, how strange soever it may appear to vulgar Minds; who are more terrified by the least Irregularity which happens before their Eyes, than by Consequences more remote, but infinitely more fatal, which flow from one false Principle adopted by a People. Every Man has his own particular Mode of viewing Objects presented to his Mind, different from every other. We should see the Fate of a Citizen changed, by the Removal of his Cause from one Court of Judi-

cature to another; and his Life and Liberty depending upon Chance, either from some false Ideas, or the Perverseness of his Judge: We should see the *same* Crimes punished *differently*, at *different* Times, by the *very same* Court of Judicature; if they will not listen to the invariable Voice of the fixed, established Laws, but follow the deceitful Inconstancy of their own arbitrary Interpretations.

154. The Disorders which may possibly arise from a *strict* and *close* Adherence to *the Letter* of *penal* Laws, are by no Means comparable to those, which are produced by the *arbitrary Interpretation* of them. The Errors proceeding from the *first* are only *temporary*, and will oblige the Legislator to make, some-times, easy and necessary Corrections in such *Words* of the Law as are capable of a *double Meaning*. However, it will prove a Bridle to curb that *licentious* Method of *interpreting*, and *deciding* at *their own Discretion*, which may prove fatal to every Citizen.

155. If the Laws are not *exactly* and *clearly* defined, and understood *Word by Word*; if it be not the sole Office of a Judge, to *distinguish*, and lay down *clearly*, what Action is conformable to the Laws, and what is repugnant to them: If the Rule of *just* and *unjust*, which ought to govern alike the ignorant Clown, and the enlightened Scholar, be not a *simple Question* of Matter of Fact for the Judges; then the Situation of the Citizen will be exposed to strange Accidents.

156. By making the *penal* Laws always *clearly* intelligible, *Word by Word*, every one may calculate truly, and know exactly the Inconveniencies of a bad Action; a Knowledge which is *absolutely* necessary for restraining People from committing it; and the People may enjoy Security, with respect both to their Persons and Property; which ought ever to remain so, because this is the *main Scope* and *Object* of the Laws, and without which the Community would be dissolved.

157. If the Power of *interpreting* Laws be an Evil, there is an Evil also which attends the *Obscurity* of them, and lays us under the Necessity of having Recourse to their Interpretation. This Irregularity is still greater, when the Laws are written in a

Language *unknown* to the People, or expressed in *uncommon* Phrases.

158. The Laws ought to be written in the *common vernacular Tongue*; and the Code, which contains all the Laws, ought to be esteemed as a Book of the utmost Use, which should be purchased at as *small* a Price as the Catechism. If the Case were otherwise, and the Citizen should be ignorant of the Consequences of his own Actions, and what concerns his Person and Liberty, he will then depend upon some few of the People, who have taken upon themselves the Care of preserving and explaining them. Crimes will be less frequent, in *proportion* as the Code of Laws is more *universally* read, and *comprehended* by the People. And, for this Reason, it must be ordained, That, in all the Schools, Children should be taught to read *alternately* out of the Church Books, and out of *those* which contain the Laws.

159. Q. 2*d*, *Which are the best Means to be used, when a Citizen is to be taken into Custody, and also to convict him of a Crime?*

160. That Person will violate the *personal Security* of every Citizen; who shall allow a Court of Judicature, (which is obliged to act according to the Laws, and has the Power of imprisoning a Citizen) to deprive *one Man* of his Liberty, under some frivolous Pretence, and to leave *another* at large, notwithstanding the most clear Evidence of his Guilt.

161. To confine a Citizen is a Punishment, which differs from all other Punishments in this, that it inevitably *precedes* the judicial Declaration of the Crime.

162. But this Punishment cannot be inflicted, except where there is a great Probability that a Citizen has committed a Crime.

163. Consequently, the Law ought to *specify* exactly the *distinguishing Marks* of *that* Crime, which should make a Man liable to be put under Confinement, and should subject the Party accused to this Punishment, and to the *verbal Examinations*, which are likewise a Species of Punishment. As for instance:

164. The Voice of the People, which accuses him; his Flight; his own preceding Confession, whilst at Liberty; the Evidence

of his Accomplice in the same Crime; the Threats, the known Enmity between the accused Party and the offended, the very Fact itself, and *other similar Marks*, will afford sufficient Reason why a Citizen ought to be taken into Custody.

165. But these Proofs ought to be *specified* by the Law, and *not* by the Judges, whose Sentences are always averse to civil Liberty, if they are not deduced from the general Rule, which is in the Code of Laws, upon whatever Occasion it may so happen.

166. When the Prison shall be less dreadful; that is, when Humanity and Compassion shall reach even the Prisons themselves, and shall penetrate the *callous Hearts* of the Officers of Judicature; then the Laws may be satisfied with *these specific Marks*, and order any Person into Custody.

167. There is a Difference between taking into Custody, and shutting up in Prison.

168. To take a Man into Custody is nothing more, than to guard the Person of a Citizen accused of some dangerous Crime, until it can be discovered, whether he is guilty or not; consequently, Confinement ought to be as short, and as gentle as possible; a *limited* Time ought to be fixed for it, *proportioned* to the Time *requisite* for preparing the Process to be laid before the Judges. The Strictness of the Confinement ought to be no greater, than what is necessary to prevent the Escape of the Offender, or for the Discovery of Proofs of the Crime alledged against him. The Affair therefore ought to be *finally* determined as soon as possible.

169. The Man, who has been under Confinement, and afterwards cleared himself of what was laid to his Charge, ought not to be *subject to Infamy*. Amongst the Romans, we see that Citizens, who had been accused in Court even of capital Crimes, yet were honoured, and raised to the principal Posts in the State, after they had proved their Innocence.

170. The Confinement of a Prison is the Consequence of the final Determination of the Judges, and serves instead of Punishment.

171. We ought not to confine in the same Place, 1*st*, Him,

who is accused of a Crime upon *Suspicion* only; *2dly*, He, who is *convicted*; *3dly*, He, who is *condemned*. He who is charged on *Suspicion*, is kept only in Custody, and the other two are confined in Prison. But this Imprisonment will be only a Part of the Punishment to *One* of them; but the *Other* must suffer the Punishment *itself* he is condemned to.

172. To be taken into Custody is not to be considered as a Punishment, but as an Expedient to secure the Person of a Citizen accused: Which Expedient assures him, at the same Time, of Liberty, if he be not really guilty.

173. To be put under Arrest by the Articles of War, is no Dishonour to any Member of the Military Corps. It ought to be the same among the Citizens, with respect to *Civil* Confinement.

174. The detaining a Person under Confinement changes into *Imprisonment*; if the Party accused should be found *guilty*; consequently there should be *different* Places of *Confinement* for all three.

175. Here is a general Proposition for Calculation, in order to *evince with Certainty* the Truth of the Crime committed; as for Instance, when the Proofs of any Fact depend on each other; that is, when the Proofs of the Crime can neither be *demonstrated*, nor the *Truth* of them *affirmed*, otherwise than of *one* by *another*. When the *Truth* of *many* Proofs *depends* upon the *Truth* of *one* Proof only, then the *Number* of Proofs neither *increases* nor *diminishes* the Probability of the Fact; because, *at that Time*, the *Force* of *all* the Proofs *centers* only in the *Force* of *that Proof*, upon which all the rest *depend*; and if this *one Proof* should not be *valid*, then all the *others* depending upon that *one* will be instantly *invalidated* too. But when the Proofs are *independent* on each other, and every particular Proof *confirms* the *same* Truth, then the *Probability* of the Fact *increases* according to the *Number* of the Proofs; because, the Falsehood of *one* Proof does not infer the *Falsity* of another. Perhaps it will appear strange to some Persons, that *I* make use of the Word *Probability*, when *I* speak of Crimes; which, in order to *deserve Punishment*, ought to be *undoubtedly certain*; yet it ought here to be con-

sidered, that moral Certainty is only *Probability*; which is termed *Certainty*; because, every Man of Sense is obliged to acknowledge it *as such.*

176. The Proofs of Crimes may be divided into two Species, *perfect* and *imperfect. I* call those *perfect,* which exclude all *Possibility* of shewing the Innocence of the Party accused; and those *imperfect,* which do not exclude such Possibility. One single *perfect* Proof is sufficient to confirm the Justice of the Condemnation which was passed upon the Malefactor.

177. With respect to *imperfect* Proofs, their Number should be so great, as to form a *perfect* Proof; that is, the *Sum Total* of all such Proofs ought to exclude all *Possibility* of proving the Innocence of the Party accused; though each Proof, *separately* taken, does not exclude it. We must add to this, that *imperfect* Proofs, which the Party accused is not able to *invalidate* in his Defence, though his Innocence ought to give him *the Means* of doing it; in such a Case, become *perfect.*

178. Where the Laws are precise and clear, there the *Office* of a Judge *consists* only in *ascertaining* the Fact.

179. To investigate the Proofs of a Crime, a Quickness of Apprehension is required, and in order to sift out from these Disquisitions the *final Result,* there ought to be a *Precision* and *Clearness* of Ideas; but, in order to judge by this *final Result* of the whole, nothing more is required but plain good Sense, which will be a more certain Guide, than all the Knowledge of a Judge, who is accustomed to find every one guilty.

180. That Law, therefore, is highly beneficial to the Community where it is established, which ordains that every Man shall be judged by his Peers or Equals. For when the Fate of a Citizen is in Question, all Prejudices arising from the Difference of Rank or Fortune should be stifled; because they ought to have no Influence between the Judges and the Parties accused.

181. But if the Crime extends to the Prejudice of a third Person, *one Moiety* of the Judges ought to be taken from the *Peers* to the Party accused, and the *other Moiety* from the *Peers* to the Party offended.

182. It is also just, that the Party accused should have the Liberty of excluding a *certain Number* of his Judges, upon any *Suspicion* of Partiality. Where the Party accused has the Benefit of this Right, in that Case he, who is guilty, will seem to condemn himself.

183. The Sentences of the Judges, as well as the Proofs of the Crimes, ought to be communicated to the People; that every Citizen might say, *He lives under the Protection of the Laws*; a Sentiment, which inspires Courage in the Citizens, and is of the greatest Utility to a Sovereign, who has his *real Interest* at Heart.

184. It is highly necessary in all Laws, *to specify exactly* the principal Rules upon which the *Credibility* of the Evidence depends, and the *Strength* of the Proof required for every Crime.

185. Every Man of good Sense, that is, whose Ideas have a Connection with each other, and whose Sensations sympathize with the Sensations of those who are like himself, is qualified to be a Witness. But the Credit due to his Evidence will be exactly *in Proportion*, as he *is interested* in declaring, or concealing the Truth. Credit must be given to Witnesses in every Case, where they have no Reason to give a false Testimony.

186. There are People, who estimate among the *Abuses* of Words, *those* which have *stolen secretly* into Use, and have already *taken strong Root* in worldly Transactions. That Observation is worthy of Remembrance, which induced Legislators to abolish the Evidence of a Malefactor after Condemnation. Such a Citizen is reckoned as *dead in Law*, say the Legislators, and a *dead Man* is incapable of producing any Fact. If the Evidence of a Malefactor, after Sentence of Condemnation only, should be no Obstacle to the judicial Course of Law, why do not they allow him a little more Time, even after Condemnation, for the Sake of Truth, and the terrible Destiny of the unfortunate Man; that he might either justify himself, or others who are accused, if he can but produce *new Proofs*, which may alter the Nature of the Fact?

187. Formalities are necessary in the Administration of Justice, but they must never be appointed in such a Manner by

the Laws, as may prove fatal to Innocence, otherwise they would occasion great Inconveniences.

188. Therefore we may admit the Testimony of *any Person*, who has *no Reason* to be a false Witness. By these Means the *Credibility* of the Evidence, will be *greater* or *less*, *in Proportion* to the Hatred, or Friendship, or Connections, or Differences, *subsisting* between the *Witness* and the *Party* accused.

189. One Evidence alone is not sufficient. When the Party accused *denies* that which a single Evidence *affirms*, Truth remains *in Suspense*, and the Right that every one has to be esteemed *innocent*, will turn the Balance, in such a Case, on the Side of the *Party* accused.

190. The Credibility of a Witness is of so much the *less* Weight, as the Crime is *more* horrible, and the Circumstances of it are *less* probable. This Rule may be applied also in Cases of Witchcraft, or Acts of wanton Cruelty.

191. Whoever obstinately refuses to answer such Questions as are put to him by the Court, deserves Punishment; which ought to be appointed by the Law, and chosen out of the most rigorous of those which are already established, to the End that the *Guilty* might not screen themselves from being exposed as a *publick Example* to the People, which they ought to be. This particular Punishment is unnecessary, when no Doubt can be made that the Party accused has really committed the Crime he stands charged with; for Confession is no longer necessary, when other evident Proofs demonstrate that he is guilty. This last Case is the most common; because the Evidences generally depose the *chief Circumstances* in criminal Cases, which the Guilty *refuse* to confess.

192. Q. 3. *Whether the Torture of the Rack does not violate the Rules of Equity; and whether it produces the End proposed by the Laws?*

193. The Torture of the Rack is a Cruelty, established and made use of by many Nations, and is applied to the Party accused during the Course of his Trial, either to extort from him a Confession of his Guilt, or in order to clear up some Contradictions, in which he had involved himself during his Examina-

tion, or to compel him to discover his Accomplices, or in order to discover other Crimes, of which, though he is not accused, yet he may *perhaps* be guilty.

194. (1.) No Man ought to be looked upon as *guilty*, before he has received his judicial Sentence; nor can the Laws deprive him of *their* Protection, before it is proved that he has *forfeited all Right* to it. What Right therefore can Power give to any to inflict Punishment upon a Citizen at a Time, when it is yet dubious, whether he is *innocent* or *guilty*? Whether the Crime be known or unknown, it is not very difficult to gain a thorough Knowledge of the Affair by duly weighing all the Circumstances. If the Crime be known, the Criminal ought not to suffer any Punishment but what the Law ordains; consequently the Rack is quite unnecessary. If the Crime be not known, the Rack ought not to be applied to the Party accused; for this Reason, *That the Innocent ought not to be tortured*; and, in the Eye of the Law, every Person is innocent whose Crime is not yet *proved*. It is undoubtedly extremely necessary, that no Crime, after it has been proved, should remain unpunished. The Party accused on the Rack, whilst in the Agonies of Torture, is not Master enough of himself to be able to declare the Truth. Can we give more Credit to a Man, when he is light-headed in a Fever, than when he enjoys the free Use of his Reason in a State of Health? The Sensation of Pain may arise to such a Height, that, after having subdued the whole Soul, it will leave her no longer the Liberty of producing any proper Act of the Will, except that of taking the shortest instantaneous Method, in the very twinkling of an Eye, as it were, of getting rid of her Torment. In such an Extremity, even an *innocent* Person will roar out, that he is *guilty*, only to gain *some Respite* from his Tortures. Thus the very same Expedient, which is made use of to distinguish the *Innocent* from the *Guilty*, will take away the *whole Difference* between them; and the Judges will be as uncertain, whether they have an *innocent* or a *guilty* Person before them, as they were before the Beginning of this *partial* Way of Examination. The Rack, therefore, is a sure Method of condemning an *innocent* Person of a weakly Constitution, and of acquitting a *wicked Wretch*, who depends upon the Robustness of his Frame.

195. (2.) The Rack is likewise made use of to oblige the Party accused to clear up (as they term it) the Contradictions in which he has involved himself in the Course of his Examination; as if the Dread of Punishment, the Uncertainty and Anxiety in determining what to say, and even gross Ignorance itself, common to both *Innocent* and *Guilty*, could not lead a timorous *Innocent*, and a *Delinquent*, who seeks to hide his Villanies, into Contradictions; and as if Contradictions, which are so common to Man even in a State of Ease and Tranquillity, would not increase in that Perturbation of Soul, when he is plunged entirely in Reflections, how to escape the Danger he is threatened with.

196. (3.) To make use of the Rack for discovering, whether the Party accused has not committed *other* Crimes, besides *that* which he has been *convicted* of, is a certain Expedient to *screen every Crime* from its *proper* Punishment: For a Judge will always be discovering new Ones. Finally, this Method of Proceeding will be founded upon the following Way of reasoning: *Thou art guilty of one Crime, therefore, perhaps, thou hast committed an Hundred others: According to the Laws, thou wilt be tortured and tormented; not only because thou art guilty, but even because thou mayest be still more guilty.*

197. (4.) Besides this, the Party accused is tortured, to oblige him to discover his Accomplices. But when we have already proved, that the Rack cannot be the proper Means for searching out the Truth, then how can it give any Assistance in discovering the Accomplices in a Crime? It is undoubtedly extremely easy for him, who accuses himself, to accuse others. Besides, is it just to torture one Man for the Crimes of others? Might not the Accomplices be discovered by examining the Witnesses, who were produced against the Criminal? by a strict Inquiry into the Proofs alledged against him, and even by the Nature of the Fact itself, and the Circumstances which happened at the Time when the Crime was committed? In short, by all the Means which serve to prove the Delinquent guilty of the Crime he had committed?

198. Q. 4. *Must Punishments be proportioned to Crimes, and how are we to fix the Proportion?*

199. A Time ought to be fixed by the Law for collecting the Proofs, and whatever is necessary for carrying on the Prosecution of great Crimes; that the Guilty might not be able to stave off the Punishment they merit for any Length of Time, nor perplex the Affair. When all the Proofs shall be collected, and the Certainty of the Crime shall be known; Time and Means ought to be allowed the *Guilty*, for his Justification, if he is able to make it. But this Interval should be but short, lest Delays should prejudice the good Effect of the Punishment; which ought to follow the Crime as speedily as possible; a Method which is esteemed one of the most powerful Expedients for preventing People from committing Crimes.

200. That the Punishment should not seem to proceed from the Violence of one, or many, who rise up against a Citizen, it ought to be public, as speedy as the Good of the Community requires, and as moderate as possible; and according to the Circumstances, proportioned to the Crime, and precisely *expressed* in the Laws.

201. Though Laws cannot punish the Intention; yet it cannot be said, that an Action, which is a *Prelude* to a Crime, and which *demonstrates* the violent Tendency of the Will to compleat that Crime in the very Act, should not deserve Punishment, though more moderate than any of those, which are established for a Crime already committed in Fact. Punishment, in this Case, is requisite, for this Reason, that it is highly necessary to *prevent* even the very *first Approaches* to a Crime; but as, between the *first* Attempts, and the *Completion* of a Crime, there might be some *Interval*; therefore it would not be amiss to leave the *greater* Punishment for the Crime *already completed*, in order to give some Encouragement to a Beginner in Wickedness; which may perhaps deter him from *completing* the Crime, he had just entered upon.

202. The same Punishment likewise must not be decreed for the Accomplices in any Villany, who are only *Accessory* to it, as for the Principals, who *actually committed* the Fact. If many Persons shall agree to hazard a Danger in Common, in that Case, the greater the Danger is, the more they will strive to bring every

One into an equal Share of it. The Laws, which punish the *Principals* in a Crime with more Severity than those who are barely *accessory* to it, will prevent the Danger from being *equally* divided amongst the whole Confederacy, and will render it more difficult to find a Man who would take *the Whole* upon *himself*, in the Execution of any *concerted* Villany. For the Danger he exposes himself to, will be *greater*, just in the Proportion of that *greater* Degree of Punishment allotted for him, to that *smaller* Degree of Punishment *decreed* for the *rest* of his Confederates. There is only one Case, in which we can make an Exception to this general Rule; which is, when the Perpetrator of a Crime receives a *peculiar* Reward from his Confederates: In such a Case, as the *Difference* in point of *Danger* is recompenced by the *Difference* in point of the *Emolument*, his Punishment ought to be *equal* to that of the *whole Body* of the Confederates. These Considerations may seem extremely refined and delicate; but we ought to reflect, how essentially necessary it is, that the Laws should leave as little Room as possible, for *Confederates* in Villany to *agree* among themselves.

203. There are some States, which dispense with the Punishment of a *Confederate* in any great Crime, provided he *impeaches* his Accomplices. Such an Expedient has its Inconveniencies, when practised on some particular Occasions. A fixed standing Law, which promises *Pardon* to any Accomplice who *reveals* a Crime, ought to be preferred to a timely *particular* Discovery of it, on some particular Occasion. For such a Law may prevent the *Combination* of a *Crew* of Villains by striking such a Terror into all, as may prevent any one of them from taking the Danger *wholly* upon *himself*. But we ought afterwards to *observe this Promise sacredly*; and give full Assurance of taking *every Person* under Protection, who shall *rely* upon the *good Faith* of this Law.

204. Q. 5. *What is the proper Estimate of the Degrees of Crimes?*

205. The Intent of well-regulated Punishments, is not merely to torment a sensible Being: They are ordained for this wise End; which is, to prevent a Criminal from doing *farther* Injury to the Community for the future; and to *deter* his fellow Citizens

from committing the *like* Offences. For this Reason, *such* Punishments, and *such* a *Mode* of inflicting them, ought to be selected, as will make the *deepest* and most *durable* Impression on the Minds of the People, and at the same Time with the *least* Cruelty to the Body of the Criminal.

206. Who can read, without being struck with Horror, the History of so many barbarous and useless Tortures, invented and executed without the least Remorse of Conscience, by *People* who assumed to themselves the *Name of Sages*? Who does not feel within himself a sensible Palpitation of the Heart, at the Sight of so many Thousands of unhappy Wretches, who have suffered, and still suffer: *frequently* accused of Crimes, which are *difficult, or impossible to happen*, proceeding often from *Ignorance*, and some-times from *Superstition*? Who can look, I say, upon the Dismembering of these People, who are executed with *slow* and *studied* Barbarity, by the *very Persons* who are *their Brethren*? Countries and Times, in which the most *cruel Punishments* were made use of, are those, in which the most *inhuman Villainies* were perpetrated.

207. That a Punishment may produce the *desired* Effect, it will be sufficient; when the *Evil* it occasions exceeds the *Good* expected from the Crime, including in the Calculation the *Excess* of the Evil *over* the Good, the undoubted *Certainty* of the Punishment, and the *Privation* of all the *Advantages* hoped for from the Crime. All Severity *exceeding* these Bounds is *useless*, and consequently *tyrannical.*

208. Wherever the Laws have been extremely severe, they have either been altered, or the Impunity of the Criminals arose from the very Severity of the Laws. The *Degrees* of Punishment ought to be referred to the present *Situation* and *Circumstances* in which every People *finds* itself. In *Proportion* as the *Minds* of those who live in a Community become *enlightened*, the *Sensibility* of every Individual *increases*; and if Sensibility increases amongst the Citizens, then the *Severity* of Punishments must *abate* in Proportion.

209. Q. 6. *Whether the Punishment of* Death *is really useful*

and necessary in a Community, for the Preservation of Peace and good Order?

210. Proofs from Fact demonstrate to us, that the frequent Use of capital Punishment never mended the Morals of a People. Therefore, if *I* prove the *Death* of a Citizen to be neither *useful* nor *necessary to Society in general, I* shall confute *those* who *rise up against* Humanity. *I* repeat here, *to Society in general*; because the Death of a Citizen can *only* be useful and necessary in *one* Case; which is, when, though he be *deprived* of Liberty, yet he has *such Power* by his *Connections*, as may *enable* him to raise Disturbances dangerous to the publick Peace. This Case can happen only, when a People either loses, or recovers their Liberty; or in a Time of Anarchy, when the *Disorders* themselves hold the *Place* of Laws. But in a Reign of Peace and Tranquillity, under a Government established with the united Wishes of a whole People; in a State well fortified against external Enemies, and protected within by strong Supports; that is, by its own internal Strength and virtuous Sentiments rooted in the Minds of the Citizens; and where the whole Power is lodged in the Hands of a Monarch; in such a State, there can be *no* Necessity for *taking away the Life* of a Citizen. The twenty Years Reign of the Empress *ELIZABETH PETROVNA* gives the Fathers of the People a more illustrious Example for Imitation than a Reign of the most shining Conquests.

211. It is not the *Excess* of Severity, nor the *Destruction* of the human Species, that produces a powerful Effect in the Hearts of the Citizens, but the *continued Duration* of the Punishment.

212. The Death of a Malefactor is not so efficacious a Method of deterring from Wickedness, as the *Example continually remaining* of a Man, who is deprived of his Liberty for *this End*; that he might *repair*, during a Life of *Labour*, the *Injury* he has done to the Community. The Terror of Death, excited by the Imagination, may be more strong, but has not Force enough to resist that *Oblivion*, so natural to Mankind. It is a general Rule, that rapid and violent Impressions on the human Mind, *disturb* and *give Pain*, but do not *operate* long upon the *Memory*. That a Punishment, therefore, might be conformable with Justice, it

ought to have *such* a Degree of Severity only, as might be sufficient to *deter* People from committing the Crime. Thence *I* presume to affirm, that there is no Man who, upon the least Degree of Reflection, would put the *greatest possible* Advantages he might flatter himself with from a Crime *on the one Side*, into the Balance against a Life *protracted* under a *total* Privation of Liberty, *on the other.*

213. Q. 7. *What Punishments ought to be inflicted for different Crimes?*

214. He who disturbs the publick Peace, who refuses to submit to the Laws, who breaks through those Ties, by which People are united in Society, and reciprocally defend each other, ought to be excluded from the Community; that is, to become *politically dead.*

215. There ought to be stronger Motives for the *Expulsion* of a *Citizen*, than of a *Stranger.*

216. A Punishment which declares a Man *infamous*, is a Mark of the publick *bad* Opinion, which deprives a Citizen of the Esteem and Confidence before reposed in him by the Community, and which expells him from the Fraternity existing between *Members* of the *same* Country. The *Infamy* inflicted by the Laws, ought to be the very same with that which *results* from universal Morality; for if an Action, which Moralists term *indifferent*, should be declared *infamous* by the Laws, then this bad Consequence would follow, that Actions, which for the common Good ought to be deemed *infamous*, will quickly cease to be reckoned so.

217. Great Care ought to be taken not to inflict corporal and painful Punishments upon those, who are infected with the Vice of Enthusiasm, either by pretending to Inspiration, or by counterfeiting a false Appearance of Sanctity. This Vice, founded upon Pride, and puffed up by Self-conceit, will derive *Glory*, and *fresh* Nourishment from the *very* Punishment itself. There have been Instances of this in the late *secret Chancery where such Persons used to come voluntarily on particular Days, merely for the Sake of suffering Punishment.*

218. *Infamy* and *Ridicule*, are the *only* Punishments which ought to be employed against these *pretendedly* inspired, and *counterfeit* Saints. For these may *abase* their *Pride*; and wise Laws, by opposing *those* Forces with Forces of the *same Kind*, will scatter, like Dust, that Admiration of these *false Doctrines*, which may *nestle* in the *weak* Minds of the Populace.

219. *Infamy* ought not to be inflicted upon a *Number* of Persons at once.

220. A Punishment ought to be *immediate*, *analogous* to the *Nature* of the Crime, and *known* to the Publick.

221. The *sooner* the Punishment succeeds to the Commission of a Crime, the *more useful* and *just* it will be. *Just*; because it will spare the Malefactor the torturing and useless Anguish of Heart about the *Uncertainty* of his Destiny. Consequently the Decision of an Affair, in a Court of Judicature, ought to be finished in as little Time as possible. *I have said before, that Punishment immediately inflicted is most useful*; the Reason is, because the *smaller* the Interval of Time is, which passes between the Crime and the Punishment, the *more* the Crime will be esteemed as a *Motive* to the Punishment, and the Punishment as an *Effect* of the Crime. Punishment must be *certain* and *unavoidable.*

222. The most certain Curb upon Crimes, is not the *Severity* of the Punishment, but the absolute Conviction in the People, that Delinquents will be *inevitably* punished.

223. The *Certainty* even of a small, but *inevitable* Punishment, will make a *stronger* Impression on the Mind, than the *Dread* even of *capital* Punishment, *connected* with the Hopes of escaping it. As Punishments become *more* mild and moderate; Mercy and Pardon will be *less* necessary in Proportion, for the Laws themselves, at such a Time, are replete with the *Spirit* of Mercy.

224. However extensive a State may be, *every Part* of it must depend upon the Laws.

225. We must endeavour to exterminate Crimes in general, *particularly* those which are *most* injurious to the Community: Consequently, the *Means* made use of by the Laws to deter

People from the Commission of every Kind of Crimes, ought to be the *more* powerful, in proportion as the Crimes are *more* destructive to the Publick Good, and in proportion to the *Strength* of the Temptation, by which *weak*, or *bad* Minds may be *allured* to the Commission of them. Consequently, there ought to be a *fixed* stated *Proportion* between *Crimes* and *Punishments*.

226. If there be two Crimes, which injure the Community *unequally*, and yet receive *equal* Punishment; then the *unequal* Distribution of the Punishment will produce this *strange Contradiction*, very little *noticed* by any one, though it frequently happens, that the *Laws* will punish Crimes, which *proceed* from *the Laws themselves*.

227. If the *same* Punishment should be inflicted upon a Man for killing an *Animal*, as for killing *another Man*, or for *Forgery*, the People will soon make no *Difference* between *those* Crimes.

228. Granting the Necessity and Conveniency of *uniting* People in *Societies*, we may *arrange* Crimes by a *Scale*, beginning from the *highest*, quite down to the very *lowest*; in which, the *first* Degree will consist of *those*, which tend to the *final* Dissolution, and *immediate* Ruin of the Community; and the *last*, of the *least* Provocation, which can be given to any *Individual* in the *Society*. Between these two *Extremes* will be comprehended all *Actions*, contrary to the *Good* of the Community, which are termed *Criminal*, decreasing *almost* imperceptibly from the *first*, or *highest* in this Scale, to the very *last* or *lowest*.

It would suffice, if on *these Scales* should be marked regularly, by *Degrees*, all Actions deserving Blame, which belong to each of the four Species, which *We* have already enumerated in the seventh Chapter.

229. *We* have allotted the *first* Degree to *those* Crimes, which *tend* directly and immediately to the *Destruction* of the Community, and to the Injury of him, who is the *Head* of it; which are of the greatest *Importance*; because they are of all others the *most Fatal* to the Community; these are termed the *Crimes of High Treason*.

230. Next to this *first* Degree of Crimes follow *those*, which are *destructive* of the Security of *Individuals*.

231. It is indispensably necessary, that Criminals of *this* Degree should suffer the greatest of Punishments. Attempts against the Life and Liberty of a Citizen, are *Crimes* of the *most* atrocious Nature. In this Class are not only comprehended *Assassinations*, and *Murders* committed by the Populace; but even the *same* Acts of Violence committed by Persons of any *Rank* or *Dignity* whatsoever.

232. Also Robberies attended *with* Violence, or *without* it.

233. Personal Offences against the Honour of a Citizen; that is, which *tend* to deprive a Citizen of that *just Share* of Respect, which he has a Right to demand from others.

234. With regard to Duels, it may not be unnecessary to repeat again, what many have affirmed, and what others have wrote upon that Subject: That the *best Expedient* for preventing *these* Crimes, is, to punish the *Aggressor*; that is, the *Challenger*, who gave *Occasion* for the Duel, and to acquit the other as *innocent*, who was *compelled* to defend his Honour, without having given *any Cause* for the Challenge.

235. Smuggling of Goods is a *Real* Robbery of the State. This Crime took its *Origin* from the *Law itself*: For the *higher* the *Duties* are, the *greater* the Profit is which arises from *Smuggling*. Consequently, the Temptation is the *stronger*; which is still *more increased* by the *Opportunities* of doing it, where the *Circumference* to be guarded is of *a great Extent*, and when contraband Goods are *small* in *Bulk*. The Forfeiture of the contraband Goods, together with such other Goods as are found along with them, is *very just*. Such a Crime deserves severe Punishment; such as *Imprisonment* proportioned to the *Nature* of the Crime. The Imprisonment for a *Smuggler* ought not to be the *same*, as for a *Highway-man* or a *Murderer*; and the most *proper* Punishment seems to be, *to oblige the Offender to labour for the Publick, the Produce of which should be calculated, and settled according to the Value of that Sum, of which he intended to defraud the Revenue.*

236. We ought here to mention *Bankrupts*, or those who *fail*

in Trade on account of *Debt.* The Necessity of *good Faith,* in Contracts for the *Safety* of Commerce, obliges the Legislator to allow *Creditors* the *proper Means* for obtaining *Payment* from their *Debtors.* But it is necessary to make a Distinction between the *fraudulent* and the *honest* Bankrupt. The *honest undesigning* Bankrupt, who can *shew* evidently, that either the Breach of Promise in his own *Debtors,* or *Losses* which have disabled them from making good their *Payment*; or *Misfortunes,* which human Prudence can neither *foresee* nor *prevent,* have ruined his Fortune; such a One ought not to be *treated* with the *same* Rigour as the *fraudulent* Bankrupt. For why should he be *thrown into Prison*? Upon what Account should he be deprived of *his Liberty,* the only *Property* that is *left* him? Why should he be subject to a *Punishment,* which is only *proper* for Criminals; and be compelled, through Despair, to *repent* of his *Honesty*? Let his *Debt,* if you please, stand *charged* against him, till his Creditors are intirely satisfied: Let him be denied the Liberty of *removing* into another Country, without Leave from *those* to whom he is *indebted*; and let him be *compelled* to employ his *Industry* and *Abilities* to effect such a *Change* in his Situation, as may *enable* him to make a *clear Discharge of his Debts.* That Law, therefore, is not to be justified, which deprives him of his Liberty, without the *least* Benefit to his *Creditors.*

237. We may, I think, be able to distinguish, on all Occasions, a Fraud attended with aggravating Circumstances, from a *great* Oversight; and a *great* Oversight from a *small* Oversight; and *this last* from perfect *Innocence*; and, by *this Distinction,* proportion the *Measure* of the Punishment provided by the Laws.

238. A wise and provident Law might prevent the greatest Part of these *fraudulent* Bankruptcies, and provide *proper* Expedients to guard against those Accidents, which may befall the *honest industrious Trader.* A publick *Register* for all mercantile *Contracts,* and free Liberty for every Citizen to *inspect* it on Occasion, and to act accordingly; and a *Fund* raised by a prudent Contribution of the Merchants; out of which the *unfortunate,* though *careful* Trader, might be properly assisted; *provided* these

Establishments bring with them many great Advantages, and occasion no Difficulty in the Execution.

239. Q. 8. *Which are the most efficacious Means of preventing Crimes?*

240. It is better to *prevent* Crimes, than to *punish* them.

241. To *prevent* Crimes, is the *Intention*, and the *End* of every *good* Legislation; which is nothing more than the Art of conducting People to the *greatest* Good, or to leave the *least* Evil possible amongst them, if it should prove impracticable to *exterminate* the whole.

242. If we forbid many Actions, which are termed *indifferent* by the *Moralists*, we shall not prevent the Crimes, of which they *may* be productive, but shall *create* still *new* Ones.

243. Would you *prevent* Crimes? order it *so*, That the Laws might rather favour every *Individual*, than any particular Rank of Citizens, in the Community.

244. Order it so, that the People should fear *the Laws*, and *nothing* but the Laws.

245. Would you prevent Crimes? order it so, that the *Light of Knowledge* may be *diffused* among the People.

246. A Book of good Laws is nothing but a Bar to prevent the Licentiousness of injurious Men from doing Mischief to their fellow Creatures.

247. There is yet another Expedient to *prevent* Crimes, which is by *rewarding* Virtue.

248. Finally, the *most sure*, but, at the same Time, the *most difficult* Expedient to mend the Morals of the People, is a perfect System of Education.

249. In this Chapter will be found Repetitions of what has been said before; but they, who shall examine the Case with the least Attention, will perceive, that the Subject itself required it; and besides, it is very allowable to *repeat* more than once, whatever may be *useful* to Mankind.

Chap. XI

250. A Society of Citizens, as well as every Thing else, requires a certain fixed Order: There ought to be *some to govern*, and *others to obey*.

251. And this is the Origin of every Kind of Subjection; which feels itself more or less alleviated, in Proportion to the Situation of the Subjects.

252. And, consequently, as the Law of Nature commands *Us* to take as much Care, as lies in *Our* Power, of the Prosperity of all the People; we are obliged to alleviate the Situation of the Subjects, as much as sound Reason will permit.

253. And therefore, to shun all Occasions of reducing People to a State of Slavery, except the *utmost* Necessity should *inevitably* oblige us to do it; in that Case, it ought not to be done for our own Benefit; but for the Interest of the State: Yet even that Case is extremely uncommon.

254. Of whatever Kind Subjection may be, the civil Laws ought to guard, on the one Hand, against the *Abuse* of Slavery, and, on the other, against the *Dangers* which may arise from it.

255. Unhappy is that Government, which is compelled to institute *severe* Laws.

256. *Peter the Great* ordained, in the Year 1722, that Persons who were insane in Mind, and those who tortured their Vassals, should be put under the Tutelage of Guardians. This Injunction is executed with regard to the Objects of the first Part of it; the Reason why it is not put in Force with respect to the Objects of the last Part, is *unknown*.

257. In Sparta Slaves could not obtain the least Satisfaction in the Courts of Judicature: And the Extreme of their Unhappiness consisted in this, that they were not only the Slaves of *one* individual Citizen, but at the same Time of the *whole* Community.

258. Among the Romans, in Case of maiming a Slave, Regard was only paid to the Damage done by it to the Master. It was esteemed *equal* by them, whether a Wound was inflicted on a

Beast, or on a Slave: Nothing was taken into Consideration, but only the *Diminution* in the Price of each: And even that turned to the *Interest* of the Master, *not* of the injured.

259. Among the Athenians, whoever treated a Slave with Cruelty, was punished with great Severity.

260. A great Number of Slaves ought not to be infranchised all at once, nor by a general Law.

261. A Law may be productive of public Benefit, which gives some *private* Property to a Slave.

262. Let us finish all this, by repeating that *fundamental Rule*; that the government which most resembles that of Nature, is that, whose particular Disposition answers best to the Disposition of the People, for whom it is instituted.

263. However it is still highly necessary to prevent those Causes, which so frequently incited Slaves to rebell against their masters; but till these Causes are discovered; it is impossible to prevent the like accidents by Laws; though the Tranquillity, both of the one and of the other, depends upon it.

Chap. XII

264. *Of the Propagation of the human Species in a State.*

265. Russia is not only *greatly* deficient in the *number* of her Inhabitants; but at the same Time, extends her Dominion over *immense* Tracts of Land; which are neither peopled nor improved. And therefore, in a Country so circumstanced, *too much* Encouragement can never be given to the *Propagation* of the human Species.

266. The Peasants generally have twelve, fifteen, and even twenty Children by one Marriage; but it rarely happens, that one *Fourth* of these ever attains to the *Age* of Maturity. There must therefore be some Fault, either in their Nourriture, in their Way of Living, or Method of Education, which occasions this *prodigious* Loss, and disappoints the *Hopes* of the Empire. How flourishing would the State of this Empire be, if we could but ward off, or *prevent* this fatal Evil by proper Regulations!

267. You must add too to *this*, that two Hundred Years are now elapsed, since a *Disease* unknown to our Ancestors was imported from America, and *hurried* on the Destruction of the human Race. This Disease spreads *wide* its *mournful* and *destructive* Effects in *many* of our Provinces. The utmost Care ought to be taken of the Health of the Citizens. It would be highly prudent, therefore, to stop the Progress of this Disease by the Laws.

268. Those of Moses may serve here for an Example. LEVITIC. chap. xiii.

269. It seems too, that the Method of exacting their Revenues, *newly* invented by the Lords, diminishes both the *Inhabitants*, and the *Spirit of Agriculture* in Russia. Almost all the Villages are *heavily* taxed. The Lords, who seldom or never *reside* in their Villages, lay an Impost on every Head of one, two, and even five Rubles, without the least Regard to the *Means* by which their Peasants may be able to *raise* this Money.

270. It is highly necessary that the Law should prescribe a Rule to the Lords, for a more judicious Method of raising their Revenues; and oblige them to levy *such* a Tax, as *tends least* to separate the Peasant from his House and Family; this would be the Means by which Agriculture would become more extensive, and Population be more increased in the Empire.

271. Even now some Husbandmen do not see their Houses for fifteen Years together, and yet pay the Tax annually to their respective Lords; which they procure in Towns at a vast Distance from their Families, and wander over the whole Empire for that Purpose.

272. The more happily a People live under a Government, the more easily the Number of the Inhabitants increases.

273. Countries, which abound with Meadow and Pasture Lands, are generally *very thinly* peopled; the Reason is, that *few* can find Employment in those Places: But arable Lands are much *more* populous; because they *furnish* Employment for a *much greater* Number of People.

274. Wherever the Inhabitants can enjoy the Conveniencies of Life, there Population will certainly increase.

275. *But a Country, which is so overwhelmed with Taxes, that the People, with all their Care and Industry, can with the utmost Difficulty find Means for procuring a bare Subsistance, will, in length of Time, be deserted by its Inhabitants.*

276. Where a People is poor for no other Reason, but because they live under oppressive Laws, and esteem their Lands not so much a *Fund* for their Maintainance, as a *Pretence* for their Oppression; in such Places, the Inhabitants cannot increase. They have not the Means of Subsistance sufficient for themselves, how then can they think of yielding a Part of it to their Offspring? They are not able to take Care of *themselves*, even in their *own* Illness; how then can they bring up, and look after *Creatures*, which are in a State of *continual* Illness, that is, *Infancy*? They bury their Money in the Earth, and are afraid to let it circulate; and they fear to appear rich, because their Wealth might expose them to Persecution and Oppression.

277. The Ease of asserting, and the Incapacity for thoroughly examining an Affair, have induced many to affirm, *That the poorer the Subjects live, the more numerous their Families will be; and the heavier the Taxes are, the more readily they will find the Means of paying them.* These are two Sophisms, which ever did, and ever will bring Destruction upon Monarchies.

278. The Evil is almost incurable, when the Depopulation of the Country has been of long standing, from some internal Defect in the Constitution, and a bad Administration. The People drop off there by an imperceptible and almost habitual Malady. Born in Languor and Misery, under the Oppression, or false Maxims adopted by Government, they see themselves destroyed frequently, without perceiving the Causes of their Destruction.

279. In order to re-establish a State stripped in such a Manner of its Inhabitants, it will be in vain to expect Assistance from the Children, which may be born in future. This Hope is totally over: People in their Desart have neither Courage nor Industry. Lands, which might feed a whole People, can scarce yield Food for a single Family. The common People in those Parts have no *Share* even in that, which is the *Cause* of their

Misery; that is, the Lands which lie *fallow* and *uncultivated*, with which the Country abounds; either some of the principal Citizens, or the Sovereign, insensibly ingross the *whole Extent* of these desert Countries. The ruined Families have *left* their Oppressors the *whole* for *Pastures*, and the laborious Man has nothing.

280. In such Circumstances, the same Method ought to be followed through the whole Extent of that Country, which the Romans practised in one Part of theirs. To *do*, in a Scarcity of Inhabitants, what they *did* in a Superfluity of them, to *divide* the Lands amongst the Families which *had none*, and to enable them to cultivate and improve them. This Division ought to be made without Loss of Time, as soon as ever one Man can be found who would undertake it on those Terms, that not a Moment might be lost before the Work is begun.

281. Julius Cæsar gave Premiums to those who had many Children. The Laws of Augustus were more forceable. He imposed Penalties upon those who refused to marry, and increased the Premiums of those who married, and also of those who had Children. But *these* Laws are not consistent with *those* of our orthodox Religion.

282. In some Countries particular Privileges are granted to married Persons: For Instance, that the Overseers, and petty Justices in Villages, must be elected out of the married People only. Unmarried Persons, and those who have no Children, are neither qualified to transact publick Business, nor to preside in the Village Courts. He who has the most Children, takes the highest Place in that Court; and that Peasant, who has more than five Sons, is exempt from all Taxes.

283. Among the Romans, unmarried People were excluded from receiving Legacies bequeathed by the Last Wills of Strangers; and married Persons, who had no Children, were entitled only to a Moiety.

284. The Benefits which a Husband and Wife are able to leave reciprocally by Will to each other, were limited by Law. If they had Children by one another, they could bequeath each other their whole Substance; but, if they had none, they could

only inherit the tenth Part after the Death of either, in consideration of their Marriage. And if they had Children by a former Marriage, they were allowed to bequeath each other as many tenth Parts as they had Children.

285. If a Husband absented himself from his Wife, upon any other Account than that of the publick Service, he was not allowed to inherit her Effects.

286. In some Countries, a certain Pension is appointed for those who have ten Children; and a larger for those who had twelve. But the Point does not consist in rewarding Fecundity only in married People; their Lives ought also to be made as easy as possible; that is, the Careful and Industrious ought to enjoy the Means of supporting themselves and their Families.

287. Temperance in the People conduces greatly to Population.

288. It is generally ordained by the Law, that Fathers should unite their Children in Marriage. But what Advantage will arise from this, if Oppression and Avarice should, in an illegal Manner, usurp the Authority of a Father? Fathers ought rather to be encouraged to unite their Children in Marriage, and not to be debarred the Power of marrying their Children according to their own Judgment.

289. With regard to Marriages, it would be highly necessary, and of great Importance, to define once *clearly* and with *Certainty*, the *Degree* of Consanguinity in which Matrimony is allowed, and the *Degree* in which it is forbid.

290. There are Countries where the Law [in case of Want of Inhabitants] gives the Freedom of Citizens to Foreigners; or those who are illegitimate, or born only from a Mother who is a Citizen: But when they have acquired a sufficient Number of Inhabitants by these Means, they admit them no longer.

291. The Savages of Canada burn their Prisoners of War; but if they have any vacant Huts, with which they can accommodate the Prisoners, they incorporate them with their own Nation.

292. There are People who, after the Conquest of other Nations, unite in Marriage with the Conquered: Thus they

attach the conquered People to themselves, and increase their Numbers.

Chap. XIII

293. *Of handicraft Trades, and Commerce.*

294. There can be neither skilful Handicraftsmen, nor a firmly-established Commerce, where Agriculture is neglected, or carried on with Supineness and Negligence.

295. Agriculture can never flourish there, where no Persons have any Property of their own.

296. This is founded upon a very simple Rule: *Every Man will take more Care of his own Property, than of that which belongs to another; and will not exert his utmost Endeavours upon that, which he has Reason to fear another may deprive him of.*

297. Agriculture is the most laborious Employment a Man can undertake. The *more* the Climate induces a Man to shun this Trouble, the *more* the Laws ought to animate him to it.

298. In China, the Emperor Bogdo-Chan is informed annually of that Husbandman, who has distinguished himself most in his Profession, and makes him a Mandarine of the Eighth Order. That Sovereign begins every Year to open the Ground with a Plough, with his own Hands, and with the most magnificent Ceremonies.

299. It would not be improper to give a Premium to those Husbandmen, who bring their Fields into better Order than others.

300. And to the Handicraftsmen, who distinguished themselves most by their Care and Skill.

301. This Regulation will produce a Progress in the Arts, in all Parts of the Country. It was of Service, even in our own Times, in establishing very important Manufactories.

302. There are Countries, where a Treatise of Agriculture, published by the Government, is lodged in every Church, from which the Peasant may be able to get the better of his Difficulties, and draw proper Advantage from the Instructions it contains.

303. There are Nations inclined to Laziness. In order to

exterminate Laziness in the Inhabitants, arising from the Climate, such Laws are to be made, as should deprive those, who refuse to work, of the Means of Subsistance.

304. All Nations inclined to Laziness are arrogant in their Behaviour; for they who do not work esteem themselves, in some Measure, Rulers over those who labour.

305. Nations who have given themselves up to Idleness, are generally proud: We might turn the Effect against the Cause from which it proceeds, and destroy Laziness by Pride itself.

306. For Government may be as strongly supported by *Ambition*, as it may be endangered by *Pride*. In asserting this, we need only represent to ourselves, on the one Hand, the innumerable Benefits which result from *Ambition*; such as, Industry, Arts, and Sciences, Politeness, Taste, *&c.*; and, on the other, the infinite Number of Evils arising from *Pride*, in some Nations; such as Laziness, Poverty, Disregard for every thing; the Destruction of Nations, who accidentally fall into their Power, and afterwards the Ruin of themselves.

307. As *Pride* induces some to shun Labour, so *Ambition* impells others to excell all the rest in Workmanship.

308. View every Nation with Attention, and you will find, that arrogant Pride and Laziness, most commonly, go Hand in Hand together.

309. The People of Achim are haughty and lazy: Such amongst them as have no Slaves of their own, hire one, if it be only to carry a small Bag of Rice a hundred Paces. They would look upon it as a Disgrace, if they should carry it themselves.

310. The Women in India think it a Scandal to learn to read: This Business, they say, belongs to the female Slaves, who chaunt the Hymns in their Temples.

311. A Man is not poor, because he has nothing; but because he will do no Work. He who has no Estate, but will work, may live as well as he, who has an annual Income of a Hundred Rubles, but will do no Work.

312. A Tradesman who has taught his Children his Art, has

given them such an Estate, as increases in proportion to their Number.

313. Agriculture is the first and principal Labour, which ought to be encouraged in the People: The next is, the manufacturing our own Produce.

314. Machines, which serve to shorten Labour in the mechanick Arts, are not always useful. If a Piece of Work, wrought with the Hands, can be afforded at a Price, equally advantageous to the Merchant and the Manufacturer; in this Case, Machines which shorten Labour, that is, which diminish the Number of Workmen, will be greatly prejudicial to a populous Country.

315. Yet, we ought to distinguish between what we manufacture for our Home-consumption, and what we manufacture for Exportation into foreign Countries.

316. Too much Use cannot be made of this Kind of Machines in our Manufactures, which we export to other Nations; who do, or may receive the same Kind of Goods, from our Neighbours, or other People; especially those who are in the same Situation with ourselves.

317. Commerce flies from Places where it meets with Oppression, and settles where it meets with Protection.

318. The Athenians did not carry on that extensive Commerce, which might have been expected from the Labour of their Slaves, the great Number of their Seamen, the Power which they had over the States of Greece, and, what exceeded all, the excellent Regulations of Solon.

319. In many Countries, where all the Taxes are farmed, the *Collection* of the Royal Revenues *ruins* Commerce, not only by its Inequality, Oppression, and extreme Exactions, but also by the *Difficulties* it occasions, and the *Formalities* it requires.

320. In other Places, where the Duties or Customs are *collected* upon the *good Faith* of the Importers, there is a wide Difference in respect of the Conveniencies for Traffick. One Word in Writing transacts the greatest Business. The Merchant is under no Necessity of losing Time in Attendance; nor obliged

to employ *Clerks*, on purpose to remove the Difficulties started by the *Financiers*, or be *compelled* to submit to them.

321. The Liberty of Trading does not consist in a Permission to Merchants of doing whatever they please; this would be rather the *Slavery* of Commerce: What *cramps* the Trader, does not *cramp* the Trade. In free Countries the Merchant meets with innumerable Obstacles; but in despotic Governments he is not near so much thwarted by the Laws. England prohibits the Exportation of its Wool; she has ordained Coals to be imported to the Capital by Sea; she has prohibited the Exportation of Horses fit for Stallions; she obliges Ships, which Trade from her Plantations in America into Europe, to anchor first in England. By these, and such like Prohibitions, she *cramps* the Merchant; but it is for the *Benefit* of Commerce.

322. Wherever there is Trade, there are Custom-houses also.

323. The Object of Trade, is the Exportation and Importation of Goods, for the Advantage of the State: The Object of the Custom-houses, is a certain Duty, exacted from the same Exportation and Importation of Goods, for the Advantage likewise of the State; for this Reason a State ought to preserve an exact Impartiality between the Custom-house and the Trade, and to make such proper Regulations, that these two might never clash with each other: Then the People will enjoy there free Liberty of Commerce.

324. England has no Tarif, or fixed Book of Rates with other Nations: Her Tarif changes, as we may say, at every Session of Parliament, by the particular Duties, which she lays on, or takes off.

Strongly jealous of the Trade which is carried on in Her Country, She rarely engages herself in Treaties with other States, and depends on no Laws, but Her own.

325. Some Countries have made Laws, perfectly well calculated to humble those States, which carry on the Commerce of Oeconomy. They are forbidden to import any Commodities, except what are Raw, and not manufactured; and even those must be the Growth of their own Country; and they are pro-

hibited from trading thither in any Vessels, but what are constructed in that Country, from whence they come.

326. The State, which imposes these Laws, ought to be in a Condition to carry on the Trade itself with Ease, and without the Assistance of others; otherwise it would, at least, do *equal* Injury to itself. It is better to be concerned in Trade with such a Nation, as exacts little, and which the Necessity of Trade renders in some Measure attached to us: With such a People, who from their extensive Views, or Traffick, know where to dispose of their superfluous Merchandize; who are rich, and can take off a great Stock of Commodities; and who will pay for them in ready Money; who, if we may express ourselves in this Manner, are *necessitated* even by Interest to be *honest*; who are *pacifick* from *Principle*; who aim at *Profit*, but not at *Conquests*. It is better, *I* say, to be concerned with *such a Nation*, than with others, who are always *our Rivals*, and will grant us *none* of these Advantages.

327. It would be still more injurious to a State; if, in order to sell its Commodities, it should confine itself to one Nation only, upon this weak Pretence, that it will take off all our Goods at a fixed Price certain.

328. The true Maxim is, not to exclude any People from trading with us, without very important Reasons.

329. In many Countries Banks are established with good Success; which, by their Credit, have created *such new Signs* of Valuation, as have increased the Circulation. But, in order to establish the Credit of such Institutions under a monarchical Government, these Banks ought to be annexed to such *charitable Foundations*, as are esteemed *sacred*, and *independent of the Government*; and which have a *Grant* by Letters Patent, with which no Person *can*, or ought *to interfere*; such, for Instance, as *Hospitals*, *Orphan-Houses*, *&c.* that all Persons might be *persuaded*, and *firmly trust*, that the Sovereign will never violate the *sacred character* of *those Places*; nor incur the *Guilt of Sacrilege*, by seizing their Money.

330. One of the best Writers upon Laws gives us his Sentiments in the following Words. *People, incited by what they see*

practised in some Dominions, imagine, that it would be expedient to have Laws, which should encourage the Nobility to ingage in Commerce. This would be the Means of ruining the Nobility, without the least Advantage to Commerce. The Practice indeed is extremely wise in those Countries, where Merchants, though not ennobled, are yet capable of attaining the Rank of Nobility; they have the Hopes of obtaining that Rank, without labouring under the Inconveniencies, which actually attend it. They have not a more certain Method of rising above their present Profession, than by carrying it on with the utmost Assiduity, or meeting with such Success, as is generally accompanied with an affluent Fortune. It is repugnant to the true Spirit of Trade, that the Nobility should engage in it under a monarchical Government. It would be fatal to the Cities, as the Emperors Honorius and Theodosius affirm; and would destroy the Facility of buying and selling between the Merchants and the Plebeians. It is equally contrary to the Spirit of monarchical Government, for the Nobility to engage in Trade. The Custom allowed to the Nobility, in some Countries, of engaging in Trade, is one of the Means, which contributed most to weaken the Monarchical Government.

331. There are People, however, of a different Opinion; who judge, that such Noblemen may be permitted to Trade, as are not actually in the Service of the Government; but still with this Restriction, *that they conform themselves, in every Thing, to the Laws of Commerce.*

332. Theophilus seeing a Ship freighted with Merchandize for his Consort Theodora, ordered it to be burnt. *I am an Emperor, said he to her, and thou makest me a Master of a Vessel; which Way shall poor People be able to earn a Livelihood, if we turn Traders?* He might have added, "Who will be able to "restrain us, if we turn Monopolists? Who can compell us to "make good our Contracts? The Courtiers, following our Ex-"ample, will do the same; they will be more rapacious, and more "unjust than we are. The People confide in our Justice, but not "in our Opulence: The great Number of Taxes, which reduce "them to Misery, are convincing Proofs of our own Necessities."

333. When the Portuguese and Spaniards lorded it over the

East-Indies, Trade there produced such lucrative Branches, that their Sovereigns thought proper to seize upon them themselves. This destructive Measure ruined their Settlements in that Part of the World. The Viceroy of Goa granted exclusive Privileges to different Persons. No one can ever confide in such Sort of People; the Trade was ruined by the continual Change of the Parties, to whom it was intrusted. No one gave himself the least Concern about such a Kind of Trade; nor cared in how ruinous a Condition he left it to his Successor. The Profit centered in few hands, and was not sufficiently diffused.

334. Solon made a Law at Athens, that the Person of a Debtor should not be arrested for Debts on civil Contracts. This Law is very useful for the common domestick Affairs of the Citizens; but *We* ought not to follow it in Affairs relative to Commerce. For as Merchants are frequently obliged to intrust *large* Sums of Money for *very short* Times, to *give* them, and to *receive* them back; the *Debtor* ought in Justice to be always punctual to the Time appointed for the Payment; which implies a Power of *arresting* his Person. In Disputes arising from common civil Contracts among the Citizens, the Law ought not to allow the Arrest of the Person; because it sets a greater Value upon the *Liberty* of one Citizen, than the *private Interest* of another. But in *commercial Contracts*, the Law ought to set a *greater* Value upon the *Interest* of the *whole* Community, than upon the Liberty of a *private* Citizen. Yet this does by no Means exclude such Restrictions and Limitations, as Humanity and good Policy require.

335. That Law at Geneva is highly praise-worthy, which excludes all the Children of those who lived or died insolvent from the Magistracy, and even from a Seat in the great Council; unless they discharged the Debts contracted by their Parents. The happy Effect resulting from this Law produces a general Confidence for the Merchants, for the Magistrates, and for the City itself. The particular Credit of every Individual has, in that Place, the same Force as the united Credit of the Publick.

336. The Rhodians extended this Law much farther. Amongst them a Son could not possibly avoid the Payment of

his Father's Debts, even though he should relinquish all Right to his paternal Inheritance. This Law of Rhodes was calculated for a State founded in, and supported by Commerce. The very Nature, therefore, of their Constitution seems to have required *this Exception* to be annexed to the Law, for the Encouragement of Commerce, *That all Debts contracted by the Father, after the Son had commenced Trader upon his own Account, should not affect, or deprive him of what Property he had acquired after that Period of Time.* A Merchant ought always to know thoroughly the Extent of his Contracts, and to conduct himself so, as never to exceed his capital Stock.

337. Xenophon is of Opinion, "that a Premium should be "allowed to such of the Prefects of Trade, as terminated soonest "all Processes relating to Commerce." He seems to have foreseen the Necessity of the Consular Jurisdiction.

338. Affairs relating to Trade will hardly admit of the Delay occasioned by judicial Formalities. They are Actions produced *every Day* in Commerce, from which others of the *same Nature* must *every Day* invariably follow. They ought therefore to be *every Day* decided. The Case is quite different with respect to *temporal* Affairs, which chiefly influence *future* Events, and which happen *but rarely*. We generally marry *but once*; we do not make our *Wills*, or *bequeath* Gifts *every Day*, and we can be of Age *but once*.

339. Plato affirms, that in a City which carries on no Commerce by Sea, there is no Occasion for Half the Number of civil Laws; which is extremely right. A maritime Trade introduces People of *various* Nations into the *same* Place; a great Number of *Contracts*, *different* Kinds of Commodities, and different Methods of Gain: Consequently, in a trading City, there are *fewer* Judges, and *more* Laws.

340. The Law, which confiscates the Effects of any Stranger to the Sovereign's Use in whose Territories he happens to die, and deprives the right Heir of his Inheritance; and the Law, which appropriates to the Sovereign, or his Subjects, the Cargo of a Ship wrecked upon their Coasts, are alike ill-judged and inhuman.

341. The Grand Charter, or *Magna Charta* of England, forbids the Seizure of the Lands or Revenues of a Debtor, if his moveable or personal Effects are sufficient to discharge his Debts, and he is willing to resign them to his Creditors; In such a Case, all his Effects are valued as *ready Money*. This Charter does not prevent the *Lands* and *Revenues* of an Englishman from being valued *as ready Money*, in the same Manner as his personal Effects. The Intention of this Prohibition was to protect the Debtor from the Hardships he might be exposed to from the Severity of his Creditors. Justice becomes *Oppression*, when strained so far beyond the *Bounds* of Equity, in Seizures for Debts, as to *deprive* the Debtor of that *Security*, which every Man has a *Right* to demand; and if *one Species* of Wealth is alone sufficient for the Payment of his Debts, there is no absolute Necessity for seizing *another*. And as *Lands* and *Revenues* are seized for the Payment of Debts, where no other Effects remain sufficient to satisfy the Creditors, it should seem, that *they* ought not to be excluded from the *Number* of those Signs, which are *valued as ready Money*.

342. The Proof of Gold, of Silver, and of Copper, in Coin, likewise the Impression and the intrinsick Value of the Coin, ought always to be regulated by *one fixed Standard*, which should never *be varied* upon any Occasion; for *every Alteration* in the Coin *injures the Credit* of the State. Nothing ought to be so much *exempted* from Alteration, *as that* which is the *common Measure* of every Thing. Commerce, in its very Nature, is extremely uncertain, and it is highly injurious to add a new Degree of Uncertainty to that, which arises from the very Nature of the Thing itself.

343. There are Laws in some Countries, which prohibit the Subjects to sell their Lands, lest they should transport the Purchase-money into foreign Countries. These Laws might be of use at that Time, when the Wealth of any Country was so circumstanced, that it could not be transported to another without the utmost Difficulty. But since, *by the Invention of Letters of Exchange*, *Wealth* is, in some Measure, no longer the *sole Property* of any *particular* Country, and can with so much Ease *be trans-*

ferred from one Country to another; that ought to be termed *a bad Law*, which does not permit the Owner to dispose of *his Lands* as he thinks proper, and the Situation of his Affairs requires, just *as freely*, as he can *dispose* of his Money. This Law is bad too for this Reason, that it gives the Preference, in point of Advantage, to the *personal* over the *landed Estate*; because it prevents *Foreigners* from *settling* in that Country; and, finally, because it may be *easily eluded.*

344. It ever happens, that whoever forbids that which Nature itself dictates, or unavoidable Necessity requires, such a one will do nothing more, than only *reduce* those who practise it to be *dishonest.*

345. In commercial Countries, where great Numbers depend intirely upon their Art, the State is frequently obliged to provide for the Necessities of the Ancient, the Infirm, and the Orphans. A well-regulated State draws a Fund for their Subsistence from the very Arts themselves; it gives Work to some in proportion to their Abilities; and it teaches others to work, which is itself an Employment.

346. An Alms bestowed on a Beggar in the Street, can never acquit a State of the Obligation it lies under, of affording all its Citizens a certain Support during Life; such as wholesome Food, proper Cloathing, and a Way of Life not prejudicial to Health in general.

Chap. XIV

347. *Of Education.*

348. The Rules of Education are the fundamental Institutes which train us up to be Citizens.

349. Each particular Family ought to be governed upon the Plan of the great Family; which includes all the Particulars.

350. It is impossible to give a general Education to a very numerous People, and to bring up all the Children in Houses regulated for that Purpose; and, for that Reason, it will be proper to establish some *general Rules*, which may serve *by Way of Advice* to all Parents.

1.

351. Every Parent is obliged to teach his Children the Fear of God, as the Beginning of all Wisdom, and to inculcate into them all those Duties, which God demands from us in the ten Commandments, and our orthodox Eastern Greek Religion, in its Rules and Traditions.

352. Also to inculcate into them the Love of their Country, and to enure them to pay due Respect to the established civil Laws, and to reverence the Courts of Judicature in their Country, as those, who, by the Appointment of God, watch over their Happiness in this World.

2.

353. Every Parent ought to refrain *in Presence* of his Children, not only from *Actions*, but even *Words* that *tend* to Injustice and Violence; as for Instance, *Quarelling*, *Swearing*, *Fighting*, *every Sort of Cruelty*, and *such like Behaviour*; and not to allow those who are about his Children *to set them such bad Examples.*

3.

354. He ought to forbid his Children, and those who are about them, the *Vice* of *lying*, though even *in jest*; for *Lying* is the most pernicious of *all Vices.*

355. We shall add here, for the Instruction of every Man in particular, what has been already printed, and serves as *a general Rule* for the Schools already founded, and which are still founding by *Us*, for *Education*, and for the *whole* Society.

356. *Every one ought to inculcate the Fear of God into the tender Minds of Children, to encourage every laudable Inclination, and to accustom them to the fundamental Rules, suitable to their respective Situations; to incite in them a Desire for Labour, and a Dread of Idleness, as the Root of all Evil, and Error; to train them up to a proper Decorum in their Actions and Conversation, Civility, and Decency in their Behaviour; and to sympathise with the Miseries of poor unhappy Wretches; and to break them of all perverse and froward Humours; to teach them Oeconomy, and what-*

ever is most useful in all Affairs of Life; to guard them against all Prodigality and Extravagance; and particularly to root a proper Love of Cleanliness and Neatness, as well in themselves as in those who belong to them; in a Word, to instill all those Virtues and Qualities, which join to form a good Education; by which, as they grow up, they may prove real Citizens, useful Members of the Community, and Ornaments to their Country.

Chap. XV

357. *Of the Nobility.*

358. The Husbandmen, who cultivate the Lands to produce Food for People in every Rank of Life, live in Country Towns and Villages. *This is their Lot.*

359. The Burghers, who employ their Time in mechanick Trades, Commerce, Arts, and Sciences, *inhabit the Cities.*

360. *Nobility* is an Appellation of *Honour*, which distinguishes all those who are adorned with it from every other Person of *inferior Rank.*

361. As amongst Mankind there were *some more* virtuous *than others*, and who at the same Time distinguished themselves *more* eminently by their *merit*, the People in ancient Times agreed to dignify the *most* virtuous, and the *most* deserving, by this *honourable Appellation, or Title*, and determined to *invest* them with *many Privileges* which are *founded* upon *the Principal Rules of Virtue and Honour* above mentioned.

362. They proceeded still farther, and regulated by Law *the Means* by which *this Dignity* might *be obtained* from the Sovereign, and pointed out *those bad Actions* by which it *might be forfeited.*

363. *Virtue* with *Merit raises* People to the *Rank of Nobility.*

364. Virtue and Honour ought to be the Rules, which prescribe *Love for their Country*, *Zeal for its Service*, *Obedience and Fidelity to their Sovereign*; and continually suggest, *never to be guilty of an infamous Action.*

365. There are few Ways which lead so directly to the Attainment of Honours, as the military Service. To defend their

Country, and to conquer its Enemies, is the first Duty, and Proper Employment of the Nobility.

366. But though the military Art is the most ancient Way of attaining the Rank of Nobility; and though the military Virtues are essentially necessary for the Existence and Support of the State;

367. Yet still Justice is no less required in Time of Peace than in War; and the State would be destroyed without it:

368. And from hence it proceeds, that this Dignity is not attached solely to the Nobility; but may be acquired by the *civil* Virtues, as well as by the *military*.

369. Whence it still follows, that no one can lose the Rank of Nobility, but he who forfeits it by a Conduct directly opposite to the *Rules of Virtue and Honour*, on which his Dignity was founded; and by such means renders himself unworthy of that Appellation;

370. And the Honour and Preservation of the Purity of that Dignity require, that he, who by his ill Conduct has violated the *Rules* on which his Title is founded, should be excluded, after Conviction, from the Number of the Nobility, and be deprived of that Dignity.

371. The Actions, which render a Man unworthy of the Appellation of *Noble*, are *Treason*, *Robbery*, *Theft* of all Kinds, the *Violation of Oaths*, or his *solemn Word given*, *false Evidence*, which he either *gave* himself, or *suborned* others to give; *Forgery* of false Deeds, Letters, or any such Kind of Writings:

372. In a Word, *every Fraud* contrary to *Honour*, especially those *Actions*, which *degrade* a Man, and bring him into *Contempt*.

373. And the Preservation of Honour intire, consists in the *Love of their Country*, and *Observance of all its Laws and Duties*: From whence will follow,

374. *Praise* and *Glory*, especially to *that Race*, which can reckon up among *their Ancestors more* of such Persons, who were *adorned* with *Virtue*, *Honour*, *Merit*, *Fidelity* and *Love to their Country*, and consequently *to their Sovereign*.

375. And the Prerogatives of the Nobility ought to be founded on all the above-mentioned Qualifications, which compose the very *Essence* of the Appellation of *Nobleman.*

Chap. XVI

376. *Of the middling Sort of People.*

377. *I* have mentioned in the xvth Chapter, *that those People who inhabit the Cities, apply themselves to handicraft Trades, Commerce, Arts, and Sciences.* In whatever *State* the *fundamental Qualification* for the Rank of Nobility is established, *conformably* with the Rules prescribed in the xvth Chapter, it is no less *useful* to establish the Qualification of Citizens upon *Principles* productive of *Good Manners and Industry*, by which the People, we here treat of, will *enjoy that Situation.*

378. This Sort of People, of whom we ought now to speak, and from whom the State expects much Benefit, are admitted into the *Middling* Rank, if their *Qualifications* are firmly *established* upon *Good Manners, and Incitements to Industry.*

379. People of *this Rank* will enjoy a State of Liberty, without intermixing either with the *Nobility* or the *Husbandmen.*

380. To this Rank of People, we ought to annex all those who are neither *Gentlemen*, nor *Husbandmen*; but employ themselves in *Arts, Sciences, Navigation, Commerce,* or *handicraft Trades.*

381. Besides these, all those, who are not of the *Nobility*, but have been educated in *Schools* or *Colleges*, of what Denomination soever, *ecclesiastical* or *civil*, founded by *Us* and *Our* Ancestors:

382. Also the Children of People belonging to the Law. But as in that *third Species*, there are different Degrees of Privilege, therefore we shall not enter into a Detail of Particulars; but only open the Way for a due Consideration of it.

383. As the whole Qualification, which intitles People to this *middling* Rank, is founded upon good Manners and Industry; the Violation of these Rules will serve, on the Contrary, for their Exclusion from it; as for Instance, *Perfidiousness* and *Breach of Promise*, especially if *caused* by *Idleness* and *Treachery.*

Chap. XVII

384. *Of the Cities.*

385. There are Cities of different Kinds, and of *greater* or *less* Importance, according to their Situation.

386. In some Cities more Trade is carried on by Land, or by Water, than in others.

387. In other Cities the Merchandize is only collected together to be forwarded to other Places.

388. There are likewise some, which only serve as Places of Sale for the Products brought by the Husbandman of that and other Districts.

389. The one flourishes by Manufactories.

390. The other, lying nearer the Sea, enjoys all these and other Advantages.

391. The third Sort draws Benefit from Fairs.

392. The other are Capitals, *&c.*

393. Though there are many *different* Situations of the Cities, yet they all in general agree *in this*, that *one particular Law* is necessary for them all, *viz.* to determine *what* a City is, *who* is to be deemed an *Inhabitant* in it, and *who* are to compose the *Community* of that City, and *who* are to *enjoy* the Benefit of the Advantages arising from the natural Situation of the Place, and *how* a Person may be *admitted* a Citizen?

394. The Appellation of Citizen is *appropriated* to those who are entitled to share in the beneficial Situation of the City, by the Possession of a House and Property in it of their own. These are engaged for the Sake of their own happy Situation, and for their *Privileges* as Citizens, with respect to *Security* as to Life, Health, and Property, to pay *different* Taxes; in order to *enjoy* these Conveniencies, as well as their other acquired Wealth, without *Hindrance* or *Molestation.*

395. But those who do not give this *common Pledge*, as we may term it, are not *intitled* to the Privileges of Citizens.

396. Having fixed the *fundamental* Rules for Cities, it remains now to examine into what particular Advantages, and

what Commodities, every Kind of City may enjoy, without Detriment to the common Interest; and *what Regulations* ought to be established for their *mutual* Benefit?

397. In the Cities, where an extensive Trade is carried on, they ought strictly to observe, that *Credit*, in every Branch of Commerce, can only be *preserved* by *Honesty* in the Citizens: For Honesty and Credit are *the Soul* of Commerce; and where Art and Deceit get the *better* of Honesty, there is an *End* of Credit.

398. Towns are very necessary in the Districts, where the Husbandman might dispose of the Produce of the Land, and his own Labour, and furnish himself with whatsoever he has occasion for.

399. The Cities of Archangelgorod, of St Petersburgh, of Astracan, of Riga, of Revel, and such like, are Cities and Sea Ports. Orenburg, Kachta, and many other Cities, carry on other Kinds of Trade: Whence we may clearly perceive, how great an *Analogy* the *Situation* of Places bears to the *civil* Regulations; and that, without a thorough Knowledge of all the *particular* Circumstances, it is impossible to make the *Situation* of every City *beneficial.*

400. With respect to the *exclusive* Trade of Companies of Artificers, and the Establishment of Companies for Trade in Cities, the Question is still greatly agitated, whether it is better to establish Companies of Handicraft Trades in Cities, or to reject them; and *which* of those Regulations will conduce most to the *Advancement* of Manufactories and Trade?

401. It is most certain, that the Establishment of Companies for handicraft Trades is useful, but they are sometimes injurious; particularly when the Number of Workmen is limited; for this *very* Limitation *hinders* the *Increase* of handicraft Trades.

402. In many Cities in Europe, where the Number of the Members is *not limited,* and any one may be *admitted* to the *Freedom* of the Company whenever he pleases; it has been observed, that *such Companies* contribute to the inriching of those Cities.

403. In Cities where there are few People, Companies might be of use, in order to have *able* People in handicraft Trades.

Chap. XVIII

404. *Of Inheritances.*

405. The Order of Inheritance is founded upon the Principles of the political or *civil* Law, and not upon the Law of Nature.

406. The Division of Property, the Laws respecting this Division, and the Inheritance after the Death of him who made this Division, could not have been regulated otherwise than by the Community, and consequently by the political or civil Law.

407. The natural Law enjoins the Fathers to nourish and educate their Children, but does not oblige them to make them their *Heirs.*

408. For Instance, a Father who has brought up his Son to some Art or handicraft Trade, by which he can earn his Bread, may enrich him more by that Means, than if he should leave him his small Property, which might only serve to make him idle and lazy.

409. It is true that political or civil Order often requires, that Children should inherit after their Fathers, but does not always insist upon it.

410. This Rule is *general.* To bring up their Children, is an *Obligation* of the Law of Nature; but to *give* them their Inheritance, is the *Regulation* of political or civil Law.

411. Each State has proper Laws for the Possession of Property, which answer to the Regulations of the State: Consequently, the Patrimony ought to be enjoyed according to the Manner prescribed by the Laws.

412. And a fixed inviolable Law ought to be made for the Succession to a Patrimony, that the right Heir might be easily known, and no Disputes or Complaints arise about it.

413. Every Law ought to be observed by the whole Community, and no Particular of it should ever be allowed to be violated by any private Regulation of the Citizens.

414. Since the Order of Inheritance was settled amongst the

Romans by a political Law of the State; none of the Citizens were allowed to violate it by his own *private* Will; that is, in the first Ages of Rome, no one was allowed to *make* a Will. However, it was a most cruel Circumstance, that a Man, at his last Hour, should be deprived of the Power of bestowing Favours.

415. But an Expedient was contrived to reconcile the Laws, in this Respect, with the Last Wills of Individuals. They were allowed to *dispose* of their Property by Will, in the publick Assembly; and thus each *Last Will* was, in some Measure, an *Act* of the legislative Power of that Republick.

416. In succeeding Ages, that unlimited Permission granted to the Romans, of making Bequests by Will, contributed, by imperceptible Degrees, to the Destruction of that political Ordinance, the *Partition of Lands*; and was the *chief* Cause of introducing that *great* and *fatal* Difference between the Rich and Poor. Many Shares of Land *centered* in one Owner; and some Citizens had *too much*, whilst an infinite Number of others had *nothing*, and by that Means became an *insupportable* Burden to the Publick.

417. The ancient Laws of Athens did not allow a Citizen to make a Will: Solon permitted every Citizen to do it, except those who had Children.

418. But the Roman Legislators, overawed by the imaginary Power of a Father, permitted them to make Wills even prejudicial to their Children.

419. It must be acknowledged, that the ancient Laws of the Athenians were more consonant to good Sense than the Laws of the Romans.

420. There are States, where they observe *a Medium* in all these Cases; that is, where they allow *acquired* Property to be *disposed* of by Will; but forbid a Village to be *divided* by Will into *different* Shares. And if the Inheritance of the Father by Descent, or, to speak more properly, his Patrimony, should be sold or spent, it was enacted, that a *Portion equal* to that Patrimony should be given to the lawful Heir out of the purchased or *acquired* Estate, unless he should be disqualified by Law, as

unworthy of the Inheritance. In this last Case, the next Heir *after* him was to succeed to it.

421. As the lawful Heir, so the Heir chosen pursuant to the Will of the Testator, may *accept* of, or *refuse* the Inheritance.

422. The Daughters among the Romans were excluded from inheriting by Will; for this Reason, they provided for them by *Fraud* under a *false* Name. This Law constrained People either to make themselves *infamous*, or to *violate* the Laws of Nature, which inculcate in us the Love of our Children. These are Cases which ought carefully to be avoided in constructing Laws.

423. Since nothing so much *weakens* the Force of Laws, as the Possibility of *evading* them by *Art*; *useless* Laws likewise diminish the Respect due to *useful* ones.

424. Among the Romans, Wives were permitted to be Heiresses, when it was agreeable to the Law for the *Partition* of Lands; and, when it was contrary to that Law, they were debarred the Right of Succession.

425. *My* Opinion in this Affair inclines more to the Division of Property; as *I* esteem it *My* Duty to wish, that every one should have a *Competency* sufficient for his *Livelihood.* Besides, Agriculture, by this Method, will arrive to greater Perfection; and the State will receive more Benefit from several *Thousands* of Subjects, who enjoy a *moderate* Competency, than from a few *Hundreds* who are *immensely* rich.

426. But the Division of Property should not be prejudicial to ancient *general Rules* (at a Time for regulating the Laws) as *much*, or perhaps *more* conducive to the Preservation of the whole State; which Rules should therefore not be laid aside, without due Consideration.

427. The Division according to the Number of Peasants, which has been hitherto customary, is detrimental to Agriculture, and falls heavy with respect to Taxes, and reduces the last Partakers to Poverty; but, on the Contrary, the Division of an Inheritance into certain Portions is agreeable with the Preservation of all these fundamental Rules, and with the *general* and *particular* Interest of every one.

428. A Person under Age is a Member of the *domestic Family*, and not of the *Community*, till he attains the Age of Maturity: It is necessary, therefore, to regulate the Guardianship of such *Minors*; as for Instance,

429. 1*st*, For Children which are left Orphans at the Death of their Parents, and have not yet attained the Age of Maturity; and therefore cannot be intrusted with the *full Power* over their Fortune, lest they should *squander* it away before they come to *Years* of Discretion.

430. 2*dly*, So likewise for *Lunaticks*, or those who have *lost* their Senses.

431. 3*dly*, Also for People in the like unhappy Circumstances.

432. In some free States, the Laws allow the nearest Relations of a Man, who has squandered away the *Moiety* of his Fortune, or has contracted Debts to the *Amount* of that Moiety, to sequester the *other Moiety* of it. The Revenues of this remaining Moiety are divided into *two* Parts; *one* Part is allowed him for his Support, and the *other* is appropriated to the Payment of his Debts; and, at the same Time, he is restrained from selling or mortgaging it deeper. When his Debts are discharged, the Fortune, which his Relations held for him in Trust, is given back for his own Benefit, in case he should reform his Manners; but if he should persist in his former Course of Life, they allow him only the Income of it.

433. It is necessary to establish Rules adapted to every one of these Cases, that the Law might preserve every Citizen from such Acts of Violence, and such Extremities, as may happen in those Circumstances.

434. The Laws which intrust the Guardianship of a Child to the Mother, consider most the Preservation of the remaining Orphan; and those which intrust it to the nearest Heir, attend most to the Preservation of the Fortune.

435. In Nations corrupt in their Manners, the Legislators intrusted the Guardianship of an Orphan to the Mother; and in those where the Laws could place a Confidence in the Manners of the Citizens, they gave the Guardianship to the Heir of the Fortune, and sometimes to both of them.

436. Women, among the Germans, were never permitted to be without a Guardian. Augustus made a Law, "That those "Women who had borne three Children should be exempted "from the Power of Guardianship."

437. The Roman Laws permitted the Bridegroom to make Presents to his Bride, and the Bride to do the same to the Bridegroom, *before* Marriage; but *after* Marriage, that Practice was forbidden.

438. A Law of the Western Goths ordained, "That the "Bridegroom should not make a Present to his future Spouse of "more than the *tenth* Part of his Fortune; and that, in the first "Year of their Marriage, he should make her no Present at all."

Chap. XIX

439. *Of the Composition of Laws.*

440. The whole Body of Laws ought to be divided into three Parts.

441. The first Part is to be intitled *Laws.*

442. The second is to be denominated *the momentary Regulations*, which depend upon Circumstances.

443. The third is to be named *the Injunctions.*

444. Under the Word *Laws* are comprehended all the *fundamental Institutions*, which ought never to be altered, and the Number of such can never be large.

445. Under the Denomination of *momentary Regulations*, is comprehended that *Order* by which all Affairs are to be carried into Execution, and the different Instructions and Institutions which relate to them.

446. The Word *Injunctions* includes in it whatever is made upon some Emergency, and what is only occasional, or relates to some particular Person, and may be *altered at any Time.*

447. Every Subject, according to the *Order* and *Place* to which it belongs, is to be inserted separately in the Code of Laws. —For Instance, Judicial, Military, Commercial, Civil, or the Police, City and Country Affairs, &c. &c.

448. Each Law ought to be written in so clear a Style, as to be perfectly intelligible to every one; and, at the same Time, with great Conciseness: For which Reason Explanations, or Interpretations, are undoubtedly to be added (as Occasion shall require), to enable the Judges to perceive more readily the *Force* as well as *Use* of the Law. The martial Law is full of Examples of the like Nature, which may easily be followed.

449. But the utmost Care and Caution is to be observed in adding these Explanations and Interpretations; because they may, sometimes, rather *darken* than *clear up* the Case; of which there are many Instances.

450. When Exceptions, Limitations, and Modifications are not absolutely necessary in any Law, in that Case it is better not to insert them: For *such* particular Details generally produce still *more* Details.

451. If a Legislator desires to give his Reason for making any particular Law, that Reason ought to be *good*, and *worthy* of the Law. Amongst the Roman Laws, there is one, which determines, that a blind Man should not plead in a Court, for this Reason, because he does not see *the Insignia* of the Magistracy. This Reason is extremely weak, when so many better might be given.

452. Laws ought not to be filled with subtile Distinctions, to demonstrate the quick Parts of the Legislator; they are made for People of *moderate* Capacities, as well as for those of *Genius*. They are not a *Logical Art*, but the simple and plain Reasoning of a Father, who takes Care of his Children and Family.

453. *Real* Candour and Sincerity ought to be *displayed in every Part* of the Laws, and as they are made for the Punishment of Crimes, they ought consequently to *include* in themselves the greatest *Virtue* and *Benevolence*.

454. The Style of the Laws ought to be simple and concise: A *plain direct* Expression will be always better understood, than a *studied* one.

455. When the Style of Laws is *tumid* and *inflated*, they are looked upon only as a Work of *Vanity* and *Ostentation*.

456. Laws ought not to be wrote in Words of a *vague indeter-*

minate Meaning, an Instance of which is here produced. "The "Law of one Greek Emperor punishes that Man with Death, who "shall purchase a freed Man like a Slave, or *who shall disquiet* "*him.*" Such a vague indeterminate Expression as *disquiet* ought not to be made use of. The *Disquiet* we give a Man depends wholly upon the *Degree of Sensibility* he is endued with.

457. The Style of the Code of Laws of Czar Alexis Michailowiz, of blessed Memory, is in general clear, simple, and concise. We listen with Pleasure when Extracts are quoted from it; no one can mistake the Meaning of what he hears: The Words in it are understood even by Persons of middling Capacities.

458. Laws are made for the whole Body of the People: It is the Duty of every Individual to act conformably to them; consequently, it is absolutely necessary that every Individual should understand them.

459. The *sublime*, or lofty, and elevated Expressions, are studiously to be avoided; nor should one unnecessary Word be added in the Construction of a Law; that every one, at first Sight, might readily and clearly comprehend its Meaning.

460. Due Care is likewise to be taken, that, amongst the Laws, there should be none which do not answer the End they were made for; that is, none which abound in Words, and are deficient in Sense; which, in their Contents, are trifling, and in their Style, *bombast.*

461. Laws which prescribe *those* Actions as highly *necessary*, which partake *neither* of Vice *nor* Virtue, are subject to this pernicious Consequence, that they oblige People, at the same Time, to esteem Actions *unavoidably necessary* as *unnecessary* ones.

462. Laws for pecuniary Mulcts or Fines, which mark precisely the Sum of Money payable for particular Offences, ought at least to be re-examined every *fifty Years*; because the Payment of that Sum, which at one Time was a *sufficient* Penalty, may be *none at all* at another; for the Value of Money changes, in proportion to the Quantity of Wealth in a Nation. There was once a whimsical fellow at Rome, who gave a Box on the Ear to

all he met, and paid every one immediately *five and twenty Pence*, which was the *Mulct* inflicted by the Laws for that Offence.

Chap. XX

463. *Of the different Statutes which require Explanation.*

464. (*A.*) The Crime of High-treason.

465. Under this Denomination are comprehended *all* Crimes against the Safety of the Sovereign and the State.

466. The Style of all Laws ought to be expressed in *clear* and *concise* Terms; but there are none which require *more* Precision and Conciseness in their Construction, and *more nearly concern* the Security of the Citizens, than the Laws relating to *the Crime* of High-treason.

467. The Liberty of a Citizen is endangered by nothing so much as by judicial and oblique Accusations in general. How dangerous then would it be, if this important Statute should remain *obscure*? For the Liberty of a Citizen depends chiefly upon the *Goodness* and *Excellency* of the penal Laws.

468. The penal Laws are not to be intermixed with the Laws, which regulate the judicial Forms.

469. If the Crime of High-treason is laid down in the Laws in *vague indefinite* Terms, it will then be productive of an Infinity of different Abuses.

470. The Chinese Laws, for Instance, decide, That whoever does not shew *proper Respect* to the *Sovereign* is to be punished with Death. But as they do not *define* what is *not shewing proper Respect*, in that Case any Thing will furnish a Pretext for taking away the Life of whoever they please, and destroying the whole Family of any Person whom they chuse to ruin.

Two Persons commissioned to write the *Court Gazettes*, having inserted in the Account or Description of an Affair of no Consequence, some Circumstances which proved not to be *strictly true*; it was declared, that to *lie* in the *Court Gazettes* is to be wanting in *the Respect due to the Court*; and they were both put to Death.

One of the Princes of the Blood having *inadvertently* put some Mark upon a Memorial signed by the Emperor, it was decided, that he did not shew *due Respect* to *Bogdo-Chan*; which occasioned a most horrible Persecution against the Prince and his whole Family.

471. To denominate an Action *High-treason*, which is absolutely *not so*, is a most flagrant Abuse of the Law. A Law of the Roman Emperors prosecuted those as guilty of *Sacrilege*, who questioned the *Merit* of any Person to whom they thought proper to give an Employment, and consequently condemned them to die.

472. Another Law declared those guilty of *High-treason*, who coined false Money; but they are to be considered as no more than *Robbers* of the State. Thus the Ideas of Things, *different* in their Nature, are confounded.

473. To affix the Name of *High-treason* to a Crime of a different Nature, is only to lessen the Horror for the Crime of High-treason.

474. A Roman Governor wrote Word to an Emperor, that a Process was preparing against a Judge for *High-treason*, who had pronounced a Sentence contrary to the Ordinances of that Emperor; the Emperor replied, that, in his Reign, the Crimes of *indirect* High-treason were *not* to be admitted in Courts of Judicature.

475. There was a Law among the Romans, which ordained, that whoever should throw any Thing, though by Accident, against the Images of the Emperors, should be punished as guilty of *High-treason*.

476. There was a Law in England, which declared all those guilty of *High-treason* who should *foretell* the Death of the King. In the last Illness of that King, no Physician dared to inform him of the Danger he was in: We may presume, that they acted in the same Manner with respect to the Cure.

477. A Man *dreamed* that he killed a King: That King ordered him to be put to Death, declaring that he would not have dreamed of it in the Night, if he had not often *meditated* upon it in the Day-time. This was a terrible Act of Tyranny; for though

he had even *intended* it, yet he had not *attempted* to put his Design in Execution. The Laws are not obliged to punish any Acts but external or *overt* Acts only.

478. When a great Number of Crimes were included in the Term *High-treason*, it became unavoidably necessary to *distinguish* and *proportion* the Punishment to the *Nature* of the respective Crime; it was therefore, at last, decreed, that no Crimes should be *deemed* High-treason, but those which *indicated an Intention* against the Life and Security of the Sovereign, and against the State and such like; to which Crimes they annexed the severest Punishment.

479. This Kind of Actions does not happen every Day; many People may have an Opportunity of taking Notice of them: A false Accusation with *respect to Facts* may be easily cleared up.

480. *Words*, accompanied with *Actions*, partake of the *Nature* of those Actions; therefore, a Man who goes to publick Places to excite the Subjects to Rebellion, will be guilty of *High-treason*; because the *Words*, accompanied with the *Action*, partake of its *Nature*. In this Case the Laws do not punish for the *Words*, but for the *Action* committed, at the Time when the *Words* were made use of. *Words* are never imputed as a *Crime*, unless they *prepare*, or *accompany*, or *follow* the *criminal Action*. He who tortures *Words* into a *Crime* worthy of Death, perverts the whole Order of Things: *Words* ought to be esteemed only the *Sign* of a Crime, worthy of capital Punishment.

481. Nothing renders the Crime of *High-treason* more dependent upon the *arbitrary* Interpretation and *Will* of another, than when *indiscreet Words* are the *Subject* of it. Words *spoken* in Conversation are so subject to *arbitrary* Interpretations, and *so great* a Difference subsists between *Indiscretion* and *Malice*, and so *little* between *indiscreet* and *malicious* Expressions, that the Law can by no Means subject *Words* to capital Punishment; at least, without *expressly specifying* those *particular Words* which it declares treasonable.

482. And, consequently, *Words* do not form the *Essence* of a Crime; they frequently signify *nothing* of *themselves* but by the

Tone of Voice they are pronounced with. Frequently a Repetition of the *same Words* does not give the *same Sense*; this *Sense* depends upon the *Connexion* with what *preceded* or *followed*. Sometimes *Silence* expresses *more* than *Words*. There is nothing so *equivocal* and *uncertain*, as this whole Affair about *Words*. How then can so capital a Crime as *High-treason* be made of *Words*, and punished in the *same* Manner as the very *Action* itself? I mean not to lessen the Indignation which every one ought to have for *those*, who try to *tarnish* the Glory of their Sovereign; but will say this, that simple corrective Punishment will *suit better*, on these Occasions, than the *Charge of High-treason*, which is always terrible even to *Innocence* itself.

483. *Writings* contain Things, which are more durable than *Words*; but if they do not *lead* to the Crime of *High-treason*, they cannot, *of themselves*, constitute the *Essence* of High-treason.

484. Satirical Writings are prohibited in Monarchies; but they make them *a Misdemeanor* subject to the *Police* of the Town, and not *a Crime*: And great Care ought to be taken, in the Examination of *these Libels*, how we *extend it farther*; representing to ourselves, that Danger of *debasing* the human Mind by *Restraint* and *Oppression*; which can be productive of nothing but *Ignorance*, and must *cramp* and *depress* the *rising Efforts* of Genius, and destroy the *very Will* for Writing.

485. Slanderers ought to be punished.

486. In many States, the Law obliges all Persons, under Pain of capital Punishment, to discover even those Conspiracies which they know of *only by Hearsay*, and *not* by any Communication with the Conspirators. It is highly necessary that this Law should be executed with the *utmost Severity*, in Cases of the *highest Degree* of Treason.

487. And it imports us greatly not to confound the *different* Degrees of this *Crime*.

488. (*B.*) *Of Judgments by particular Commissions.*

489. The most useless Thing to sovereign Monarchies is, to nominate sometimes *particular* Judges, or *Commissioners*, to try some of their Subjects. Such Judges ought to be *virtuous* and

upright Men; that they might not think to justify themselves by *their Orders*, by some *secret Interest* of the State, by the *Choice* made of *their Persons*, and by their *own Fears*. So little Benefit accrues from Trials by *Commissioners*, that it is not worth the Trouble of altering the *common* Forms of Trial for that Purpose.

490. This Method too may be productive of an Abuse highly dangerous to the publick Safety. Of this we shall here produce an Instance. In England, in the Time of some of their Kings, they judged the Members of the House of Peers by *Commissioners* chosen out of the same Body; and by this Method they put to Death whatsoever Peers they pleased.

491. Among *Us* they often embroiled the Discussion of an Affair by nominating *such Kind* of Judges, both by their Opinion in that Affair, and the judicial Sentence consequent upon it.

492. However there is a wide Difference between collecting all the Informations and Circumstances relative to any Affair whatsoever, and giving our Opinion, or judging that Affair.

493. (*C.*) *Rules necessary, and of great Importance.*

494. In such a State as *Ours*, which extends its Sovereignty over so many different Nations, to forbid, or not to allow them to profess *different Modes* of Religion, would greatly indanger the Peace and Security of its Citizens.

495. And the most certain Means of bringing back these wandering Sheep to the true Flock of the Faithful, is *a prudent Toleration* of other Religions, not repugnant to our orthodox Religion and Polity.

496. The human Mind is irritated by Persecution, but the Permission to *believe* according to *one's Opinion*, softens even the most *obdurate* Hearts, and draws them gradually from their *inveterate* Obstinacy, by *stifling* those Disputes; which are detrimental to the *Tranquillity* of the State, and the *Union* of the Citizens.

497. We ought to be extremely cautious in the Examination of Persons accused of *Witchcraft* and *Heresy*. Accusations of these two Crimes may break terribly in upon the Tranquillity, Liberty, and Welfare of the Citizens; and prove the Source of

innumerable Acts of Tyranny, unless *Bounds* are set to them by the Laws. For as this Kind of Accusation does not directly strike at the Actions of a Citizen, but the imaginary Idea which People form of his Character, it becomes highly dangerous, in proportion to their *Ignorance*; and, in that Case, a Citizen will always find himself in Danger; because neither the *most* exemplary Behaviour in Life, nor the *most* conscientious Discharge of every moral Duty, can protect him against the Effects of Suspicions of these Crimes.

498. In the Reign of the Greek Emperor Manuel Comnenus, the Protestator was accused of a Conspiracy against the Emperor, and of making use of certain *secret Inchantments, which rendered People invisible.*

499. They write in the History of Constantinople, that after a Revelation was published, that a miraculous Power had ceased by the *magical Art* of a particular Person, both he and his Son were condemned to die. Upon how many different Circumstances did this Crime depend, which a Judge was obliged to unravel? 1*st*, That the Miracle had ceased; 2*d*, That, at the Time of this Cessation of the Miracle, *magick Art* had been practised; 3*d*, That this *Inchantment* could put a Stop to the Miracle; 4*th*, That the Man accused was a *Conjuror*; 5*th*, and lastly, That *he* had done this *Act of Inchantment.*

500. The Emperor Theodore Lascaris ascribed his Illness to *Inchantment.* Those who were accused of it had no other Way of proving their Innocence, but *by handling a red-hot Iron without burning themselves.* They joined here, to the most *uncertain Crime* in the World, the most *uncertain Proofs* for its Discovery.

501. (*D.*) *How can we know, when a State approaches to its Fall, and entire Dissolution?*

502. The Corruption of every Government generally begins by the *Corruption of its fundamental Principles.*

503. The fundamental Principles of a Government are not only corrupted, when they extinguish that Idea of the State ingrafted in the Minds of the People by the Law, which may be termed the *Equality* prescribed *by the Laws*; but even then, when this *Idea of Equality* shall take root in the People, and grow to

such a Pitch of Licentiousness, that every one *aims* at being *equal* to him, who *is ordained* by the Laws *to rule over him.*

504. If they do not shew Respect to the *Sovereign*, to the *Courts of Judicature*, and to *Governors*; and if they do not respect the *Ancient*, neither will they respect *Fathers*, nor *Mothers*, nor *Masters*; and the State insensibly will run to ruin.

505. When the fundamental Principles of Government are corrupted, then the *Regulations* introduced in it are termed *Hardships*, or *Severities.* The established *Rules* are termed *Restraints*; what was *Caution* before, is *now* termed *Fear.* The *Property* of particular Persons constituted, in former Times, the *Wealth of the People*; but now the *Wealth of the People* becomes the *Inheritance* of *particular Persons*, and the Love of their Country vanishes.

506. In order to preserve the *fundamental Principles* of a well-regulated Government inviolate, the State ought to be supported in its present Grandeur; and this State will fall to Decay, if its fundamental Principles should be *altered.*

507. There are two Kinds of Corruption; the first is, when *the Laws are not observed*; the second when *the Laws are so bad, that they corrupt themselves*; and the Evil then is *incurable*; because the *Remedy* of the Evil is to be found only in *itself.*

508. A State may change also two different Ways; either because the Constitution of it *mends*, or because the *same* Constitution *corrupts.* If the *fundamental* Principles in a State are preserved, the Constitution of it *mends*; but if the fundamental Principles of it are destroyed, the Constitution *changes*, and then it *corrupts.*

509. The *more* capital Punishments increase, the *more* a State is in Danger of Destruction; for capital Punishments *increase* in Proportion to the *Corruption* of Manners, and Corruption of Manners produces the *Ruin* of a State.

510. What destroyed the Reign of the Posterity of Cina and Sunhy, says some Chinese Author, is this: "That those Sove-"reigns, not content with the general Inspection of Affairs, "which alone become a Sovereign, would govern every Thing

"immediately by themselves, and brought all the Causes before "themselves, which ought to have been decided by the different "Courts of Judicature, instituted for that Purpose."

511. A Monarchy is destroyed, when the Sovereign imagines, that he displays his Power more by *changing* the Order of Things, than by adhering to it, and when he is more fond of *his own Imaginations* than of *his Will*, from which the Laws proceed, and have proceeded.

512. It is true, there are Cases, where Power ought and can exert its full Influence, without any Danger to the State. But there are Cases also, where it ought to act according to the *Limits* prescribed by itself.

513. The supreme Art of governing a State consists in the *precise* Knowledge of *that* Degree of Power, whether *great* or *small*, which ought to be exerted according to the *different* Exigences of Affairs: For, in a Monarchy, the Prosperity of the State depends, in Part, on a mild and condescending Government.

514. In the best constructed Machines, Art employs the *least Moment*, *Force*, and fewest Wheels possible. This Rule holds *equally good* in the Administration of Government; the most *simple Expedients* are often the *very best*, and the *most intricate* the *very worst*.

515. There is a certain Facility in the Method of governing: It is better for the Sovereign to *encourage*, and for the Laws to *threaten*.

516. That Minister is ill qualified for his Office, who shall always tell you, "That the Sovereign is displeased; that he is "unexpectedly prevented; that he will act as he pleases."

517. It would be a grievous Misfortune to a State, if no one should dare to represent the Danger of some future Accident; nor excuse his bad Success, proceeding from ill Fortune; nor presume to speak his Mind freely.

518. But if any one should inquire, *When* a Sovereign ought to punish, and *when* to pardon? this is a Point which can be more easily *felt* than *prescribed to*. When *Lenity* is dangerous; the

Dangers arising from it are extremely *obvious*. It is easy to distinguish *Lenity* from that *Weakness*, which brings the Sovereign into an Aversion for punishing, and into such a Situation, that he cannot himself *decide whom he ought to punish*.

519. It is certain, that a *high* Opinion of the *Glory* and *Power* of the Sovereign, would *increase* the *Strength* of his Administration; but a *good Opinion* of *his Love of Justice*, *will increase it at least as much*.

520. All this will never please those Flatterers, who are daily instilling this pernicious Maxim into all the Sovereigns on Earth, *That their People are created for them only*. But *We* think, and esteem it *Our* Glory to declare, "That *We* are created for *Our* "People;" and, for this Reason, *We* are obliged to Speak of Things just as they ought to be. For God forbid! that, after this Legislation is finished, any Nation on Earth should be more just; and, consequently, should flourish more than Russia; otherwise the Intention of *Our* Laws would be totally frustrated; an Unhappiness *which I do not wish to survive*.

521. All the Examples and Customs of different Nations, which are introduced in this Work, ought to produce no other Effect, than to co-operate in the Choice of those Means, which may render the People of Russia, humanly speaking, the *most happy* in themselves of any People upon Earth.

522. Nothing more remains now for the Commission to do, but to compare every Part of the Laws with the Rules of these Instructions.

CONCLUSION

523. *Perhaps some Persons may object, after perusing these Instructions, that they will not be intelligible to every one. To this it may be answered: It is true, they will not be readily understood by every Person, after one slight Perusal only; but every Person may comprehend these Instructions, if he reads them with Care and Attention, and selects occasionally such Articles as may serve to direct him, as a Rule, in whatever he undertakes. These Instructions ought to be frequently perused, to render them more familiar: And*

every one may be firmly assured, that they will certainly be understood; because,

524. Assiduity *and* Care *will* conquer *every Difficulty; as, on the Contrary,* Indolence *and* Carelessness *will* deter *from every laudable Attempt.*

525. *To render this difficult Affair more easy; these Instructions are to be read over once, at the Beginning of every Month, in the Commission for composing the New Code of Laws, and in all the subordinate Committees, which depend upon it; particularly the respective Chapters and Articles intrusted to their Care, till the Conclusion of the Commission.*

526. *But as no perfect Work was ever yet composed by Man; therefore, if the Commissioners should discover, as they proceed, that any Rule for some particular Regulations has been omitted, they have Leave, in such a Case, to report it to* Us, *and to ask for a Supplement.*

The Original signed with Her Imperial Majesty's *own Hand, thus,*

CATHERINE.

Moscow, *July* 30.
1767.

THE FIRST

SUPPLEMENT

TO THE

GRAND INSTRUCTIONS.

Chap. XXI

527. *Of good Order, otherwise termed Police.*

528. The Order in general in a State is frequently understood by the Term *Police.*

529. *We Ourselves* will explain in this Chapter what *We* mean here by the Term *Police.*

530. To the Care of which every Thing appertains, which conduces to the Preservation of *good Order* in a Society.

531. The Institutes of this *Department* are intirely of a *different* Kind from the rest of the Civil Laws.

532. There are a Kind of Criminals, whom the *Laws punish.*

533. There are others whom they only *correct.*

534. The first Sort are subject to the Rigour of the Law, and the other to its Authority; the former are excluded from the Society, the latter, on the contrary, are *compelled* to live in the Society, according to the *established Rules.*

535. The *Objects* of the Police are *Affairs,* which may happen every Hour, and are generally Matters of little Consequence; and, therefore, judicial Formalities are here quite unnecessary.

536. The Police is continually taken up with particular Details, or with Trifles; consequently Affairs which require a great Length of Time, in order to their being thoroughly examined into, are by no Means fit to come under the Cognizance of *this Department.* In many Places, Affairs, after the Expiration of a certain limited Number of Days, are sent to those Courts of Judicature, to which they belong.

537. The Actions of the Police ought not to be in the least tedious; and they are exercised in Cases, which happen over and

over again every Day. And, consequently, the great Punishments can have no Place here; and the great Examples of Justice are not made for *this Department*.

538. *Regulations* are more necessary for it than *Laws*.

539. The Persons, who belong to it are always under the Eye of the civil Magistracy, and the wise Regulations of the Police prevent them from the Commission of great Crimes.

540. For this Reason *High Violations* of the Laws ought not to be confounded with the *simple Violation* of the Police: These Things must not be *ranked* in the *same* Order.

541. From hence it follows, for Instance, that the Action of a *certain Sultan*, who ordered a *Baker to be impaled*, who had been detected in a Fraud, is the Action *of a Tyrant*, who does not know how to execute Justice but by *exceeding the Measure of Justice itself*.

542. It is extremely necessary to separate those Cases, in which the Police ought to *punish*, from those, in which *it* ought only to *correct*.

543. It is not sufficient to find out Disorders, and to contrive *Means* to prevent them: *It* ought, besides, to look with a watchful Eye, that those *Means* should be put in Execution at the very Instant the Cases happen.

544. And this is a Part of the Argument proposed to be resolved here; which, in many Countries, is totally neglected; however, *without it*, the *other* Parts of the Chain, (if one may make use of the Expression) which connect the Government of the whole State, will fall into Disorder.

545. Exactly the same Confusion has happened in the Regulations of *this Department*, as with *that* Number of Houses, which *compose* a City, *where* the *Plan of the Ground* was not regularly *marked out* before the People *began* to build. When People begin to build in a City so circumstanced, every one fixes upon a Spot, which he thinks most convenient, without the least Regard either to the *Symmetry* or *Extent* of the Place he had selected: Whence a *Heap* of Edifices are *huddled* together, which can hardly ever be brought into a *regular* Form by the

Efforts and careful Attention of *whole Ages*. The Laws for the Preservation of good Order are equally *liable* to the *same* Irregularities.

546. The Number of those Regulations increases, in proportion to the Necessities of the State; but to bring them into such *regular* Order, that they might always be *properly* carried into Execution, without *any Difficulty, or Obstruction*; will be the *Masterpiece of Science*, with respect to *this Offspring* of the Laws.

547. These Regulations ought to be divided into two Species.

548. The first contains in itself the *Police* of the City.

549. The second, the Police of the Country.

550. This last has neither *Objects*, nor *Extent* equal to the first.

551. In these Departments, *particular* Care and Attention ought to be given to what follows here below.

552. (1.) Not to allow any Thing which may disturb the Celebration of divine Service in Places appointed for that Purpose, and that *Order*, and proper *Decorum* should be *observed* by the Citizens, at the Time of the *Procession with the Cross*, and such like *Rites* and *Ceremonies*.

553. (2.) Purity of Manners is the *second* Object for the Preservation of good Order, and comprehends in itself whatsoever is necessary to repress Luxury, to deter from Drunkenness, to put a Stop to the Progress of prohibited Games, to regulate the publick Bagnios, and publick Spectacles, in order to restrain the Licentiousness of *those People*, who lead *bad* Lives, and to drive out of the Community *those*, who *cheat* the People, under the *Denomination* of Magicians, Fortune-tellers, Prophets, and such like *Impostors*.

554. (3.) Health is the *third* Object of the Police, which obliges *it* to extend *its* Care to the Salubrity of the Air, the Cleanliness of the Streets, Rivers, Wells, and Water-Springs; and to the *Quantity* of Provision of *Eatables* and *Drinkables*; and, finally, to those *common* Maladies which increase among the People, as well as to those which are *contagious*.

555. (4.) To the most watchful Care for the Conservation of

every *Species* of *Corn*, even before the Harvest, and for the Preservation of Cattle, and Meadows for their Pasture, of Fisheries, *&c. It* ought to prescribe *general* Rules for all *these* Things according to their *various* Circumstances, and direct *what* Precautions *ought* to be taken for the *future.*

556. (5.) To the *Security* and *Firmness* of Buildings, and *such* Rules as are *proper* to be observed in *this Case*, by the different Artists and Workmen, upon whom the *Strength* and *Goodness* of the Building *depends*: To the Preservation of Pavements, of the Decoration, and Ornaments of Cities; of *free Way* in the Streets for *Passengers*, who either *walk* or *ride*; of the *general Rates* for Carriage of Goods or Persons; of the Inns, *&c.*

557. (6.) The Tranquillity of the People requires, that *sudden Accidents* should be prevented, as well as *other Casualties*; such as *Fires*, *Robberies*, &c. And therefore certain Rules are prescribed for the Preservation of this Tranquillity; such, for Instance, as to put out *all Fires* at the *appointed* Hours, to *shut up* their Houses, to set such Vagabonds and Persons *to work*, as can *give no Account* of themselves, and shew *which Way* they gain a *Livelihood*; or to *expell* them the City; to forbid such Persons to carry Arms, who have *no Right* to do it, *&c.*; to prohibit *unlawful* Assemblies, or *rendezvous*, and to forbid the Dispersion of *seditious*, or *scandalous Libels*. To endeavour, at the Ending of the Day, to preserve the Town in *Peace* and *Safety*, and, in the *Night*-time, to *light* the Streets, *&c.*

558. (7.) To regulate and establish *one true Weight* and *Measure*, and to prevent the Practice of any *Kind* of *Fraud.*

559. (8.) Servants hired by the Year, and those who work by the Day, compose an *Object* of this Department, both to *keep* them to their Duty, and likewise to enable them to *obtain* their *just* Due *punctually* from those who hire them.

560. (9.) Finally, Beggars, and *particularly* such of them as are *sick*, or *impotent*, come under the Care of *this Administration.* In the *first* Place, to set those to work, who beg for Charity, but have the *Use* of *their Limbs*; and, at the same Time, to give a *certain* Maintenance, and the *Means* of Cure, to *those* who are *sick* or *impotent.*

561. As the *Intention* and *End* of the Institution of this Administration is *good Order*, and *Decency* in general, in the *Dwellings* of the Citizens, it evidently follows, that *every* Member of the Society, of *whatsoever Rank* he may be, is *dependent* upon *this* Administration.

562. Where the Limits of the Power of the *Police* end, there the Power of the *civil* Jurisdiction begins.

563. For Instance, *the Police* takes a Thief, or Criminal, into Custody: *It* examines him, but *it* recommends the *Decision* of the Business to that Court of Judicature which his Case properly belongs to.

564. From the whole of what has been mentioned above, it evidently appears, that this Administration ought not to inflict severe Punishments on the Delinquents. It is sufficient, in order to curb Licentiousness, and to keep the Affairs intrusted to its Care in proper Order, that its Punishments should consist in *Corrections*, *Amercements*, and such other Penalties as bring Shame and Infamy upon those who are guilty of bad and scandalous Actions, and to keep up a due Respect and Obedience in all the other Inhabitants to this Administration.

565. There is an established Rule in the Courts of Judicature, not to judge of any Affairs, except those which are brought before them *regularly*, and *in due Form*, in order to be heard.

566. On the Contrary, the *Business of the Police* is to *discover* Crimes, leaving the *Decision* of all *criminal* Cases to the other Courts of Judicature, to which *It refers* them for *that Purpose*.

The Original signed with *Her Imperial Majesty's* own Hand, thus,

CATHERINE.

St. Petersburgh,
February 28, 1768.

THE SECOND

SUPPLEMENT

TO THE

GRAND INSTRUCTIONS.

Chap. XXII

567. *Of the Expences, Revenues, and publick Management of the Finances; that is, of the Oeconomy of the State, otherwise termed the Direction of the Exchequer.*

568. Every one here ought to say to himself, *I am a Man, and think myself interested in every Thing which affects Mankind.*

569. And consequently, (1.) *The Man* ought not, nor ever can be forgotten.

570. (2.) There is very little done by *Man*, which is not done for *Man*; and, for the most Part, all Things are done by *him.*

571. The first of these two last Expressions requires the greatest possible *Notice* and *Attention*, from the *Dignity* of its *Object.*

572. The second requires *much Gratitude*, and sincere *Benevolence*, to the *pains-taking Labourer.*

573. A Man, whatever he should *happen* to be, whether a Sovereign or a Plowman, a Handicrafts-man or a Merchant; whether he who eats the *Bread of Idleness*, or he, who, by his Industry and Labour, gives him *the Means* of doing it; whether the Governor or the Governed; every *Individual* of *all these* is still but a *Man.* This one *emphatical Word* gives already a perfect Idea of all his Necessities, and of all the Means of supplying them.

574. How many more *Wants* must that Multitude of People still *labour under*, who are united in one common Cohabitation in a State.

575. Whatever occasions the publick *Expences* of a State, is here termed the *Necessities* of the State, and consists in the following Particulars.

576. The Preservation of the entire State:

(1.) By maintaining the *Means* for its Defence; that is, the Land and maritime Forces, the Fortresses, Artillery, and every other Necessary that belongs to it.

577. (2.) By preserving the interior Order, Quiet, and Safety of *every one* in particular, and *of all* in general; by maintaining Persons for executing Justice, keeping good Order, and inspecting into the different Establishments, which conduce to the *general Good.*

578. (3.) By *Means* which conduce to the publick Utility; such for Instance, as the Building of Cities, making Roads and Drains, scouring Rivers, the Regulation of Schools, Infirmaries, and other innumerable Objects, the Particulars of which the Conciseness of this Work does not permit *Us* to describe.

579. (4.) Decency requires, that Affluence and Magnificence should surround the Throne, as the Source of Prosperity to the whole Community; from which flow Rewards, Encouragements, and Bounties; for all which, *Expence* is not only *necessary* but *highly* useful.

580. After this short Description of the Expences of the State, it is now proper to speak of its *Revenue*, and the *Means* of collecting it in the *Manner least* burthensome to the Publick.

581. Taxes are an *Offering*, which every Citizen *makes*, in order to preserve his own peculiar *Welfare*, *Safety*, *Life*, and *Property*; as was remarked above.

582. But (1*st*,) On what Objects ought Taxes to be imposed?

583. (2*d*,) How are they to be made least burthensome to the People?

584. (3*d*,) How to levy them with the least Expence?

585. (4*th*,) How to prevent Frauds in the Revenue?

586. (5*th*,) How they are to be directed?

587. These are the Questions necessary to be resolved, though attended with great Difficulty.

588. Remarks upon the (1*st*). Politicians reckon five Objects, on which Imposts are generally laid.

(I.) Persons

(II.) Property.

(III.) Family Improvements, which are made use of by the People.

(IV.) Goods exported and imported.

(V.) Deeds, Bonds, *&c.*

589. Upon the (2*d*). Taxes, which are esteemed least burdensome, are those, which are paid voluntarily, and without Constraint, and regard all the Inhabitants of a State in General, and increase *in proportion* to the Luxury and Prodigality of *each* Individual.

590. But, in order to render the Imposts less sensibly felt by the Subjects, this ought, at the same Time, to be constantly observed as a general Rule, *Never to allow of a Monopoly on any Pretence whatever*; that is, never to grant the Privilege of any particular Trade to any one, *exclusive of every other Person.*

591. Upon the (3*d*). The Diminution of the Expence, in levying those Imposts, requires a particular Consideration with respect to those Trifles, where the Duty, sometimes, is not worth the Expence of collecting it, which should be excluded from the Number of Taxables.

592. Upon the (4*th*). The more *substantial* the People shall happen to be, the *more able* they will find themselves to pay the Taxes *faithfully*.

593. It may be mentioned here, that, in general, there are Taxes; which, from their very Nature, are subject to many Difficulties, and Inconveniencies; the Means of preventing which ought to be discovered. Others, where the Expence of collecting the Duty exceeds the Revenue arising from it, are of very little Consequence.

594. At the same Time, the Reason, why Deficiencies happen in some Places, deserves strictly to be inquired into.

595. Is it because the Circulation of Money is less there, than in other Places?

596. Or is it, because the Exportation of their Superfluities becomes burdensome?

597. Or, because the People are still deficient in Arts, and handicraft Trades?

598. Or, because they have very few Means of acquiring Wealth?

599. Or, does it proceed from Laziness, or from excessive Oppressions?

600. It follows now to speak upon the (5*th*). Of the Direction of the Finances of the State, or the Oeconomy, which is otherwise termed *the Direction of the Exchequer*: But *We* comprehend all this under the Denomination of *the Oeconomy of the State.*

601. It has been shewed, that five Objects are reckoned up as subject to Imposts for raising the Revenue. But the *Imposts* in a State are like *Sails* upon a Ship, *destined* for her safe *Run* by a *sure* Track, and *safe* Arrival at her *intended Port*; and not for *overwhelming* her whilst continually *floating* upon the Waves, till *she founders at last in the Depth of the Abyss.*

602. Whoever considers *the Oeconomy of the State*, with respect to the Revenue in Money only, sees only the *final Expence* of it, and does not comprehend the *principal foundations* on which it rests. But he, who examines the *whole Affair* with Attention, and penetrates into the *Interior* of it, will find out the principal *Foundations*, *Objects*, and *Ways* and *Means* which are *most useful* to the State.

603. What are the *first Foundations*, which support *this Oeconomy* by their Strength and Firmness? Nothing, certainly, *but the People.*

604. Hence follows, (1*st*,) The Necessity of encouraging the Increase of Population, in order to produce a greater Number of People in the State.

605. (2*d*,) Of employing them usefully in whatever is necessary, according to the Number of People, and the Extent of the Countries; and of encouraging and assisting the different Arts and Employments, in proportion to the different Degrees of *their* being *necessary* or *beneficial.*

606. Here *Agriculture* claims the *first* Place; for as *it alone* nourishes the People; if duly improved, it may bring them into

such a happy Situation, that they will soon be Possessors of *all other* Conveniencies. Without Agriculture there will be *none of the first Materials* for the Use of the Manufacturer, or handicraft Tradesman.

607. The Duty of the *Oeconomy of the State*, is to find out Means for encouraging the Proprietors of Lands.

(1.) That they might reap the *Profit* of the Goodness of the Land of every Kind, *arising* from whatever *Produce* it should yield them.

(2.) That they might endeavour to increase *Fruits*, *Forests*, *Trees*, and every other Kind of *Growths* that cover the Surface of the Earth.

(3.) That they might encourage the Propagation of every *Kind* of Animals, and of every *Species* that *creeps* upon the Earth, and *flies* in the Air; which *serve for the Improvement of Land*, and which *reciprocally* gives them *Subsistence*.

(4.) That they might employ, for *their Benefit*, the Metals, Salts, Stones, and *other Minerals* and *Fossils*, which conceal themselves within the Earth, and which we *pluck* out, by our Labour, from the *very Bowels of it*.

(5.) And likewise *Fish*, and, in *general*, whatever lives in the Water.

608. Hence is derived the *Root* and *Foundation* of Commerce. By Commerce all these Things are brought into Circulation within the State, or are exported into foreign Countries.

609. The inland, or Home Trade, cannot properly be called Commerce; it is nothing more, than a *simple Circulation in the same Spot*.

610. True Commerce, *emphatically* so called, is *that*, by the *Means of which* a State procures from foreign Countries whatever Things are necessary, which it does not produce itself, and sends out *in Return* its *own Superfluities*.

611. But Exportation and Importation of Goods are subject to *different* Laws, according to the *Difference* of their Object.

612. The foreign Trade is not always the same.

613. Trade, which is well regulated, and carried on with Care

and Assiduity, animates, and supports every thing. If it be *foreign*, and the Balance is on *Our* Side; and, if Inland, and the Circulation has *no* Obstacles, nor shackles which restrain it; then, *in both Cases*, Trade inevitably ought to bring a *general* and *constant* Abundance to the People;

614. From whence arise Riches; which are, (1*st*,) *Natural*, or *acquired*.

615. (2*d*,) *Real*, or *Imaginary*.

616. In the Number of *natural* Riches, *We* may reckon the natural *Genius* of the Inhabitants; which, after it is *enlightened*, and incited and animated by Zeal, may extend far, and by its *extensive* Progress, bring *great* Utility to the State, and no *little* to Individuals.

617. Countries, which have been examined with Attention, and cultivated with Care, yield rich Harvests, and a plentiful Sufficiency of all the Necessaries and Conveniences of Life.

618. *Acquired* Riches are those, which are produced by Care and Application, indefatigably exerted in handicraft Trades, Manufactures, Arts, and Sciences.

619. Encouragement will conduce greatly to farther Improvement, and more perfect Knowledge in every Branch of these, and more Industry in the Execution of their Productions.

620. One ought also to esteem as *acquired* Wealth, the convenient inland Navigation through *Canals*, *cut* for that Purpose in Places, which, without *those*, are *inaccessible* to Vessels. The *Extent* of foreign Commerce by Sea, the *Improvement* of Land Carriage, both as to Facility and Safety, by *constructing*, *re-building*, and keeping in *good* and *solid Repair*, publick Roads, Bridges, and Ferries.

621. The Number of Particulars, which belong to this Head, is so *extensive*, that the *principal ones* only are here mentioned; but still even these, according to the *Necessities* and *different Circumstances* of Things, are always subject to Alteration. However, this will be sufficient to give an Idea of what *We* mean under the Denomination of *the Oeconomy of the State*. The rest remains for the Consideration of those, who will engage in the

Execution of this *important* Part, in order to penetrate into the Depth of it.

622. Of the Riches in a State some are *real*, and others *imaginary*.

623. The real ones are either immoveable, or moveable.

624. They belong either to the Sovereign, or to Individuals.

625. The Riches of the Sovereign are either *simply* his own *Lordships*, such as *certain* Lands, or *Possessions*, belonging *to him*, in the *same* Manner as to any *other particular Lord*; or, as *Sovereign* Lord over whatever the publick Wealth consists of, which *he possesses by virtue of that Appellation which he derives immediately from God.*

626. The *Wealth* of *Individuals* consists in whatever they enjoy as Citizens; whose Property is the *Foundation* of the *real Riches* of the State by *these two Methods*,

(1*st*,) By the *Produce* of every Kind of those Persons, who enter into Trade, and which comes into the *Home Circulation.*

(2*dly*,) By *Taxes*, which an *honest* Man cannot pay otherwise, than by the Means of *this Produce.*

627. The real *Riches*, which consist in the Revenues, are either *constant* or *occasional*, and belong equally with the Lands, either to the *Sovereign* or to *Individuals.*

628. The Revenues, which belong to the Sovereign, are likewise of *two Species*; either as belonging to *him*, as a *particular* Lord, or as to the *Head* of the State.

629. The Sovereign possesses the *first* in his own proper *Right.*

630. But, *as Sovereign*, he reckons,

(1*st*,) *The Income of all the Property in the State in its full Extent.*

(2*dly*,) The *Taxes* upon whatever the State possesses.

631. This *last Branch* of the Revenue *a wise Sovereign* never increases, without *extreme* Reluctance; and whenever *he* is *compelled* to do it, he takes particular Care that the Taxes should be regulated in *proportion* to the *Wealth* of the Subjects; and that it

should never *exceed* the *Measure* of their Abilities, nor lay a *greater* Burden upon the Citizens, than they can naturally support, or than ought, in *strict Equity*, to be *exacted* from them.

632. In collecting the Taxes, the *greatest Exactness* ought to be observed, as well as the *greatest Moderation and Humanity*.

633. We ought to observe here, that Gold and Silver, which represent alternately the Commodities, and the Signs of whatever can be made use of in Exchange, are procured either from the Mines, or by Commerce.

634. Gold and Silver are considered either as the *first simple* Material*, or as a Thing *constructed by Art*†.

635. Commodities or Goods, and every Species of moveable Property, are frequently the *Object* of the *interior* Circulation, and of *that Trade* which is carried on with foreign States.

636. And in this Case, especially with respect to *foreign* Trade, it is highly necessary to examine, whether the Traffick with the *first Raw Materials*, together with the *Manufactures* constructed from them; or whether *the One* or *the other* of them is carried on by *our own People*?

637. *Real* Wealth might be greatly increased by that, which is *imaginary*.

638. *Imaginary* Wealth is *founded* upon *Credit* or *Confidence*; that is, upon the ingrafted and received *Opinion* of the *faithful* and *punctual* Payment of a Debt, when it becomes due, and of the Ability of the Person who is to pay it.

639. *Credit*, or *Confidence*, may be either *that* of the *whole Body of the People*, which is visible in *national Banks*, and in the *Circulation* of some *Signs*, which from *good Regulations* of Government have *acquired the Force* of Credit; or from *Confidence* in *particular* Persons, either as *Individuals*, or as *united in a Company*.

640. As *Individuals*, they may, by their *Integrity*, *upright Conduct*, and *extensive Views*, become *Bankers*, not only for *one State*, but even for *the whole Universe*.

641. Individuals may unite together into great or small

* Bullion. † Bullion coined, which is Money.

Bodies, in *mercantile Companies*, and then the *personal Credit* of Individuals increases the *Credit* of the Public.

642. But the Conveniences of *natural* and *acquired* Wealth, both *real* and *imaginary*, are not confined within the Limits of the *present* Time; they *extend* even to the *Future*, by supplying, in *Time of Need*, the certain *Means* for augmenting the Revenue. These also constitute an Offspring of *the Oeconomy of the State.*

643. These *Means*, or *Expedients*, are exactly circumstanced like *publick Credit*; a *wise Use* of them *enlarges*, but *the Abuse* as certainly *destroys* them.

644. It is injurious to a State, when it is *totally* ignorant of *these Expedients*, or when it has *continual Recourse* to them. It ought to *seek* for them, as if it could not *do* without them: But, on the *other Hand*, it ought never to make use of them, except in Time of *absolute* Necessity, and even *then* too but *sparingly*, and with *such Precaution*, as if no *new ones* could be found out in future.

645. And the true principal Foundations *of the Oeconomy of the State* lead us to this prudent Management.

646. The general *Oeconomy of the State* is divided into *political* and *domestick.*

647. The *political* comprehends the whole Body of the *People* and *Affairs*, and a *distinct Knowledge* of *their Situations*, *their Ranks*, and *their Employments.*

648. The whole System of Affairs, both as to *Particulars* and in *general*, is necessary to be thoroughly known, that one might judge of their *reciprocal Relation* to each other, in order to make *them altogether* useful to the Community.

649. The *domestick Oeconomy* comprehends the following Objects, with respect to the principal Foundations of *the Oeconomy of the State.* It ought to preserve the Sources of the Revenue *untouched*, to make them, if possible, yield *more abundantly*, and to draw *Supplies* from them, without *exhausting* or reducing them to *Penury.*

650. With respect to *the national Wealth*, it ought to preserve

the Lands in a well-cultivated State, and to endeavour to *better them* by Improvement;

651. To *defend just* Rights, to collect *the Revenue* in *such a Manner*, that nothing might be *lost*, which ought to be *brought* into the publick Exchequer:

652. And that, at the Time of discharging the publick Expences, every Part of *the Revenue* should be applied to *those Disbursements* for which it was *appropriated.*

653. That the *Sum-total* of the Expences might not, if possible, *exceed* the *Revenue*;

654. And that the *Accounts* should always be *regularly kept*, and proved by *clear indisputable Vouchers.*

655. From the whole of what *I* have said here upon *the Oeconomy of the State*, it evidently appears, That *this* very *simple* and very *natural* Division, and the Assemblage and Connection of *general* Ideas, *clear* and *intelligible* to all, *lead* to the *direct determinate* Meaning of *that Expression*, which is of *so much Importance* to the *whole* Community: That in this Chapter, *all* the Parts enter *one into another*, according to the *Propriety* of that *reciprocal* Relation, which *they bear* to each other: That there is not *one* amongst them which does not *depend* upon the *rest*, and that a *single* Connection only of *all* these Parts may *establish, strengthen*, and *perpetuate* for ever, the *Safety* of the State, the *Prosperity* of the People, and the *Glory* of the Sovereign.

The Original signed with Her Imperial Majesty's own Hand, thus,

CATHERINE.

ST. PETERSBURGH,
April 8, 1768.

NOTES

LETTER I

Peter the Great is appropriately mentioned in the first line of this book, for it was his spirit that inspired Catherine and her projected code. "He raised his country", wrote the translator of 1768, "to her present envied height, and made her the arbitress of those very nations from whom she had so lately received law, and of whom she had been so long the contempt and scorn." Catherine's tributes to him were numerous and sincere, as both sections of this volume show.

Voltaire had studied Peter when writing on Charles XII of Sweden, and was now fresh from that history of Russia under his rule which Shuvalov had commissioned him to write. To Shuvalov in January 1761 he sent a quatrain which he afterwards recalled as follows:

> Ses lois et ses travaux ont instruit les mortels;
> Il les rendit heureux, et sa fille l'imite.
> Jupiter, Osiris, vous eûtes des autels,
> Et c'est lui seul qui les mérite.

"Le seul nom de Pierre-le-Grand", he declared, "vaut mieux que ces quatre vers." Trained by his study of Peter, Voltaire's insight into the potentialities of Russia was far more profound than that of his critics. After Tottleben's raid on Berlin, Frederick the Great petulantly wrote to him: "I shall not read the history of these barbarians, I would fain be unaware that they live in our half of the globe".

"Rousseau's prophecy" followed his own attack on Peter (*Contrat social*, II, viii) for westernising those who were by nature Russians. "Il a empêché ses sujets de devenir jamais ce qu'ils pourraient être, en leur persuadant qu'ils étaient ce qu'ils ne sont pas.... Les Tartares, ses sujets ou ses voisins deviendront ses maîtres et les nôtres." Voltaire both understood the present and judged the future far better, as the coming war with the Turks was to show. (Cp. Letters XXXIII, LVIII.)

LETTER II

This letter of thanks for the *Philosophie de l'histoire* appears to be represented in the Petersburg archives by a draft, written by Catherine, which exceeds it in length and has nothing in common with it except the reference to the Abbé Bazin. It contains an important statement about Russia and the contemplated code of laws. (*Sb*. x, 35.)

"Je dois rendre justice à la nation: c'est un excellent terrain, sur lequel une bonne graine prend bien vite; mais aussi il nous faut des axiomes incontestablement reconnus pour vrais. Tout autre trouvera à qui parler, quand la traduction française des principes qui doivent servir de base à nos nouvelles loix sera achevée; je prendrai la liberté de vous l'envoyer, et vous verrez que grâce à de pareils axiomes cette pièce a obtenu le suffrage de ceux pour qui elle était composée. J'ose tout augurer de la réussite de cet important ouvrage, vu la chaleur dont chacun est rempli pour cette confection. Je pense que vous vous plairiez au milieu de cette table où l'orthodoxe assis entre l'hérétique et le musulman écoutent tous les trois paisiblement la voix d'un idolâtre et se concertent souvent tous les quatre pour rendre leur avis supportable à tous. Ils ont si bien oubliés la coutume de se griller réciproquement que s'il y avait quelqu'un d'assez malavisé pour proposer à un député de bouillir son voisin pour plaire à l'être suprême, je réponds pour tous qu'il n'y en a pas un seul qui ne répondrait: il est homme comme moi, et selon le premier paragraphe de l'instruction de S. M. I. nous devons nous faire le plus de bien possible, mais aucun mal."

LETTER III

Late in 1762, Catherine appointed a commission of five secular and two clerical members to settle the ecclesiastical questions which had done much to make her husband unpopular. This was the prelude to a resumption of secularisation. Against the measures mentioned in the postscript to Letter IV, ecclesiastical privilege found a daring champion in Archbishop Arsenius of Rostov, north-east of Moscow. Arsenius used the ceremonies of preparation for the enshrinement of the bones of Demetrius, a predecessor, to launch a tremendous attack upon the enemies of God and despoilers of the church (Feb. 1763). This he followed up by an explicit indictment of Catherine, addressed to the Holy Synod, the board which Peter had established to govern the Russian church. Catherine accepted the challenge. Within a month, Arsenius had been condemned by the Synod, degraded, and banished to a monastery near Archangel.

LETTER VI

Catherine's letter passed through the hands of the Prince Galitsin, her representative in Paris. She explained the "metropolitan" thus: "Les métropolites ne diffèrent des autres évêques et archevêques que par une cape blanche; celui-ci l'a reçue pour m'avoir couronnée".

LETTER IX

Here the *Instruction* definitely enters the *Correspondance*. In 1766, answering the letter of 11 August in which D'Alembert will give no account of Parisian literary quarrels ("Il ne faut point entretenir les Dieux de la querelle des Rats et des Grenouilles"), Catherine begins: "Mes principales occupations depuis deux ans se réduisent à copier et à apprécier les principes du président de Montesquieu. Je m'applique à l'entendre, et j'efface aujourd'hui ce que je trouvais très bien hier". (*Sb.* x, 131.)

LETTER XII

"L'imprimé" which Catherine sent to Voltaire may well have been a manifesto on the dissensions in Poland, where Catherine somewhat later published a declaration which our representative in Warsaw described as written with consummate prudence. Prince Galitsin then sent a copy to Voltaire, who replied that he had had it from the empress three months earlier. Among the Dissidents to whom the Poles refused the rights of citizenship, the majority were Greek Catholics who rejected the *filioque* clause in the Nicene Creed. Stanislaus Poniatowski, whom Catherine and Frederick had placed upon the throne, was powerless to obtain from the Polish diet the liberal concessions that he desired. The bishops, however, had been induced to bring in a bill mitigating the former oppression and permitting the Dissidents to repair their churches, and the *liberum veto* had been restored—"the death's wound for the Republic", as the king declared with tears. Henceforward, as since the decline of Poland set in, a single dissentient could frustrate all the legislation of a session.

LETTER XIV

To answer a proposal of marriage from overseas with an appreciation of erotic literature and thanks for the stamp might be the spiritual equivalent of this letter—the most amazing in the whole collection. Catherine had given the Philosophers full notice of her great effort in their joint crusade. Voltaire, with "an intellect the sharpest, swiftest of the world", was the supreme master of the art of complimenting, and a Disraeli in complimenting crowned heads. No man was more ready to say to Catherine, "We authors, Ma'am", or to lay on flattery with a trowel. "Je suis idolâtre de trois choses", he wrote soon after to Vorontsov, "de la liberté, de la tolérance, et de votre Impératrice." Letter LXXXIV, perhaps the most compelling begging letter ever written, shows what he could say of the *Instruction*. Yet the long letter and bulky enclosure from an empress who is plainly an authoress eager for recognition are dismissed with a quatrain and two light compliments. Why?

LETTER XV

An interesting letter, for (1) it shows Catherine receiving the education of travel as never before while the Grand Assembly is in the making, and (2) it poses the question of her sincerity or insincerity with regard to her letters.

Voltaire's assiduity in complimenting the empress is shown by the fact that he wrote twice to Vorontsov at the Hague with "une brochure sur les panégyriques", which was unmistakably his own. Vorontsov duly sent all to an unknown excellency (10 May) for submission to Catherine who had already received them from the author. (*Sb.* x, 179.)

LETTER XVII

This is a brisk belles-lettristic treatment of the first of the two major crises in the period covered by the *Correspondance*. The papal nuncio had appeared in the Polish diet to urge its members to make no surrender to the Dissidents. They were almost unanimously in favour of a law proposed by the bishop of Cracow, inflicting ruin and perpetual infamy upon all who should thenceforward even speak for toleration. The Russians forced them to be tolerant and happy by seizing the estates of the bishop, haling him to "the fatal castle of Schlüsselburg" and overawing the diet by a display of irresistible force. The sequel was a Turkish war which, for geographical reasons, was likely to cost Russia countless lives, as in fact it did.

LETTER XVIII

Catherine's inoculation was a signal and daring defiance of the quasi-Christian fatalism which constituted the chief barrier to progressive monarchy in Russia. At the same time she bid for that good repute in the West which formed one object of her connection with Voltaire. The design to make importation of goods and men into Russia easier by representing the country as civilised neither began nor ended with her, but no ruler pursued it more consistently and resourcefully than she did.

LETTER XX

In order to help on the good work, Voltaire enclosed a memorandum by a French officer in favour of reviving the "chariots of Cyrus", which he continued to urge Catherine to adopt. (See Index.)

LETTER XXIII

The Turkish war, which Russia had not sought, but which she had provoked by her policy in Poland, dominates the *Correspondance* for at least three years. The league of the southern or Catholic powers, both Bourbon and Habsburg, had threatened the Continental balance of power. If Russia were to dominate Poland and conquer northern Turkey she would tilt it still further the other way. This Britain, with some misgivings, encouraged, but the German powers insisted upon the partition of Poland as the price of their consent to the spoliation of the Turk. France had too many internal embarrassments to interfere openly. Voltaire's function was to give Catherine moral support and to plead her cause at the bar of western opinion.

LETTER XXIV

With this letter Catherine assumes the office of head of a press bureau, which it was her duty to fulfil so long as Russia remained at war. Deceit became for her a branch of tactics. Her aim was the normal aim of keeping neutrals neutral at the least and lowering the enemy force by persuading him that her own was invincible. (Cp. Letter LI.) The remoteness and strangeness of Russia have always favoured such attempts. Peter ascribed to a divine miracle the mystification of the western peoples—"there are certain matters which they are powerless to discern"—and Catherine drew large drafts upon the polite credulity of Voltaire. In point of fact, Russia was not exempt from the ordinary fate of nations who go to war—waste of men and money and increased taxation. "The year 1704 alone", writes Kluchevsky in his translated *History of Russia*, IV, 132, "saw introduced new taxes upon land, upon weights and measures, upon agricultural teams, upon varieties of head-dress, upon boots, upon peasant souls, upon stage drivers' earnings (a tenth), upon sowings, upon reapings, upon horse and cattle hide-tannings, upon bees, upon bathhouses, upon mills, upon taverns, upon rents, upon market stands, upon timber fellings, upon ice cuttings, upon graves, upon fountains, upon stove-pipes, upon marine arrivals and departures, upon ships, upon firewood, upon sales of provisions, upon water-melons, upon cucumbers, and upon (to quote from a list of the day) 'nuts and other such small ingatherings'." Taxation of religious beliefs was added, and "toll taken of the beard and whiskers through means of which the Russian of old was fain to assimilate his features to those of the Deity". Cp. Letter CLIV (1776): "Nous sommes...très occupés à réparer nos pertes" and the long list of war taxes removed in March 1775. (*Sb.* XIX, 452 etc.)

LETTER XXV

Catherine's draft contains several additional paragraphs of interest. Among them: "Puisque l'envie de faire cause commune contre les barbares est passée aux autres puissances de l'Europe, la Russie seule cueillera ces lauriers-ci, et son attention à bien battre ses ennemis ne sera point distraite par des combinaisons de campagnes concertées aux-quelles souvent il n'y a eu que les ennemis qui aient gagné". And "Je suis bien aisé, monsieur, de ce que mon instruction a votre approbation; je doute qu'elle ait celle du saint-père et du mufti; les cardinaux devraient prendre ce dernier pour pape: ils sont présentement si bien avec lui. Ce serait aux ultramontains à le proposer".

Catherine further declares Riga the equal of German universities for the German language, but otherwise below them. If and when Voltaire meets her at Constantinople "je tâcherai en attendant d'étudier un compliment grec que je vous ferai. Il y a deux ans que je savais quantité de phrases tartares et arabes à Cazan, ce qui faisait un grand plaisir aux habitants de cette ville, qui, pour la plupart, sont de cette nation, bons musulmans, bien riches, et qui bâtissent une magnifique mosquée en pierre depuis mon départ".

LETTER XL

Catherine's account of the campaign of 1769 may be compared with that of Edmund Burke in the *Annual Register*. Russia, he believes, will acquire Moldavia, Wallachia and the lower Danube. If her own subjects do not rebel nor foreign powers step in, she may destroy the Turkish empire. The enterprise of the Russian fleet, despite its poor showing in England, "is indeed a remarkable aera in naval history....The attempt is great, bold and manly". Great successes are not to be obtained by the precise rules of vulgar calculation. But to Russia, "the want of inhabitants is its great and principal want". Tartar ravages must have cost Russia many lives, "besides their ruining the infant colony of New Servia and spoiling the noble province of the Ukraine; a province by much the finest and most fertile that Russia is possessed of". "In number of troops, in discipline, in marine, even in pecuniary resources, Russia seems much superior. The Turks derive their advantages from the difficult nature of their pontic country; from the jealousy of other European states, and from the unsettled state of the throne in Russia."

While still Grand Duchess, Catherine had noted the necessity of peace and population for the vast empire of Russia, which needed people so sorely that her polygamous heathen subjects should not be Christianised by force. "Pour l'extérieur", she continued, "la paix nous met la balance à la main bien plus que les hasards d'une guerre toujours ruineuse." (*Sb.* VII, 85.)

LETTER LXVIII

To check Catherine's roseate reports, we may turn to those furnished to their governments by the representatives of foreign powers writing at the same place and time. The Prussian has little to say, because Frederick was concerned with the number of men whom Catherine could put into the field, rather than with the way in which they were paid and recruited. The French and Austrian wrote with more anti-Russian prejudice than information. The British, Lord Cathcart, did his best to send accurate accounts to a court which favoured Russia. He wrote (11 January 1771): "Both (Russian) armies disgusted; officers of all ranks retiring and refusing to serve; men harassed by sickness, fatigue and bad regulations more destructive than the sword of the enemy; recruiting fatal to a country of vast extent not peopled. A fleet in the Archipelago ill-constructed, ill-commanded and ill-paid. Division among the officers and sickness among the sailors; Dardanelles inattackable; blockade of Constantinople ineffective. Infinite expense, violences in Poland; no proper steps towards pacification, though the Czartoriskys are willing to do whatever is desired....No means to raise money by loans to any extent abroad; no means to raise money at home by additional taxes, as the poor and middling would be crushed before the rich would begin to bleed; dangerous to government were the rich to be squeezed. Treasure not exhausted but very much diminished. Bank resource overstrained, and which may recoil as all the taxes will soon be paid in paper; specie much debased and become extremely scarce. The reimportation of it totally prohibited, to prevent the coinage of the King of Prussia and others, who have taken advantage of the baseness of the Russian coin". Only providence, he held, could save Russia from greater misfortunes. (*Sb.* XIX, 166.)

The *Annual Register* for 1770, which speaks of "the glare of success", concludes that Count Tottleben had been defeated in Armenia and had since been engaged in a confused civil war in Georgia for or against "the celebrated Prince Heraclius...and a Prince Solomon". "The Russian accounts give a pompous list of conquered places, as if taken from the Turks, though they are most of them places of no consequence and unknown, or else that belonged to the Georgians. It is probable that the principal end of this expedition was to gain a thorough knowledge of the country, to foment dissensions...and, under the colour of friendship and religion, to prepare that slavery for the bravest nation in Asia, which the avowed enmity of the Turks and Persians was never able fully to accomplish."

The plague against which the three great powers formed cordons of troops on the frontiers of Poland broke out in villages across the Turkish border. Its victims in southern Poland were reckoned at 250,000. One village lost all its inhabitants in a single day. The frontier fortress of Kamjeniec, the Polish counterpart to Choczim, was abandoned for several months, and the Russians dared not enter it.

LETTER LXIX

Voltaire alludes first to his *Épître au roi de la Chine* and second to his *Questions sur l'Encyclopédie*, which, however, contain no article on *Reconnaissance*. The reference to Catherine imports that the Egyptians have not adopted the Turkish alphabet, and will, the author hopes, shake off the Turkish yoke, thanks to the empress of Russia. She in reply (Letter LXXII) hopes that the fall of her enemy, Choiseul, will increase Voltaire's immunity from punishment for his writings.

LETTER LXXIII

Christian VII of Denmark, unostentatiously influenced by a pupil of the "philosophers", Struensee, had recently dismissed his minister Bernstorff, granted liberty of printing and shown zeal for a liberal *régime*. Catherine, fearing French intrigue, sent him a severe rebuke.

LETTER LXXV

The mainspring of this long letter, with its playful reference to Rousseau, and light touch upon every other string that could stir Voltaire to do battle for Russia, is doubtless the prospect of yet another campaign. The statement that the Austrian internuncio had been done to death at Constantinople is an addition to Catherine's draft. Voltaire, meanwhile, wrote to a great Paris hostess that the odds were on the fall of Constantinople within the year.

LETTER LXXVI

Catherine, hastening to answer two lost letters of Voltaire, acknowledges a new compliment in his *Questions sur l'Encyclopédie* (cp. note on Letter XCIV). Unhappily, Voltaire's incense enveloped a new idol at the first spark.

Par votre esprit vous étonnez le sage,
Qui cesserait de l'être en vous voyant

dates from a time when Voltaire could know little of Catherine except that she admired his writings.

LETTER LXXIX

Within seven years, Voltaire was urging two abbés to come to what he believed to be his death-bed. (Letters 10187, 10188 and note.)

LETTER LXXXIII

The draft of this letter preserved at Petersburg contains, as is not uncommon, a paragraph which is absent from that which Voltaire's literary executors published as having been received. But in this case Voltaire's Letter LXXXVI shows that it or something like it reached him, and as the subject matter is interesting it is reproduced in full.

"Si le chevalier de Boufflers, qui est allé faire le chevalier errant incognito parmi les prétendus confédérés, enlève vos montres de Ferney, j'espère que vous aurez assez de crédit sur lui pour vous les faire rendre. Soyez assuré que ce sera avec bien du plaisir que je me prêterai à encourager vos fabricants et leur fabrique. Je crois qu'il ne serait point impossible de faire passer de leurs ouvrages à la Chine; mais il faudrait pour cela quelque marchand instruit qui sût les allures du commerce de Kiachta; c'est la place frontière de la Russie où ce commerce se fait. Il y a cinq ans à peu près qu'à Moscou et à Tobolsk il s'est établi quelques faiseurs de montres dans l'intention d'en envoyer à la Chine; cependant, je crois qu'ils se sont bornés jusqu'ici au débit intérieur de cet empire-ci. Le transport de Moscou jusqu'à Selenguinsk se fait par eau, et les frais du transport sont très-modiques. Je fais revoir le tarif de la douane du commerce de la Chine, dans l'intention de l'alléger pour favoriser l'exportation et l'importation. Les prix que vous marquez sont si modiques que ces ouvrages, fabriqués chez vous, ne peuvent qu'avoir un grand débit."

Young Boufflers, "son of...the mistress of King Stanislas", had visited Voltaire in 1764, travelling incognito as a French artist.

LETTER XCIV

Voltaire complimented Catherine, at the expense of her predecessors, Alexis in particular, by writing: "Il a été avantageux à un empire plus vaste que l'empire romain d'être longtemps dans le chaos: car, tout étant à faire, il était plus aisé de bâtir un édifice que d'en réparer un dont les ruines seraient respectées".

LETTER CVII

Fax-hall means Vauxhall, the famous gardens which with Newmarket constituted what some Continental reformers thought most worthy of transplantation from English social life.

LETTER CIX

Catherine's riches or poverty, like those of Russia, puzzled many observers, and the problem survived her. Sir George Macartney, a shrewd and unbiassed British minister in Petersburg, wrote in 1765 that her private treasure amounted to 7,000,000 roubles (at a time when the rouble was about five shillings in value) and increased daily, that specie was extremely scarce, that the peasants buried it, but that none the less, in that land of paradoxes, goods were dear beyond all conception. The mines in eastern Siberia and elsewhere sent the privy purse 600,000 roubles in a year and besides these many belonged to the treasury. At her accession Catherine had divided the public funds from her own, but the separation was only apparent and the people "egregiously deceived".

LETTER CXI

The "adventure of Copenhagen", which brought Denmark and Britain to the verge of war, particularly interested Catherine both for political and personal reasons. Apart from the fact that eighteen months earlier the Danes had been her docile clients, the history of their queen largely duplicated her own. A princess of north German stock, marrying in girlhood, changing her communion, her language, her attendants, espousing an impotent or indifferent husband more or less insane, becoming enamoured elsewhere, complicating the succession, supplanting the monarch—there was much besides humanity which made Catherine eager to check the vengeance of royalties and priests on the queen and Struensee—but in vain. (Cp. Letter CXIV.)

LETTER CXVIII

The gap in Catherine's letters may perhaps be filled by one based on her draft preserved at Petersburg and dated from its contents "August 1772".

"Monsieur, en réponse à votre lettre du 1er d'auguste, je vous envoie un mémoire sur ma guerre avec la sainte congrégation de la Propagande: vous ne vous doutiez pas apparemment de ce petit démêlé-là. Ces gens voudraient me faire accroire, comme dit la chanson, *que je ne suis pas le maître dans ma maison quand ils y sont*; mais difficilement ils me persuaderont. Leurs arguments ne valent pas même ceux de Moustapha et des bandes à écharpes blanches de Pologne. J'espère que cette vétille ne vous mettra point en colère contre moi; au reste ne me boudez point, j'aime trop à être bien avec vous.

"Si la paix se fait, je reviendrai à mon code; cette paix se traite à Fokchani; mais jusqu'ici il n'y a rien encore de décidé. Je suis fâchée de la petite mésaventure arrivée à notre ami Ali-bey. Notre-Dame de Czenstochowa s'est mise à coqueter avec le général-major prince Golitsine; j'ai reçu un courrier avant-hier où il me mande que cette forteresse s'est rendue à discrétion. Le nonce du pape, Durini, part furieux de Varsovie, parce que l'incrédulité des Polonais a empêché les miracles de cette image, fertile en pareilles productions."

LETTER CXXX

As drafted, Catherine's letter contained two further paragraphs of no little interest. Between the first and second sentences she wrote: "J'aurais tâché de l'apaiser sur-le-champ, si vous ne m'aviez envoyé un mémoire de ce M. Aubry pour lequel vous souhaitez une patente d'associé de l'Académie de Saint-Pétersbourg. Par là vous m'avez mise en négociation avec tous les savants possibles, et ce Congrès n'a pas été plus heureux que celui de Fokchani, quoiqu'il n'ait pas donné lieu à d'aussi mauvais propos. Avec peine ai-je réussi à faire donner la réponse ci-jointe à M. Aubry. Il me semble qu'il y a un peu d'humeur dans les réflexions de nos académiciens; il me paraît qu'ils auraient pu dire simplement: Nous n'avons guère pensé jusqu'ici à ce que vous nous proposez, quoique nous eussions la chose sous nos yeux tous les jours; mais nous vous envoyons ce que nous en avons trouvé dans notre bibliothèque, et parce que l'impératrice nous demandait une réponse, *ergo* nous l'avons faite telle quelle".

This refers to the *Séance* of 30 January, when the Academy discussed Voltaire's appeal on behalf of Aubry, and refused to make him an External Member for reasons set out in *Sbornik*, XIII, 305, 306.

Further, before speaking of her comedies, Catherine deals vigorously with D'Alembert's repeated applications on behalf of her French prisoners. "J'ai reçu de M. d'Alembert une seconde et troisième lettre sur le même sujet; l'éloquence n'y est pas épargnée: il a pris à tâche de me persuader de relâcher ses compatriotes; mais n'y a-t-il de l'humanité que pour nos compatriotes? Que ne plaide-t-il pour les prisonniers turcs et polonais, dupes et victimes des premiers; ces gens-là sont plus malheureux que ceux-ci. Il est vrai que les vôtres ne sont pas à Paris; mais aussi pourquoi l'ont-ils quitté? Personne ne les y a obligés. J'ai envie de répondre que j'en ai besoin pour introduire les belles manières dans mes provinces."

LETTER CXL

The threat of the Pugachev insurrection to Catherine s throne was most formidable, for it seemed for a time as hard to suppress as was the contemporary rebellion in America, and for the same reasons. The demonstration that over a vast region the people were ready to kill the gentry and burn their houses removed many of Catherıne's illusions. At the same time it contributed to the strengthening of her power, since the frightened gentry took refuge behind the throne, instead of making the Tsardom their own instrument of government. Catherine confronted rebellion as bravely as did George III.

LETTER CXLII

This letter is dated "Le 4/15 mars 1774" both in the reprint of Catherine's draft of what was to be sent and in the reprint of what Voltaire presumably received. But it differs from the draft in that it contains an acknowledgment of a lost letter of Voltaire's which makes the date at the head merely misleading. Late in March or early in April should therefore be substituted.

LETTER CXLVIII

Voltaire's questions about the "baisemain des prêtres" occurred presumably in a letter or letters which have been lost. Travellers observed that the Russians would spit at the sight of a "pope", to keep off the devil, and then kiss his hand. Always poor, often ill-educated, lacking roots among the people, since they were largely a clan apart, the married village priests held a lower place in social esteem and influence than perhaps any other clergy in the world. The *Annual Register*, in describing the murder of Archbishop Ambrosius, affirmed the exact opposite.

LETTER CLII

When Ségur suddenly gained a Franco-Russian commercial treaty in 1787, he boasted with truth that he had accomplished what his country had vainly attempted during forty years.

LETTER CLIV

The "pertes" of which Voltaire had spoken to Catherine in a lost letter were doubtless those of Turgot, "qui en moins de deux ans, avait gagné les suffrages de toute l'Europe", and De Lamoignon, "digne héritier d'un nom cher à la France", as he informed the Landgrave of Hesse-Cassel. These two philosopher-ministers fell on 11 May. Who knows, Voltaire asked Frederick, whether France will not have new cases like La Barre's, and her "philosophers" follow her Huguenots into Prussia? To a friend he declared that this "mainmorte gothe, visigothe et vandale" made the remainder of his days mere bitterness, spent "dans un faubourg de l'enfer". The Landgrave, at the feet of whose "philosophie sérénissime" Voltaire would fain prostrate himself, replied that the eyes of statesmen were turned towards America, "a fine country but a very long sea-voyage", where he hoped that his 12,000 men would help to compel the rebels to return to their duty.

Catherine's opinion of the French language agreed with that of Wesley, who thought it a reed to an organ beside the Italian. The sense suggests that the word always printed "sage" was intended by her to be "sèche".

LETTER CLVII

The sobriety with which Catherine, here and in Letter CLIV, speaks of the work of legislation contrasts strikingly with the enthusiasm of ten years before. At the same time it is notable that she persists. The legislation of 1775 in itself acquits her of the charges of seeking nothing but self-advertisement or being merely "une commenceuse". It was an attempt, though by no means a wholly successful attempt, to apply the principles of the *Instruction* to the provincial administration of Russia, and it shaped that administration for many years.

LETTER CLIX

Voltaire's *Prix* had already elicited from Catherine the appreciation in Letter CLVIII and from Frederick the dictum, "L'homme est une espèce assez méchante, à laquelle il faut partout des principes réprimants, ou sa méchanceté foncière renverserait toutes les bornes de l'honnêteté et même de la bienséance". To La Harpe Voltaire described his object as to aid humanity and reason by proposing the best method of reforming the abominable French criminal law, which also sullied many German states. Condorcet read and re-read it. He declared that France was hopeless, but that the example of all Europe might exert some small influence upon her.

THE INSTRUCTION

§ 3. The word "citizen" is a programme in itself—a programme realised for a moment after the fall of the Tsardom. These first five sections lay the foundation of Catherine's edifice: Religion inculcates mutual good: good comprises patriotism and the rule of law: law should be natural, and—implied in the word "citizen"—the individual is to be active in the state, not a mere subject. Catherine then proceeds to show that for Russia "natural" means "European", and the way is clear for herself and the citizens to do their religious duty by giving her the best European laws. In § 7 "facilités" seems nearer to the Russian than "means".

§§ 8–10. This demonstration that Russia belonged to the number of "great states" amounted to a defence of her autocracy. Montesquieu lays down (*Esprit des Lois*, VIII, xix): "Un grand empire suppose une autorité despotique dans celui qui gouverne". The *Instruction* softens *despotique* into *souveraine*, and omits some of Montesquieu's reasons, e.g. the need for terrifying distant officials into diligence, and for rapidity of legislation to cope with accidents, "qui se multiplient toujours dans l'état à proportion de sa grandeur".

§ 13. Having proved her own absolutism indispensable to Russia and re-baptised it, in the French text, by the name which Montesquieu gave to limited, constitutional monarchy, Catherine here reconciles it with natural liberty. The inevitable criticism is Diderot's. The only true sovereign, he holds, is the nation: a good code must begin by making the monarch swear to the law. The empress of Russia is certainly a despot; whatever the true end of her government, it makes all liberty and property depend upon one person.

"L'action héroïque d'un bon despote, c'est de lier un bras à son successeur; et c'étoit là la première question à proposer à la commission."

Diderot, like Mazzini, was "heedless of the stumbling-blocks of practice", and from the practical point of view this dictum ranks with his advice to civilise Russia by introducing a colony of Swiss. But his record proves that Catherine discussed the theory of her work and that with frankness and good temper. "You can tell her the truth", he declared, "she is the true wife of Henri IV." She admitted that three successive Elizabeths could have enslaved England for centuries, and she convinced him that if she could she would create a parliament on the English model forthwith.

§ 26. "En Russie, c'est le Sénat qui est le Dépositaire des Loix", because (cp. § 99) Peter the Great had wisely established the rule of law, and had provided administrative and judicial organs which minimised the number of appeals to the sovereign himself. Pokrovsky (III, 73, etc.) maintains that Catherine had failed to understand Montesquieu's devices for hoodwinking the French censors, and that she was thus misled into prescribing for Russia the institutions of limited monarchy. Her object, however, seems to have been one which autocrats must always find difficult of attainment—to reconcile their own power of uttering laws with their incapacity to visualise every principle and to remember every precedent. Struensee in Denmark tried to throw upon the Colleges (departmental boards) the duty of holding up any royal decree which might clash with existing legislation, but the weakness of such a procedure is obvious. Ill-considered legislation, however, is by no means confined to autocracies, nor, as the Prussia of Frederick the Great may demonstrate, is it necessarily attached to them.

§ 28. The first three lines, being nonsense, should disclose something of the origin of the text. The version printed by the Senate press in

April 1768 is sun-clear. "Si l'on demande: Qu'est-ce que le Dépôt des Loix? Je réponds, le Dépôt des Loix est cette Institution", etc. "Dépôt" appears to be a fair equivalent for a Russian word meaning repository, and the English might go on, "I answer that the repository is the particular instruction in obedience to which", etc. It may fairly be assumed that no one, Russian or English, who had the French version before him would have produced the section as it stands. Whether a Russian or an Englishman would be the more likely to misapprehend a simple metaphor and wander so far afield in the hope of making good may be debated.

Diderot, writing in 1773, objected that the French *parlement* had been such an institution, but it had ceased to exist. In Russia the Senate was only a voice crying in the wilderness, and one day a Herod would silence it. Even in London corruption ruled.

§§ 36–38. From the original MS. there have been deleted Montesquieu's opening words (XI, iii): "Il est vrai que dans les démocraties le peuple paraît faire ce qu'il veut; mais...".

§ 39. The *Instruction* reproduces a paragraph of Montesquieu's, XI, vi, "De la constitution d'Angleterre", down to the concluding clause which is added by Catherine in Russian. (Chechulin, p. 9, n. 1.) Such an insertion may suggest that the emendation came from a Russian-speaking counsellor at a conference over which the empress presided. § 44 was altered by her to its present form in consequence of a written criticism by Bibikov, who could not understand why perfection should rather be desired than hoped for. (*Sb.* X, 76.)

§ 79. Diderot argued that men were more ready to hazard honour than life and life than fortune. Fines therefore were the ideal punishment. Infamy should seldom be inflicted, since it condemned a man to do evil. A dead assassin was good for nothing, and there were so many public works! Banishment, which amounted to introducing a malefactor into a neighbour's house, violated the law of nations.

§ 86. Literally, "the imagination of the people is affected by this great punishment just as it would have been affected by the small one".

§ 91. Montesquieu (VI, xii) wrote, "Ils se sont accoutumés au despotisme". The Russian and French official versions substitute "violence".

§ 95. Montesquieu (VI, xvi) wrote, "En Angleterre"; and this he contrasts with "En Moscovie, où la peine des voleurs et celle des assassins sont les mêmes, on assassine toujours. Les morts, y dit-on, ne racontent rien".

§ 101. Diderot objected that the decisions of the courts stifled the laws and should never be printed or quoted. There should be no third to law and reason. Commentators on the scriptures had made a thousand heresies.

§ 111. Montesquieu begins his chap. II, "On entend dire sans cesse qu'il faudrait que la justice fût rendue partout comme en Turquie". The alteration is significant because (i) the statement would have been untrue of Russia, where the Turk was too well known; (ii) praise of the hereditary enemies might be dangerous; (iii) Europe, despite § 6, did not include Russia, where men spoke of "Russia and Europe" and where the word for "German" and for "foreigner" were the same. Cp. § 402. The literal translation runs, "It is often heard that in Europe they say...".

§ 123. I.e. England, where the *peine forte et dure* was preserved as in § 124. After swearing obedience to the empress and her heir, the deputies who were assembled in the cathedral at Moscow to legislate, kissed the cross and gospels and then subscribed the oath.

§ 127. The empress wrote the final sentence, in amplification of Montesquieu, XI, vi, par. 18.

§ 145. This section and the next replace quotations from Beccaria occupying four times as much space in the original MS.

§ 148. This high claim for the Legislator moves Diderot to an elaborate criticism of the whole *Instruction*. Catherine, he declares, unconsciously takes up the sceptre which at the outset she laid down. She has not established an order of succession, or a system of taxation, or rules for the making of war, or discussed the emancipation of the serfs. "Ignore-t-elle qu'il n'y a ni vraie police, ni loix, ni population, ni agriculture, ni commerce, ni richesse, ni science, ni goût, ni art, où la liberté n'est pas?"

§ 253. The French version begins, "Par conséquent, nous devons éviter de rendre des gens SERFS". Diderot complains that all the theoretical investigations of the age have led to nothing, since despotism was extending on every side. "Nous sommes encore bien loin du moment où l'on lira à la tête d'un édit: 'Louis, Frédéric, Catherine par la grâce de ses sujets', et non par la grâce de dieu; cette innovation immortalisera le premier souverain qui la fera".

§ 258. Montesquieu wrote (XV, xvii, 5): "La loi de Moïse était bien rude: 'Si quelqu'un frappe son esclave, et qu'il meure sous sa main, il sera puni: mais s'il survit un jour ou deux, il ne le sera pas, parce que c'est son argent'. Quel peuple que celui, où il fallait que la loi civile se relâchât de la loi naturelle!"

According to Pokrovsky (III, 72) Catherine was attracted by the phrase, but transferred the fact to Rome, for fear of displeasing the clergy. This seems highly doubtful. Deliberately to falsify a passage from a well-known book would be no less impudent than unwise. A careless transcriber might have overlooked the fact that while the preceding paragraph of Montesquieu treats of Rome, in this the subject is different. The probable explanation is that § 258 is not a reproduction of Montesquieu as many other sections are, but is based upon the facts that, until modified by Christian influence, the Roman law gave masters the rights in question.

§ 260. This sensible rule is interpreted by Pokrovsky (III, 73) as an astonishing perversion of Montesquieu's warning (xv, xviii, 4) which was given in the interests of a republic. Pokrovsky represents Catherine's dictum as a mere platitude designed to please the proprietors. Catherine, like several of her successors, was shocked by the existence of serfdom but failed to convince the gentry.

§ 267. This adaptation of Montesquieu's, XIV, xi, 6, enunciates a disputable fact, since those who went to America for gold and brought back "the pox" were seldom if ever men of the north. "On vit la plupart des plus grandes familles du midi de l'Europe périr par un mal qui devint trop commun pour être honteux, et ne fut plus que funeste" —these are Montesquieu's words.

§ 276. Montesquieu wrote (XXII, ii, 4) of a despotism, "La tyrannie et la méfiance font que tout le monde y enterre son argent", and declared that the practice was universal in Algiers. A British minister in Petersburg during Catherine's early years ascribed the scarcity of specie in Russia to a like cause.

§ 281. The concluding sentence replaces the earlier version: "But Julius Caesar and Augustus did not know the Christian law. All these laws [i.e. those in Montesquieu's long chapter XXIII, xxi, 'Des lois des Romains sur la propagation de l'espèce'] can only serve as examples in so far as they agree with our Orthodox institutions". (Chechulin.)

§ 298. Cp. note on § 470.

§ 301. Montesquieu, XIV, ix, continues: "Elle a servi de nos jours en Irlande à l'établissement d'une des plus importantes manufactures de toile qui soit en Europe".

§ 302. Originally written "In England", but altered by the empress. (Chechulin.)

§ 319. Originally written "In France", but altered by the empress. (Chechulin.) Broadly speaking, Montesquieu praises England by name and blames France by implication: Catherine often prefers periphrases for both.

§ 325. This is an important section for the light which it throws both upon the authorship of the text and upon Russian commercial policy in the 'sixties. The French text is verbatim from Montesquieu, XX, viii, I. The Russian translates this, but in so doing turns "font le commerce d'économie" into language which renders "carry on [their] domestic trade" an easy and almost inevitable rendering. This suggests that "carry on the commerce of oeconomy" came directly or indirectly from Montesquieu and not directly from the Russian. If so, was Montesquieu the refuge of a puzzled Russian or a puzzled Englishman, or both? The historical importance of the passage is due to the fact that when Catherine was composing the *Instruction* she was also deciding the question whether or no to continue the close commercial ties with England. Montesquieu's next paragraph, which is § 326, might have been written to advise her, and she obeyed. In 1766 she conceded better terms than the British merchants or the government had dared to hope for.

§ 330. The change from the original, which began "President Montesquieu", seems not to have been made by the empress. (Chechulin.)

§ 337. "Consular Jurisdiction" is a very loose rendering of "procédure verbale".

§ 343. "Tout ce que vous dîtes là est fort beau; pourquoi avez-vous donc fait le contraire?" This was among the caustic comments of Diderot which made Catherine really angry when she found it in his library in 1785. He had probably written it in 1774, at a time when Pugachev's rebellion had already supplied the answer to his question. It called forth a defence by Catherine of her *Instruction*, which in eighteen years, she claimed, had not only done no harm but "tout le bien qui s'est fait, et dont tout le monde convient, est fait des principes établis par cette instruction". She was warranted in maintaining to Grimm that legislation by a Diderot would have ruined everything.

§ 356. This section is extracted from Betsky's report of 1764 on the education of the young of both sexes. (Chechulin.) To set about rooting a proper love of cleanliness and neatness in those who belong to a child might be difficult, whether the tutor's duty be construed as to teach its father to be neat or to teach the child to love to see him neat. The French version inculcates the precept not only for the child's own person "mais aussi à l'égard de tout ce qui les environne". A later French version reads "ceux qui les entourent". The Russian would appear to cover persons or things belonging to them.

§§ 378–383. The French versions are superior in putting all this into the future. A Russian translator should have known better than an English that this "middling rank" was a project, not a reality. We may pertinently ask with Diderot whether the excluded person was to become a serf?

§ 394. Perhaps "burgess" would be a better rendering, so that "citizen" might be kept for wider use as in § 3. The French has "citoyen" here and "concitoyen" earlier. The Russian word used here has, like "tradesman", acquired a tinge of contempt.

§§ 398, 399. Here the English falters—"might" for "may", and "Situation" in the second case for "Statute", the French in each case being perfectly clear. This last mistake would perhaps be more easily made by a non-Russian unaware of the double meaning of a Russian word than by a Russian. For a Russian could not fail to understand what the empress meant to say, and could hardly assume that "Situation" covered both senses.

§ 426. The translator has again mistaken the meaning of the Russian text and produced nonsense. Read, "to other general principles of legislation".

§§ 434, 436. The translation, which dispenses with some of the aid that a reference to Montesquieu could give, renders the Russian somewhat clumsily. "Which has been left an orphan", "women having three children", "from guardianship" would be better.

§ 435. An amazingly bold quotation for Catherine to make, at a time when many supposed that she ruled only till Paul came of age.

§ 470. Montesquieu consistently writes "l'Empereur". The Russian, here as in § 298, renders this "Bogdochan". It appears in the French version as "le Bogdochan". The translator into English writes in perplexity "the Emperor Bogdo Chan".

A Russian would perhaps be less likely than a non-Russian to be led astray thus.

§ 491. Nonsense. French: "Chez nous on a confondu souvent la commission remise à de pareils juges d'instruire certains procès, et de donner simplement leurs avis, avec le pouvoir de prononcer une sentence dans les formes sur cette affaire". Is the translator a non-Russian struggling with what he cannot construe and hoping for the best?

§ 498. "Protestator" faithfully follows the Russian text: the French has "Protostrator".

§ 510. Likewise the Russian rendering of the French "Soüi".

§ 520. The draft of this section included an appeal to history which Catherine made on more than one occasion. "We are created for our people, and to be convinced of this we need only reflect on the miraculous way in which God has placed the sceptre of this empire in our hands."

§ 541. As Diderot tells the story, the cadi left the table of the French ambassador for a brief space, and replied to his host's enquiry that he had had the fraudulent baker thrown into his own oven. The defence was that the man had robbed the most unfortunate section of the people, those who bought bread by the pound. "Vous faites rouer celui qui brise le coffre-fort du financier, et vous ne voulez pas que je fasse brûler celui qui vole le pain du pauvre." Diderot further makes the pertinent observation that the history of a nation cannot be read in its laws, for these may not be carried out. When Rome had only the twelve tables she had morals, when she had achieved the civil code she had none.

§ 560. This section, which derives from Bielefeld, shows how far Catherine was prepared to go in the enunciation of state socialism. The Supplements presumably received less outside criticism than the *Instruction* proper, which had been far longer in incubation.

§ 588. What are "Family Improvements"? Presumably an attempt has been made to grapple with two Russian words which are correctly rendered by the French "les productions du pays".

§ 637. Catherine here follows Bielefeld, who shows the usefulness of state debts, in spite of the contrary opinion of Montesquieu. (Chechulin.)

In his conclusion, Diderot emphasises the absence of any provision for emancipation:

"Or sans affranchissement", he continues, "ou sans liberté, point de propriété; sans propriété, point d'agriculture; sans agriculture, nulle force, nulle grandeur, nulle opulence, nulle prospérité.

"Mais l'Impératrice a l'âme grande, de la pénétration, des lumières, un génie très étendu; de la justice, de la bonté, de la patience et de la fermeté; et pour me servir de ses propres mots, l'arbre qu'elle ne peut renverser à brasse-corps, elle le fait tomber en lui coupant peu à peu les racines; elle est magnifique sans être dissipatrice; elle jouit d'une bonne santé; elle a quarante-quatre ans, et elle m'a dit, promis qu'elle vivroit jusqu'à quatre-vingt. Il n'y a rien dont on ne vienne à bout avec le tems et un assemblage aussi rare d'excellentes qualités.

"Il est impossible que les maisons d'éducation et autres, si elles subsistent, ne changent la face de son Empire. On alloit voir à Lacédémone la manière dont la jeunesse y étoit élevée; je ne désespère pas qu'on ne fasse un jour le voyage en Russie pour un même motif, et que Dieu veuille qu'elle finisse promptement et avec gloire sa guerre contre les Turcs. La mort de cent Turcs ne compense pas le sang d'un seul Russe; et tous les lauriers de la guerre ne dédommageront jamais son empire de la perte d'une année de son Règne."

EVENTS OF 1762–77 RELEVANT TO THE CATHERINE-VOLTAIRE LETTERS

YEAR	PHILOSOPHY	BRITAIN	CONTINENT	RUSSIA
1762	Diderot: *Neveu de Rameau* Rousseau: *Contrat Social* and *Emile* Gluck: *Orfeo*	Warburton attacks Wesley and "enthusiasm" *Jan.* War with Spain Successive captures of Martinique, Havana and Manila *Nov.* Preliminaries of Fontainebleau with France	Calas broken on the wheel at Toulouse Attack on Jesuits (Choiseul and Pompadour) *May.* Spain invades Portugal Sweden makes peace with Prussia *June–Oct.* Prussian victories in Germany	Platon compiles Catechism *Feb.* New Tsar, Peter III, frees nobles from serving State *May.* Peace with Prussia, yielding all conquests *June.* Alliance with Prussia. War with Denmark *July.* Peter forced to abdicate, and murdered Catherine succeeds (July 18) Gregori Orlov favourite: Panin minister Daria Saltikov denounced for cruelty 21 *Sept.* "Je ne crois pas que Cathérine II jouisse longtemps de la mort de son mari" (Voltaire)
1763	Boswell meets Johnson Febronius upholds rights of Councils and bishops Institution of village schools in Prussia *Ossian* completed Voltaire completes his work on Russia under Peter I and writes on Tolerance	*Feb.* Peace of Paris *April.* Bute resigns Wilkes struggle begins Friction with Spain about logwood	*Feb.* Peace of Hubertusburg ends Seven Years' War French *parlements* begin struggle with crown about taxation: autocracy challenged	Catherine transfers Church possessions to a Commission Panin frustrates Empress' marriage with Orlov, countenanced by Bestuchev

764	Beccaria on Crime and Punishment Voltaire: *Dictionnaire philosophique portatif*, which he repudiates, and *Corneille* Walpole: *Castle of Otranto* Goldsmith: *Traveller* D'Alembert declines invitation to Russia	*Jan.* Prince of Brunswick = Princess Augusta Monmouth girl burned for murdering mistress *Oct.* "Cheap victory" of Buxar	Pope upholds Jesuits Pombal burns Malagrida Fourteen Frenchmen burned alive for cattle maiming *April.* Death of Mme de Pompadour *May.* Polish diet accepts Biron succession in Courland *Sept.* "Unanimous" election of Stanislaus Poniatowski France takes Réunion *Dec.* Jesuits dissolved in France	"Nothing can be more critical than the situation of the government" (Annual Register) *Mar.* Influx of silver and gold from Siberia *April.* Treaty of alliance with Prussia *June.* Catherine founds school of arts for 300 boys and St Cyr for 150 girls *July.* Mirowitz' attempt for Ivan VI leads to Ivan's death and his own execution Catherine facilitates great Prussian purchases of saltpetre Russians fail to gain rights for Dissidents in Poland but drive Confederates into Turkey Little Russian autonomy reduced
1765	Tull represents activity in agricultural improvement Percy's *Reliques* Watt's observations Blackstone: *Commentaries* Pope sanctions devotion of the Sacred Heart Anderson's *History of Commerce* Abbé Chappe's account of journey to Tobolsk Rousseau visits Berlin	*March.* Stamp Act. Rockingham Whigs replace Grenville and Bedford Fall of Bedford favours negotiation with Russia Health of George III precarious Spitalfields weavers threaten riot and secure redress Somerset woman burned for poisoning husband Clive again governor of Bengal	Calas cleared, thanks to Voltaire La Barre tortured for insulting religion France helps Genoa to garrison Corsica: Paoli agrees Constitutional struggle in France continues *July.* Prussian East India Co. at Emden *Aug.* Joseph II succeeds Francis I as Emperor and as co-regent with Maria Theresa. His brother Leopold inherits Tuscany and introduces reforms *Dec.* Death of Dauphin	Catherine buys Diderot's library, establishes an orphan-house in Moscow, endows Academy of Sciences, favours Agricultural Society and Academy of Polite Arts Panin attempts to form a Northern System to counteract the Southern Family Pact and Franco-Austrian alliance. Britain refuses eventual hostility against the Turks

Year	Philosophy	Britain	Continent	Russia
1766	Goldsmith: *Vicar of Wakefield* Cavendish discovers hydrogen Sieur de Bougainville sets off round the world *Dictionnaire philosophique* and other works burned at La Barre's execution Euler endowed by Catherine Turgot's physiocratic treatise	*Feb*. Stamp Act repealed *Mar*. Prince of Wales inoculated *July*. Chatham-Grafton ministry Commercial treaty with Russia ratified Pretender not recognised by Pope and other sovereigns Bread riots, notably in Devon	Hoffmann repeatedly tortured at Stockholm *March*. Prince of Orange comes of age *May*. Lally executed *July*. La Barre executed French and Spanish navies developed France acquires Lorraine on death of King Stanislaus Many Lorraine families emigrate France breaks with Geneva Russian ambassador, Prince Repnin, appears to dominate in Poland D'Aranda introduces secular education into Spain Spain revolts against foreign domination Risings against her dominion overseas reported Anti-Turkish revolts in Georgia, Egypt and Cyprus	*May*. Great carousal at Petersburg, followed by masquerade
1767	Lessing: *Minna von Barnhelm*	Clive quits India: chaos until Hastings arrives Bread riots	Several royal deaths from small-pox *Jan*. French coerce Geneva Jesuits expelled from Spain, the Sicilies and Parma Frederick renews the Russian alliance Denmark arranges with Russia provisionally the exchange of Paul's rights over Holstein Revolt in Montenegro, false Peter III Many Confederations in Poland *Oct*. Extraordinary diet, under Russian influence Paoli sets up government in Corsica	Commissioners at Moscow active in preparing for legislation Rebellion of Orenburg Cossacks repressed

1768	Sterne: *Sentimental Journey* Captain Cook's voyage Pallas' journey through Siberia Voltaire completes *Guerre civile de Genève*	Sir Joshua Reynolds founds Royal Academy Chatham resigns: Government business in confusion Wilkes centre of politics Christian VII traverses many counties Britain attempts to prevent Russo-Turkish War which is incited and partly sustained by France	Genoa cannot suppress Paoli: France buys Corsica Maria Theresa renounces Silesia Pope confiscates Parma; France seizes Avignon; Naples invades Papal States Royal inoculations at Vienna *March*. Polish diet ends peacefully, but Confederates in Podolia take Bar. Russian war against many Confederations generally successful *Aug*. Russians storm Cracow Jacquerie near Kiev suppressed by Russians *Oct*. Mustafa III declares war. Obreskov imprisoned	Catherine provides 5000 roubles annually for translations into Russian Russians pursue Confederates to Balta in Turkey. "Unquestionably many Turkish subjects perished" (Lord Cathcart) *Oct*. She and Paul are inoculated by Dr Dimsdale Many mines discovered in Siberia Russia offers 7000 men to defend Corsica against France Legislative Commission much interrupted by Turkish war Daria Soltikov degraded and immured for cruelty
1769	French controversy about Shakespeare English prominence in the arts—Wedgwood, Flaxman, Arkwright, Boulton and Watt, etc. Robertson: *Charles V*	*Jan*. *Letters of Junius* *Feb*. Expulsion of Wilkes from Parliament Negotiations for Anglo-Russian alliance fail Naval aid to Russia—officers and harbourage *Oct*. Part of the Russian fleet in the Humber *Nov*. British ambassador effects *rapprochement* between Panin and Orlov	Death of Clement XIII *March*. Joseph II at Rome during conclave. He investigates Austrian Italy *May*. Ganganelli becomes Clement XIV. He upholds Jesuits: Bourbons keep Avignon and Benevento French East India Co. bankrupt and suspended Dauphin contracted to Archduchess Maria Antonia, but Dutch and British prevent rearrangement of Netherlands Confusion and devastation in Poland. Russians supreme after repulse of Turks *Aug*. Cordial meeting between Frederick and Joseph II at Neisse	*Feb*. Tartars under Krim Gherai ravage New Serbia In spring and summer Turks resist successfully near Choczim on Dniester and Tartar raids continue. Russians take Azov *Sept*. New Grand Vizier, "Moldovanghi", incurs disasters which cause submission of Moldavia and Wallachia to Russia. Mustafa "Ghazi" (Conqueror), after early success, orders the Greeks of those provinces to be exterminated New war taxes and Council of Seven with Catherine presiding Military Order of St George instituted "Hermitage" built

Year	Philosophy	Britain	Continent	Russia
1770	Immanuel Kant "awakened by Hume" Holbach (atheist): *Système de la nature* Hargreaves' spinning-jenny Voltaire: *Questions sur l'Encyclopédie* (completed 1772)	*Jan.* North's ministry Burke on the Present Discontents Collision with Spain about Falkland Islands Danger of war with Spain and France Russian sailors at Portsmouth, many deaths Russian fleet sheltered at Port Mahon *Aug.* Renewed efforts to secure Russian alliance and to mediate for peace	San Domingo earthquake Intense constitutional struggle in France, also dearth and Corsican disturbances *May.* Dauphin's wedding: 3000 reported killed or injured French chastise Tunis *Aug.* Danes bombard Algiers Struensee gains secret influence, startling reforms follow *Sept.* Frederick and Joseph II meet at Neustadt Prussians coerce Danzig *Oct.* Austrians seize Zips *Nov.* Plague raging at Constantinople *Dec.* Choiseul receives *lettre de cachet* Ali Bey heads successful revolt in Egypt	Moldavia and Wallachia lost in winter campaign. Tartars and Confederations active Rumiantsov wins great victories near the Pruth, at the Larga (July 18) and at the Koghul (Aug. 2) and clears Wallachia. Bender and other fortresses fall and the Budziak Tartars submit. Meanwhile Alexis Orlov and the fleet rouse the Greeks and distract Turkish forces, but suffer defeat and abandon the Morea to its fate *July.* Turkish fleet annihilated off Chesmé, but Dardanelles not forced *Oct.* Prince Henry of Prussia's visit begins Menace of prospective army of observation in Hungary influences Russian policy. Frederick and Catherine begin a secret correspondence
1771	Unitarians founded Smollett: *Humphrey Clinker* Abbé Raynal: *Histoire des Indes*	*Jan.* Falklands question settled *Feb.* British warning to Russia that Prussia and Austria are plotting annexations in Poland Parliamentary debates may be reported First Roman Catholic Relief (in Ireland) *June.* Anglo-Russian alliance breaks down on question of subsidies to Sweden	Austria postpones anti-Russian intervention *Jan.* Recalcitrant members of *parlement* banished: many to villages Maupeou creates simplified *parlements* Adolf Frederick of Sweden dies: Gustavus III more dangerous Polish Partition—Kaunitz and Joseph II overcome Maria Theresa	*Feb.* Panin declares that Russia has no aggrandisement in view *April.* Turks release Obreskov Russians fail in Bulgaria; Turks, more conspicuously, in Wallachia. Giurgevo thrice changes hands Russians force lines of Perekop and swiftly conquer Crimea Fleet makes no conquest, but harms Levant trade and ravages coasts Difficulty in raising loans abroad

			Three powers suppress Confederations Plague spreads to Southern Podolia France reduces army *Nov.* King of Poland kidnapped but escapes Great outcry against the Confederates *Dec.* Toulouse *parlement* exculpates *les Sirven* Ali Bey successful and threatening	Rising in favour of Paul plotted At Petersburg, many galleys with munitions destroyed by fire At Moscow, pestilence and murder of archbishop. Many inhabitants reported slain by troops. Orlov's visit *Dec.* Secret treaty with Prussia regarding Poland
1772	Death of Helvétius *Morning Post* founded Rutherford describes nitrogen Agricultural innovations by Coke of Holkham	Friction with Denmark caused by imprisonment of Queen, sister of George III Britain seeks alliance with Russia, countenancing acquisitions on the Black Sea, but not passage to the Mediterranean *July.* Partition treaty ascribed to Count Zachary Chernishev Britain offers co-operation with Russia against Gustavus III, and does not oppose the partition of Poland *Oct.* Russia renews alliance negotiations Britain opposes a partition of Sweden and condemns Frederick's treatment of Danzig	*Jan.* Struensee overthrown by *coup d'état*: reactionary *régime* Great dearth in the Low Countries *Feb.* Polish Partition. Secret treaty of Petersburg Confederates surprise Cracow *April.* Ali Bey crushed in Egypt. His progress in Syria continues Prussian forces plunder Poland *Aug.* Surrender of Czenstockowa ends Polish war *Coup d'état* of Gustavus III *Sept.* 30. Powers announce First Partition of Poland *Oct.* Frederick II forms a company for commerce	Plague reported fatal to 60,000 Russians Catherine buys a great diamond for more than £100,000 and diamonds as war rewards for 100,000 roubles Government buys up iron on credit for sale to Britain for cash Re-enactment of prohibitions against gold imports (except Dutch ducats) and against speaking on religion or politics *April.* Armistice arranged *July.* Peace commissioners at Fokshani. The Russian terms proving too high, a further meeting takes place at Bucharest *Aug.* 4. Partition treaties with Austria and Prussia signed Catherine prepares against surprise by Gustavus III *Sept.* Vasilchikov succeeds Gregori Orlov as favourite

Year	Philosophy	Britain	Continent	Russia
1773	Goethe: *Götz von Berlichingen* Goldsmith: *She Stoops to Conquer* Montgolfier's balloon Pombal's emancipation policy Pope suppresses Jesuits	Sliding-scale for corn imports Naval armament in reply to that of France Britain declines to purchase Russian alliance by subsidy to Denmark North's Regulating Act for India Hastings Parliament upholds religious tests in Universities	Alliance of Sweden with France Avignon restored to Pope Beaumarchais attacks Maupeou's *parlement* Bread riots in France *Nov.* Exchange treaty between Denmark and Russia carried out General commercial crisis in Europe *May.* Polish diet accepts Partition *Nov.* Treaties ratified Frederick conscripts new subjects and banishes poorer Jews. He shelters Jesuits Turks reform army. Ali Bey perishes Prussia and Austria arm by land; France and Spain by sea	Catherine attempts to embellish towns and improve rural housing. She employs Sir C. Knowles to form Baltic fleet. She supports British merchants during the commercial crisis. She shelters Jesuits. She provides for Petersburg a great spectacle—the capture of Giurgevo Russians fail to take Silistria or Varna. They abandon Paros. Their Georgian enterprise fails The Astrachan Tartars quit the empire The rebellion of Pugachev (Cossack: false Peter III) in S.E. Russia becomes formidable Great supplies of silver come from Siberia *Oct.* Paul marries Wilhelmina of Hesse Biron's son succeeds in Courland Catherine munificent to Panin and Rumiantsov. Orlov gives her a diamond worth 500,000 roubles
1774	Chesterfield: *Letters to his Son* Goethe: *Sorrows of Werther* Priestley discovers oxygen Density of the earth determined	Boston riot. Boston Port Act Clive's suicide Wilkes Lord Mayor and M.P. Quebec Act	*Jan.* Mustafa III succeeded by his brother *May.* Death of Louis XV from small-pox French royal family inoculated *Aug.* Turgot finance minister Polish Permanent Council established Jesuits expelled from Poland	Potemkin succeeds Vasilchikov as favourite Death of Gen. Bibikov Civil servants unpaid Tartars defeated: Turks collapse *July.* Investment of Shumla and Peace of Kutchuk-Kainardji Disaffection rife, especially at Moscow

			Oct. Spain declares war on Morocco *Nov. Parlement* restored, with restrictions Morocco declares war on the Dutch	*Sept.* Pugachev captured
1775	Sheridan: *The Rivals* Beaumarchais: *Le Barbier de Seville*	American war begins Britain attempts to hire Russian troops	Spanish failure at Algiers; Florida Blanca replaces D'Aranda French military and naval reform Turks cede Bukovina to Austrians	*March.* Abolition of war-taxes—many concessions *Nov.* Statutes for provincial administration "Vis-à-vis de cela, je ne regarde *l'Instruction*...que comme une bavardage" (Catherine) Loan to the devastated provinces Autonomy of Zaporogian Cossacks abolished
1776	Adam Smith: *Wealth of Nations* American Declaration of Independence	Prohibitory Act against American commerce	Turgot's reforms and dismissal (May 11) Spanish attack on Sacramento	*April.* Prince Henry's visit Death of Paul's consort *May.* Marriage with the Princess of Würtemberg arranged Friction with Crimean Tartars Zavadovski replaces Potemkin as favourite
1777	Sheridan: *School for Scandal* Franklin in France John Howard on prison reform Birmingham tailors' workshop for strikers	Washington in extremities at Valley Forge British surrender of Saratoga: French unofficial share in the war	*June.* Necker financial director-general Fall of Pombal *Rapprochement* of Spain and Portugal Franco-Swiss alliance Death of Bavarian Elector	Zoritch replaces Zavadovski as favourite Potemkin rules Southern Russia

INDEX

Académie (Petersburg), 320
Acalziké (Armenian fortress), 68
Accessories, 246, 247
Achaï (on the Taman peninsula), 124
Achim, 263
Achmet IV, 200, 205
Agriculture, 262, 264, 303, 304
Akkermann (*see* Belgorod)
Alembert (D') (philosopher second only to Voltaire, mathematician and encyclopaedist), x, xi, xiv, xxi, 6, 9, 13, 76, 77, 173, 312, 320
Alep (Haleb, Aleppo), 77, 118, 130
Alexis, Mandement de (du révérendissime Père en Dieu... archevêque de Novgorod-la-Grande) (skit on quarrels between French clergy and *Parlement*, 1765, when *Parlement* burnt a circular letter "au pied du grand escalier"), 8, 9
Alexis Michailoviz (1645–76, i.e. "son of Michael" the first Romanov Tsar), xxix, 284
Algarotti ("one of the first *beaux-esprits* of his age"—Carlyle), 180, 183, 185
Ali-Bey, Grand Vizier, 59, 61, 70, 88, 101
Ali "d'Égypte" (rebel), 71, 78, 81, 83, 94 sqq., 106, 109, 113, 118, 123, 128, 130, 134, 138, 143, 165, 173, 187, 320
Alton (on the Taman peninsula), 124
Ambition, support of government, 263
Ambroise (Archevêque de Moscou), 135, 141, 144, 321
America, revolt in, 321, 322, 326
Anatolie, 81
Andrinople (Adrianople, often spoken of by Voltaire), 28 sqq., 50, 192
Anecdote sur Bélisaire (two pieces by Voltaire, "par l'abbé Mauduit, qui prie qu'on ne le nomme pas"), 17
Angleterre (*see* England), 49, 80, 87, 105, 324
Anson (explorer and admiral), 136
Arcadie (Arkadia, sea-port north of Navarino), 55
Archangelgorod (gorod = town), 277
Argenson, Comte d', 28
Arkwright, Richard, x
Arsène, Évêque de Rostou, q.v., 5, 312
Astracan, 100, 277
Athènes, 42, 71, 123, 128, 178, 279
Athenians, 257, 264, 268
Atméidan, de Stamboul (place of the hippodrome), 96, 183, 186, 188
Aubri (secretary), xxi
Aubry, ingénieur, 175, 177, 320
Augustins, 4
Augustus, Emperor, 260, 282
Avignon (papal territory, symbolic of papacy), 33, 38
Azem, visir, 78
Azof (key to the Don), 28, 31 sqq., 42, 45, 59, 101, 124, 132

Babadaki (Babadagh, S.W. of Ismail, S.E. of Braila), 87
Bagdat, fort (in Mingrelia), 67
Baisemain des prêtres, 203 sqq., 321
Balada, 50, 143
Balk, M. de, xxi, 1, 50, 143
Bankrupts, 253, 254
Banks, 266
Baptism, 193
Barrat, peintre, 206
Baschkis (Bashkirs), 194
Bawer, Général (Bauer, Prince Ferdinand's quartermaster-general; employed by Catherine in Finland and Bessarabia; confused by Gunning with Kar), 81
Bazin, Abbé de (one of Voltaire's *noms de plume*, used for his *Philosophie de l'histoire* which became the introduction to *L'Essai sur les mœurs*), 2 sqq., 9, 17, 19, 20, 311
Beccaria, x, xxiv, xxv, xxvii
Beggars, 298
Belgorod (Akerman, fortress at Dniester mouth), 69, 78

Belisaire (by Marmontel, condemned in 1767 by the Paris Theological Faculty, translated by Catherine), 18, 19
Bender (fortress on the Dniester), 57, 61 sqq., 80, 82, 83
Berdoni (in E. Sparta), 55
Bernstorff, Count J. H. E. B., 317
Bessarabia, 58, 60, 123
Betzky, M. de (Actual Privy Councillor), 176, 327
Bibikov, Général (Catherine's adviser, her agent in the legislative commission, commander against Pugachev), 194, 324
Bielefeld, Baron, xxvi, 329
Boswell, James, x
Boufflers, Chevalier de (believed to be sent by France to command Polish confederates), 118, 318
Bourdillon, Joseph (*nom de plume* of Voltaire for writing on the dissensions of the Polish churches—an essay condemned at Rome, Dec. 1768), 19
Bourjak, le (Budzak, Bessarabia), 69
Brahilof (near Braila, to the south-west), 57, 62, 63, 66, 78, 86
Bramcamp (Amsterdam connoisseur; Catherine said to have spent more than 100,000 guilders, £9000–£10,000), 146
Brückner, Alex., xx, xxxii
Bucharest, 46, 86, 131, 173, 177
Buckinghamshire, Earl of, xx, xxiii
Buildings, police and, 298
Bulgar (Bolgarie, ruined town near the Volga rediscovered under Peter), 173
Burghers, 273, 327
Burke, Edmund, 316
Byzance (*see* Constantinople)

Cabarda (Kabardia, buffer-state between Russia and Turkey, north of the Caucasus), 36
Caffa (chief town in Crimea), 122, 124, 126, 132
Calamata (on south coast of the Morea), 55
Calas (family of victim of judicial murder, for whom Voltaire secured redress), 6 sqq., 10, 11
Canada, 261
Canals, 305
Candide, 22, 48, 100, 101, 159, 163
Capital punishment, 224, 249, 250, 251
Capucins, 4, 54
Carouzel (the "carousal" of May 1766 occupied more than a column of the *Annual Register*), 3, 4, 87
Caterinimbourg (Ekaterinburg, also Jek. or Yek., beyond Urals, founded 1721), 129
Cathcart, Lord (on Russia in 1770–1), 316, 317
Catherin (pun—a religious sect in Albigensian times—Schnitzler), 53
Catherine I (1725–7), 48
Catherine II (1729–96), and Voltaire, ix; appearance and characteristics, ix; and Voltaire, xi, xiii, xiv; authenticity of her letters, xv–xxi; advance in power, xxii, xxiii; her *Instruction*, xxiii–xxx; Turkish war, xxx; *1763:* admiration for Peter I, 1. *1765:* no verse-maker, 2; her debt to Voltaire, 2; the bee her emblem, 4; she replaces Capuchins with Augustinians, 4; coerces Bishop Arsenius, 5; has bought Diderot's library, 7; praises Peter for tolerance, 8. *1766:* contributes towards the Sirven family, 11; quotes from her *Instruction*, 12. *1767:* will not be deified, 13; intervenes in Poland, 14; on miracles, 15; is draining Petersburg, 16; sends her *Instruction*, 16; at Casan realises legislative difficulties, 17. *1768:* on inoculation, 21; sends MS. translation of her *Instruction*, 22; on Turkish war, 22; sends a fur coat, 23. *1769:* on French detractors, Saratov colonists and Russian prosperity in spite of Turks and Polish confederates, 30; Azov taken, 32; New Servia not much injured, 35; Cabarda conquered, 36; *Instruction* banned at Paris, 36; Moldavia conquered, 38; on the Orlovs, 39; on her naval expedition, 40; Bucharest taken, 41; people of Galatzo pursue the Turks, 42. *1770:* progress in war, gaiety in Petersburg, 44;

Catherine II (*cont.*)
Giurgi taken, 46; Turkish ineptitude, 50; war-chariots, 54; progress in Greece, 55; hopes for her code of laws, 57; Romanzow's victories, 60, 61; victory in all fields, 62; Tartars weakening, 64; Russia's resources, 65; Ismailof taken, 65; Tottleben in Caucasus, 67; on Tartar submission, 69; on Turkish desertion to Russians, 70; Kilia-Nova taken, 71; Chesmé, 71; on Chesmé, 74–6; Akkermann taken, 78; Prince Henry's visit, 80; Bender and Lemnos taken, 80; on war progress, England, and the masquerade, 86; on the Sultan and his brother, 91; on the Chinese, 92. *1771:* derides l'Abbé Chappe, 95; buys Ferney watches, 95; on Russia and France, 98–101; on the Chinese, 102; on progress beyond the Danube, and on Gustavus III, 103; on prospect of peace, 111; on progress and polemics, 112, 113; homage to Peter, 115; Crimea invaded, 120; and conquered, 122; more conquests, 124; would have peace, 125; returns to Code, 126; on conflagrations, 127; Crim Tartars submit, 128; on her garden, 129; on the campaign, 131; on the murder of Archbishop Ambrosius, 135; on Siberia, 136, 137; on Danubian victories and French volunteers in Poland, 143; on the Orlovs, 144; on her loss of pictures, 146. *1772:* on her girls' school, 152; on Russian resources, 158; on her girls' school, 160; on gardens, 163; on the armistice, 164; on the renewal of war, the partition of Poland, and the *coup d'état* of Gustavus III, 168; on comedies, 171; on D'Alembert, peace prospects and Tartar saints, 171. *1773:* on ice foundations and on the Greeks, 180; on victory beyond the Danube, 184; Romanzow retreats, 188; Paul's bride is converted, 188; on Grimm and other philosophers, 189; on Diderot, 192; on the Greek church, 193; a fresh victory, 193. *1774:* on Pugachev and Diderot, 194; on Pugachev and Tott, 196; on her constancy, 199; the Peace, 199; on Pugachev, 202; on kissing priests' hands, 203. *1775:* on Pugachev and resumption of legislation, 205. *1776:* on French politics and on her legislation of 1775, 209. *1777:* on Tasso and Homer, 211; on the *Instruction* and legislation, 211; on criminal law, 212; on regulations for finance, 213; her *Instruction*, 214–309. Notes *passim*; drafts of letters, 311, 315, 318–20; parallel documents, 315–17, 319; Diderot's tribute, 329
Cazan (beyond the Volga, *not* in Asia, destroyed by Pugachev), 17, 109, 173, 194, 315
Chappe, l'Abbé (sent by Louis XV to Tobolsk, 1760–2; observed transit of Venus, and much genuine barbarism), 95, 120, 142
Chariots de guerre, chars de Cyrus, etc., 28, 29, 45, 48, 51, 54, 57, 64, 71, 142, 143, 187, 314
Chatham (Pitt), xvii
Chaumeix, Abraham (Paris schoolmaster, *convulsionnaire*, q.v., attacked the *Encyclopaedia*, which was stopped, went to Moscow), 2, 4 sqq.
Chesmé (Tchesmé, Russia's greatest naval victory), 74, 75, 99, 115, 129
Chinese, Chinois, les (*see* Kienlong), 91, 100, 102, 105, 107, 112, 220, 221, 262, 285, 291, 318
Choczin (Chotin, south of middle Dniester), 38–41, 50, 317
Choiseul, Duc de, 94, 96, 97, 113, 126, 136, 317
Christian VII (*see* Danemarck)
Circassie, 33, 36, 45
Cities, citizens, 276 sqq., 322, 323, 327
Clazomène (*see* Chesmé), 74, 81
Code (*see* Catherine II), 238, 239
Coin, 270
Coke of Norfolk, x
Colberg (Prussian Baltic fortress), xii
Colbert, 136

Colleges (of government), 228
Cologne, gazetier de (press inconvenient to Catherine), 30 etc.
Commerce, 304, 305
Commissions, particular (judicial), 288, 289
Companies for trade, 277, 278
Condorcet, 322
Confederacy (conspiracy), 247
Confédérés (*see* Pologne)
Constantine I, 34, 76, 231
Constantinople, 40, 43, 73, 83, 88, 113, 150, 158, 162, 178, 191, 315, 318
Convulsionnaires (French fanatics who practised self-crucifixion), 127
Copenhagen, 155, 319
Corneille (Voltaire's edition to endow Corneille's grand-niece), xx, xxii, 2
Coron en Morée (on southern coast, six miles S.E. of Navarino, "the strongest place in the Morea"—British report), 55
Corruption of Government, 290, 291
Cotatıs (Koutai, in Mingrelia), 67, 77
Courts of Judicature, 217, 218, 228–31, 237, 291, 295, 299
Cracovie (Cracow, Krakau), 161, 166, 314
Creigova (Krajowa, on the Sereth, *not* the Olta), 94
Crime, 212, 223, 224, 226, 233, 246, 250, 252, 253, 255
Crime, proofs of, 241, 242, 287
Crimée (*see* Kan de), 33, 120–32 *passim*, 144
Crozat, feu M. de (collector of pictures), 168
Culloden (1746), 126
Czarskozélo (Tsarskoe selo = Tsar's village, about 15 miles S. of Petersburg), 56, 129, 163, 205, 209
Czenstokova (Polish national shrine), 162, 164, 165, 168, 171, 320
Czernischef (Count Ivan Grigorevitch Chernischev; important family), 47

Damas (Damascus), 77, 128, 130, 139, 143
Danemarck, Roi de (Christian VII, 1766–1808), 96, 101, 104, 161, 317, 319
Darmstadt, "Madame la landgrave de", 188
Darmstadt, Princesse de (bride of Grand Duke Paul), xvii, 185
Daschkof, la princesse (*née* Countess Voronzov, "who so much distinguished herself in the revolution"—British report), 108, 115, 116
Dauphin (Louis XVI), 91, 98
Debts, 268–70
Démétri, Archbishop (*see* Novgorod)
Démétrius, les (Pretenders in the Time of Troubles), 195
Denis, Mme, xviii
Despotism, 226, 323 sqq.
Diderot (most original of the Philosophers), xiii, 6, 7, 11, 12, 13, 185, 189, 190, 192–4, 196, 198, 199, 323 sqq., 328, 329
Dimsdale, Dr Thos., M.P. (1712–1800, Quaker, pensioned and made a baron by Catherine for inoculation services, 1768), 21
Dissidents (Greek and Lutheran Poles), 178, 313, 314
Dolgorouky (Prince Basil, by Chernichev's influence commanding second army, "called a beast by all parties"—British report), 117, 120, 122, 123, 128
Don (Tanaïs), 32, 36, 202
Donskoi (convent at Moscow), 135
Duels, 253
Duménil, avocat, 201, 203 sqq.
Durini, nuncio, 320

East Indies, 268
Education, 255, 271–3
Egypt (*see* Ali d'Égypte), 53, 58, 63, 73, 317
Elisabeth (Petrovna, i.e. "Peter's daughter", Tsarina, 1741–61), xi, xii, 5, 249
Elizabeth, Queen, 323
Encyclopaedia Britannica, xv
Encyclopédie (the great French; cp. "Chaumeix"), xiii, xxvi, xxx, 5, 144, 149
Encyclopédie, Questions sur l' (by Voltaire, 1770–2, 9 vols.), 89, 95, 98, 100, 102, 106, 112, 125, 131, 134, 136, 138, 142, 317, 318

England (*see* Angleterre), 265, 270, 325 sqq.
Enthusiasm, vice of, 250
Erzerom, 43, 73, 77
Espagne (*see* Spaniards), 15
Espagne, Roi d', Charles III (on inoculation), 116
Esprit des Lois (*see* Montesquieu)
Essai sur l'Histoire générale, Voltaire's, 2
Essen, Lieutenant-général, 131, 143
Euler (Leonhard, of Basel, Curator of the Berlin Academy; his works comprise 16,000 quarto pages), 201
Evidence, 231, 240, 242, 243
Expenditure, principle of, 309

Falconet (French sculptor), 166, 176, 186, 189
Fax-hall, 149, 319
Ferney ("mes colons de F."), xii, xxii, 10 etc., 89, 93, 95, 105, 106, 114, 115, 118, 119, 125, 138, 142, 172, 197, 211, 318
Finances, 300–9, 319
Fines, 284, 324
Fires, and police, 298
Fokschan (Fokshani on the Moldavian-Wallachian frontier), 167, 175, 177, 320
Frederick II, "the Great", *see* Prusse, Roi de
French (Welches), levity of, *see* Voltaire
French in Polish and Turkish armies (*see* Boufflers, Tott *and* Vioménil), 36, 139, 144, 157, 161, 162, 165, 166, 173, 320

Galatin (Swiss gentleman), 26, 27
Galatzo (on Danube), 41, 42
Gallitzin, Princes (of the great and pro-French family of Galitsin), (i) 48, (ii) 149, 312, 313, (iii) 320
Ganganelli (Clement XIV), 54, 85, 163, 200
Gazette (*see* Cologne, Avignon) Gazette de France, etc., 41, 49, 57, 66, 67, 91, 167
Geneva, xii, 19, 47, 52, 148, 151, 268
Geoffrin, Madame (brilliant Parisian hostess; friend of Poniatowski), 34
George III, 321
Georgia, 43, 44, 58, 63, 317
Gérard, Balthasar, 144
Germans, women among, 282
Gibraltar, 40, 42
Giorgiova, 139, 147, 164
Girsova, fort, 143
Giurgi (*see* Giorgiova, Gorgora), xxx, 46, 131, 139, 143
Glébof, Général-major, 86
Goa, 268
Goethe, x
Goldsmith, Oliver, x
Golitsine (*see* Gallitzin)
Gorgora (*see* Giurgi), 103, 139, 164
Greeks, 53, 55, 56, 59, 62, 73, 78, 79, 155, 178, 180, 183
Grimm (Baron Melchior, Catherine's confidant), xiii, xvii–xx, 189–92, 198, 199, 327
Grot, Ia. K., xx
Guardianship, 281, 282
Guillaume d'Angleterre, Roi (William III), 113

Halga Sultan (or Kalga, in British despatches also Galga), 144, 160
Hargreaves, inventor, x
Health, and police, 297
Helvétius, Baron (author of *L'esprit*), 186, 189
Hémus, mont ("the Balkan"), 143, 164
Henri IV, 51, 192, 323
Henri de Prusse, Prince (brother of Frederick the Great, early acquaintance of Catherine and influential emissary), 80, 83, 87, 91, 94, 96, 98
Héraclius, Prince (victor against Persia; led Georgian insurrection, 1766), 44, 68, 317
Heresy, 289
Hesse-Cassel, Landgrave of, 321, 322
Hollandais, les, 59
Homère, 80, 211
Huber, M., 176
Husbandmen, 273, 275, 277

Ibrahim, sérasquier, 122
Ice, as foundations, 180
Imprisonment, 240
India, 263
Inheritances, 278–82
Inoculation, 21, 23, 26, 117, 314

Instruction, Catherine's (Nakaz), xxiii–xxx, 12, 16, 22, 25, 26, 31, 36, 38, 102, 113, 114, 120, 121, 124, 126, 165, 204, 205, 211 sqq., 282, 294; text of, 215–309, 311 sqq., 322, 327, 329
Ioussoupof, Prince, 211
Irkutska, 185
Isacki (on south side of Danube), 64, 111, 143
Ismaïlof (Ismail, on north side of Danube), 62, 64 sqq., 69, 72, 86
Ivan Basilewitz (Ivan the Terrible, 1533–84), 15

Jaïck (Uralsk), forteresse du (on the Ural River, more than 200 miles E. of Saratov), 202
Japan, Japanese, 220, 221, 226
Jean Kings (Jenkins; Henry Jenkins, died Dec. 1670 at Bolton, aged 169), 174, 190
Jérapkin, Lieutenant-général, 135
Jérusalem, 123, 175
Jesuits, x, xiii, 4, 188, 191
Johnson, Samuel, x
Judges, 236, 241
Julius Caesar, 260
Justi, xxvi
Justice, 228 etc., 274

Kachta (Kiachta, on the Siberian-Mongolian frontier, centre of tea trade), 277, 318
Kaffa (*see* Caffa)
Kalga (*see* Halga)
Kalmoucks, 36
Kamjeniec, 317
Kamtschatka, 136
Kan de Crimée, 61, 69, 120, 121, 126, 128, 144, 160
Kang-hi (K'ang Hsi, 1662–1723, Manchu, model of "philosophical" rule), 17
Kanton, 107, 142
Karasbasar (N.W. of Kaffa), 122
Kaunitz (Prince, Austrian statesman, "chérubin indomptable"), 189
Kertz (Kertsch, in the eastern Crimea), 122, 205
Kien-long (Ch'ien Lung, 1736–96, Manchu, another model emperor, excluded Jesuits), 85, 89, 92, 94, 97, 106, 119, 121, 163
Kilia (on the northernmost channel of the Danube), 66, 87
Kilia-Nova (at the northernmost outlet of the Danube), 72
Kiovie (Kiev), 9, 25, 50
Kissing the Cross, 232
Kluchevsky, V. O. (historian), xxiii, xxxii, 315
Kogul, ruisseau (and name of "such a victory as was never heard of before"—Carlyle), 62, 64, 66, 129
Koslof ("port sur la mer Noire", Eupatoria), 122
Kosloftsky, Prince ("lieutenant de mes gardes"), 23, 24, 81
Kouban, 36
Krémelin, de Moscou (Kreml = citadel; that of Moscow contained a vast mass of buildings), 135
Kutchuk Kainardji ("une si jolie paix", 1774), 199, 200

La Barre, Chevalier de, 28, 31, 141, 321
Lacédémoniens (*see* Greeks)
La Harpe, M. de, 204, 322
Lally, xxx
Lameri, actor, 189
Lamoignon, De, statesman, 321
Larga, petite rivière (Moldavia), 61
La Rivière, M. (sent by Galitsin to help in legislation; too late; disgusted), 203 sqq.
Lasalle, Sieur (artist), 108, 116
Lauterbourg (14 miles from Landau), 131
Laws, *Instruction* on, xxix, 215, 217, 218, 221, 222, 235, 237, 238, 244, 248, 255 etc., 282 etc.
Le Fort, Marc et François, 207
Lemnos, 80, 132, 136
Leo XIII, Pope, ix
Léontari (in S.W. Morea), 55
Lessing, x
Letters of Exchange, 270
Lettre sur les Panégyriques, Voltaire's ("par Irénée Aléthès, professeur en droit dans le canton suisse d'Uri"), 17, 18
Liberno (near Chesmé), 72
Liberty, 216, 219, 223, 230, 231, 233, 265
Liberum veto (derided by Voltaire, upheld by Catherine), 162

Louis XI, 130
Louis XIV, 12, 17
Louis XV, xi, xii, xxiii
Lunatics, 281
Lutzen (1632), 29
Lyon, ville de, 108

Macartney, Sir George, xxvii, 319
Machinery, 264
Mahomet, visir, 101
Mahon (*see* Port-Mahon)
Malta, 72
Man, dignity of, 300
Manifeste (see *Instruction*)
Manifeste...de Pologne, 107, 108, 113, 118
Manuel Comnenus (Eastern Emperor), 290
Maria Theresa, Empress Queen, 172
Marriage, 260, 261
Masquerade (Petersburg, 1770), 87
Masson, M., xxi
Matelina, fort, 143
Maurocordato, Prince of Moldavia, 41
Mazzini, 323
Metropolitan (Russian Church), 312
Middling rank, 275, 327
Mingrelia, 45
Minors, 281
Miracle, 290
Misistra (Mistra, in Morea, Sparta), 55
Moldavie (and Valachie, Wallachia), 38, 41, 44, 46, 50, 51, 53, 60, 123, 316
Monarchy, 216, 217, 266, 267, 288, 292, 301
Montenegrins, 53
Montesquieu, x, xxiv sqq., xxxi, 12, 312, 323–8
Montfort, régiment de, 52
Morals, 223, 224
Morée (*see* Greeks)
Morley, John (afterwards Viscount), xi, xx
Moscou, town and river, xvi, xxix, 4, 19, 50, 87, 134, 135, 140, 141, 144, 162, 202, 203, 208, 318, 325; archevêque de (*see* Ambroise)
Moscovie (*see* Russia)
Mourza, les (princes among the Tartars), 128
Moussou-Ouglou, ci-devant visir, also Moussum, 143
Moustapha (Mustafa III, 1757–73, hope of Prussia in the Seven Years' War, protector of Poland, patron of science), 22 etc., 49, 85, 90, 96, 101, 130, 186, 189, 193
Murnan, M. de, 201, 205
Murray, John, ambassadeur (procured transfer of Catherine's representative at Constantinople from prison), 85, 90

Napoli de Romanie (Nauplia), 62, 70, 74
Navarin (S.W. coast of the Morea, "Napolis, Coron, Modon and Navarino...are strong and regular fortifications erected by the Venetians"), 56, 66
Necker, x
Nicon, Patriarch (temp. Alexis, caused secession of Old Believers or Rashkolniks by his reforms, quarrelled with State and failed), 18
Niester (Dniester, scene of Moldovanghi's defeat in 1769), 36
Noailles, Duc de, 131
Nobility, 273–5
Norvège, la (subject to Danish crown), 174, 177
Novgorod, métropolitain de (formerly Novgorod the Great, 120 miles S. of Petersburg), 5, 8, 13, 14, 312

Obreskof ("mon résident" at Constantinople; imprisoned and released), 110 sqq., 116
Oczakof (commanding mouth of the Dnieper), 62
Odart (secretary), xxi
Oginski (Palatine of Wilna, cousin of Stanislaus), 139
Olitz, Comte, 103
Oliva (Cistercian monastery in Royal or Polish Prussia which Frederick wished to add to his own Prussia; as Abbot of Oliva, he would succeed to dormant rights over part of Danzig harbour of great value), 147
Olta, rivière (*see* Creigova), 94
Ordre essentiel des sociétés (by La Rivière, q.v.), 19
Orembourg (Orenburg, town and Cossack district in S.E. Russia), 194, 195, 277

Orka, fort, 122
Orlof (five brothers, Alexis and Gregori the chief, then Feodor), (ii) xxvii, (ii) 21, (ii) 26, (ii) 37, 39 (Catherine's note on), 43, (iii) 55, (i) 74, (iii) 75, (i) 77, 79, 80 sqq., 85, 92, (i) 99, 100, (i) 104, 109 sqq., 132, (ii) 135, (i) 136, 139, (ii) 141, (i) 143 sqq., (ii) 146, 161, (ii) 179, (i) 180

Panin, Nikita (Count), xxiii, xxvii
Panin, Général Comte (brother of the statesman), 202
Paoli (Corsican hero), 23
Parents, duties of, 272
Paros, 136
Partition of Poland, 168, 314
Passava (in the Morea), 55
Patras, 180
Paul, Grand Duke (Paul I), 26, 185, 188, 328
Pellemberg, Baron de, 166, 176, 180
Péloponèse, 55
Pérécop (lines fortified by the Tartars), 117, 120, 121, 123, 127, 131
Pestilence, 83, 84, 88, 140, 141, 148, 149, 317
Petersburg, xii, 16, 41, 44, 112, 114, 126, 162, 175, 183
Pettremann, J. L. (German of Cadiz), 206
Philippopolis, 29, 32
Pictet, xi sqq., xxi, 1, 26
Pierre-le-Grand, Peter the Great, Peter I (1689–1725), xii, xxi, xxviii, 1, 7, 9, 15, 33, 48, 50, 65, 101, 108, 115, 130, 145, 155, 167, 170, 172, 177, 183, 191, 204, 207, 216, 228, 234, 256, 311, 315, 323
Pierre-le-Grand, Voltaire's history of Russia under, xxi, 1
Pierre-le-Sauvage, 189
Pierre III (1762, Catherine's husband), xi, xii, xxvi, 194
Plato, 269
Platon, Archevêque de Twer, 108, 109, 115, 188
Podolie, 31
Pokrovsky, M., xxiv, xxv, xxxii, 325, 326
Polianski, M., 109, 116, 176, 178, 180
Police, 295–9
Political body (Senate, q.v.), 217, 218
Pologne (Poland), xxiii, 13, 14, 25, 29, 31, 33, 34, 107, 109, 118, 119, 125, 132, 144, 145, 162, 173, 194, 313, 314, 317, 320
Poltava, xii
Poniatowski (*see* Stanislaus)
Population, increase of, 257, 303
Port-Mahon (in Minorca, British naval base), 42, 44, 46, 87
Porto-Vitello (in the gulf of Calamata in the Morea), 55
Portuguese, 267
Potemkin, Lieutenant-général (Catherine's favourite and almost co-regent), 184
Potis (Poti, on E. coast of Black Sea), 87
Praslin, Duc de, 96
Préobrajensky, régiment des gardes, 104
Pride, as political force, 263
Prince impérial (*see* Paul)
Prix de la justice, etc., Voltaire's, 213, 322
Property, nature and division of, 228, 280, 291, 306
Prosorofski, Prince, 62
Prusse, Roi de (Frederick the Great), xi, xiv, xix, xxiii, 48, 49, 68, 85, 89, 95, 116, 138, 172, 181, 191, 192, 194, 321, 322, 324
Pruth, bataille du (1711), xxi, 62, 191; (July 1770) 66
Pugachev ("marquis de", "voleur de grand chemin", executed, 1775), xxx, 194–200, 202, 203, 205, 321, 327
Pulauski (of a Polish patriot family; kidnapped Stanislaus), 169
Punishment (*see* Capital punishment), 222, 223, 225, 226, 227, 235, 243, 244, 246 sqq., 250 sqq., 287, 324, 328

Quérard, M., xv, xviii
Questions sur l'Encyclopédie (see *Encyclopédie*)

Raguse (in Dalmatia, Turkish), 139
Rambaud, Alfred, xv
Religion, foundation of Law, etc., 215, 220, 272, 289, 297

Renne, Général, 62
Repnin, Prince, 81, 131
Revel (Reval, now Tallinn), xxviii, 277
Revenue, 264, 306, 307, 309, 319
Rhodians, 268
Riches, in a State, 305, 306
Riga, xxviii, 26, 27, 119, 277, 315
Robberies, 298
Romanzof, Comte de, maréchal (Rumiantsov, brother of Countess Bruce, Governor of the Ukraine), 60 sqq., 64, 66, 70, 71, 79, 86, 99, 103, 111, 143, 184, 188
Rome, Romans, 220, 256, 260, 279, 280, 286, 325, 326, 329
Rose, Michel, 197–201
Rostow (Rostov-Yaroslavski, c. 67 miles from Moscow, *not* Rostov-on-the-Don), 10, 11, 312
Rousseau, J.-J., "ce fou de", x, xii, xxi, 1, 98, 170, 311, 317
Russia (*see* Catherine), 215, 216, 257, 258, 293, 311, 316, 321, 323, 324

Sacrilege, 223
Saint Bernard (*see* Rousseau)
Saint-Cyr ("votre", "plus que S.-C."; Catherine's girls' school), 162, 176, 208
Saint-Priest, M. de (French envoy at Constantinople), 185, 186, 189, 191, 193
Sainte-Sophie (Constantinople), 111, 115, 175, 190
Sainte-Toloranski ("village de Lithuanie", scene of Voltaire's "Sermon du papa Nicolas Charisteski"), 116
Salomon, Prince d'Immirette, 67, 317
Saratof (on the middle Volga), 30, 33, 89, 115
Sardaigne, Roi de, Charles Emmanuel I (1730–73), 45, 78, 86
Schéripan, fort, 67
Schiumla (about 100 miles S.S.W. of Silistria), 188
Schlüsselburg (Russian Bastille), 314
Schouvalof (Schuvalov; Fieldmarshal, died Jan. 1762, leaving (i) a son, Count Andrew, 1744–89, secretary to the Legislative Commission, etc.; "busy, important and ambitious...his knowledge is of the general superficial and dictionary kind"—Cathcart; and (ii) a brother, Chief Chamberlain Ivan Ivanovitch, 1727–97), (ii) xii, (i) xv, xviii, xix, (ii) 7, (i) 12, (ii) 28, (ii) 35, (ii) 43, (ii) 46, (ii) 48, (ii) 53, (ii) 118, (ii) 213, (ii) 311
Scio, 70, 72, 74
Ségur, xvi, 321
Selenginsk (between Lake Baikal and Kiachta), 318
Sélim Ghérai (brave Khan of the Crimea; *see* Crimée), 128
Senate (Russian), 218, 228, 323, 324
Servants (police department), 298
Servie, nouvelle, 35
Sétine (Athens, q.v.), 42
Sha-Nadir, 44
Sheridan, R. B., x
Shirley, Henry, xxviii
Sibérie, ix, 136, 137, 142, 167, 169, 170, 185, 319
Silistrie (Danubian fortress on right bank), 188, 192, 194
Simeon, 18
Sinbirsk (fortified town on the Volga, S. of Casan), 202
Sinevin, Admiral, 120, 124
Sinigaglia, 148
Sirven, les (Protestant family championed by Voltaire against legal wrong), 10, 11
Slavery, x, 256
Smith, Adam, x
Smollett, Tobias, x
Smuggling, 253
Smyrna, 75, 99
Solon, 136, 264, 268, 279
Soltikof, Maréchal, 135
Soulthcha, fort, 86
Soumarokof (author "admired even in Germany"), 132
Spaniards (*see* Espagne), 80, 221, 267
Sparta (*see also* Mistra), 256
Spartiates (*see* Greeks)
Speranski, Michael, xxix
Spiridof, Amiral, 74, 75
Stamboul (*see* Constantinople)
Stanislas (ex-King of Poland, Duke of Lorraine), 318
Stanislaus Augustus Poniatowski (King of Poland 1764–95; *see* Pologne), ix, xx, 313

State, preservation of, 301
State economy, 308
Sterne, Laurence, x
Stoffeln, Lieutenant-général, 41
Stoupichin, Lieutenant-général, 184
Struensee, Dr J. F. (Count in 1771), 317, 319, 323
Suède, 173
Suède, Roi de (Gustavus III), 97, 103, 174
Sully, 51, 136

Taganrock (port on Sea of Azov, near mouth of Don), 28, 31, 33, 45, 100, 101, 105, 114, 117, 120, 121, 126
Taman (on its peninsula at mouth of Sea of Azov, shown in old maps as an island), 124
Tanaïs (*see* Don)
Tartars, 35, 36, 69, 91, 102, 122, 130, 185, 311, 315 (*see also* Halga Sultan *and* Kan de Crimée)
Tasse (Tasso), 211
Tatischeff, Michael (?), xxi
Taxes, 258, 301–3, 306, 307
Tchesmé (*see* Chesmé)
Temruk (on Taman peninsula), 124
Theodore Lascaris, 290
Thiers, ix
Tobolsk (about 750 miles E. of Moscow), 132, 318
Toleration, 12, 14, 28, 79, 178, 179, 289, 312, 313
Topana (Constantinople), 40
Torture, 231, 232, 243–5, 248
Tott, Chevalier de (ambassador to Khan of Crimea; engineer who fortified Dardanelles; vivid author), 84, 93, 95, 101, 104, 111, 118, 143, 187, 193, 195–7, 201
Tottleben, Count (restored to favour; commander in the Caucasus; amassed great riches), 45, 47, 67, 73, 77, 87, 311, 317
Traïetto, composer, 88
Treason, 234, 252, 274, 285–8
Tronchin, Dr, 30
Tunis (and Algiers), 45, 58
Turgot, x, 321
Turkish Empire, 80, 229, 230, 325
Turno (west of Giurgi), 103
Tver (Twer, on the Volga, three-fourths of the way between Petersburg and Moscow), 108, 115

Ukraine, 32, 69

Valachie (*see* Moldavie), 103
Varsovie (Warsaw), 320
Veismann (*see* Weismann)
Venice, rumours from, 68
Vioménil, de (symbolic of French aid to Poles), 144
Voltaire (1694–1778) and Catherine, his influence, xi; and Russia, xii; and Catherine, xiii, xiv; her debt to him, ii, xviii; to Pictet, xxi, xxii; and Turkish war, xxx. *1765:* knew Catherine's mother, 3; Catherine like her, 6; Shuvalovs his guests, 7. *1766:* D'Alembert piqued, 9; appeals for Sirvens, 10; admires Catherine's efforts for the Dissidents, 11. *1767:* Stanislaus tolerant, acknowledges curtly the *Instruction*, 17. *1768:* homages Catherine's Great Commission, 19; airy good wishes for Turkish war, 20. *1769:* more of the same, and thanks for pelisse, 24; homages *Instruction* and inoculation, 25; commends Galatin, 26; applauds military projects, suggests war-chariots, 27; applause, 33; encouragement, 36; applause, 38; encouragement, 40. *1770:* do., 42; do., 45; recommends Huguenot regiment, has been ill, Catherine has bought pictures at Geneva, charmed with a Galitsin, 47; encouragement, civil war at Geneva, 51; encouragement, though news discouraging, 53; do., 57; do., Catherine's Dutch loan, 58; encouragement, French levity, 63; congratulations on victory near the Pruth and in Greece, 66; sends Frederick's verses and some rumours, 68; congratulations on fresh victories by land and sea, 70; encouragement, value of victory, 72; encouragement, French levity, 76; encouragement, pity for Greeks, 78; congratulations on Scio and Chesmé, 81; and on Bender and Egypt, 83; Tott, plague, French

Voltaire (*cont.*)
armament, 84; encouragement, 85; on *Questions* and watches, 89. *1771: fêtes* in Petersburg and Paris, France pro-Turk, Ferney watches, 91; encouragement, devil's work in France, Rome and Egypt, verses to Christian VII, 95; congratulations, tribute to Choiseul, Gustavus III, watches, 97; French levity and Ferney watches, 104; Chinese, *Questions*, watches, Polish manifesto, 105; visit of Princess Dashkov, Archbishop Platon, "Lithuanian sermon", 108; visit of Polianski, 109; *Instruction*—and watches, 113; Ferney, its watches, Poland, 117; *Instruction* banned by *les Welches*, 120; conquest of Crimea, 123; Russian victory and French levity, 127; rumour and fact, congratulations, more *Questions*, 130; rumours, 132; to Mustafa, 133; asks news, French levity, 137; congratulations on health-giving news from Giurgi, 139; plague, 140; Ambrosius and La Barre, Siberia; watches, 141; attempt on Stanislaus, Russians in Switzerland, 144; congratulations and watches, 147. *1772:* plague, the *Encyclopaedia*, 148; watches, Catherine's pictures, French want of money, 150; commends a Courlander's poem, 154; current affairs, 155; Catherine's *St Cyr*, 156; has seen an Orlov, congratulations on Partition, 161; current affairs, 164; do., and Pellemberg, 165; on Siberian herons and Catherine's great diamond, 167; on Siberian rhinoceros and Russian comedy, 169; Rousseau's libel on Russia, 170; on superstition, Polish partition and Gustavus III, 171; commends Aubry, 174; commends Pellemberg, 176. *1773:* commends Aubry, 177; on toleration, 178; compliments, after fifty-two attacks of fever, 181; on the Russians and Greeks, 182; on Helvétius, 185; on partition of Turkey, 186; on Diderot and on capturing Constantinople, 190; on the reported capture of Silistria, 192. *1774:* on Pugachev and on Diderot, 195; commends Michel Rose, 197; do., 198; on Rose, 200; commends De Murnan, 201; on kissing priests' hands, 204. *1775:* commends Barrat and Pettremann, commends Marc Le Fort, 207; asks pardon, 208. *1777:* apologises for more than a year's silence, thanks for Provincial Ordinance, his *Prix de la justice et de l'humanité*, 213. Notes, especially 313, 317–32
Voncara d'Enghis, 53
Vorontsov, Count Alexander Romanovitch, 313

Waliszewski, xiv, xv, xxxii
Watt, James, x
Wedgwood, potter, x
Weights and measures, 298
Weismann, Général-major, Baron de (killed in Bulgaria 1773), 11, 143, 184
Wesley, John, x, 322
Widellin, Vice-consul de Cadix, 208
Williams, Sir Charles Hanbury, xx
Witchcraft, 243, 289
Women, among the Germans, 282
Words, as crime, 287, 288

Xenophon, 269

Yassi (Jassy), 29, 38, 41, 163
Yenikale (at extreme east of Crimea), 122

Zaïre (by Voltaire), 159
Zémire, 159
Zerbst, Princesse de (mother of Catherine), 3, 4, 6, 48, 51

Made in the USA
Monee, IL
13 September 2026

62976476R00222